D1356236

# WRINKLIES™
# BIG BOOK OF PUZZLES

This edition published in 2014 by Prion
20 Mortimer Street
London W1T 3JW



A CIP catalogue for this book is available from the British Library.

ISBN 978-1-85375 914-7

Printed in the UK by CPI Group (UK) Ltd, Croydon, CR0 4YY

10 9 8 7 6 5 4 3 2 1

The puzzles in this book previously appeared in *Brain Training Puzzles: Quick 1* and *2*, *Brain Training Puzzles: Intermediate 1* and *2* and *Brain Training Puzzles: Hard 1* and *2*

# WRINKLIES™
# BIG BOOK OF PUZZLES

*Hundreds of challenges to keep your mind active!*

PRION

# INTRODUCTION

## Question: What's grey and wrinkly and amazing?

A: You
B: Your brain
C: All of the above

If you answered A, you're our kind of wrinkly! Always pottering about, being utterly brilliant and putting the younger generation to shame. There's no doubt that you're fit as a fiddle, but have you thought about giving your brain a work-out once in a while? You'll find the puzzles in this book are great fun and won't make you feel like the class swot. Do you remember the class swot? Whatever happened to them?

If you answered B, you're obviously someone who hasn't let their faculties go to seed in your autumn years. We hope this book provides a stimulating mental challenge for you. By the way – did you know that you're amazing? Well, you are.

If you answered C, congratulations! This book should be just your cup of tea. There are three levels of difficulty including some fiendishly hard ones, for wrinklies just like you.

**Why Puzzles are great**

We all know that the brain is like a muscle – you need to use it if you want to keep it in shape. It doesn't matter how old you are, your brain is your best friend and a friend for life.

As children we learn to understand the world by playing; almost everything is a puzzle to be solved! Sadly exploring for the sake of it is not encouraged as we grow older and 'settle down'. Maybe you were lucky during your working life and had a job that challenged your brain on a daily basis, but for many of us it was mostly mind-numbing repetition.

But there's no reason why your retirement has to be a continuation of this tedium! Your time is your own once again and your brain is still hungry for a challenge – even if you don't realise it yet.

A puzzle is like a brisk walk in the fresh air. It does require a bit of motivation, a willingness to move your mental backside out of its comfy armchair. But it's always worth the effort.

In this book you'll discover a wide assortment of puzzles, some of which may appeal more than others. Remember to have a go at the puzzles you don't think you'll be especially good at, you might surprise yourself! Let's take a look at them.

## Observation

You might need to wear your specs to read the Sunday papers but that doesn't mean your powers of perception are fading. Observation is a skill that sharpens with practice, which is why hobbies like bird-watching are actually quite useful. However, if you garden isn't blessed with regular visits from two dozen species of finch, you'll find the visual puzzles in this book are a great way to train your alertness.

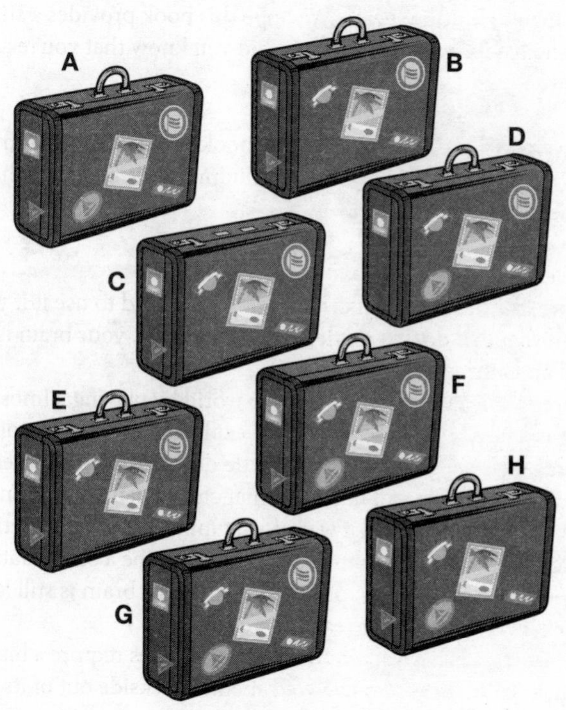

## Arithmetic

Maths isn't everyone's cup of tea, but it's been a long time since you were in school and forced to solve this type of puzzle. As an adult you've probably tackled hundreds more mental arithmetic problems than you ever did from behind a school desk. They're a lot more fun when they're not marked with red ink afterwards!

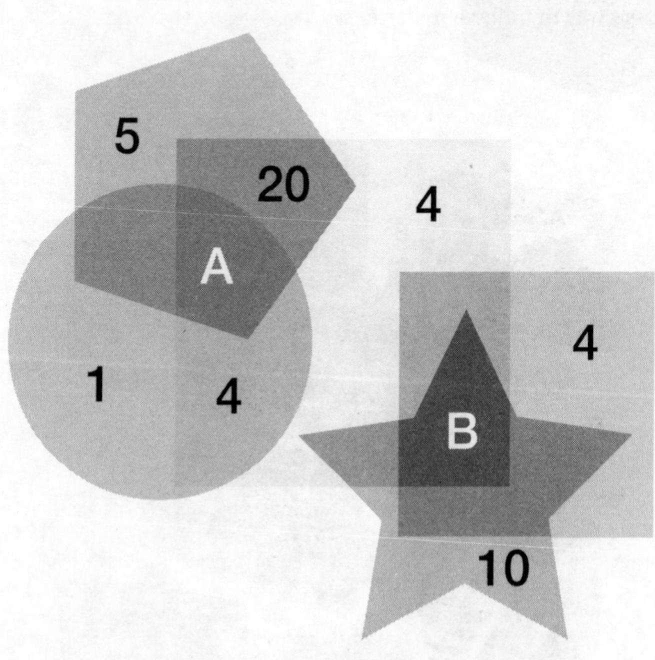

## Visualization

Never underestimate the power of imagination when solving problems. Some people are convinced that they lack a strong imagination, but in truth they just don't find a use for it in their daily lives.
Once you start using it, you'll be amazed at the creative projects you can try. Before you embark on your new career as a Rembrandt or Picasso, why not try one of these puzzles.

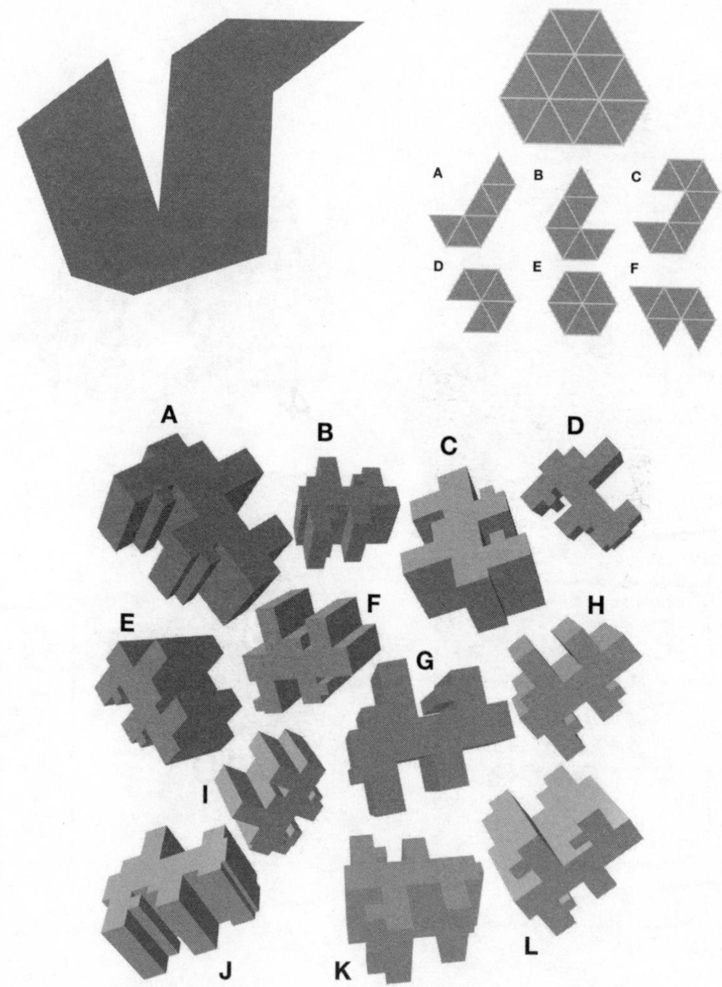

# Logic

Logic problems can often be solved by trial and error. The beauty is that once you've solved one, you acquire the mental tricks to solve similar puzzles much more quickly.

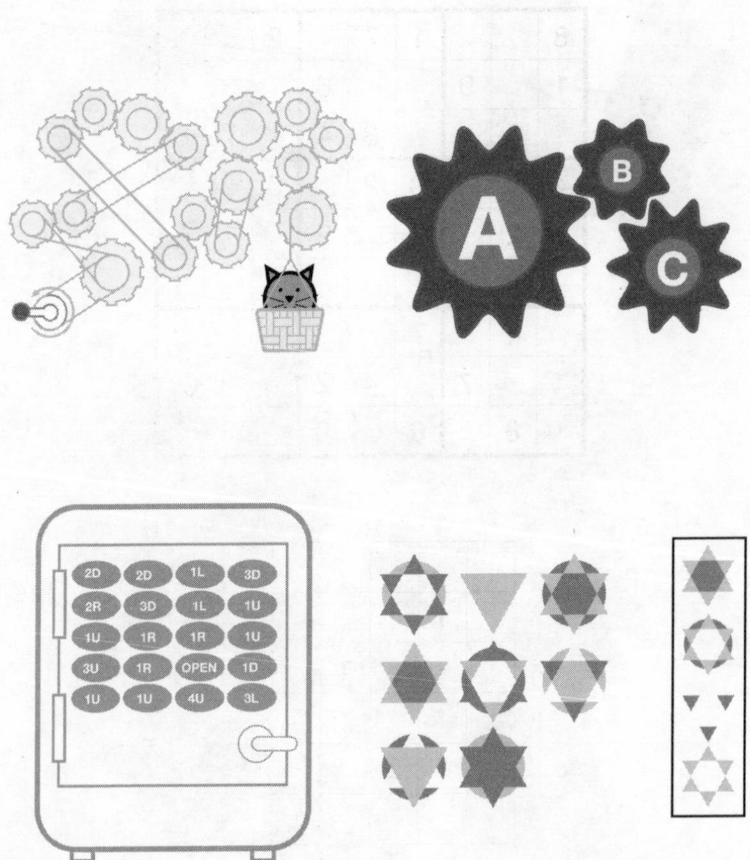

## Sudoku

It's been almost impossible to avoid these cunning Japanese logic puzzles over the last few decades. But if you still haven't had the pleasure of solving one – there's no time like the present!
Although they involve numbers, there's no arithmetic involved.
To solve a Sudoku you must simply fill in the missing squares so that each row, column and 3 x 3 box contains the numbers 1 to 9. Look out for variants – like Killer Sudoku, below.

| 8 | | | 1 | 7 | | 2 | | |
|---|---|---|---|---|---|---|---|---|
| 1 | | 9 | | | 6 | | 3 | |
| | 5 | | | 3 | 4 | | 7 | 8 |
| 4 | | | 8 | 2 | | 5 | 9 | |
| | 2 | | 3 | | 9 | | 1 | |
| | 6 | | | | | | | 3 |
| | 4 | | 7 | | | | | 2 |
| | | 7 | | 4 | 2 | 6 | 8 | |
| | 8 | | 6 | | 3 | | 4 | |

| 9 | 6 | | | 11 | |
|---|---|---|---|---|---|
| | 12 1 | 12 | | | 15 |
| 9 | 7 | | 1 | | |
| | 12 | | 11 | 9 | |
| 3 | | 2 | | | 5 |
| | 13 | | | | |

## Lateral thinking

Some puzzles force you to 'step outside the box'. It's not just a question of knowing the correct answer, you have to turn the question on its head and walk around it a few times.

Once you get into a lateral thinking state-of mind, you'll see the world differently, no matter how long you've lived in it!

## Teamwork

Some puzzles are fun to do ponder over with others – your significant other, your grandchildren or even your fellow wrinklies, there's nothing like a bit of competition to focus the mind!

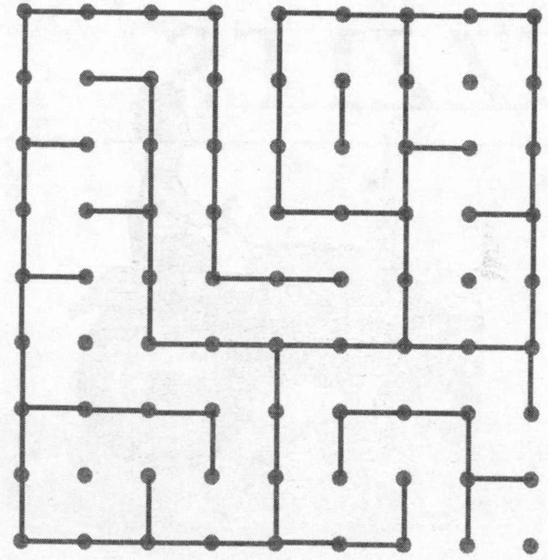

# EASY PUZZLES

**BITS AND PIECES:** How can you mend a broken heart? Here's four you can practise on. Match each half heart with its partner to make four whole ones.

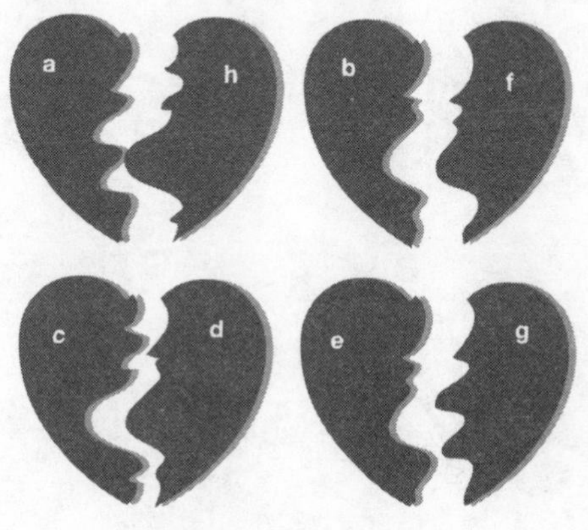


Answer on page 162

**BOXES:** Playing the game of boxes, each player takes it in turns to join two adjacent dots with a line. If a player's line completes a box, the player wins the box and has another go. It's your turn in the game below. To avoid giving your opponent a lot of boxes, what's your best move?

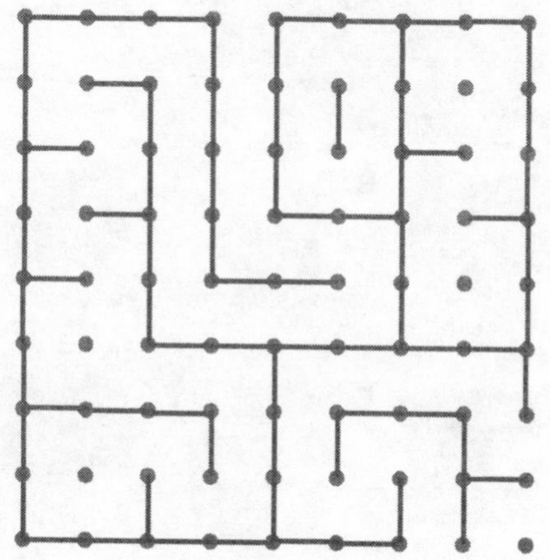

Answer on page 162

## CUT AND FOLD: Which of the patterns below is created by this fold and cut?

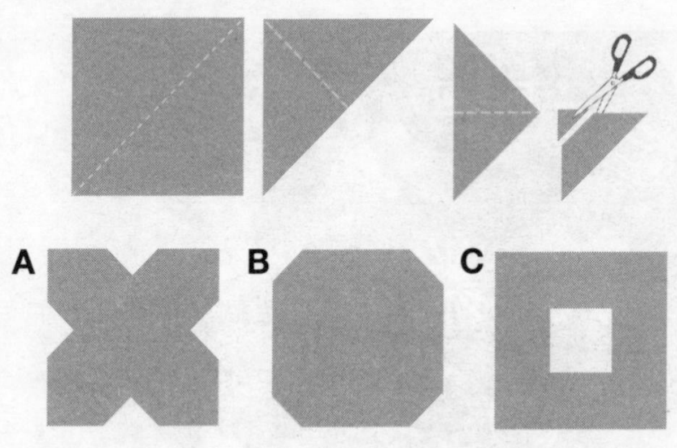


Answer on page 162

## GAME OF TWO HALVES: Which two shapes below will pair up to create the top shape?

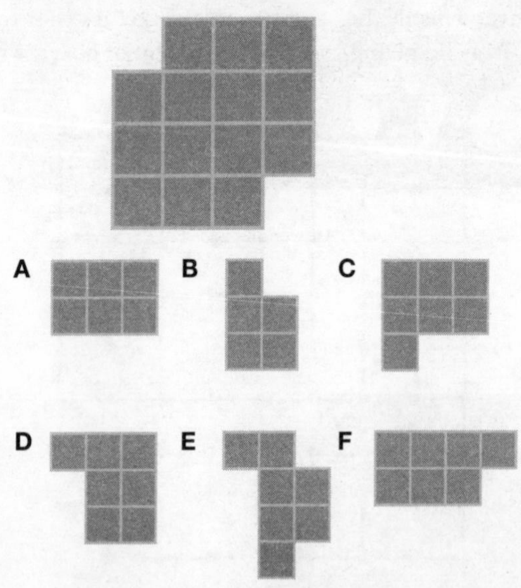


Answer on page 162

**DOUBLE DRAT:** All these shapes appear twice in the box except one. Can you spot the singleton?

Answer on page 162

WRINKLY QUOTE

'The simplest toy, one which even the youngest child can operate, is called a grandparent.'

SAM LEVINSON

**IN THE AREA:** Can you work out the approximate area that this dog is taking up?

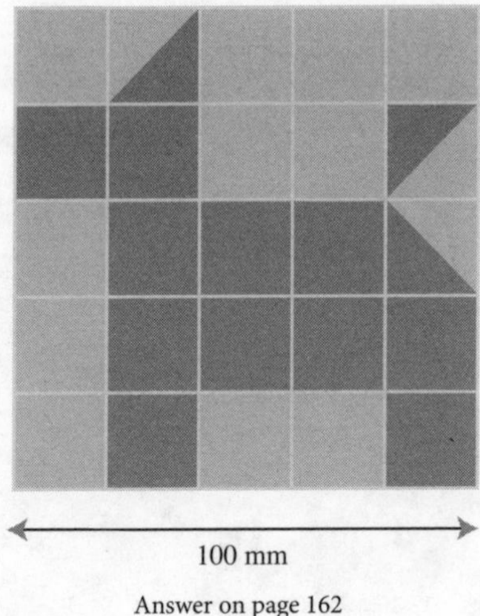


Answer on page 162

**JIGSAW:** Which three of the pieces below can complete the jigsaw and make a perfect square?

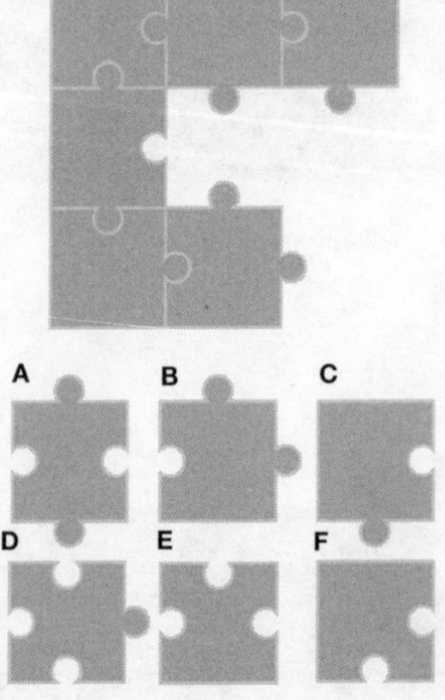


Answer on page 162

## SUM PEOPLE:

Work out what number is represented by which person and replace the question mark.

Answer on page 162

## SHAPE SHIFTING:

Fill in the empty squares so that each row, column and long diagonal contains five different symbols

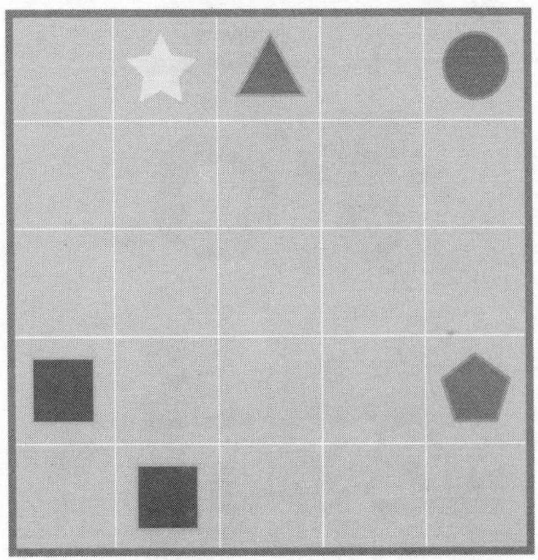

Answer on page 162

## POTS OF DOTS: How many dots should there be in the hole in this pattern?

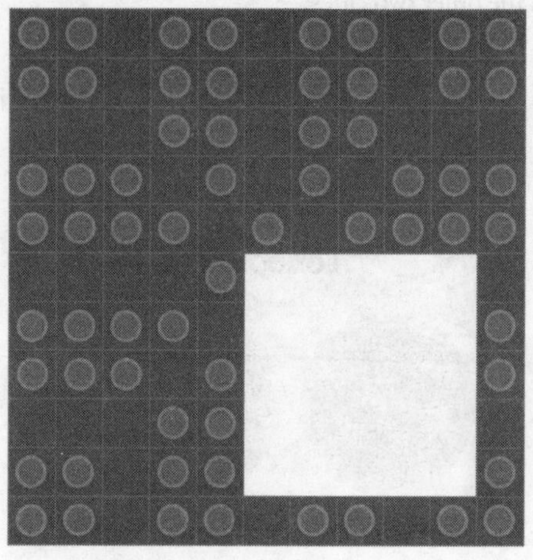

Answer on page 163

## PICTURE PARTS: Which box has exactly the right bits to make the pic?

Answer on page 163

## ODD CLOCKS: Buenos Aires is 11 hours behind Singapore, which is 7 hours ahead of London. It is 6.55 pm on Tuesday in London – what time is it in the other two cities?

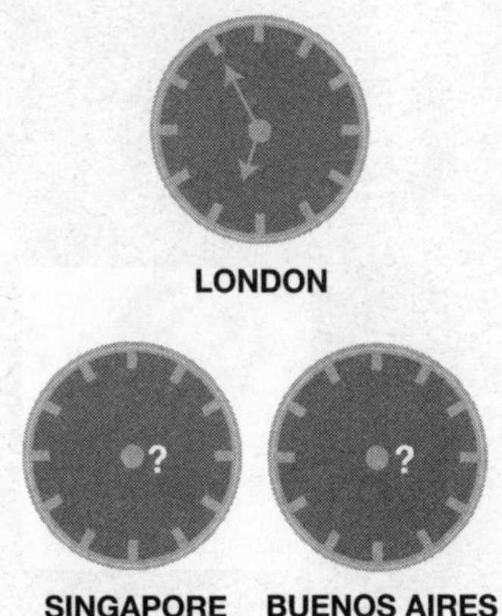


Answer on page 163

## MASYU: Draw a single continuous line around the grid that passes through all the circles. The line must enter and leave each box in the centre of one of its four sides. **Black Circle:** Turn left or right in the box, and the line must pass straight through the next and previous boxes. **White Circle:** Travel straight through the box, and the line must turn in the next and/or previous box.

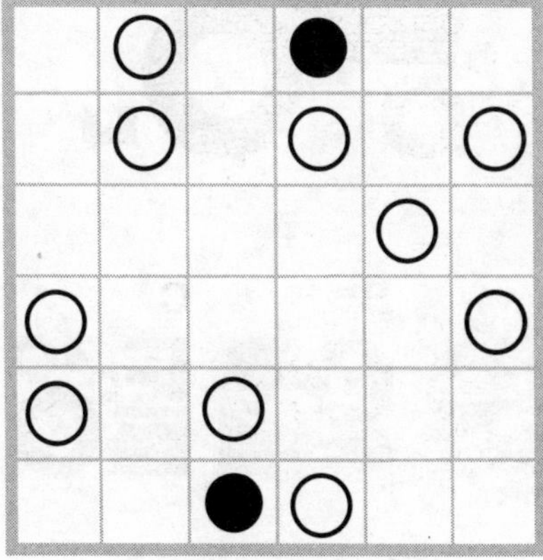

Answer on page 163

## MATRIX: Which of the boxed figures completes the set?

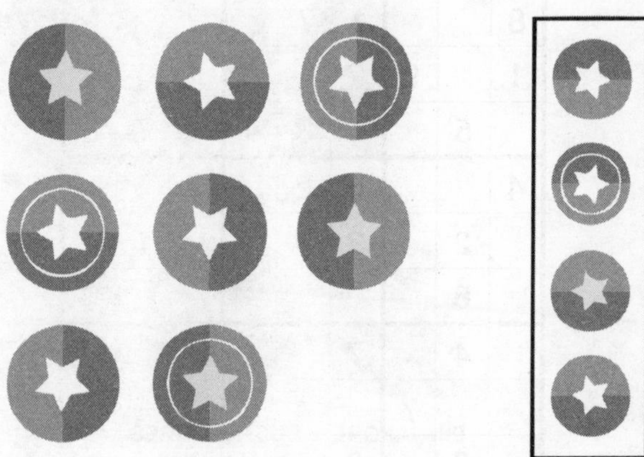

Answer on page 163

## FACE IN THE CROWD: Can you find one face in the crowd that isn't quite as happy as all the others?

Answer on page 163

**SUDOKU:** Complete the grid so that all rows and columns, and each outlined block of nine squares, contain the numbers 1, 2, 3, 4, 5, 6, 7, 8 and 9.

| 8 |  |  | 1 | 7 |  | 2 |  |  |
|---|---|---|---|---|---|---|---|---|
| 1 |  | 9 |  |  | 6 |  | 3 |  |
|  | 5 |  |  | 3 | 4 |  | 7 | 8 |
| 4 |  |  | 8 | 2 |  | 5 | 9 |  |
|  | 2 |  | 3 |  | 9 |  | 1 |  |
|  | 6 |  |  |  |  |  |  | 3 |
|  | 4 |  | 7 |  |  |  |  | 2 |
|  |  | 7 |  | 4 | 2 | 6 | 8 |  |
|  | 8 |  | 6 |  | 3 |  | 4 |  |

Answer on page 163

**RIDDLE:** An enclosure at the zoo contains both elephants and emus. If there are a total of 44 feet and 30 eyes, can you work out how many of each animal there is?

Answer on page 163

## BITS AND PIECES: Can you match the four broken tops of these vases with the bodies they belong to?

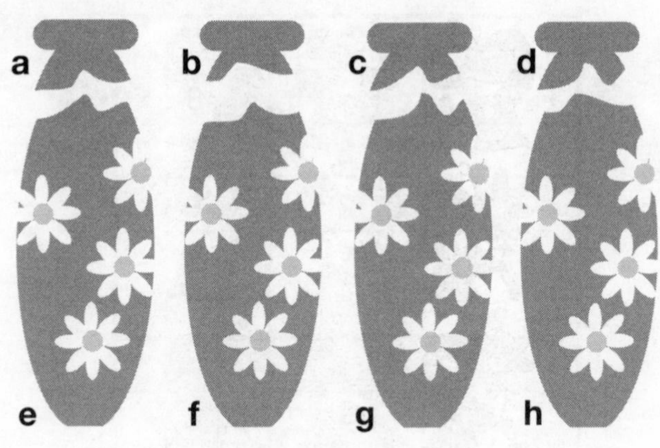


Answer on page 164

## CUT AND FOLD: Which of the patterns below is created by this fold and cut?

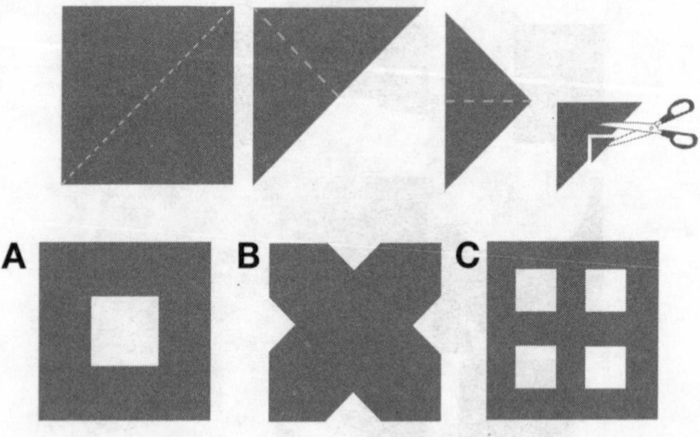


Answer on page 164

## MIRROR IMAGE: Only one of these pictures is an exact mirror image of the first one? Can you spot it?

Answer on page 164

## NUMBER JIGSAW: The nine boxes that make up this grid can be rearranged to make a number. Which number?

Answer on page 164

## MISSING LINK: What should replace the square with the question mark so that the grid follows a pattern?

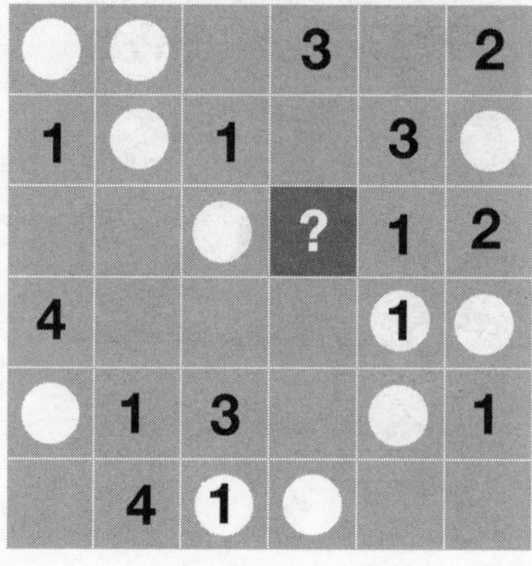


Answer on page 164

## PICTURE PARTS: Which box has exactly the right bits to make the pic?

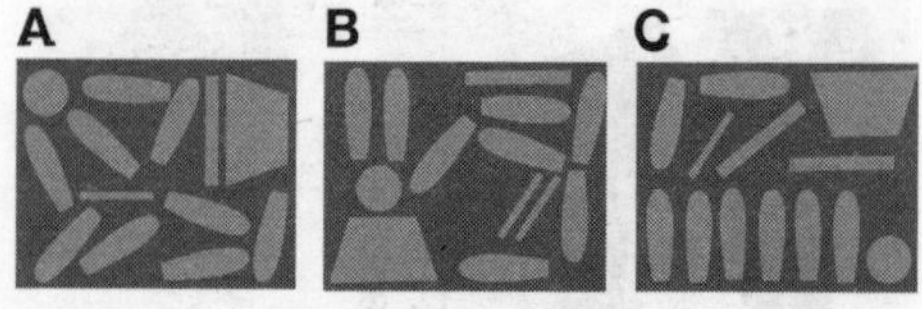


Answer on page 164

# SUM PEOPLE: 

Work out what number is represented by which person and replace the question mark.

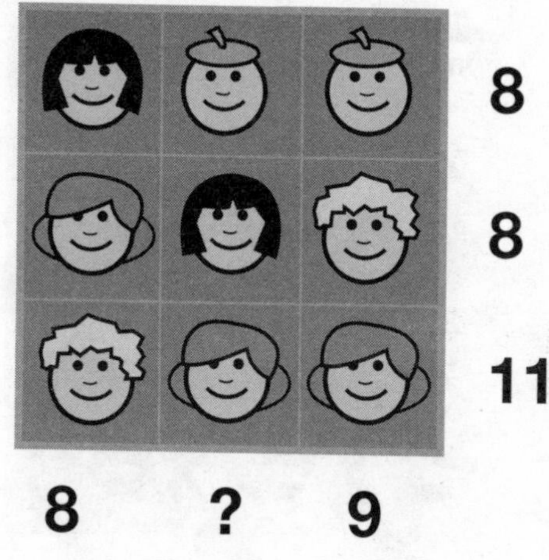


Answer on page 164

# USUAL SUSPECTS: 

Officer Lassiter is having his new uniform and kit fitted. He has the helmet badge, but not the shoulder badges yet. He has his new radio, but hasn't yet received a new tie... Can you pick him out of the group?

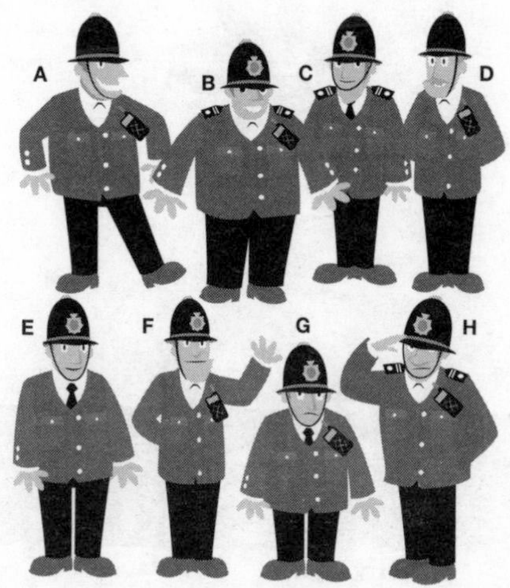


Answer on page 164

## WHERE'S THE PAIR?: Only two of these pictures are exactly the same. Can you spot the matching pair?

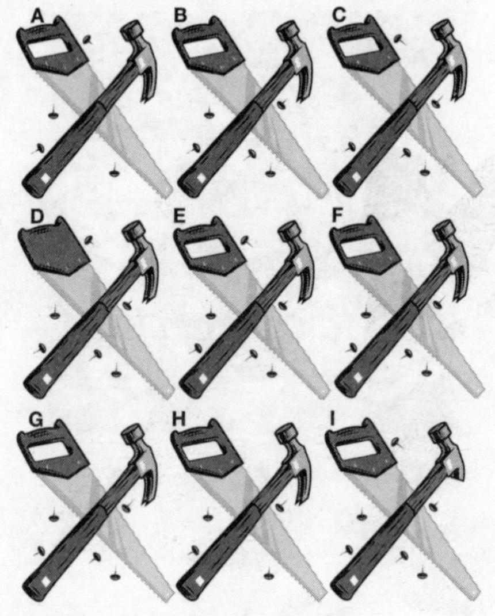


Answer on page 164

## ODD CLOCKS: Madrid is 7 hours behind Tokyo, which is 1 hour behind Melbourne. It is 6.15 am on Saturday in Tokyo – what time is it in the other two cities?

Answer on page 164

## WHERE'S THE PAIR?: Only two of the shapes below are exactly the same – can you find the matching pair?

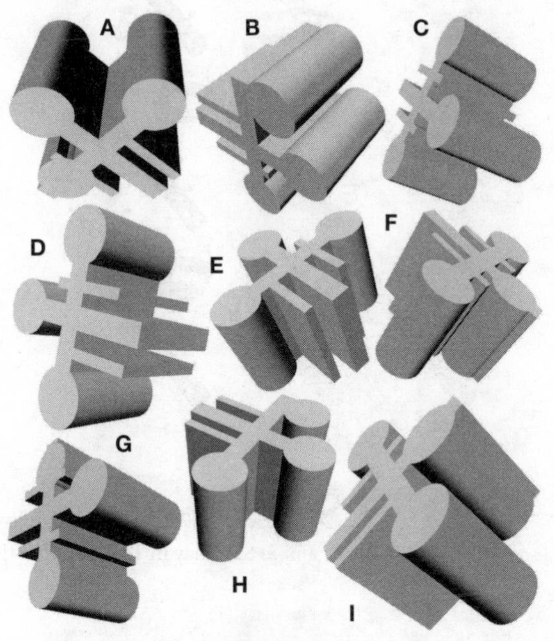


Answer on page 164

### Wrinkly Quote

"At 20 years of age the will reigns; at 30 the wit; and at 40 the judgment."

BENJAMIN FRANKLIN

# WHERE'S THE PAIR: 
Only two of these pictures are exactly the same. Can you spot the matching pair?

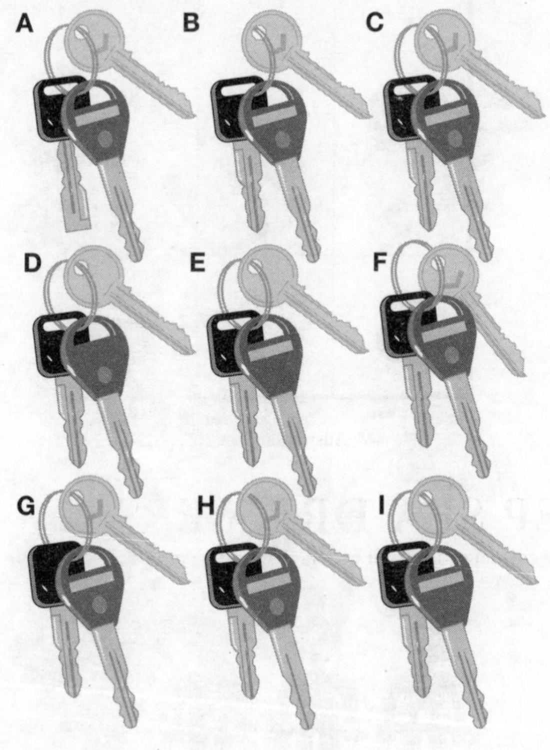


Answer on page 165

## WRINKLY QUOTE

"The point is, if I don't go to work, I don't have to get ready to go anywhere, do I… I don't have to learn anything and use my brain."

THORA HIRD

## MAGIC SQUARES:

Complete the square using nine consecutive numbers, so that all rows, columns and large diagonals add up to the same total.

| | | |
|---|---|---|
| | | |
| | | |
| 8 | 1 | 6 |

Answer on page 165

## DEEP SEA DRESSER:

Arrange this set of diver pics in the correct order from boxers to ocean-prepared.

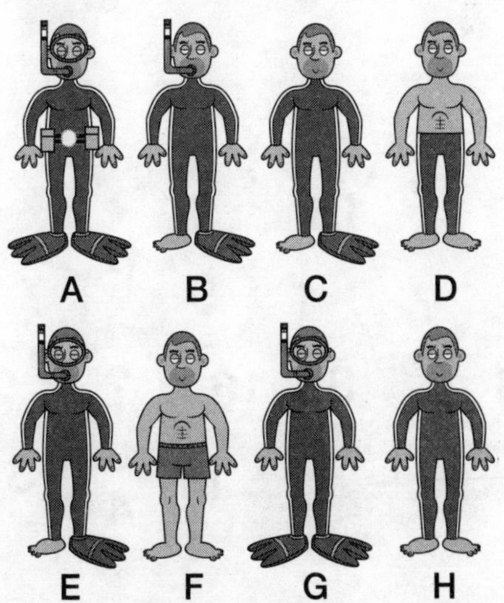


Answer on page 165

# GAME OF TWO HALVES: Which two shapes below will pair up to create the top shape?

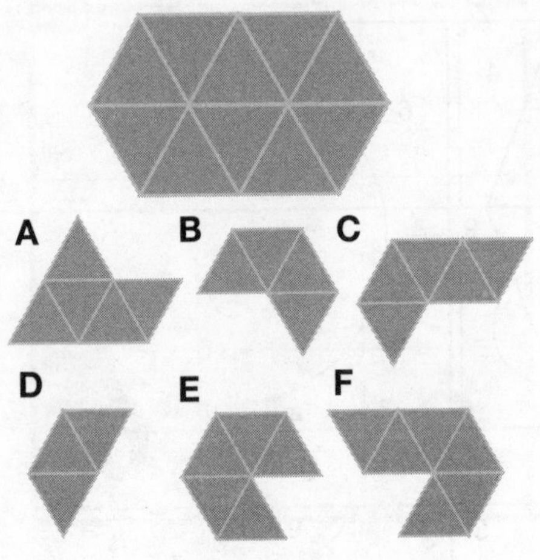


Answer on page 165

# HUB SIGNS: What numbers should appear in the hubs of these number wheels?

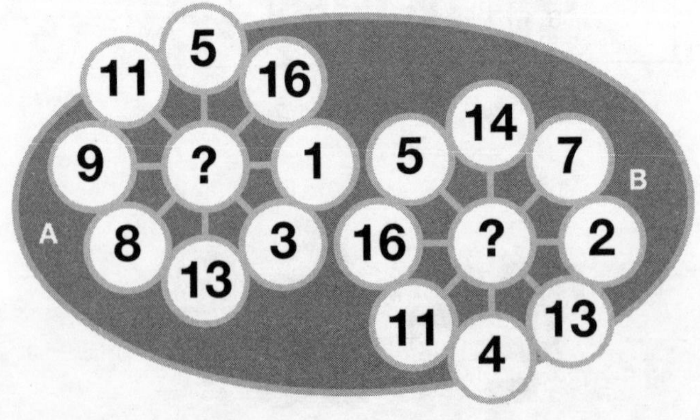


Answer on page 165

**PAINT BY NUMBERS:** Colour in the odd numbers to reveal... What?

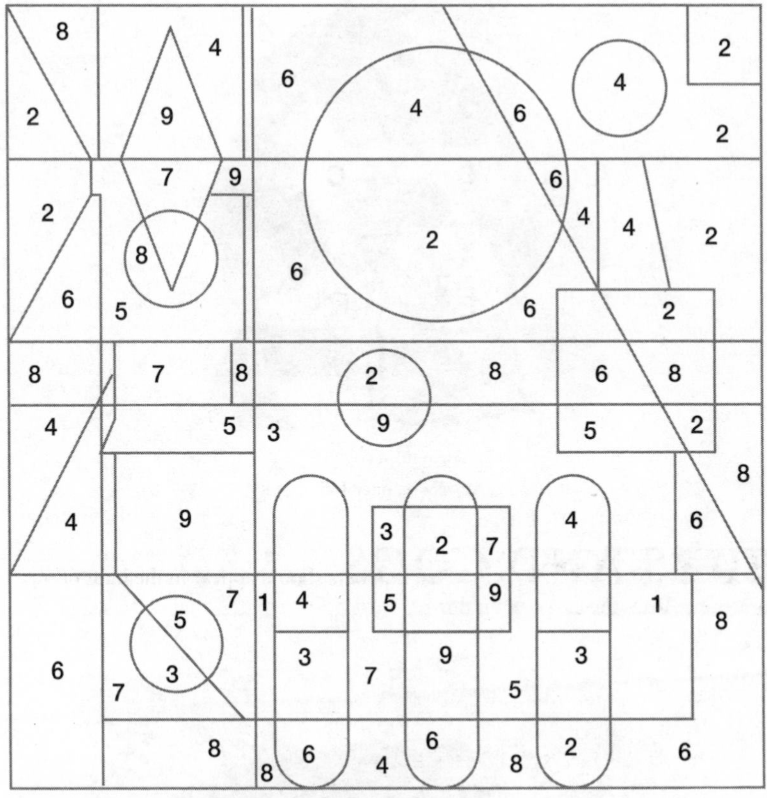

Answer on page 165

WRINKLY QUOTE

"The older I get, the less important the comma becomes. Let the reader catch his own breath."

ELIZABETH CLARKSON ZWART

## RIDDLE:

Billy bought a bag of oranges on Monday and ate a third of them. On Tuesday he ate half of the oranges he had left. On Wednesday he found he had two oranges left. How many did he start with?

Answer on page 165

## CATS AND COGS:

Turn the handle in the indicated direction... Does the cat go up or down?

Answer on page 165

## CHECKERS: Make a move for white so that eight black pieces are left, none which are in the same column or row.

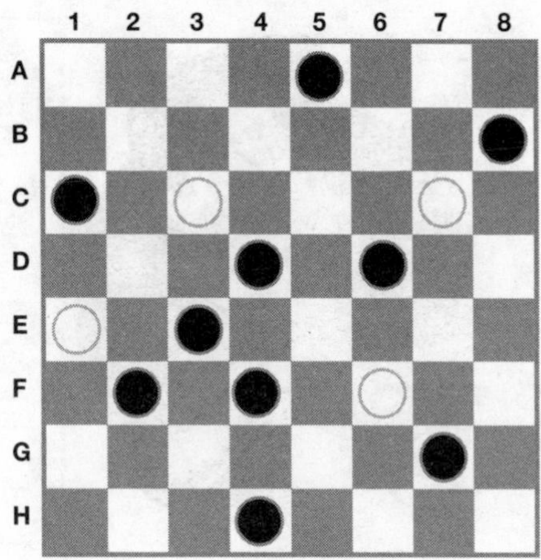


Answer on page 165

## IN THE AREA: Can you work out the approximate area this bird is taking up?

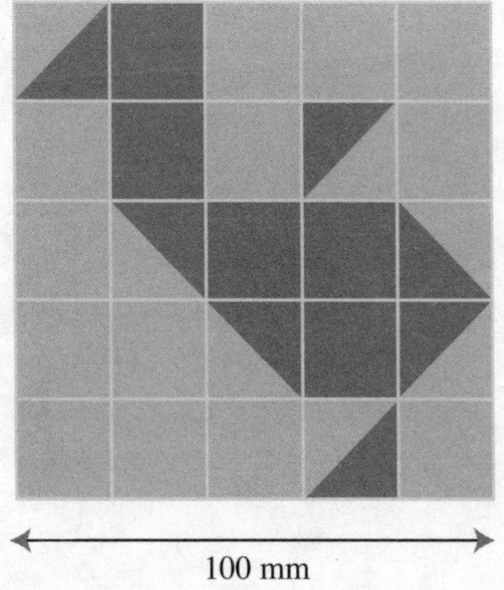


Answer on page 165

## MATRIX: Which of the boxed figures completes the set?

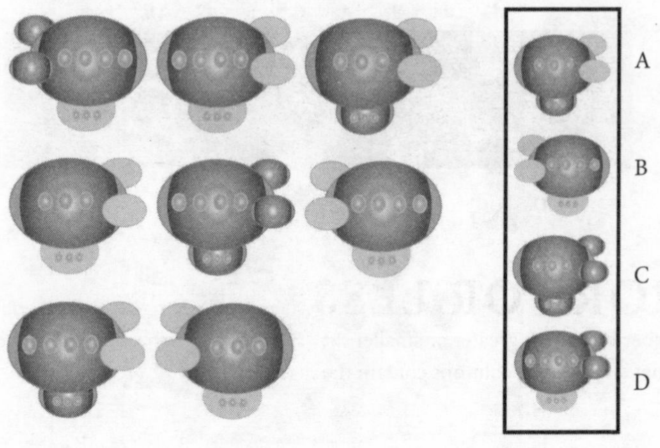


Answer on page 166

## MISSING LINK: What should replace the square with the question mark so that the grid follows a pattern?

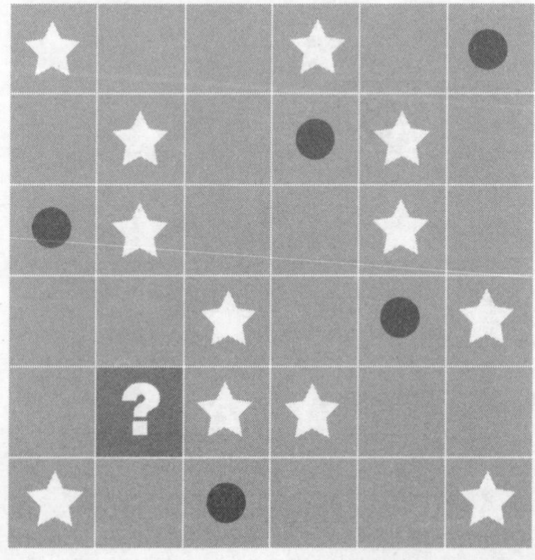


Answer on page 166

## SUM TOTAL:

Replace the question marks with mathematical symbols (+,–, × or ÷, inserting brackets where necessary) to make a working sum.

16 ? 2 ? 3 ? 1 = 6

Answer on page 166

## MORE OR LESS:

The arrows indicate whether a number in a box is greater or smaller than an adjacent number. Complete the grid so that all rows and columns contain the numbers 1 to 5.

Answer on page 166

### WRINKLY QUOTE

"My comfort is that old age, that ill layer-up of beauty, can do no more spoil upon my face."

WILLIAM SHAKESPEARE

**RIDDLE:** It's night time in your bedroom and the light has broken. You're getting dressed and need a pair of socks. You've got 10 red, 8 white and 12 grey socks in a drawer – how many do you have to pull out in the dark before you know you have a matching pair?

Answer on page 166

**BOXES:** Playing the game of boxes, each player takes it in turns to join two adjacent dots with a line. If a player's line completes a box, the player wins the box and has another go. It's your turn in the game below. To avoid giving your opponent a lot of boxes, what's your best move?

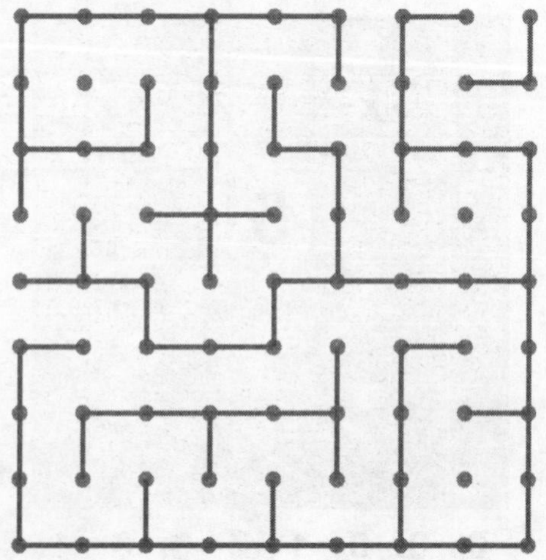

Answer on page 166

## DOUBLE DRAT: All these numbers appear twice in the box except one. Can you spot the singleton?

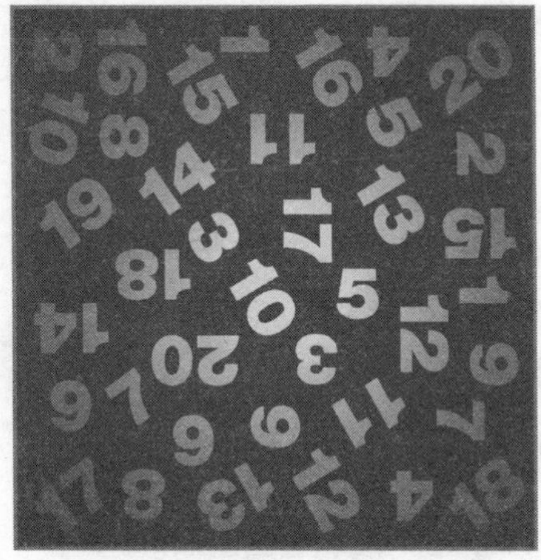

Answer on page 167

## BOATS AND BUOYS: Every buoy has one boat found horizontally or vertically adjacent to it. No boat can be in an adjacent square to another boat (even diagonally). The numbers by each row and column tell you how many boats there are. Can you locate all the boats?

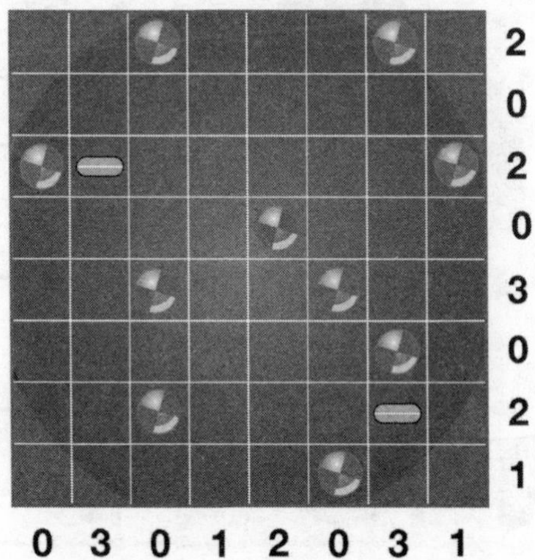


Answer on page 167

**RIDDLE:** Tony and Tina go shopping and on the way home Tina says, "Hey! If you gave me one of your bags, I'd have twice as many as you – but if I gave you one of mine, we'd have the same number!" Can you work out how many bags they each have?

Answer on page 167

**CUBISM:** The shape below can be folded to make a cube. Which of the four cubes pictured below could it make?

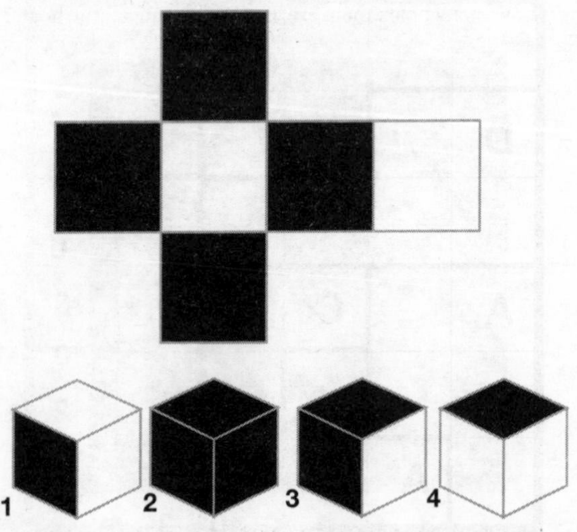


Answer on page 167

# CUT AND FOLD: Which of the patterns below is created by this fold and cut?

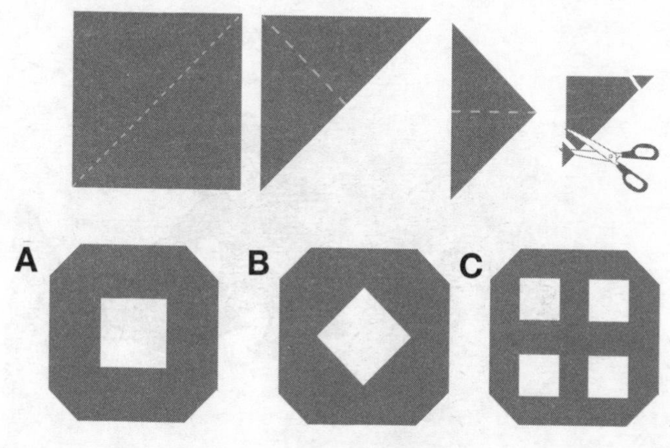


Answer on page 167

# LATIN SQUARE: Complete the grid so that every row and column, and every outlined area, contains the letters A, B, C, D, E and F

| | | | | | |
|---|---|---|---|---|---|
| | | | | F | B |
| D | | | | | A |
| | | | | D | |
| A | | C | | | |
| | | | E | | |
| | A | | | | E |

Answer on page 167

**RIDDLE:** A fish is 45 centimetres long, and its head is as long as its tail. If its head were twice as long as it really is, the head and tail together would be as long as the middle part of the fish. How long is each part of the fish?

Answer on page 167

WRINKLY QUOTE

"Age wrinkles the body. Quitting wrinkles the soul."

DOUGLAS MACARTHUR

# BITS AND PIECES: Can you match the four broken windows with the pieces of glass below?

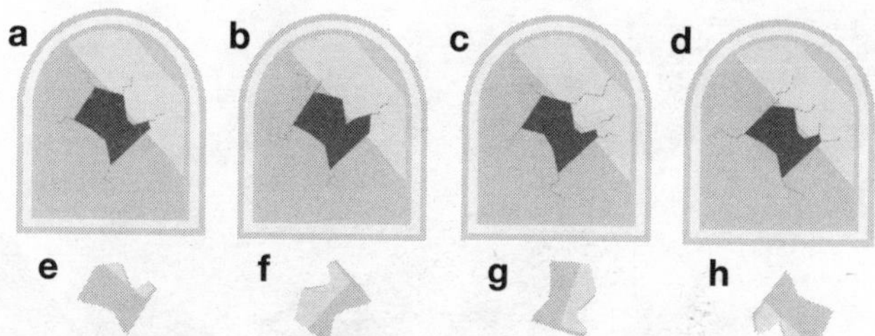


Answer on page 167

# MATRIX: Which of the boxed figures completes the set?

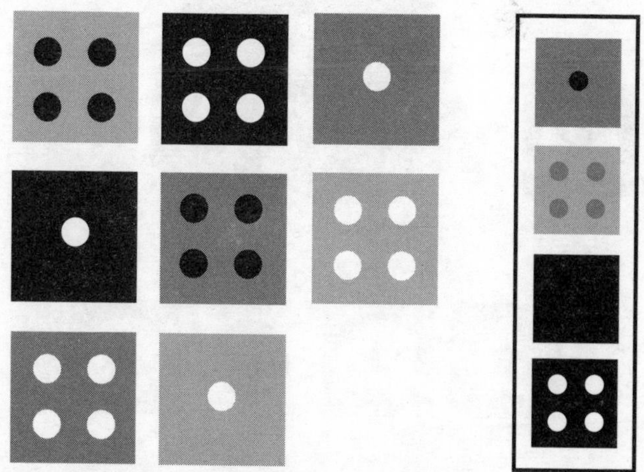

Answer on page 167

## NEXT!:

Which of the balls, A, B, C or D is the logical next step in this sequence?

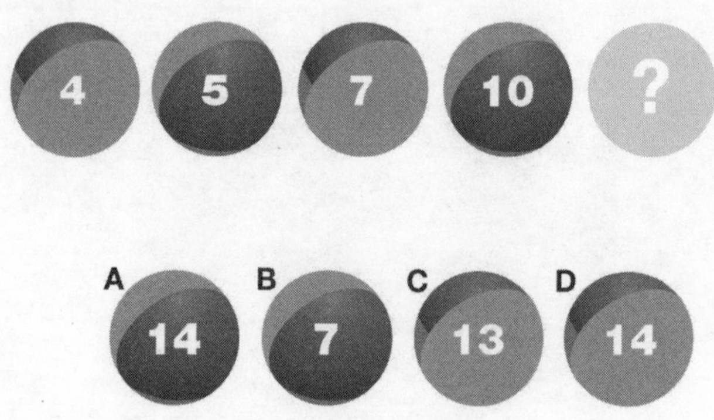


Answer on page 168

## NEXT!:

Which of the balls, A, B, C or D is the logical next step in this sequence?

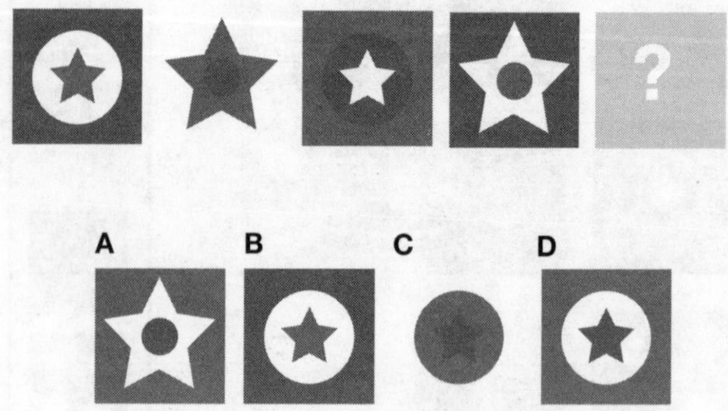


Answer on page 168

## BLOCK PARTY: Assuming all blocks that are not visible from this angle are present, how many blocks have been removed from this 6 × 6 × 6 cube?

Answer on page 168

## PICTURE PARTS: Which box has exactly the right bits to make the pic?

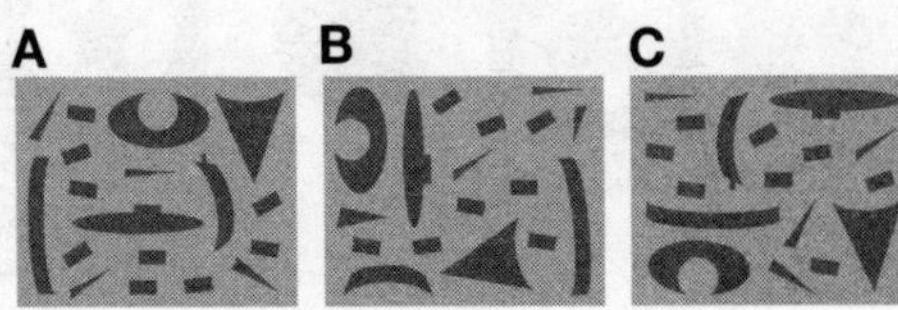


Answer on page 168

**POTS OF DOTS:** How many dots should there be in the hole in this pattern?

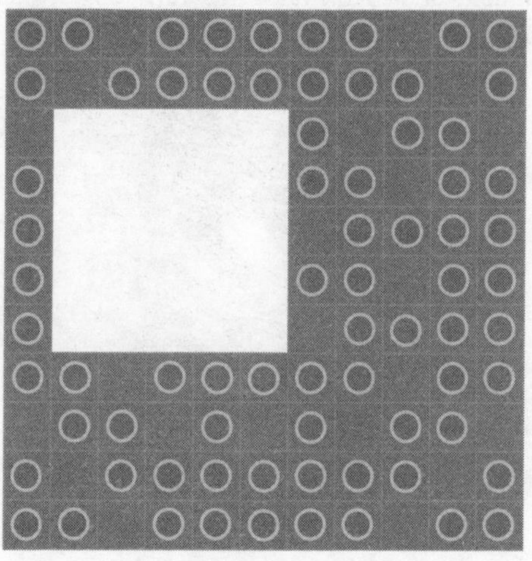

Answer on page 168

**SUM TOTAL:** Replace the question marks with mathematical symbols (+, –, × or ÷) to make a working sum.

WRINKLY QUOTE

"With age comes wisdom… and discounts."

CAR BUMPER STICKER

Answer on page 168

**RIDDLE:** You are in a room, blindfolded, with a bowl containing 50, 20, 10 and 5 dollar bills. You are allowed to take notes out of the bowl one at a time until you have four notes of the same value. What's the largest amount of cash you could end up with?

Answer on page 168

**BLOCK PARTY:** Assuming all blocks that are not visible from this angle are present, how many blocks have been removed from this 5 × 5 × 5 cube?

Answer on page 168

## BOXES:

In the game of boxes, each player takes it in turns to join two adjacent dots with a line. If a player's line completes a box, the player wins the box and has another go. It's your turn in the game below. Can you give your opponent just one box?

Answer on page 168

## DOUBLE DRAT:

All these letters appear twice in the box except one. Can you spot the singleton?

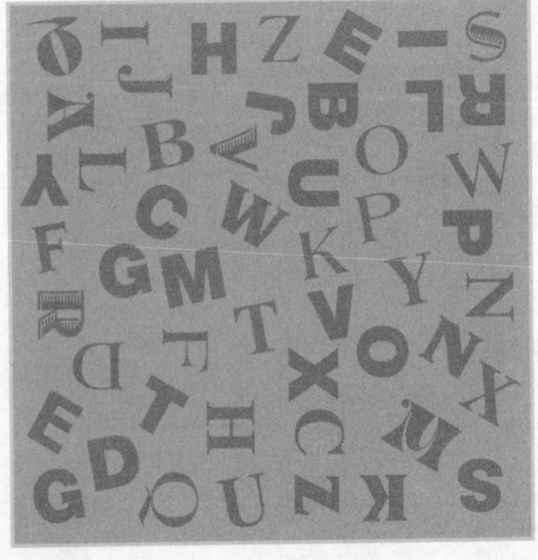

Answer on page 169

**CHECKERS:** Make a move for white so that eight black pieces are left, none of which are in the same column or row.

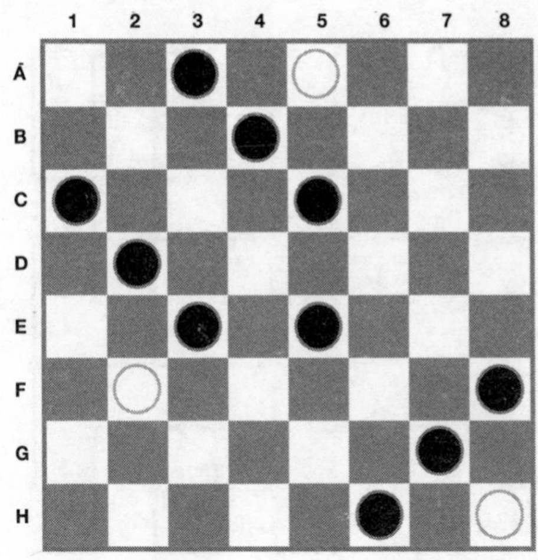


Answer on page 169

**BOXES:** In the game of boxes, each player takes it in turns to join two adjacent dots with a line. If a player's line completes a box, the player wins the box and has another go. It's your turn in the game below. Can you give your opponent just one box?

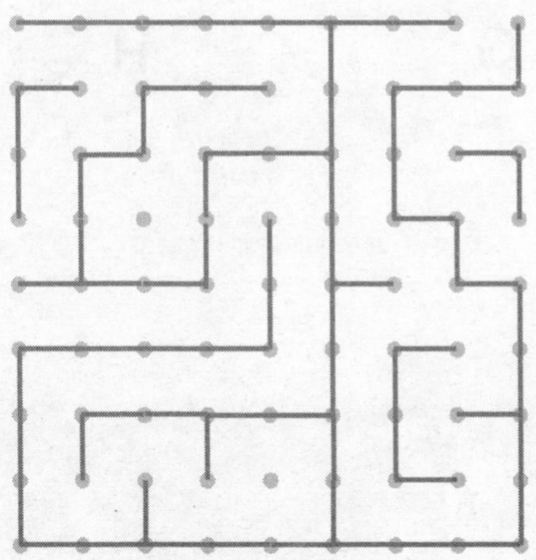

Answer on page 169

**DRESSING SNOWMAN:** Arrange this set of snowman pics in the correct order from bare ball of snow to fully fledged.

Answer on page 169

## Wrinkly Quote

"Sometimes getting older feels easy, sometimes it feels difficult. It depends how the wine is hitting you really."

RUPERT EVERETT

**RIDDLE:** Celebrity chef Gordon Ramsfoot discovered one Sunday morning that his toaster had broken and he had three hungry kids on his hands. It takes exactly one minute to toast one side of a piece of bread using the grill, but the grill only takes two pieces of bread at a time. In a terrible hurry as always, can you work out how he managed to make three pieces of toast, using the grill, in just three minutes?

Answer on page 169

**X AND O:** The numbers around the edge of the grid describe the number of X's in the vertical, horizontal and diagonal lines connecting with that square. Complete the grid so that there is an X or O in every square.

| 1 | 2 | 4 | 4 | 3 | 2 |
|---|---|---|---|---|---|
| 6 | | | | | 4 |
| 3 | | | | | 4 |
| 2 | | X | | | 3 |
| 2 | | | X | | 1 |
| 2 | 3 | 2 | 2 | 5 | 1 |

Answer on page 169

**IN THE AREA:** Can you work out the approximate area this letter Q is taking up?

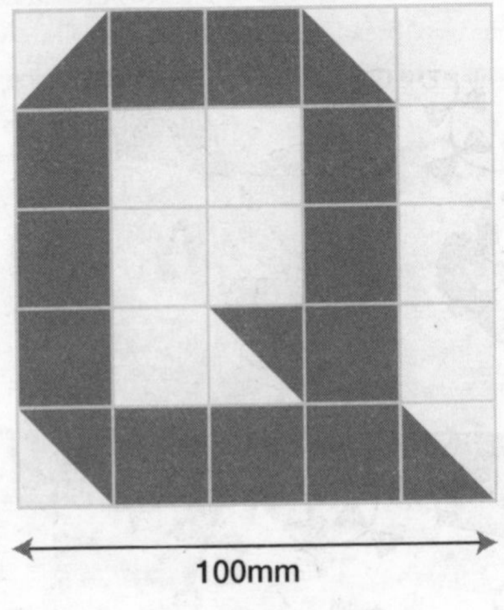


Answer on page 169

**THINK OF A NUMBER:** Officers Kaplutski and Wojowitz like a doughnut while they work. On a week long stakeout, Kaplutski ate 12 jam doughnuts and Wojowitz ate 28. What percentage of all the doughnuts eaten did Wojowitz account for?

Answer on page 169

# MIRROR IMAGE:

Only one of these pictures is an exact mirror image of the first one? Can you spot it?

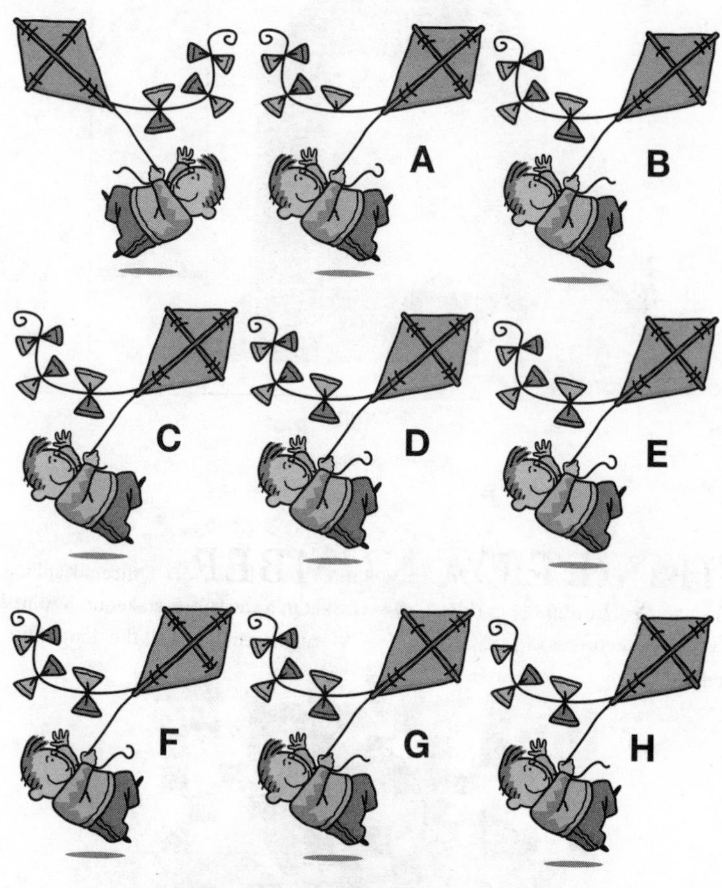


Answer on page 170

## WRINKLY QUOTE

"No wise man ever wished to be younger."

JONATHAN SWIFT

# MATRIX: Which of the boxed figures completes the set?

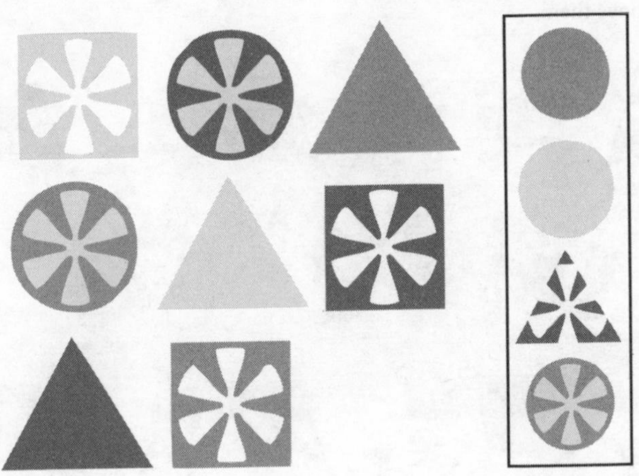

Answer on page 170

# SYMMETRY: This picture, when finished, is symmetrical along a vertical line up the middle. Can you colour in the missing squares and work out what the picture is of?

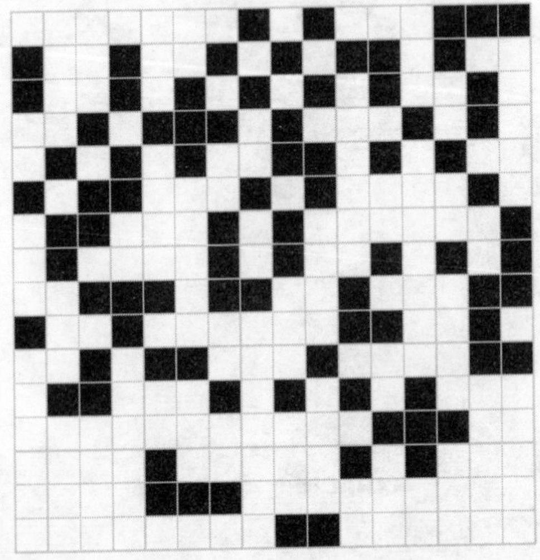

Answer on page 170

**NUMBER MOUNTAIN:** Replace the question marks with numbers so that each pair of blocks adds up to the block directly above them.

Answer on page 170

**ODD CLOCKS:** Paris is 2 hours behind Athens, which is 2 hours behind Karachi. It is 1.50 am on Sunday in Athens – what time is it in the other two cities?

Answer on page 170

## PICTURE PARTS: Which box contains exactly the right bits to make the pic?

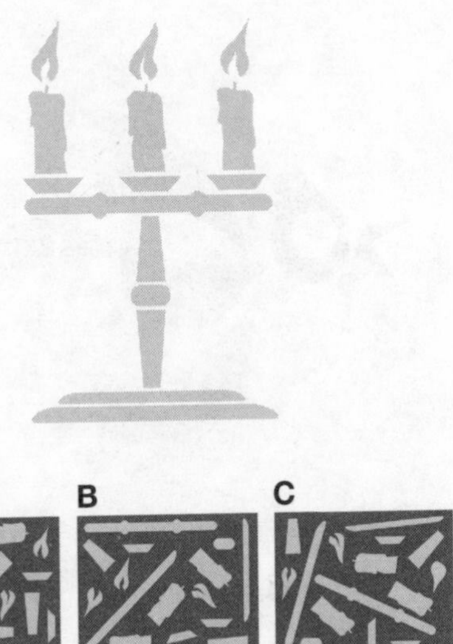


Answer on page 170

## SUM TOTAL: Replace the question marks with mathematical symbols (+, –, × or ÷, inserting brackets where necessary) to make a working sum.

Answer on page 170

# PICTURE PARTS: Which box contains exactly the right bits to make the pic?

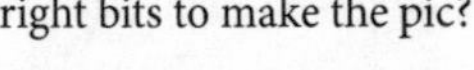

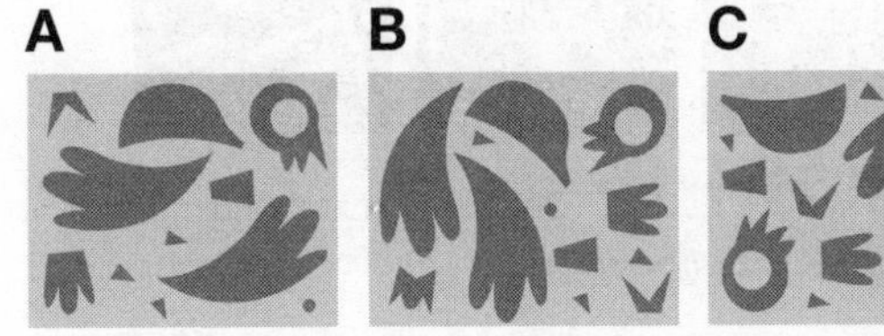


Answer on page 170

**WRINKLY QUOTE**

"I think when I'm 60, I'll finally be cool: my old man's very cool."

BONO

**SCALES:** The arms of these scales are divided into sections – a weight two sections away from the middle will be twice as heavy as a weight one section away. Can you arrange the supplied weights in such a way as to balance the whole scale?

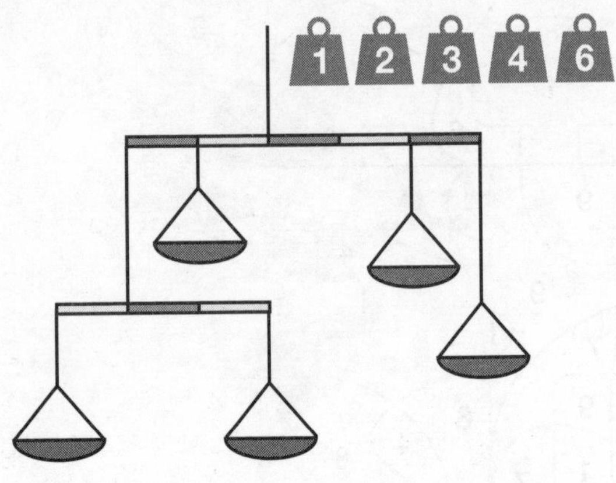


Answer on page 171

**SUM PEOPLE:** Work out what number is represented by which person and replace the question mark.

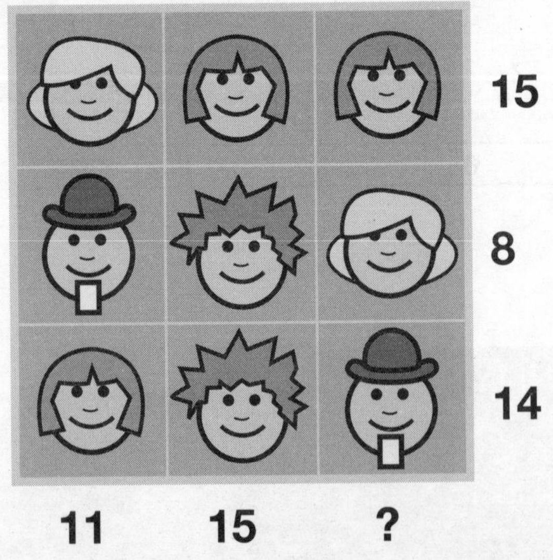


Answer on page 171

# PAINT BY NUMBERS: Colour in the odd numbers to reveal... What?

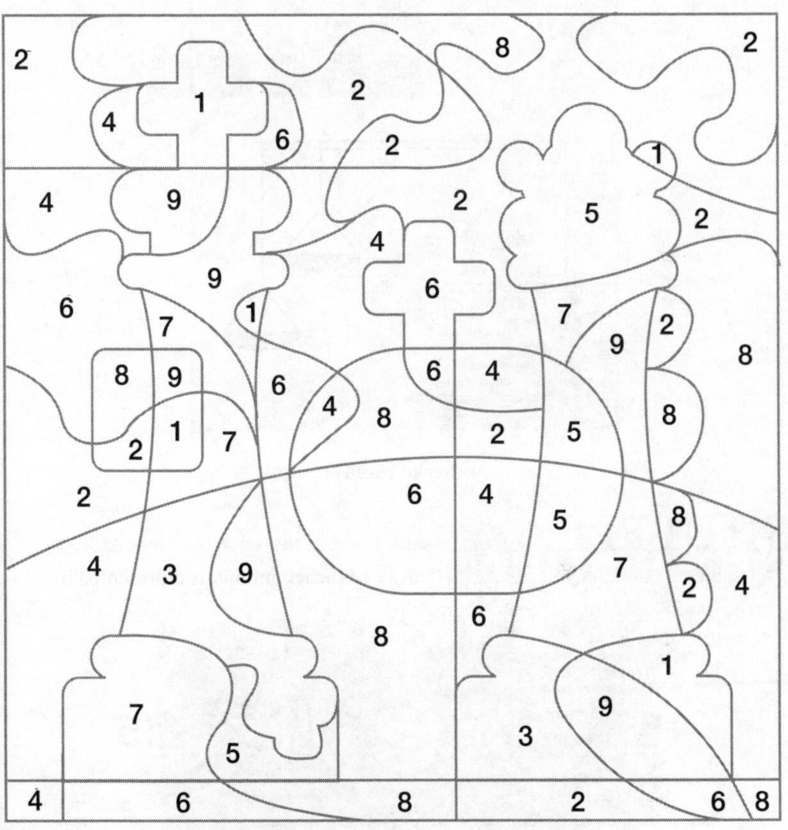

Answer on page 171

## WRINKLY QUOTE

"I'd like to be an old man with a good face, like Hitchcock or Picasso."

SEAN CONNERY

## SUDOKU SIXPACK:

Complete the grid so that every row, column and long diagonal contains the numbers 1, 2, 3, 4, 5 and 6.

| 6 |  |  |  | 1 | 5 |
|---|---|---|---|---|---|
| 2 |  |  | 4 |  | 3 |
|  |  |  |  |  |  |
|  | 6 |  |  |  | 2 |
| 4 | 2 |  |  | 3 |  |
| 1 |  |  | 5 | 2 |  |

Answer on page 171

## SHUFFLE:

Fill in the shuffle box so that each row, column and long diagonal contains four different shapes and the letters A, B, C and D.

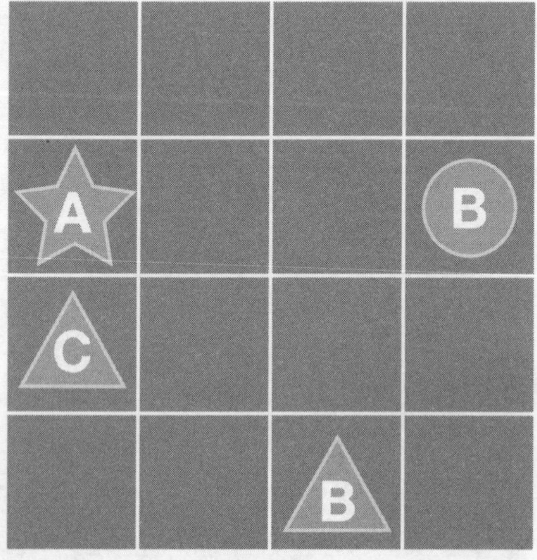


Answer on page 171

**SHUFFLE:** Fill in the grid so that each row, column and long diagonal contains four different shapes and the letters A, B, C and D.

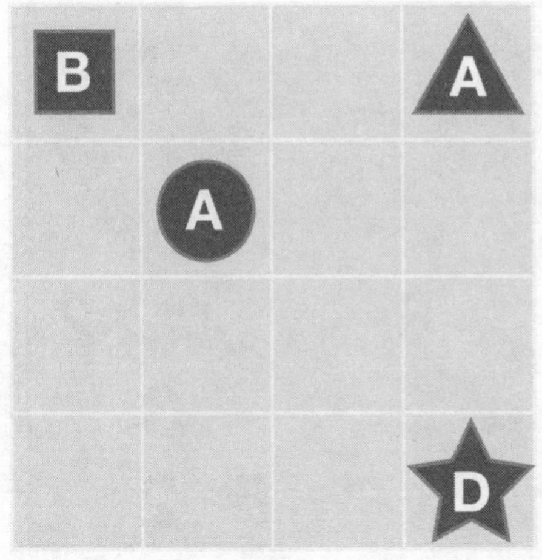


Answer on page 171

**SHAPE STACKER:** Can you work out the logic behind the numbers in these shapes, and suggest a number to replace the question mark?

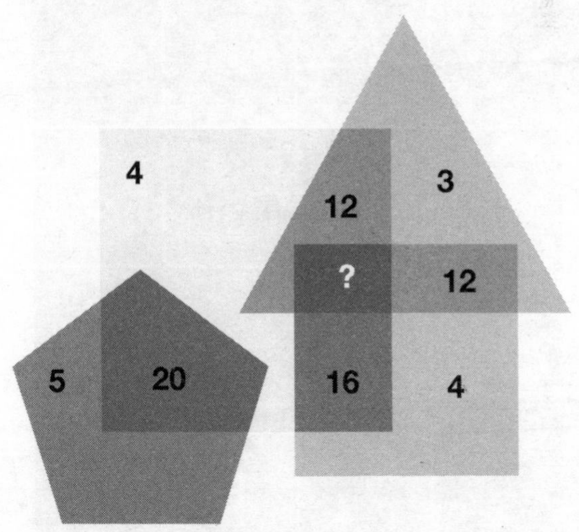


Answer on page 172

**SHAPE SHIFTING:** Fill in the empty squares so that each row, column and long diagonal contains five different symbols.

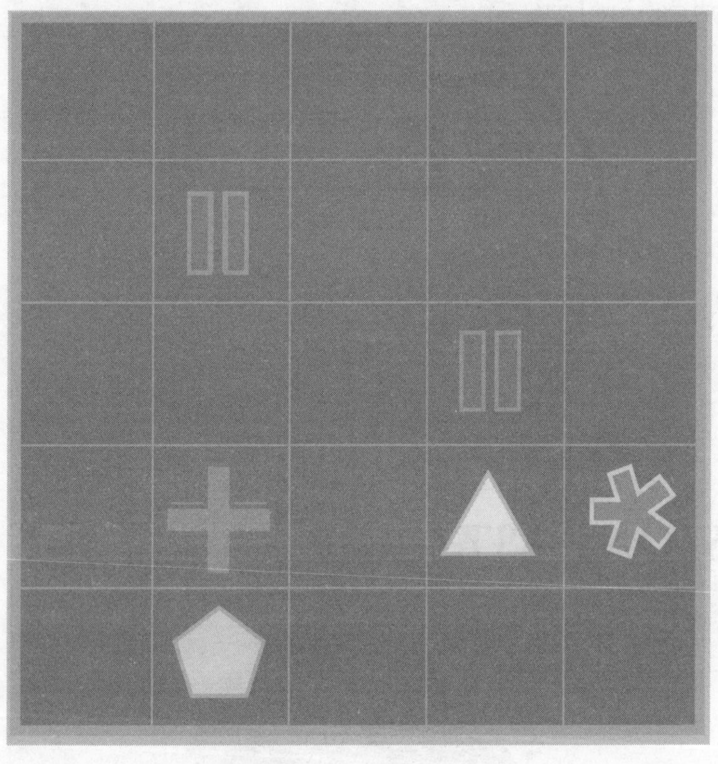

Answer on page 172

WRINKLY QUOTE

"There is nothing more liberating than age."

LIZ CARPENTER

**RIDDLE:** In my shed at home I have some hamsters and some hamster cages. If I put one hamster in each cage I'd have one hamster too many. But if I put two hamsters in each cage, I'd have one cage left over... How many hamsters and cages have I got?

Answer on page 172

**SIGNPOST:** Can you crack the logical secret behind the distances to these great cities, and work out how far it is to Karachi?

Answer on page 172

# MEDIUM PUZZLES

**BOXES:** Playing the game of boxes, each player takes it in turns to join two adjacent dots with a line. If a player's line completes a box, the player wins the box and has another go. It's your turn in the game below. To avoid giving your opponent a lot of boxes, what's your best move?

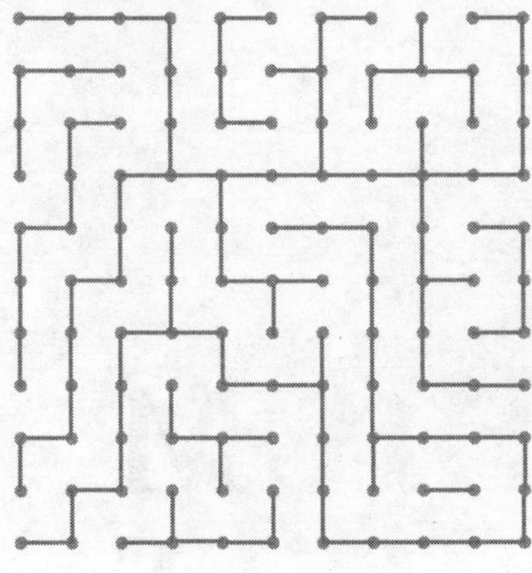

Answer on page 172

**CUT AND FOLD:** Which of the patterns below is created by this fold and cut?

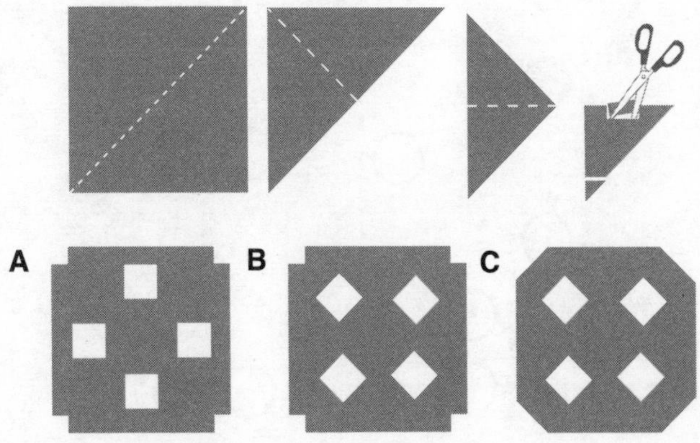


Answer on page 172

# MAGIC SQUARES: Complete the square using nine consecutive numbers, so that all rows, columns and large diagonals add up to the same total.

Answer on page 173

# MASYU: Draw a single unbroken line around the grid that passes through all the circles. The line must enter and leave each box in the centre of one of its four sides. **Black Circle:** Turn left or right in the box, and the line must pass straight through the next and previous boxes. **White Circle:** Travel straight through the box, and the line must turn in the next and/or previous box.

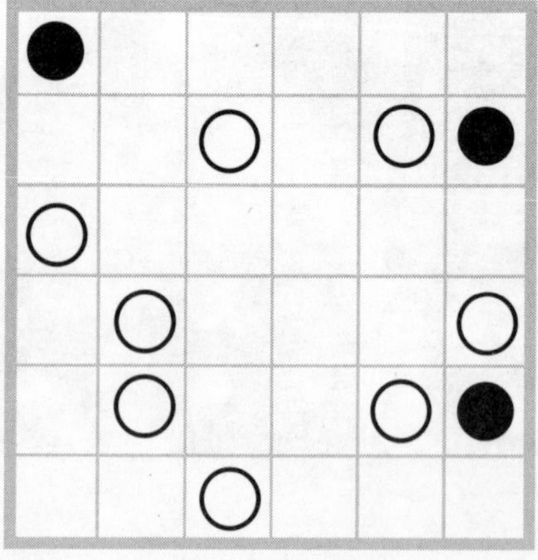

Answer on page 173

**RIDDLE:** Kitty has fallen down a well 12 metres (that's about 35 feet in old money) deep. He can jump 3 metres up. But slides back 2 metres every time he lands. How many jumps get kitty out of the well?

Answer on page 173

**THINK OF A NUMBER:** At the Sea View Guest house in Bournemouth, England over the course of one week they served 351 glasses of fruit juice with breakfast. 203 of them were orange, 31 were grapefruit, 39 were mango and 78 were apple. Can you work out what proportion of guests had citrus as opposed to non-citrus juices?

Answer on page 173

## SUM PEOPLE: 

Work out what number is represented by which person and fill in the question mark.

Answer on page 173

## TENTS AND TREES: 

Every tree has one tent found horizontally or vertically adjacent to it. No tent can be in an adjacent square to another tent (even diagonally!). The numbers by each row and column tell you how many tents there are. Can you locate all the tents?

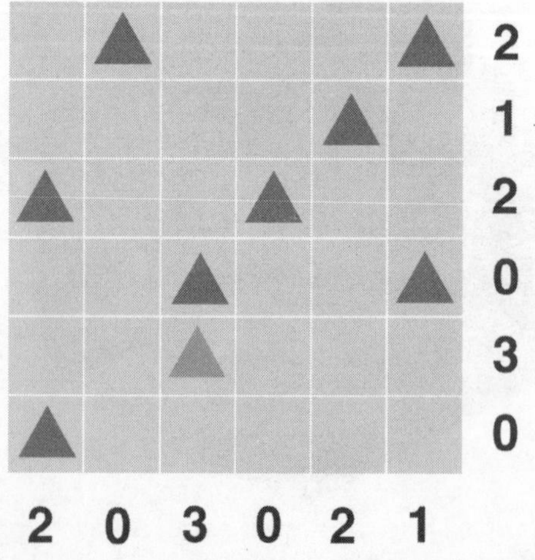


Answer on page 173

**SIGNPOST:** Can you crack the logical secret behind the distances to these great cities, and work out how far it is to Washington?

Answer on page 173

**BLOCK PARTY:** Assuming all blocks that are not visible from this angle are present, how many blocks have been removed from this 6 x 6 x 6 cube?

Answer on page 173

## WHERE'S THE PAIR:

Only two of the shapes below are exactly the same – can you find the matching pair?

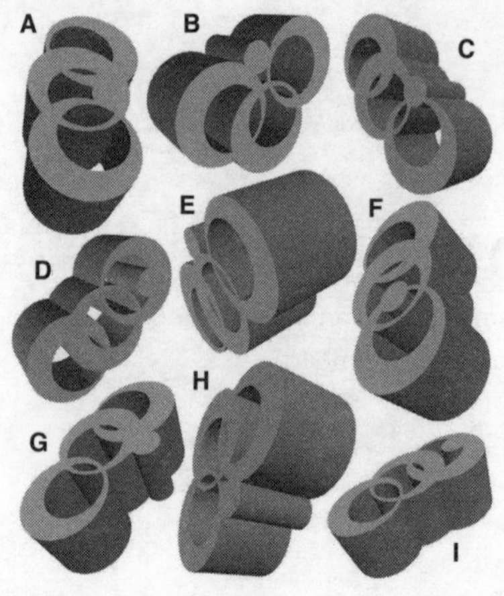


Answer on page 174

## DOUBLE DRAT:

All these shapes appear twice in the box except one. Can you spot the singleton?

Answer on page 174

## Wrinkly Quote

"Growing older is not upsetting; being perceived as old is."

KENNY ROGERS

# MORE OR LESS:

The arrows indicate whether a number in a box is greater or smaller than an adjacent number. Complete the grid so that all rows and columns contain the numbers 1 to 5.

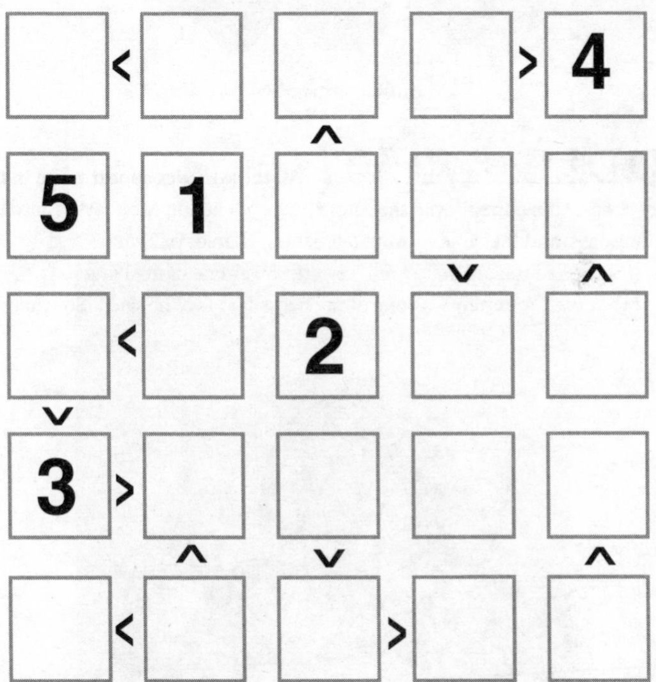

Answer on page 174

# PERCENTAGE POINT: What percentage of this grid is darker and what percentage is lighter?

Answer on page 174

# RIDDLE: Lucy met a pig and a goat in the woods and asked them what day it was, knowing full well that pigs always tell lies on Mondays, Tuesdays and Wednesdays, and that goats always tell lies on Thursdays, Fridays and Saturdays. She asked the pig first. 'Well, yesterday was one of my lying days,' he said. She asked the goat. 'Yesterday was one of my lying days too,' he said... So what day is it?

Answer on page 174

**BOX IT:** The value of each shape is the number of sides each shape has, multiplied by the number within it. Thus a square containing the number 4 has a value of 16. Find a block two squares wide and two squares high with a total value of exactly 50.

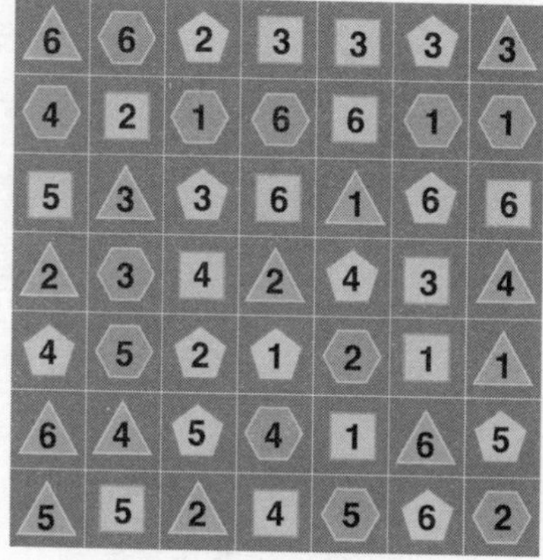

Answer on page 174

**BOXES:** Playing the game of boxes, each player takes it in turns to join two adjacent dots with a line. If a player's line completes a box, the player wins the box and has another go. It's your turn in the game below. To avoid giving your opponent a lot of boxes, what's your best move?

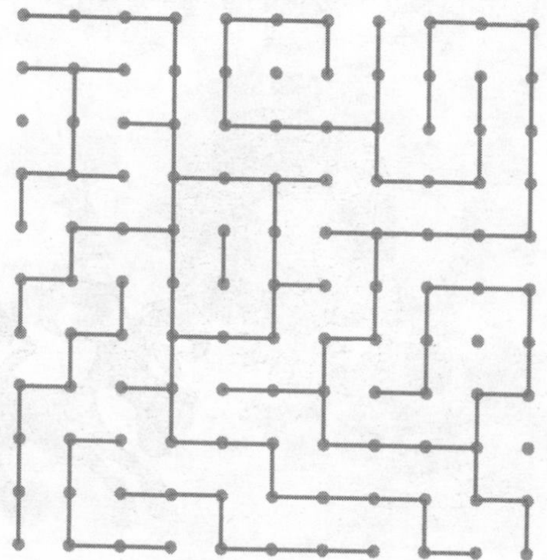

Answer on page 174

## TENTS AND TREES:

Every tree has at least one tent found horizontally or vertically adjacent to it. No tent can be in an adjacent square to another tent (even diagonally). The numbers by each row and column tell you how many tents there are. Can you locate all the tents?

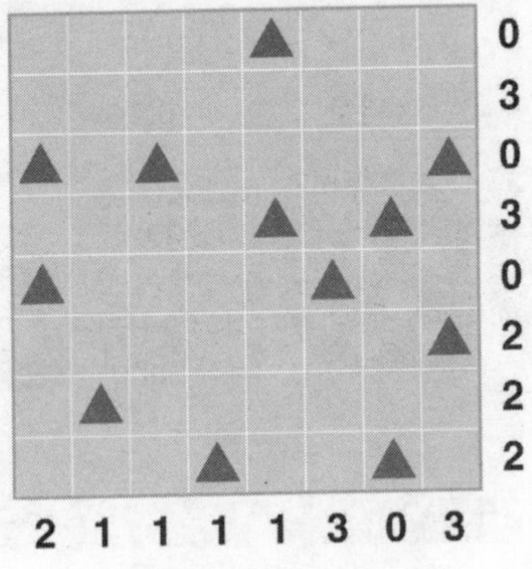


Answer on page 174

## CHECKERS:

Make a move for white so that eight black pieces are left, none of which are in the same column or row.

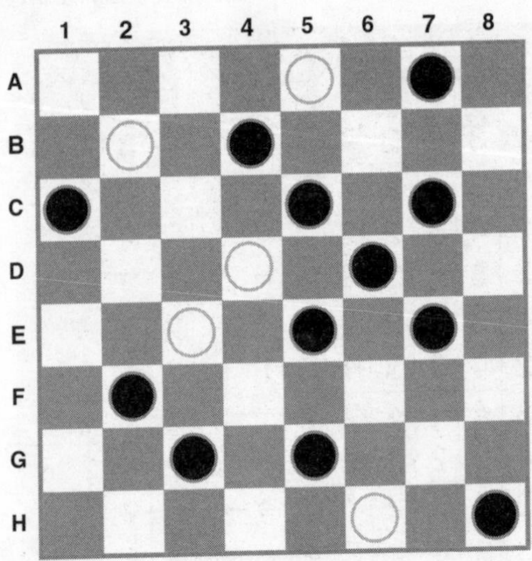


Answer on page 175

# DICE PUZZLE: What's the missing number?

Answer on page 175

# FIGURE IT OUT: The sequence 23224 can be found once in the grid, reading up, down, backwards, forwards or diagonally. Can you pick it out?

| 4 | 2 | 2 | 3 | 4 | 4 | 4 | 4 | 3 | 4 | 4 | 4 |
|---|---|---|---|---|---|---|---|---|---|---|---|
| 4 | 4 | 3 | 4 | 2 | 2 | 2 | 2 | 2 | 2 | 2 | 2 |
| 2 | 3 | 2 | 2 | 3 | 3 | 3 | 2 | 4 | 3 | 3 | 3 |
| 3 | 2 | 3 | 2 | 2 | 3 | 2 | 2 | 2 | 2 | 2 | 2 |
| 3 | 4 | 3 | 2 | 2 | 2 | 4 | 3 | 2 | 2 | 4 | 2 |
| 3 | 3 | 2 | 2 | 3 | 3 | 4 | 2 | 2 | 3 | 2 | 2 |
| 4 | 3 | 2 | 2 | 2 | 2 | 2 | 3 | 2 | 2 | 3 | 3 |
| 2 | 4 | 3 | 3 | 4 | 3 | 2 | 2 | 3 | 4 | 3 | 4 |
| 3 | 4 | 4 | 4 | 2 | 2 | 2 | 3 | 2 | 2 | 2 | 2 |
| 4 | 2 | 2 | 2 | 2 | 3 | 3 | 2 | 4 | 3 | 3 | 3 |
| 2 | 4 | 3 | 2 | 4 | 4 | 4 | 4 | 2 | 2 | 2 | 2 |
| 3 | 2 | 3 | 2 | 2 | 3 | 4 | 3 | 3 | 2 | 3 | 4 |

Answer on page 175

# GAME OF THREE HALVES:

Which three shapes below will piece together to create the top shape?

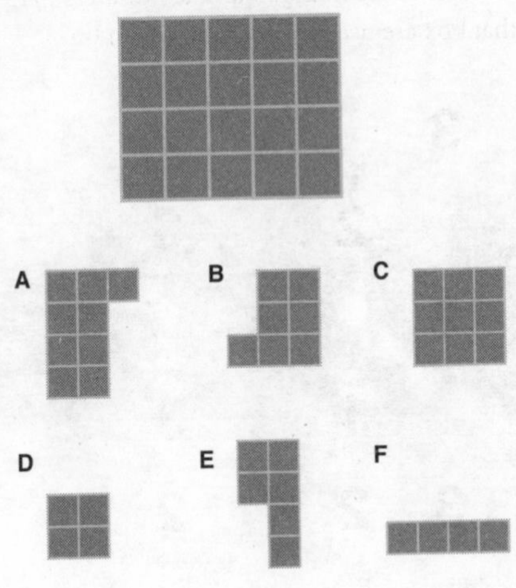


Answer on page 175

# LATIN SQUARE

Complete the grid so that every row and column, and every outlined area, contains the letters A, B, C, D, E and F.

| | | | | | |
|---|---|---|---|---|---|
| E | | | | | |
| | B | | | D | |
| | | | | | |
| C | | | A | | |
| | | | | | C |
| F | | B | | E | |

Answer on page 175

**LOOPLINK:** Connect adjacent dots with either horizontal or vertical lines to create a continuous unbroken loop which never crosses over itself. Some, but not all of the boxes are numbered. The numbers in these boxes tell you how many sides of that box are used by your unbroken line.

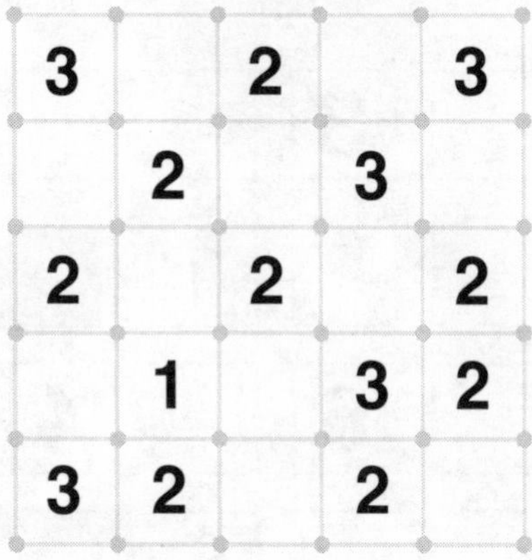

| 3 | | 2 | | 3 |
|---|---|---|---|---|
| | 2 | | 3 | |
| 2 | | 2 | | 2 |
| | 1 | | 3 | 2 |
| 3 | 2 | | 2 | |

Answer on page 175

**MASYU:** Draw a single unbroken line around the grid that passes through all the circles. The line must enter and leave each box in the centre of one of its four sides. **Black Circle:** Turn left or right in the box, and the line must pass straight through the next and previous boxes. **White Circle:** Travel straight through the box, and the line must turn in the next and/or previous box.

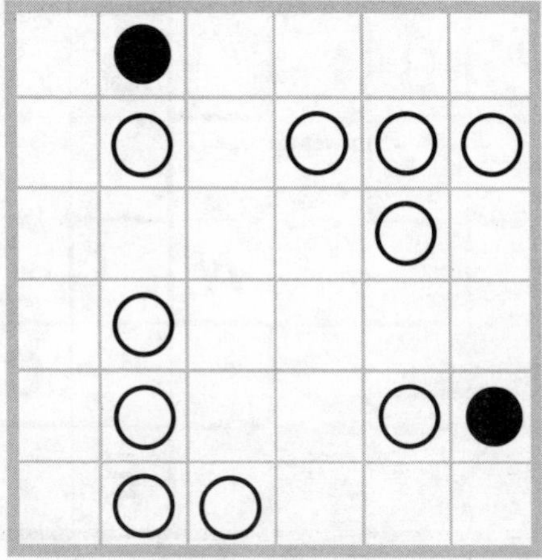

Answer on page 175

# MORE OR LESS:

The arrows indicate whether a number in a box is greater or smaller than an adjacent number. Complete the grid so that all rows and columns contain the numbers 1 to 6.

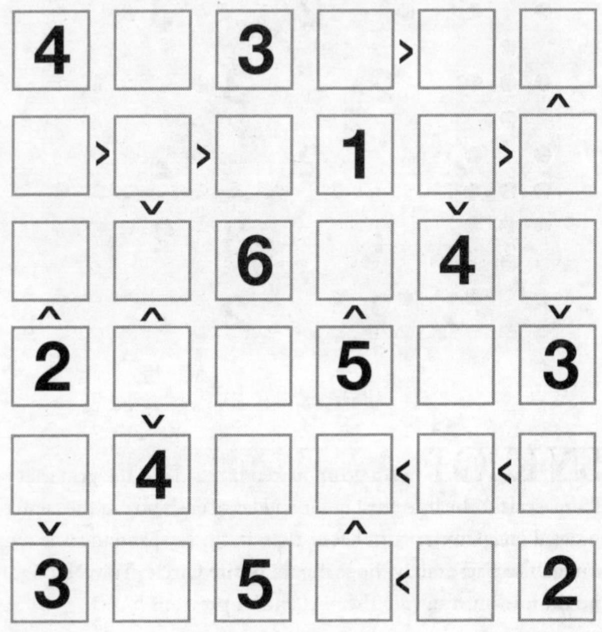

Answer on page 176

WRINKLY QUOTE

"Forty is the old age of youth, 50 is the youth of old age."

VICTOR HUGO

**POTS OF DOTS:** How many dots should there be in the hole in this pattern?

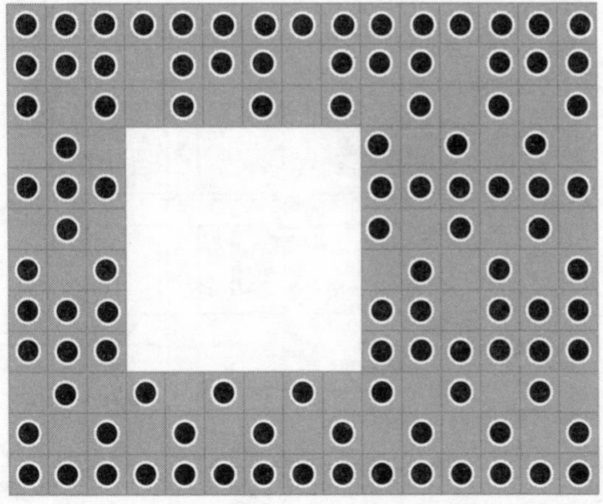

Answer on page 176

**THINK OF A NUMBER:** Little Joe was saving up for a scarf to wear to the big football match. On the first day of the month, he saved one penny, on the second, 2, on the third, 3 and so on until on the day of the match he had exactly the three pounds required to buy the scarf. What day was the game?

Answer on page 176

## SAFECRACKER:

To open the safe, all the buttons must be pressed in the correct order before the "open" button is pressed. What is the first button pressed in your sequence?

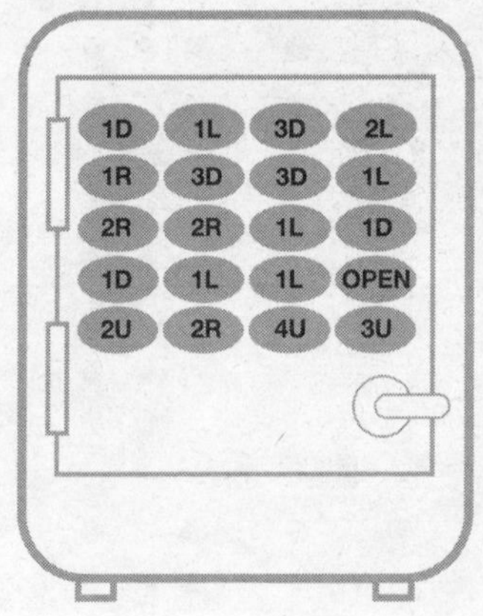


Answer on page 176

## SCALES:

The arms of these scales are divided into sections – a weight two sections away from the middle will be twice as heavy as a weight one section away. Can you arrange the supplied weights in such a way as to balance the whole scale?

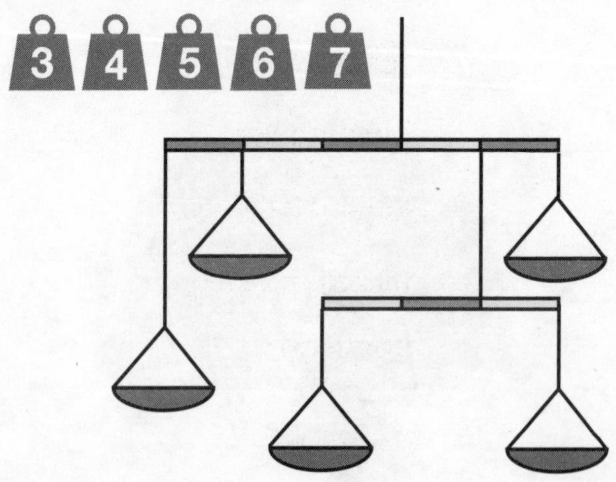


Answer on page 176

# SHAPE SHIFTING:

Fill in the empty squares so that each row, column and long diagonal contains five different numbered balls.

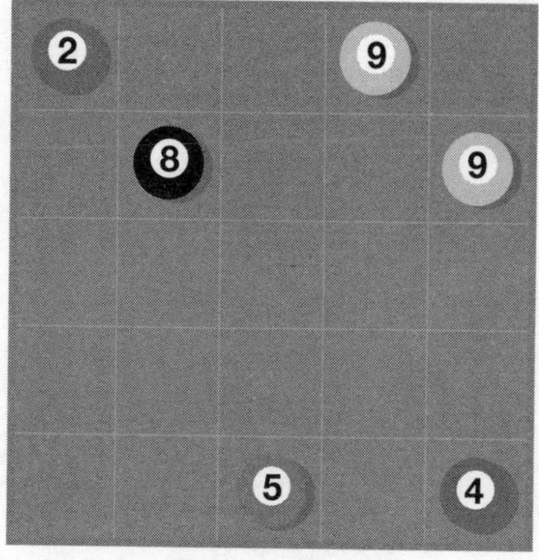


Answer on page 176

# SIGNPOST:

Can you crack the logical secret behind the distances to these great cities, and work out how far it is to Vancouver?

Answer on page 176

## SUDOKU SIXPACK: Complete the grid so that every row, column and long diagonal contains the numbers 1, 2, 3, 4, 5 and 6.

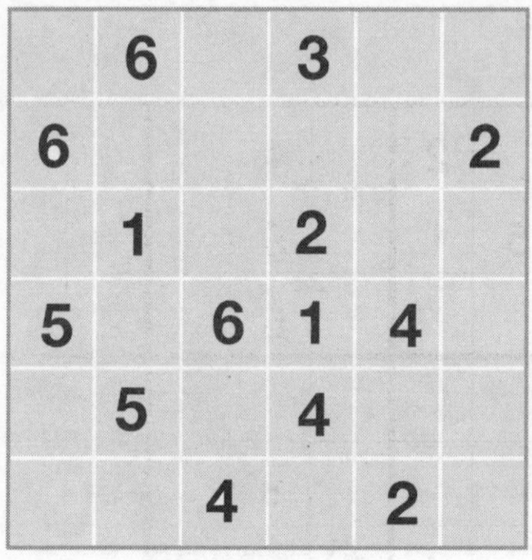

| | | | | | |
|---|---|---|---|---|---|
| | 6 | | 3 | | |
| 6 | | | | | 2 |
| | 1 | | 2 | | |
| 5 | | 6 | 1 | 4 | |
| | 5 | | 4 | | |
| | | 4 | | 2 | |

Answer on page 177

## SUM PEOPLE: Work out what number is represented by which person and fill in the question mark.

Answer on page 177

**SUDOKU:** Complete the grid so that all rows and columns, and each outlined block of nine squares, contain the numbers 1, 2, 3, 4, 5, 6, 7, 8 and 9.

| | | | | | | | | |
|---|---|---|---|---|---|---|---|---|
| | | 2 | | 1 | | 4 | | |
| | 5 | 1 | | 9 | | 7 | 3 | 8 |
| 7 | | | | 6 | | 2 | | |
| | | | | | 1 | | 4 | 5 |
| 3 | | | | 8 | | 9 | | 1 |
| 1 | | 4 | 7 | | | | | |
| | | | | 4 | | 8 | | 7 |
| 4 | | 6 | 8 | | 2 | 1 | 9 | |
| | 3 | | | | | 5 | | |

Answer on page 177

WRINKLY QUOTE

"Middle age: later than you think and sooner than you expected."

EARL WILSON

## THINK OF A NUMBER:

Officers Kaplutski and Wojowitz were counting up how many jaywalkers they had arrested in a week. Kaplutski was happy to discover he was ahead 14 to 11. Can you express the two cop's success rate as a percentage?

Answer on page 177

## VENN DIAGRAMS:

Can you work out which areas of this diagram represent Australian teetotal surfers who don't play rugby, and non-Australian beer drinking rugby players that don't surf?

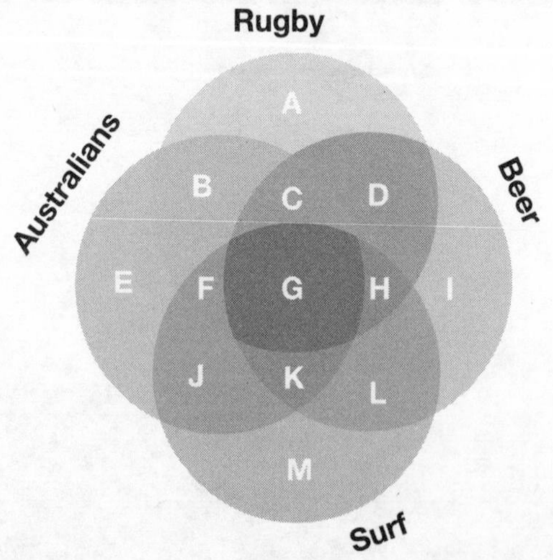


Answer on page 177

## WRINKLY QUOTE

"Like beauty, age is in the eye of the beholder."

ANON

## BITS AND PIECES: These ten pieces can be asembled to spell the name of a movie star... Who?

Answer on page 177

# FINDING NEMO:

The word NEMO can be found once in the grid, reading up, down, backwards, forwards or diagonally. Can you pick it out?

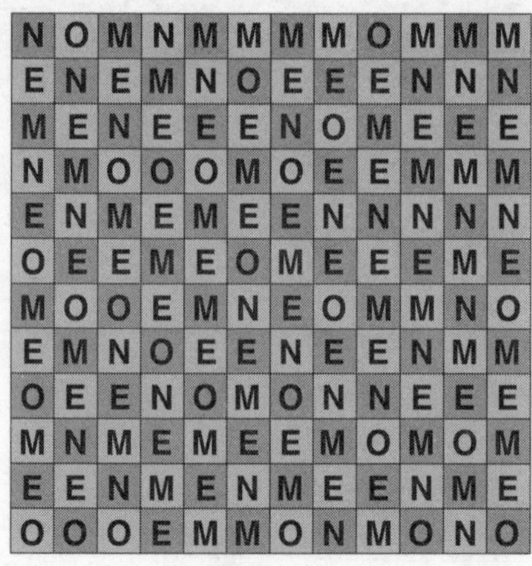

| N | O | M | N | M | M | M | M | O | M | M | M |
|---|---|---|---|---|---|---|---|---|---|---|---|
| E | N | E | M | N | O | E | E | E | N | N | N |
| M | E | N | E | E | E | N | O | M | E | E | E |
| N | M | O | O | O | M | O | E | E | M | M | M |
| E | N | M | E | M | E | E | N | N | N | N | N |
| O | E | E | M | E | O | M | E | E | E | M | E |
| M | O | O | E | M | N | E | O | M | M | N | O |
| E | M | N | O | E | E | N | E | E | N | M | M |
| O | E | E | N | O | M | O | N | N | E | E | E |
| M | N | M | E | M | E | E | M | O | M | O | M |
| E | E | N | M | E | N | M | E | E | N | M | E |
| O | O | O | E | M | M | O | N | M | O | N | O |

Answer on page 177

# MAGIC SQUARES:

Complete the square using nine consecutive numbers, so that all rows, columns and large diagonals add up to the same total.

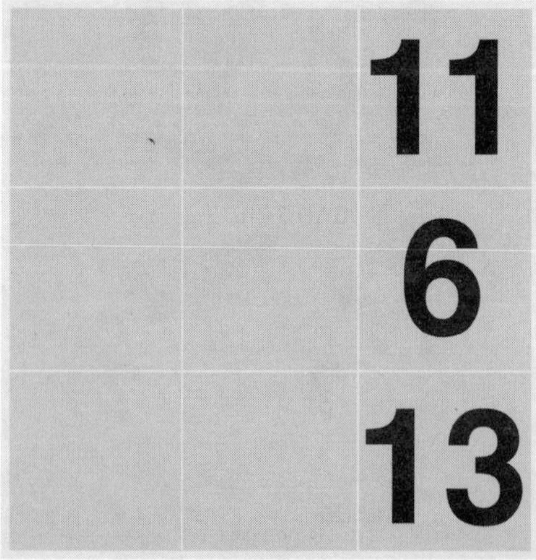

|   |   |   |
|---|---|---|
|   |   | 11 |
|   |   | 6 |
|   |   | 13 |

Answer on page 177

# MATRIX: Which of the boxed figures completes the set?

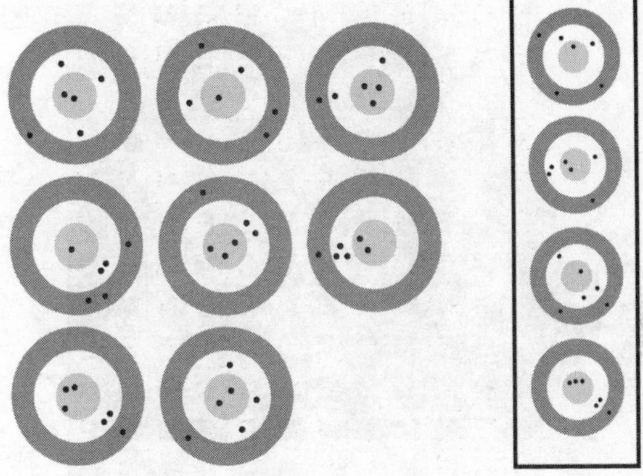

Answer on page 178

# ODD CLOCKS: Auckland is 16 hours ahead of Sao Paulo, which is 1 hour ahead of Miami. It is 2.15 pm on Saturday in Sao Paulo – what time is it in the other two cities?

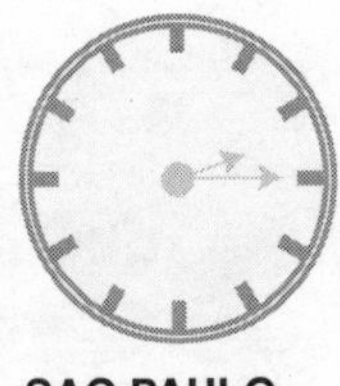

Answer on page 178

## RIDDLE:

Jessica promised Julia that she would tell her a huge piece of gossip, but it would have to wait until the day before four days from the day after tomorrow. Today is Wednesday the 3rd – when does Julia get to know?

Answer on page 178

## SAFECRACKER:

To open the safe, all the buttons must be pressed in the correct order before the "open" button is pressed. What is the first button pressed in your sequence?

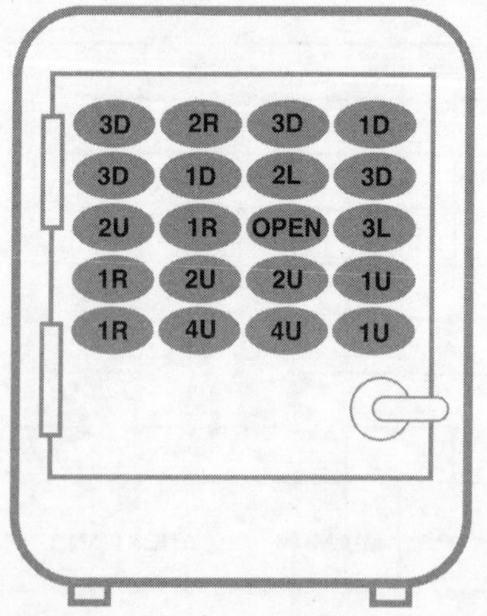


Answer on page 178

## LOGIC SEQUENCE: The balls below have been rearranged. Can you work out the new sequence of the balls from the clues given below?

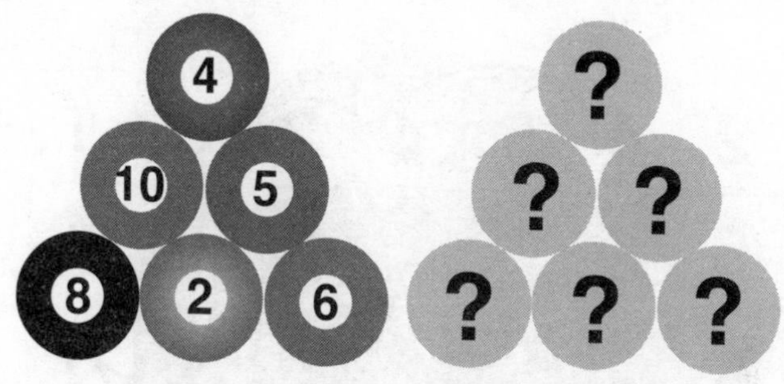


The 4 ball isn't touching the 5 or the 2.
The 8 ball is touching four others.
The 4 ball is immediately to the right of the 6.
The 10 ball is resting on two balls totalling 13.

Answer on page 178

## BOXES: Playing the game of boxes, each player takes it in turns to join two adjacent dots with a line. If a player's line completes a box, the player wins the box and has another go. It's your turn in the game below. To avoid giving your opponent a lot of boxes, what's your best move?

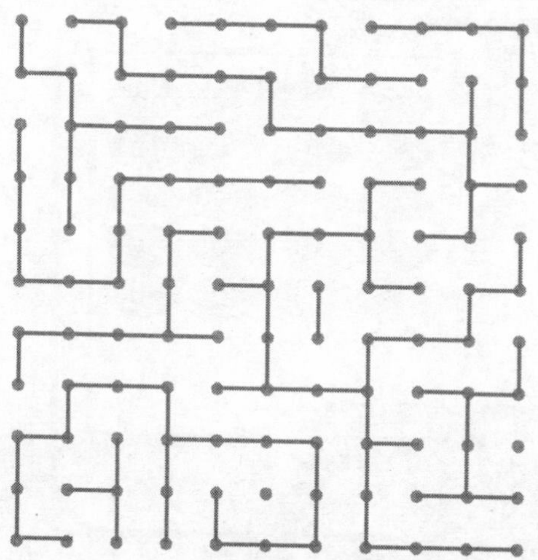

Answer on page 178

# X AND O:

The numbers around the edge of the grid describe the number of X's in the vertical, horizontal and diagonal lines connecting with that square. Complete the grid so that there is an X or O in every square.

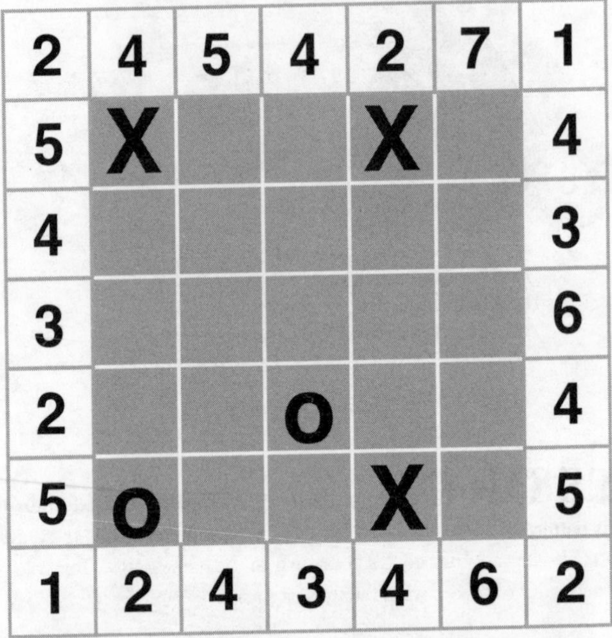

| 2 | 4 | 5 | 4 | 2 | 7 | 1 |
|---|---|---|---|---|---|---|
| 5 | X | | | X | | 4 |
| 4 | | | | | | 3 |
| 3 | | | | | | 6 |
| 2 | | | O | | | 4 |
| 5 | O | | | X | | 5 |
| 1 | 2 | 4 | 3 | 4 | 6 | 2 |

Answer on page 179

WRINKLY QUOTE

"Age is a matter of feeling, not of years."

GEORGE WILLIAM CURTIS

**PERCENTAGE POINT:** What percentage of this shape is darker and what percentage is lighter?

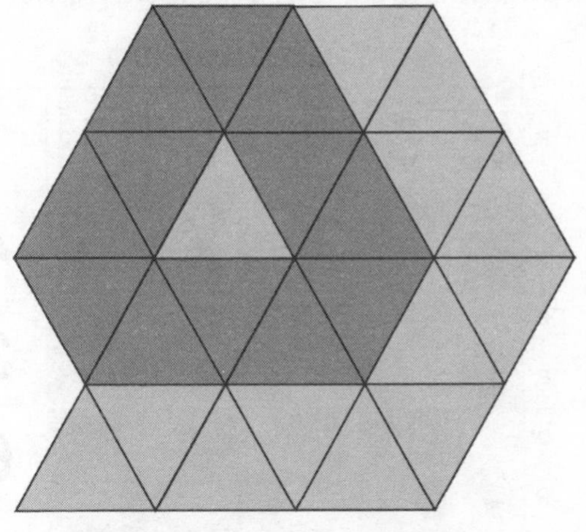

Answer on page 179

**POTS OF DOTS:** How many dots should there be in the hole in this pattern?

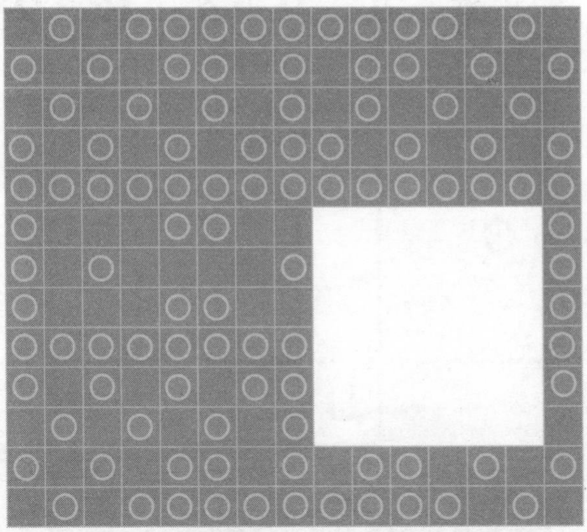

Answer on page 179

## CHECKERS: Make a move for white so that eight black pieces are left, none of which are in the same column or row.

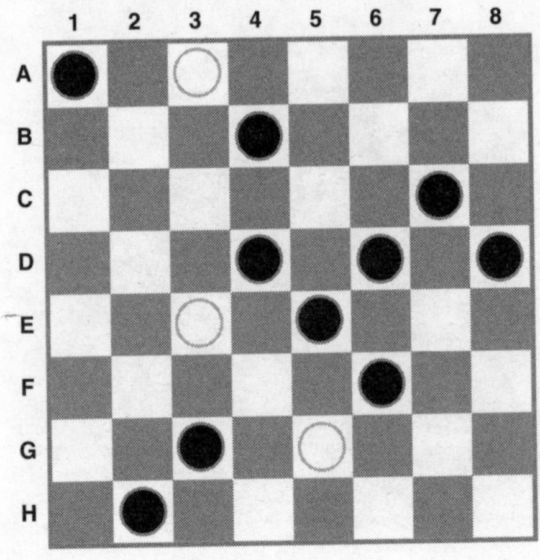

Answer on page 179

## LATIN SQUARE: Complete the grid so that every row and column, and every outlined area, contains the letters A, B, C, D, E and F.

| | | | | | |
|---|---|---|---|---|---|
| F | | | | | D |
| | | | A | | E |
| C | | | | | |
| | E | | | | |
| | | D | | | |
| E | | B | | | C |

Answer on page 179

**NUMBER MOUNTAIN:** Replace the question marks with numbers so that each pair of blocks adds up to the block directly above them.

Answer on page 179

**PICTURE PARTS:** Which box has exactly the right bits to make the pic?

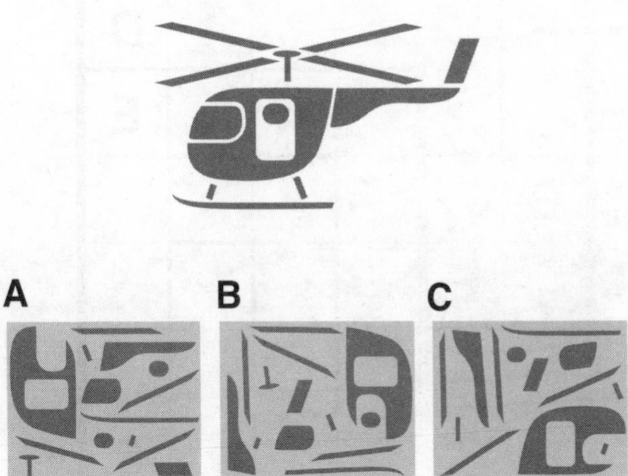


Answer on page 179

# THINK OF A NUMBER:

Belinda, Benny, Bobby, Brian and Bill entered a competition to guess how many sweets there were in a jar. Belinda said 300, Ben said 280, Bobby said 290, Brian said 250 and Bill said 260. Two guesses were just ten sweets away from the number. One guess was 40 away and another was wrong by 30. But who won?

Answer on page 180

## WRINKLY QUOTE

"The best time to start thinking about your retirement is before the boss does."

ANON

**SUM PEOPLE:** Work out what number is represented by which person and fill in the question mark.

Answer on page 180

**THINK OF A NUMBER:** Old Mother Jones loves her gummy sweets. They come in three colours: orange, red and yellow. There were exactly twice as many red sweets as yellow ones in the packet. After eating seven orange ones, she had one less orange than yellow left, and the number of orange sweets remaining represented 20 percent of the sweets she started with. How many did she start with?

Answer on page 180

# SHUFFLE:

Fill up the shuffle box so that each row, column and long diagonal contains a Jack, Queen, King and Ace of each suit.

Answer on page 180

## Wrinkly Quote

"You can be young without money, but you can't be old without it."

TENNESSEE WILLIAMS

**DOUBLE DRAT:** All these shapes appear twice in the box except one. Can you spot the singleton?

Answer on page 180

**WHERE'S THE PAIR?:** Only two of these pictures are exactly the same. Can you spot the matching pair?

Answer on page 180

## THE RED CORNER:

Use the numbers in the corners to make the central number the same way in all three cases. What number should replace the question mark?

Answer on page 180

## HUB SIGNS:

What numbers should appear in the hubs of these number wheels?

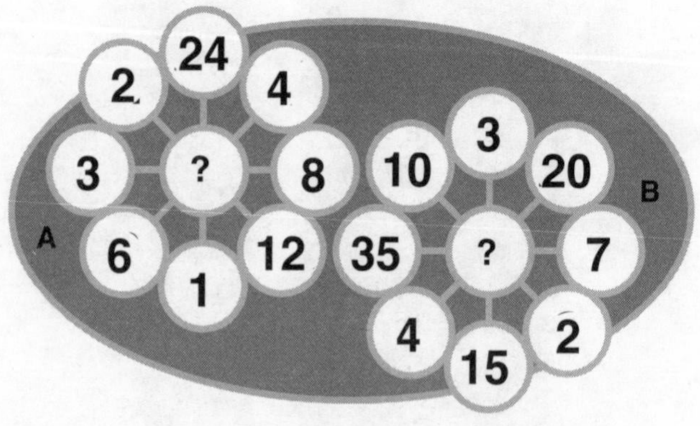


Answer on page 180

## BOX IT:

The value of each shape is the number of sides each shape has, multiplied by the number within it. Thus a square containing the number 4 has a value of 16. Find a block two squares wide and two squares high with a total value of exactly 100.

Answer on page 181

## REVOLUTIONS:

Cog A has 10 teeth, cog B has 8 and cog C has 14. How many revolutions must cog A turn through to bring all three cogs back to these exact positions?

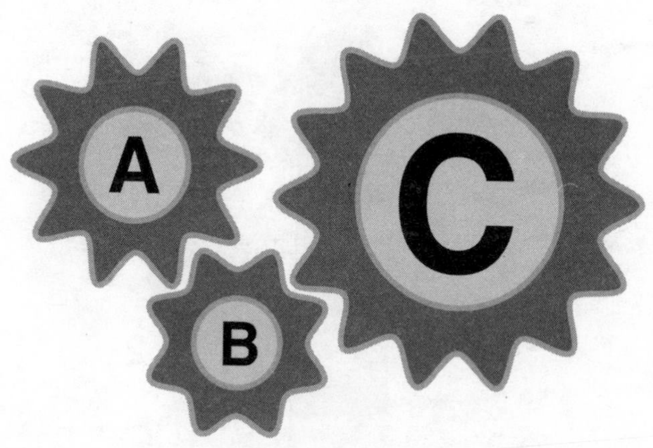


Answer on page 181

## THINK OF A NUMBER:

Ada the antique dealer was pondering her profits one day, and thinking how she could improve them. She looked at the Victorian clock she was selling for a 5% profit, and worked out that had she bought it for 10% less and sold it at the same price she would have made a £15 profit. How much did she buy it for?

Answer on page 181

## WHERE'S THE PAIR?:

Only two of the shapes below are exactly the same. Can you find the matching pair?

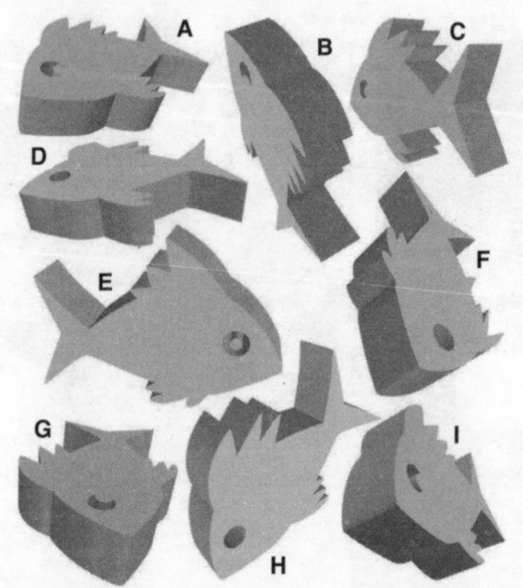


Answer on page 181

**CATS AND COGS:** Turn the handle in the indicated direction... Does the cat go up or down?

Answer on page 181

**CUT AND FOLD:** Which of the patterns below is created by this fold and cut?

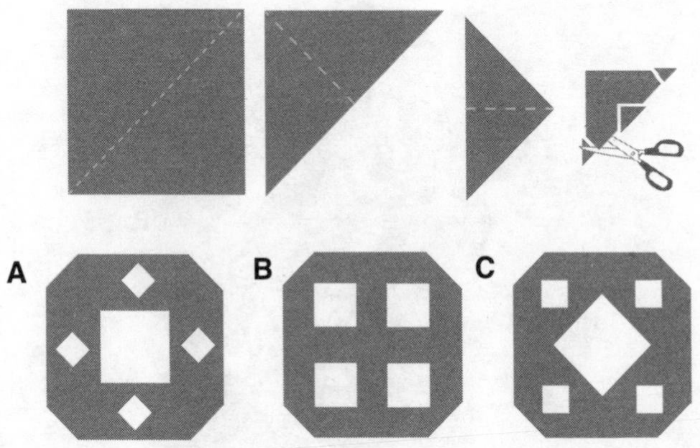


Answer on page 181

# MORE OR LESS:

The arrows indicate whether a number in a box is greater or smaller than an adjacent number. Complete the grid so that all rows and columns contain the numbers 1 to 6.

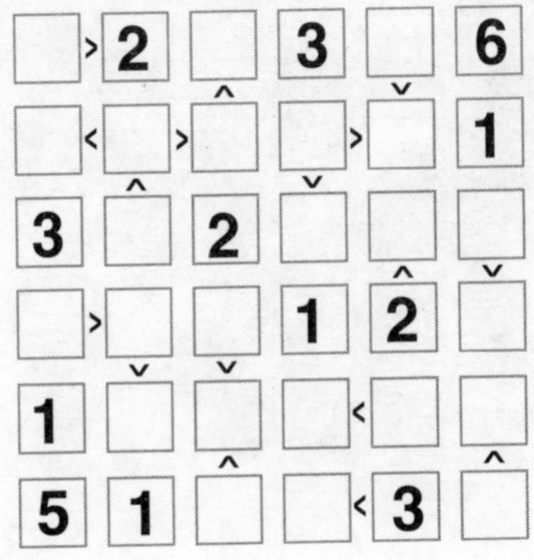

Answer on page 181

# RIDDLE:

Mr and Mrs Toggle were driving from Aystown to Beestown on vacation when Mr T accidentally ran down a signpost at a road junction. The post was fine, completely unharmed. But how do they know which way Beestown is now?

Answer on page 181

## SHAPE SHIFTING:

Fill in the empty squares so that each row, column and long diagonal contains six different symbols.

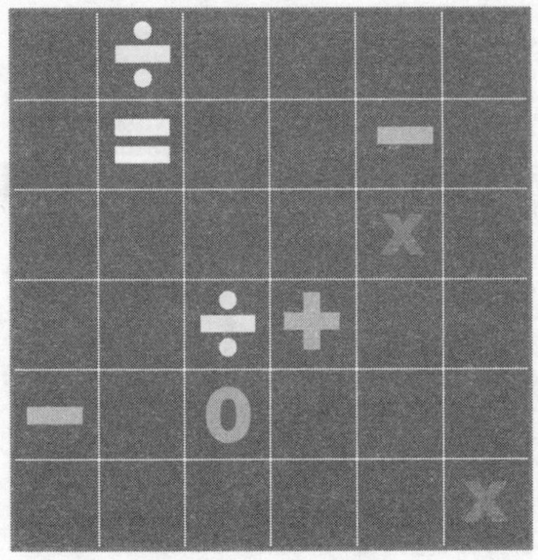

Answer on page 182

## BLOCK PARTY:

Assuming all blocks that are not visible from this angle are present, how many blocks have been removed from this 5 x 5 x 5 cube?

Answer on page 182

# DOUBLE MAZE:

Make your way from A to B without passing through any lighter squares – then do it again without passing through any darker squares!

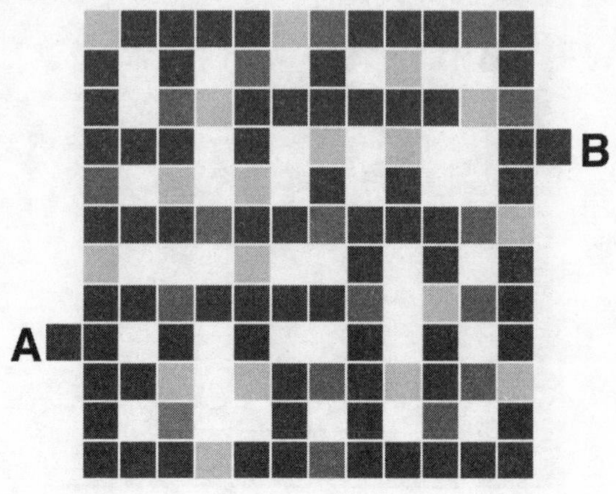


Answer on page 182

# RADAR:

The numbers in some cells in the grid indicate the exact number of black cells that should border it. Shade these black, until all the numbers are surrounded by the correct number of black cells.

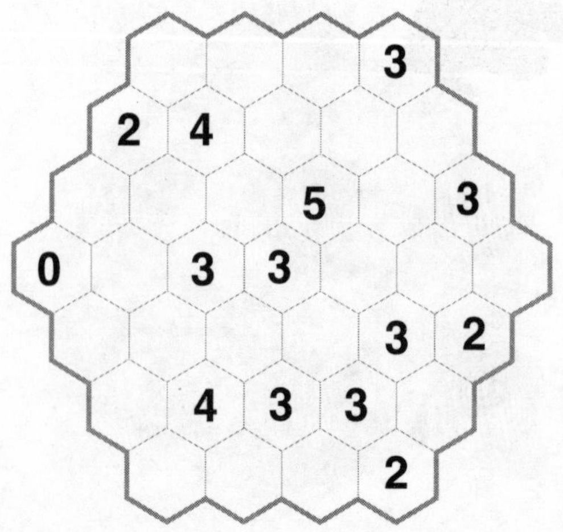

Answer on page 182

# SHUFFLE: Fill up the shuffle box so that each row, column and long diagonal contains a Jack, Queen, King and Ace of each suit.

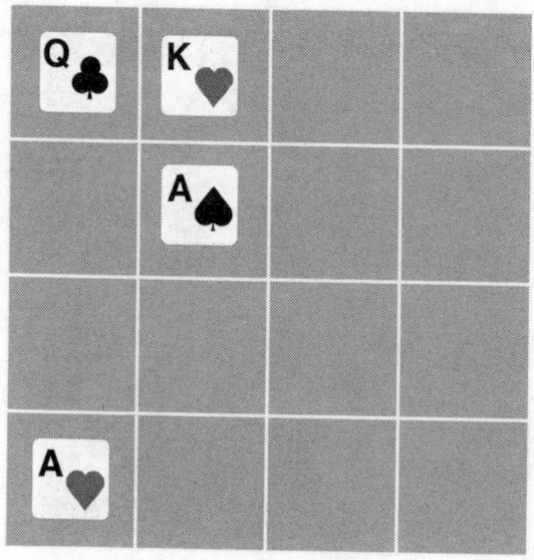


Answer on page 182

# SILHOUETTE: Which of the fish matches our silhouette?

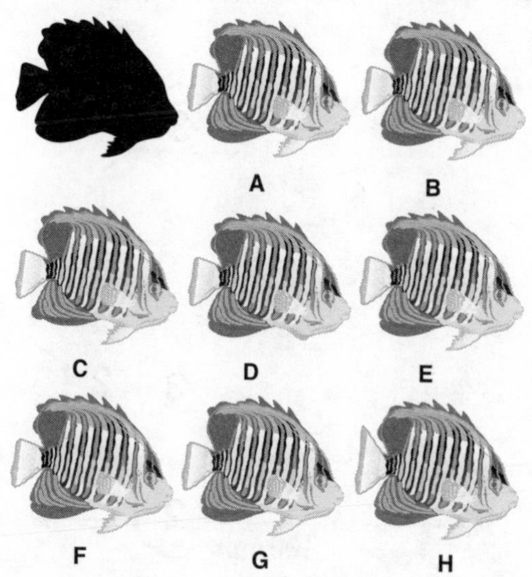


Answer on page 182

## SYMBOL SUMS: These symbols represent the numbers 1 to 4. If the central parrot in the top row represents the number 2, can you work out what the other parrots are representing and make a working sum?

Answer on page 182

## IN THE AREA: Can you work out the approximate area that this camel is occupying?

Answer on page 182

**SUDOKU:** Complete the grid so that all rows and columns, and each outlined block of nine squares, contain the numbers 1, 2, 3, 4, 5, 6, 7, 8 and 9.

| | | | | | | | | |
|---|---|---|---|---|---|---|---|---|
| 5 | 1 | | | 2 | | 4 | 9 | 8 |
| | 3 | | 1 | | 6 | | 7 | 5 |
| | 8 | | | | 4 | 6 | | |
| | 7 | 3 | | | 9 | | 8 | |
| 1 | | | | 7 | | 9 | | 2 |
| | 2 | | 3 | | 5 | 1 | | |
| | 5 | | 8 | 6 | | | 4 | |
| | 9 | 2 | | | | | 5 | 6 |
| 8 | | 4 | | 9 | 7 | 3 | | |

Answer on page 183

WRINKLY QUOTE

"I'm tired. Being older makes you tired. I quite like just sitting on the sofa."

LIZ SMITH

## SUDOKU SIXPACK: Complete the grid so that every row, column and long diagonal contains the numbers 1, 2, 3, 4, 5 and 6.

| | | | | | |
|---|---|---|---|---|---|
| | 5 | | 6 | 4 | 3 |
| 4 | | | | | 5 |
| 6 | | | | | |
| | | 6 | 1 | 5 | |
| 1 | 2 | 4 | | 3 | |
| | | 2 | | | |

Answer on page 183

## FLOOR FILLERS: Below is a plan of the entrance pathway to a theatre, complete with spaces either side for plant pots. Below it are some oddly shaped pieces of red carpet... Can you fill the floor with them?

Answer on page 183

# TENTS AND TREES:

Every tree has at least one tent found horizontally or vertically adjacent to it. No tent can be in an adjacent square to another tent (even diagonally!). The numbers by each row and column tell you how many tents there are. Can you locate all the tents?

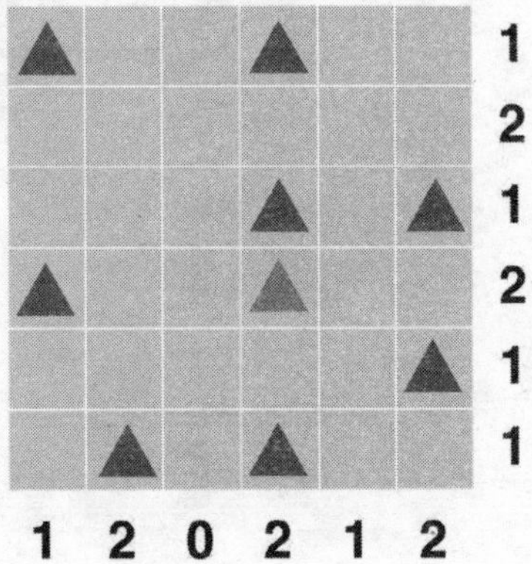


Answer on page 183

# LOOPLINK:

Connect adjacent dots with either horizontal or vertical lines to create a continuous unbroken loop which never crosses over itself. The numbers in these boxes tell you how many sides of that box are used by your unbroken line.

| | | | | |
|---|---|---|---|---|
| 3 | 2 | 2 | 2 | 3 |
| 3 | 1 | 1 | 2 | 2 |
| 3 | 0 | 2 | 2 | 2 |
| 3 | 2 | 3 | 2 | 3 |
| 3 | 1 | 2 | 2 | 2 |

Answer on page 183

## MAGIC SQUARES: Complete the square using nine consecutive numbers, so that all rows, columns and large diagonals add up to the same total.

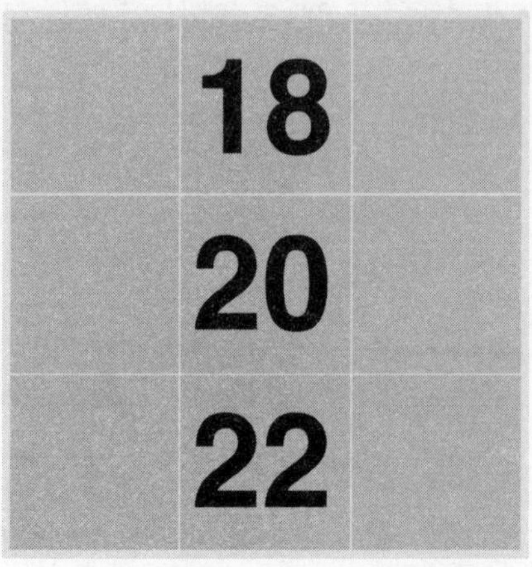


Answer on page 183

## SHAPE STACKER: Can you work out the logic behind the numbers in these shapes, and suggest what number the question mark represents?

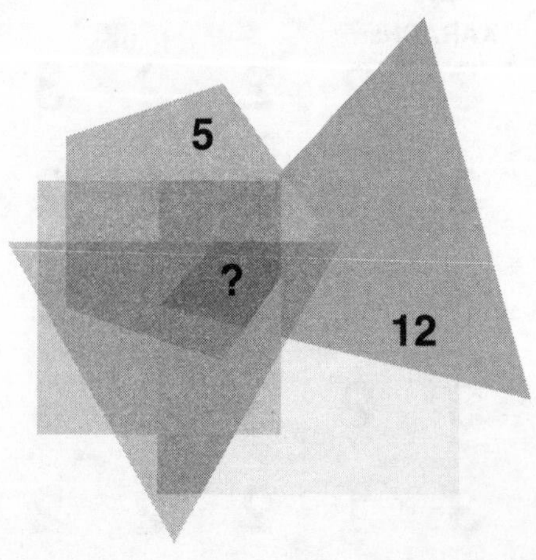


Answer on page 183

# ODD CLOCKS:

Rio is six hours behind Athens, which is two hours behind Karachi. It is 1.25 am on Thursday in Athens – what time is it in the other two cities?

Answer on page 184

## Wrinkly Quote

"Mindful that it's running out, I am determined to have the time of my life."

SHEILA HANCOCK

## SIGNPOST: Can you crack the logical secret behind the distances to these great cities, and work out how far it is to Hong Kong?

Answer on page 184

## MIRROR IMAGE: Only one of these pictures is an exact mirror image of the first one? Can you spot it?

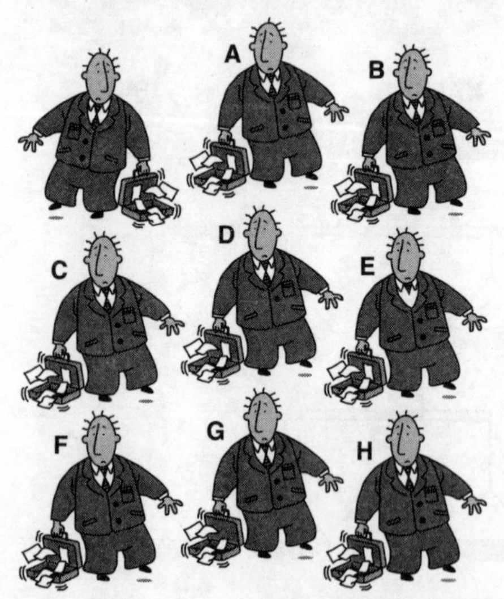


Answer on page 184

# NUMBER SWEEP:

The numbers in some squares in the grid indicate the exact number of black squares that should surround it. Shade these squares until all the numbers are surrounded by the correct number of black squares, and a number will be revealed!

| 0 | 2 |  | 5 |  | 5 |  | 5 |  | 5 |  | 2 |
|---|---|---|---|---|---|---|---|---|---|---|---|
|  | 4 |  |  | 8 |  | 8 |  | 8 |  | 5 |  |
| 2 |  | 7 | 8 |  | 6 |  | 5 |  | 5 |  | 2 |
|  | 5 |  | 8 |  |  | 6 |  | 6 |  | 3 |  |
| 4 |  | 8 |  | 7 | 6 |  | 5 |  | 4 |  | 1 |
|  | 7 |  | 7 |  | 5 |  |  | 7 |  | 5 |  |
| 3 |  | 5 |  | 4 |  | 3 | 5 |  | 8 |  | 4 |
|  | 6 |  | 4 |  | 0 |  | 3 |  |  | 8 |  |
| 3 |  | 5 |  | 4 |  | 3 |  | 6 | 8 |  | 5 |
|  | 7 |  | 7 |  | 5 |  | 6 |  | 8 |  |  |
| 3 |  | 6 |  | 8 |  | 8 |  | 7 |  | 4 | 3 |
|  | 2 |  | 4 |  | 5 |  | 5 |  | 4 |  | 1 |

Answer on page 184

# SCALES:

The arms of these scales are divided into sections – a weight two sections away from the middle will be twice as heavy as a weight one section away. Can you arrange the supplied weights in such a way as to balance the whole scale?

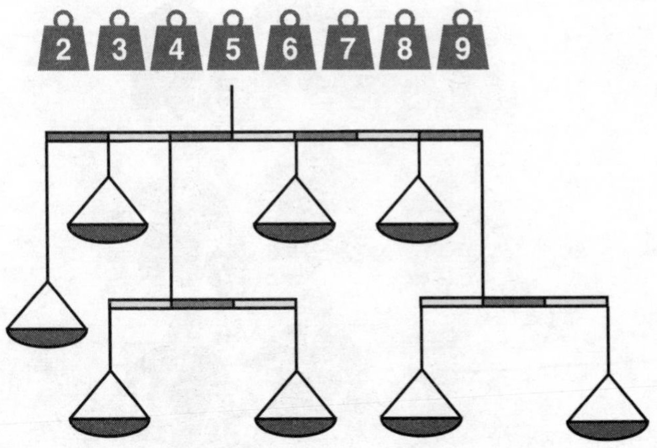


Answer on page 184

# HARD PUZZLES

# MINESWEEPER:

The numbers in some squares in the grid indicate the exact number of black squares that should surround it. Shade these squares until all the numbers are surrounded by the correct number of black squares.

| 0 | | | 1 | 2 | | | 2 |
|---|---|---|---|---|---|---|---|
| 1 | | 2 | 1 | | | | 2 |
| | | 2 | | 2 | 2 | 2 | |
| 2 | | 2 | | | | | 0 |
| | 1 | 1 | 2 | | 2 | 1 | |
| 2 | | 1 | | 2 | | 2 | 1 |
| | 3 | | | 3 | 5 | | 3 |
| 2 | | 2 | 2 | | | | |

Answer on page 184

# WHERE'S THE PAIR?:

Only two of the shapes below are exactly the same. Can you find the matching pair?

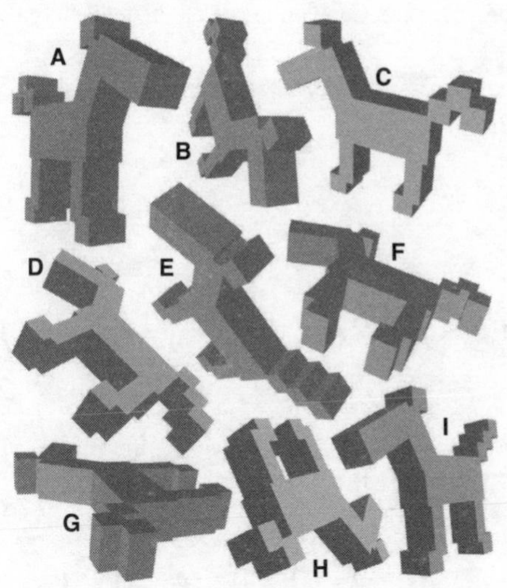


Answer on page 184

## MASYU:

Draw a single continuous line around the grid that passes through all the circles. The line must enter and leave each box in the centre of one of its four sides. **Black Circle:** Turn left or right in the box, and the line must pass straight through the next and previous boxes. **White Circle:** Travel straight through the box, and the line must turn in the next and/or previous box.

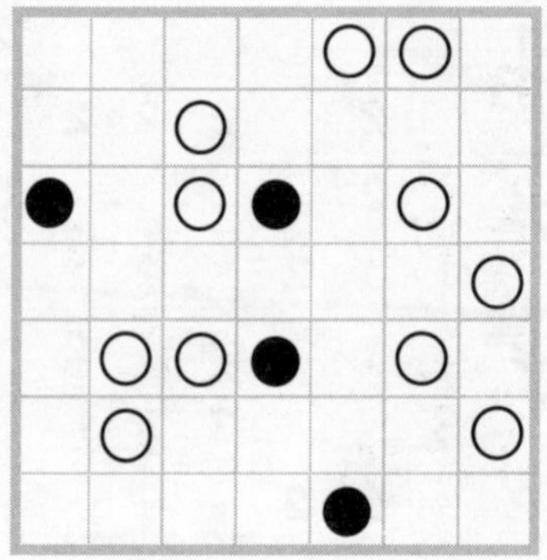

Answer on page 184

## TENTS AND TREES:

Every tree has at least one tent found horizontally or vertically adjacent to it. No tent can be in an adjacent square to another tent (even diagonally!). The numbers by each row and column tell you how many tents there are. Can you locate all the tents?

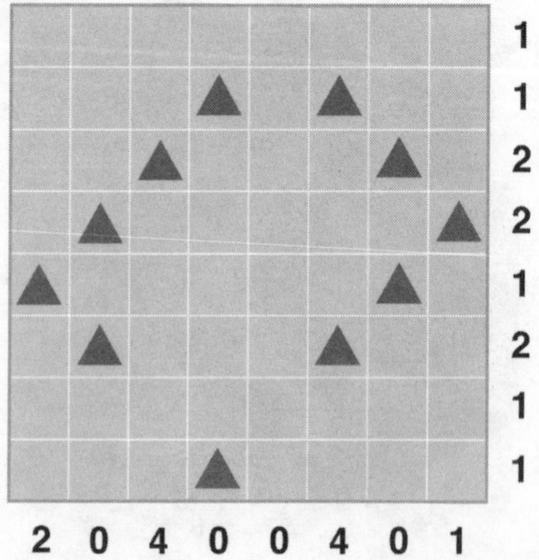


Answer on page 185

# CODOKU SIX:

Complete the first grid so that every row and column contains all the letters BCIMU and W. Do the same with grid 2 and the numbers 12345 and 6. To decode the finished grid, add the numbers in the shaded squares to the letters in the matching squares in the first grid (ie: A + 3 = D, Y + 4 = C) to get six new letters which can be arranged to spell the name of a city.

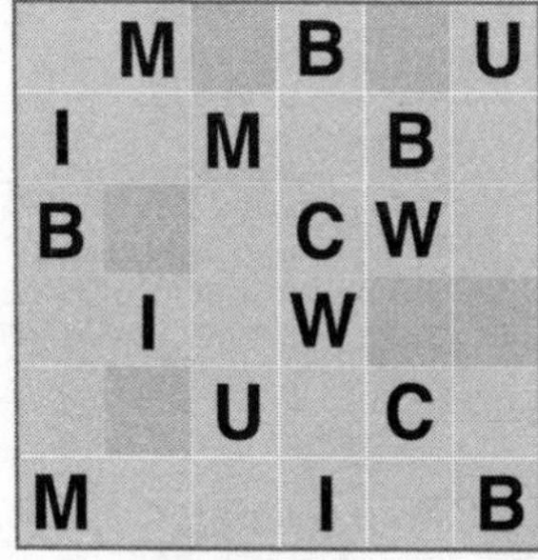

| | | | | | |
|---|---|---|---|---|---|
| | M | | B | | U |
| I | | M | | B | |
| B | | | C | W | |
| | I | | W | | |
| | | U | | C | |
| M | | | I | | B |

| | | | | | |
|---|---|---|---|---|---|
| | 1 | | 3 | | 4 |
| 3 | 6 | | | 1 | |
| | | 1 | 6 | 2 | |
| | 5 | 3 | | | |
| 2 | | 5 | | 4 | |
| | 2 | | | 3 | |

Answer on page 185

# CUBE VOLUME:

These little cubes originally made a big 5 x 5 x 5 cube measuring 20 cm × 20 cm × 20 cm. Now some of the little cubes have been removed, can you work out what volume the remaining cubes have now? Assume all invisible cubes are present.

Answer on page 185

# WHERE'S THE PAIR?: Only two of these pictures are exactly the same. Can you spot the matching pair?

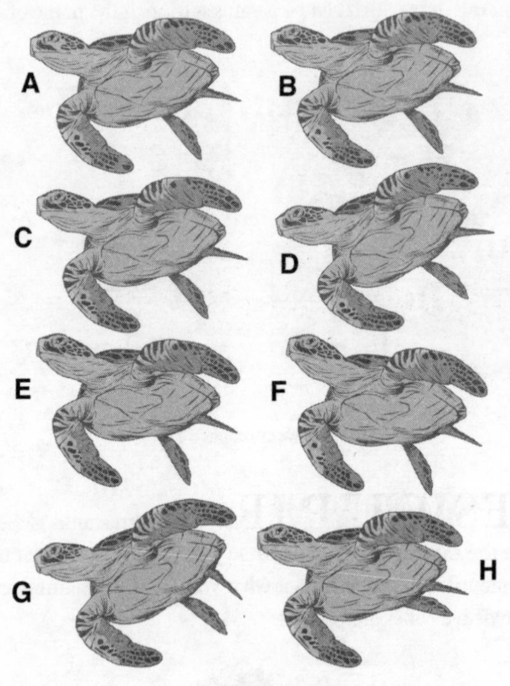


Answer on page 185

## WRINKLY QUOTE

"I remember lots of people I've known, like my grandfather, who was wild and eccentric. He often forgot to put his shoes on..."

IAN MCKELLEN

# PERCENTAGE POINT: 

Can you determine what percentage of this honeycomb is occupied by bees, and what percentage of the bees are awake?

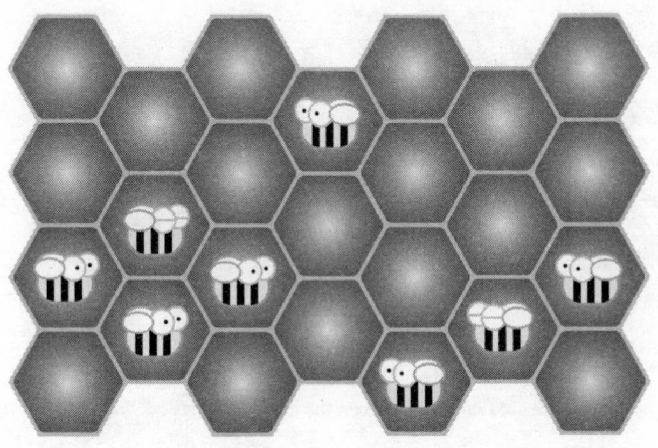

Answer on page 185

# MINESWEEPER: 

The numbers in some squares in the grid indicate the exact number of black squares that should surround it. Shade these squares until all the numbers are surrounded by the correct number of black squares.

| | | | | | | | |
|---|---|---|---|---|---|---|---|
| | 2 | 2 | | 2 | 3 | | 3 |
| 2 | | | 3 | | | | |
| | 3 | 3 | | 2 | 3 | | 3 |
| 3 | | | 3 | 3 | | 2 | 2 |
| | 3 | 4 | | | 1 | 2 | |
| 1 | | | | 3 | | | |
| 2 | 4 | 4 | 3 | | 2 | | |
| | | | 1 | 1 | | 2 | 1 |

Answer on page 185

## LOGIC SEQUENCE: The balls below have been rearranged. Can you work out the new sequence of the balls from the clues given below?

The square is immediately to the right of the X.
The circle is between the X and the triangle.
There are two balls between the circle and the star.

Answer on page 185

## A PIECE OF PIE: Can you crack the pie code and work out what number belongs where the question mark is?

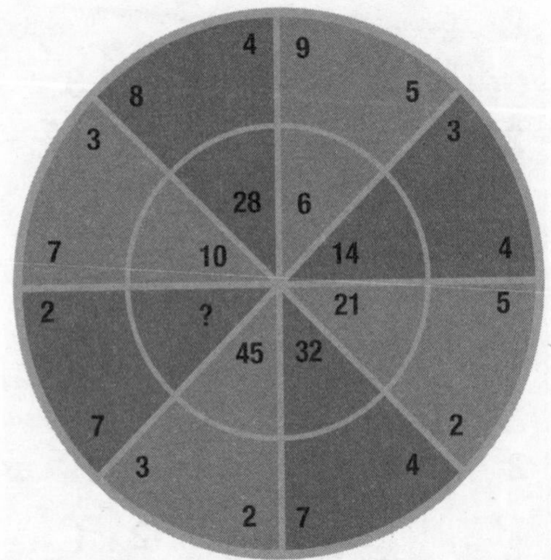


Answer on page 185

**FIVE-POINT PROBLEM:** Discover the pattern behind the numbers on these pentagons and fill in the blanks to complete the puzzle.

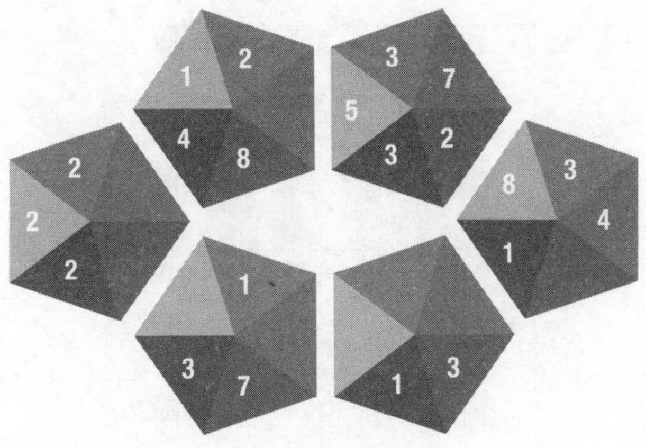


Answer on page 186

**THE GREAT DIVIDE:** Divide up the grid into four equal sized, equally shaped parts, each containing one each of the four different symbols.

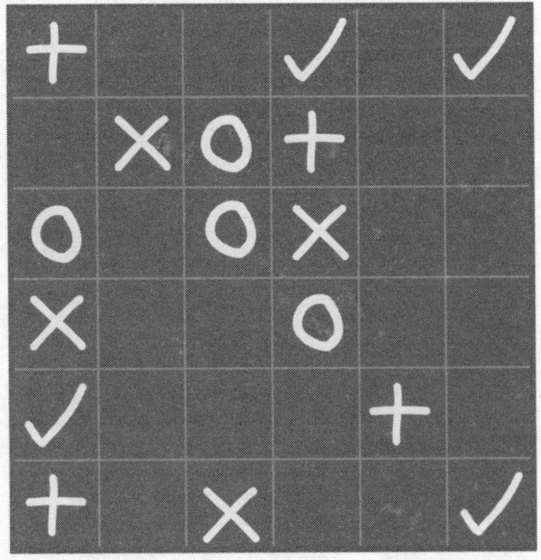

Answer on page 186

# KILLER SIX:

Complete the grid so that all rows and columns contain the numbers 1, 2, 3, 4, 5 and 6. Areas with a dotted outline contain numbers that add up to the total shown.

| | | | | | |
|---|---|---|---|---|---|
| 11 | 16 | | | 3 | 10 |
| | 4 | | 4 | | |
| 13 | 5 | | | 11 | |
| | | 6 | 4 | | 11 |
| 3 | | | 7 | | |
| | 11 | | | 7 | |

Answer on page 186

# LOOPLINK:

Connect adjacent dots with either horizontal or vertical lines to create a continuous unbroken loop which never crosses over itself. Some, but not all of the boxes are numbered. The numbers in these boxes tell you how many sides of that box are used by your unbroken line.

| | | | | |
|---|---|---|---|---|
| 3 | | 3 | 1 | 3 |
| 2 | | | | |
| 1 | 2 | 2 | | 2 |
| | 3 | | 1 | 3 |
| | 3 | 2 | | 2 |

Answer on page 186

## MASYU:

Draw a single continuous line around the grid that passes through all the circles. The line must enter and leave each box in the centre of one of its four sides. **Black Circle:** Turn left or right in the box, and the line must pass straight through the next and previous boxes. **White Circle:** Travel straight through the box, and the line must turn in the next and/or previous box.

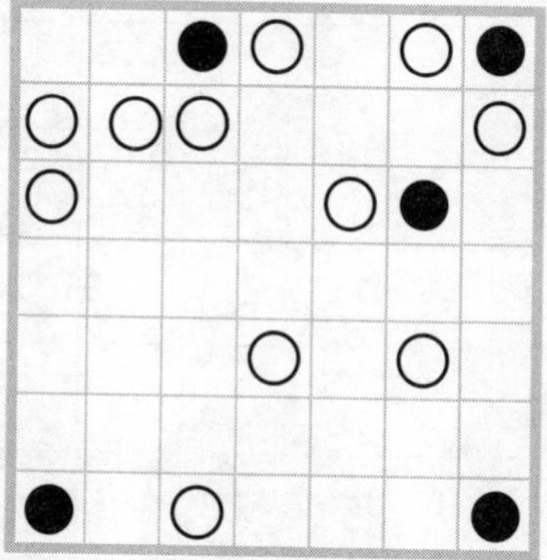

Answer on page 186

## MINI NONOGRAM:

The numbers by each row and column describe black squares and groups of black squares that are adjoining. Colour in all the black squares and a six number combination will be revealed.

| 1 | 2 | 3 | 4 | 5 | 6 | 7 | 8 | 9 | 10 | 11 |
|---|---|---|---|---|---|---|---|---|---|---|
| 5 5 | 1 1 1 1 1 | 5 5 | | 3 | 5 1 | 5 | | 1 | 1 5 | 5 |

Row clues:

| Row | Clues |
|---|---|
| 1 | 3 1 3 |
| 2 | 1 1 1 1 |
| 3 | 3 1 1 |
| 4 | 1 1 1 1 |
| 5 | 3 1 1 |
| 6 | |
| 7 | 3 1 1 1 |
| 8 | 1 1 1 1 1 |
| 9 | 1 1 3 1 |
| 10 | 1 1 1 1 |
| 11 | 3 1 1 |

Answer on page 186

# MIRROR IMAGE: Only one of these pictures is an exact mirror image of the first one? Can you spot it?

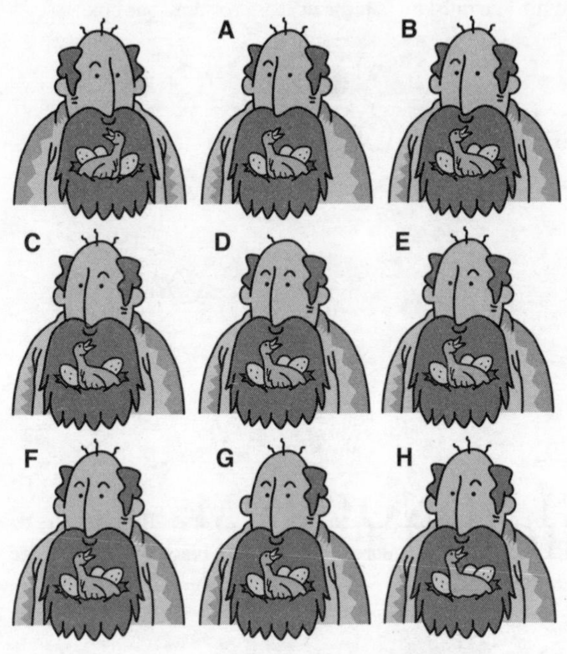


Answer on page 186

## Wrinkly Quote

"I've always totally resisted the idea of being a grandad, but now I'm beginning to warm to it."

PAUL O'GRADY

## SHAPE STACKER: Can you work out the logic behind the numbers in these shapes, and the total of A x B x C?

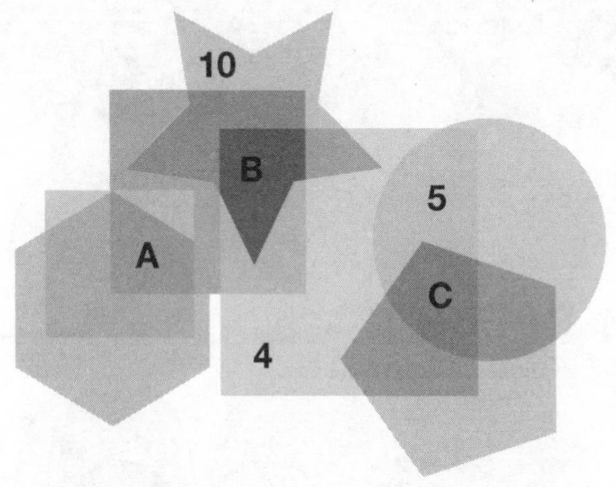


Answer on page 187

## SILHOUETTE: Which of the pics matches our silhouette?

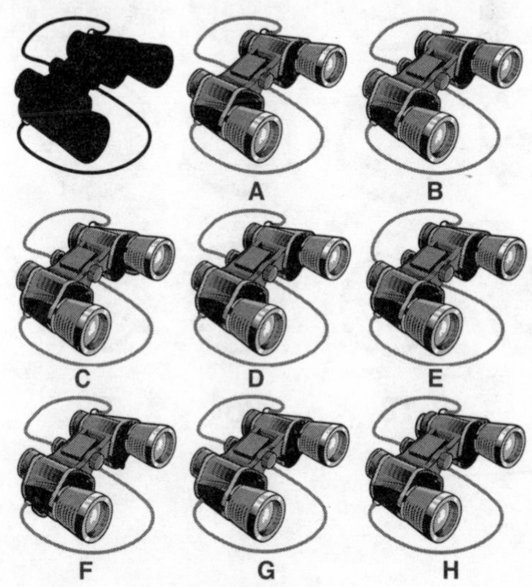


Answer on page 187

## Wrinkly Quote

"My grandfather always said that living is like licking honey off a thorn."

LOUIS ADAMIC

## SUM PEOPLE:

Work out what number is represented by which person and replace the question mark.

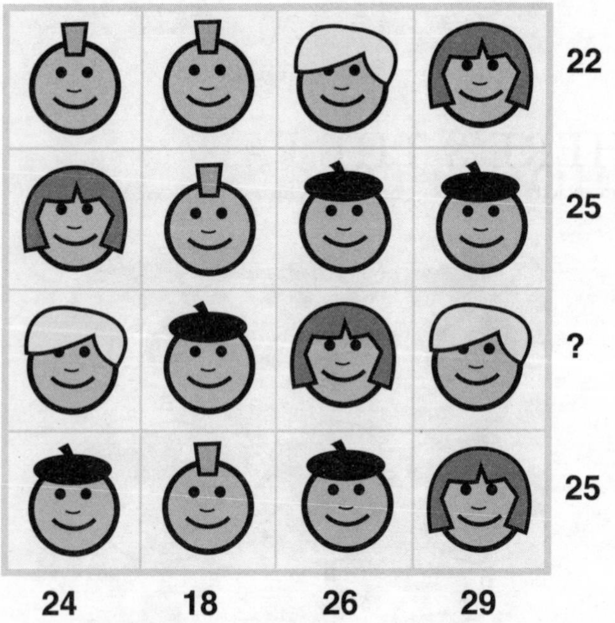


Answer on page 187

**SUM PEOPLE:** Work out what number is represented by which person and replace the question mark.

Answer on page 187

**WHERE'S THE PAIR?:** Only two of the shapes below are exactly the same – can you find the matching pair?

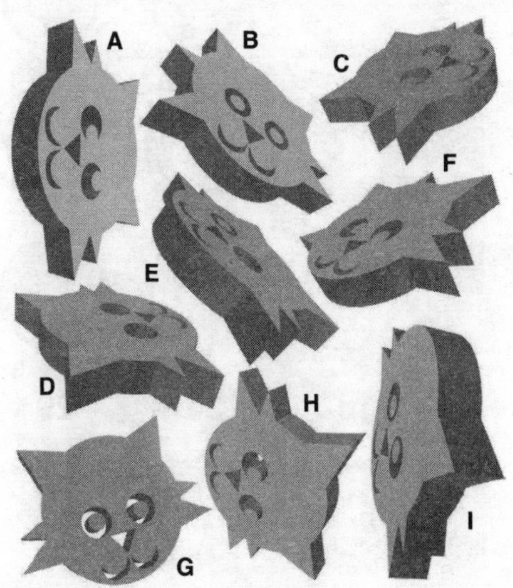


Answer on page 187

**CAN YOU CUT IT?:** Cut two straight lines through this shape to create three shapes that are identical.

Answer on page 187

**DICE PUZZLE:** Which of these dice is not like the other three?

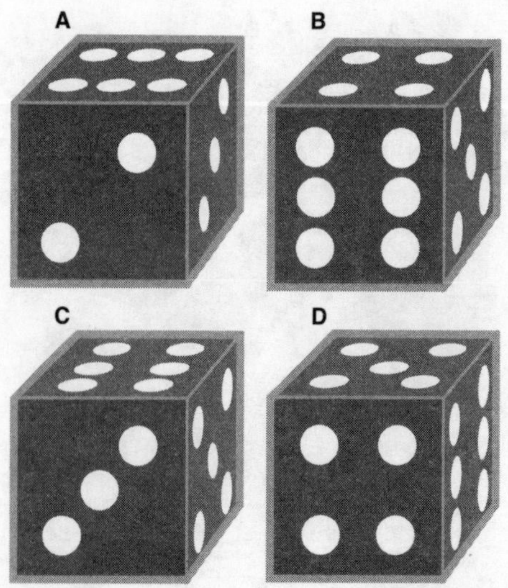


Answer on page 187

## FLOOR FILLERS: Below is a plan of a bathroom, showing the bath and other fixings, and next to it, some very oddly shaped pieces of marble. Can you arrange them to fill the floor?

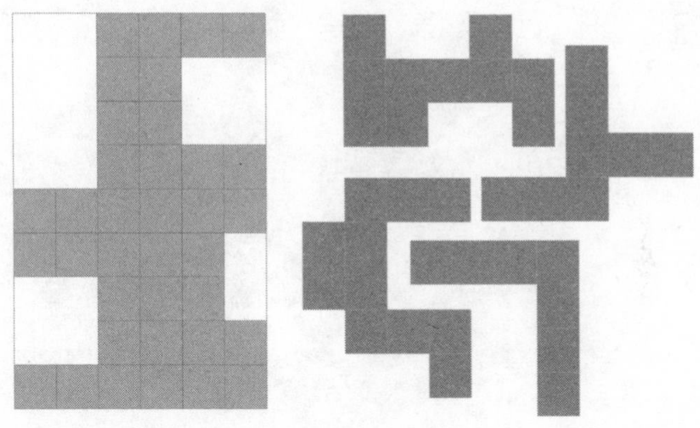

Answer on page 188

## HUB SIGNS: What number should appear in the hub of the second wheel?

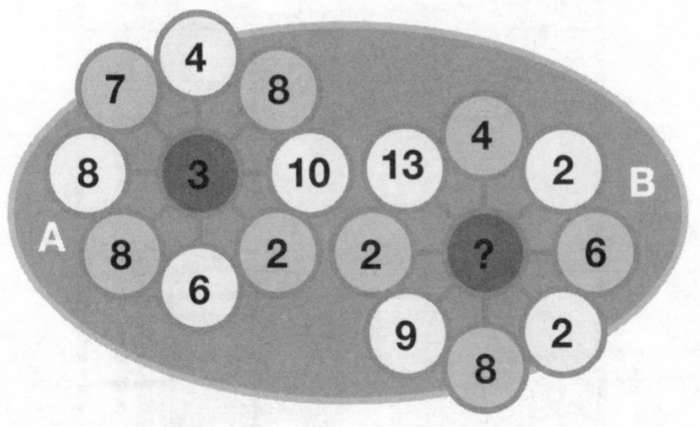


Answer on page 188

# JIGSAW: Which four of the pieces below can complete the jigsaw and make a perfect square?

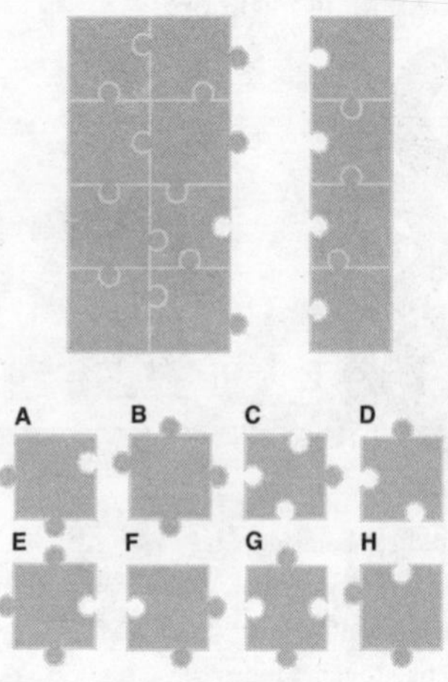


Answer on page 188

# LATIN SQUARE: Complete the grid so that every row and column, and every outlined area, contains the letters A, B, C, D, E and F.

| B | | | | | D |
|---|---|---|---|---|---|
| | | | C | | |
| | | | | | E |
| | | | | | F |
| | | | | | A |
| | | | | | |

Answer on page 188

# LOGIC SEQUENCE:

The balls below have been rearranged. Can you work out the new sequence of the balls from the clues given below?

The top three balls total 22.
The 5 ball is immediately to the right of the 6, and isn't in contact with the 4 ball.
The 10 ball touches four others, but not the 6.

Answer on page 188

# MINESWEEPER:

The numbers in some squares in the grid indicate the exact number of black squares that should surround it. Shade these squares until all the numbers are surrounded by the correct number of black squares.

| | | | | | | | |
|---|---|---|---|---|---|---|---|
| | | | 2 | | 0 | 2 | |
| 3 | 4 | 4 | | | | | |
| 1 | | | 2 | | 3 | 4 | |
| | 1 | | 1 | 3 | | | 2 |
| 1 | 2 | | 3 | 4 | | 3 | |
| 2 | | | | | 3 | 2 | 1 |
| | 4 | 5 | 5 | | 3 | | |
| 2 | | 2 | | | 2 | 1 | 1 |

Answer on page 188

## WRINKLY QUOTE

"Becoming a grandmother is great fun because you can use the kid to get back at your daughter."

ROSEANNE BARR

**BATTLESHIPS:** The numbers on the side and bottom of the grid indicate occupied squares or groups of consecutive occupied squares in each row or column. Can you finish the grid so that it contains three Cruisers, three Launches and three Buoys and the numbers tally?

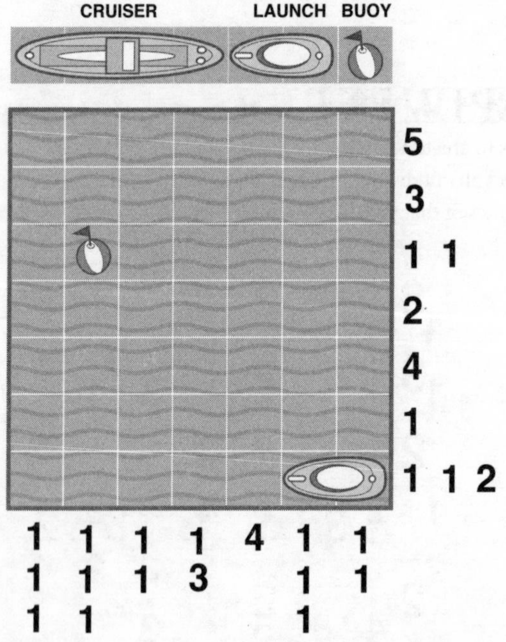


Answer on page 188

## TENTS AND TREES: Every tree has at least one tent found horizontally or vertically adjacent to it. No tent can be in an adjacent square to another tent (even diagonally!). The numbers by each row and column tell you how many tents there are. Can you locate all the tents?

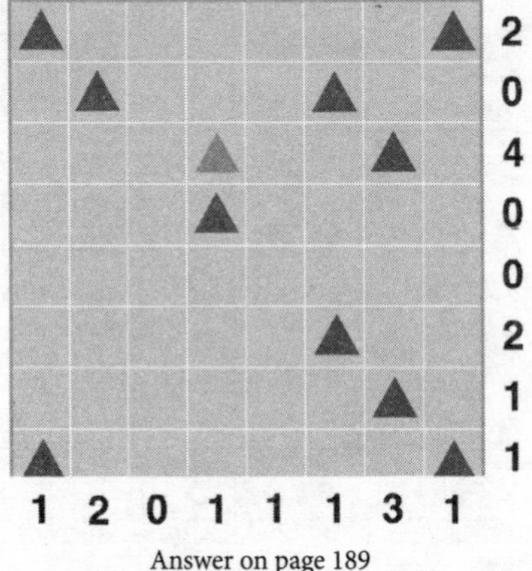

Answer on page 189

## LOOPLINK: Connect adjacent dots with either horizontal or vertical lines to create a continuous unbroken loop which never crosses over itself. Some, but not all of the boxes are numbered. The numbers in these boxes tell you how many sides of that box are used by your unbroken line.

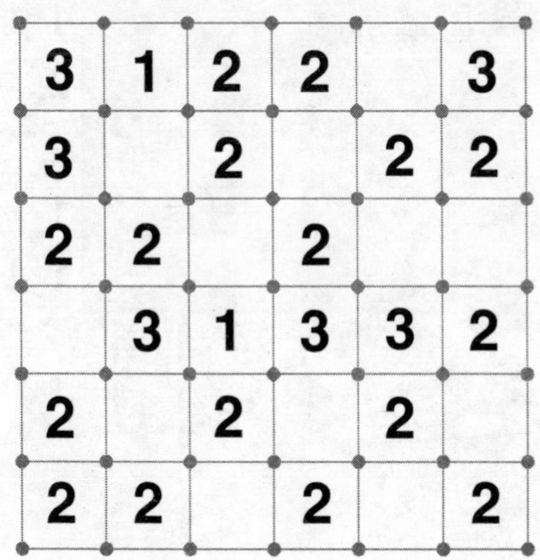

Answer on page 189

**MORE OR LESS:** The arrows indicate whether a number in a box is greater or smaller than an adjacent number. Complete the grid so that all rows and columns contain the numbers 1 to 6.

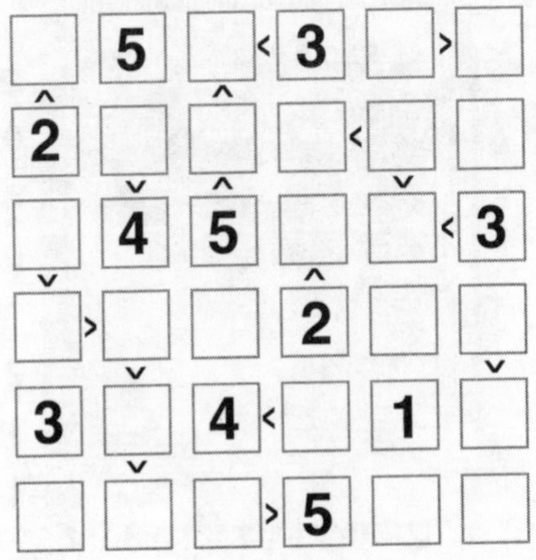

Answer on page 189

**NUMBER CHUNKS:** Divide up the grid into four equal size, equally shaped parts, each containing numbers that add up to 40.

| | | | | | |
|---|---|---|---|---|---|
| 8 | 2 | 1 | 2 | 2 | 4 |
| 6 | 3 | 1 | 1 | 6 | 3 |
| 4 | 9 | 9 | 9 | 3 | 5 |
| 5 | 7 | 1 | 5 | 5 | 5 |
| 2 | 7 | 3 | 1 | 6 | 4 |
| 9 | 7 | 3 | 2 | 3 | 7 |

Answer on page 189

# SAFECRACKER:

To open the safe, all the buttons must be pressed in the correct order before the "open" button is pressed. What is the first button pressed in your sequence?

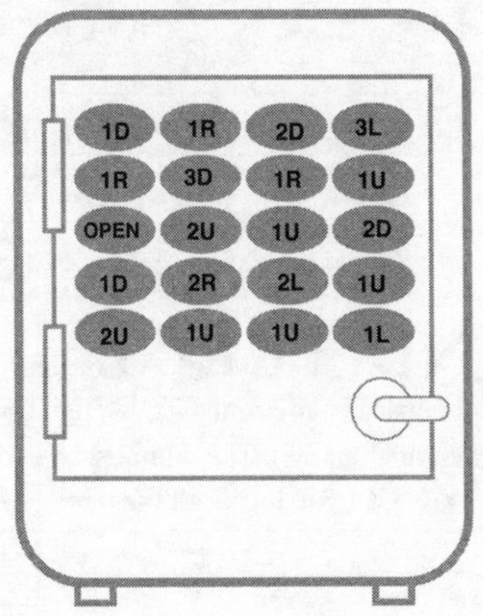


Answer on page 189

# SUDOKU:

Complete the grid so that all rows and columns, and each outlined block of nine squares, contain the numbers 1, 2, 3, 4, 5, 6, 7, 8 and 9.

| | | | | | | | | |
|---|---|---|---|---|---|---|---|---|
| | 2 | | 1 | | 8 | 3 | | |
| | | 7 | | 2 | | | | 5 |
| 4 | | | 7 | | | 1 | | |
| | | 1 | 4 | | | | | 8 |
| | 9 | | | | | 5 | | 6 |
| 2 | | | 6 | 7 | | | | |
| 7 | | 6 | 8 | | | | | 3 |
| 8 | | | | 9 | | | 2 | |
| | | | 3 | | | | 6 | 4 |

Answer on page 189

## Wrinkly Quote

"You know an odd feeling? Sitting on the toilet eating a chocolate candy bar."

GEORGE CARLIN

**TENTS AND TREES:** Every tree has at least one tent found horizontally or vertically adjacent to it. No tent can be in an adjacent square to another tent (even diagonally!). The numbers by each row and column tell you how many tents there are. Can you locate all the tents?

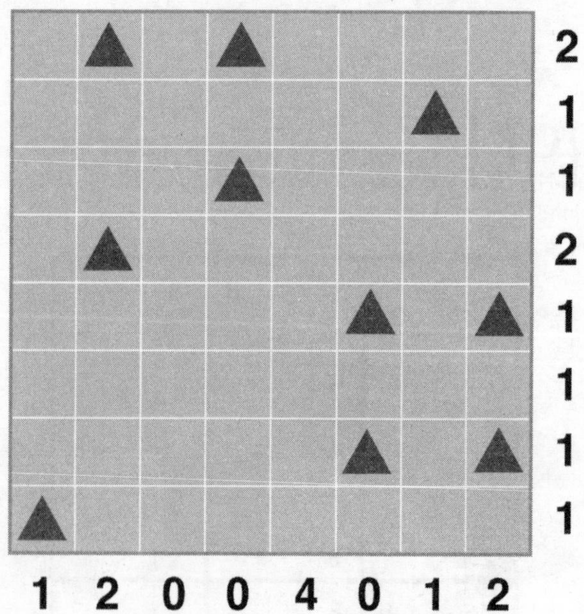


Answer on page 190

**CAN YOU CUT IT?:** Cut two straight lines through this shape to create three shapes that are identical.

Answer on page 190

**FIVE POINT PROBLEM:** Discover the pattern behind the numbers on these pentagons and fill in the blanks to complete the puzzle.

Answer on page 190

# GRIDLOCK: Which square correctly completes the grid?

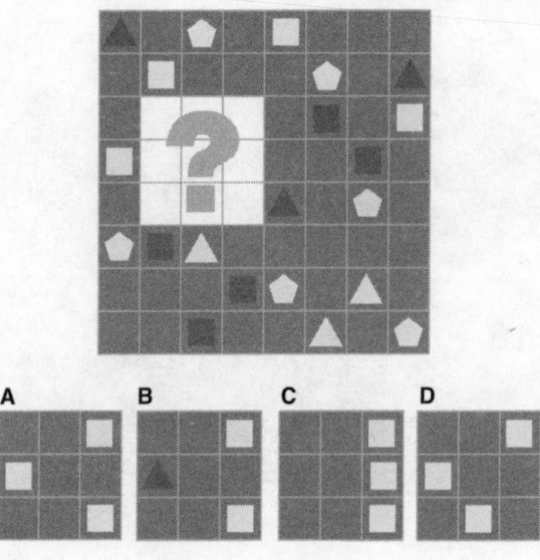


Answer on page 190

# KILLER SIX: Complete the grid so that all rows and columns contain the numbers 1, 2, 3, 4, 5 and 6. Areas with a dotted outline contain numbers that add up to the total shown. Dotted boxes can contan the same number more than once, however.

| | | | | | |
|---|---|---|---|---|---|
| 8 | | | 7 | | 10 |
| 16 | | 6 | | | |
| 3 | | **6** | 7 | 6 | |
| | 7 | | | 22 | |
| 12 | | 11 | | | 4 |
| | | | | **1** | |

Answer on page 190

## HUB SIGNS: What number should appear in the hub of the second wheel?

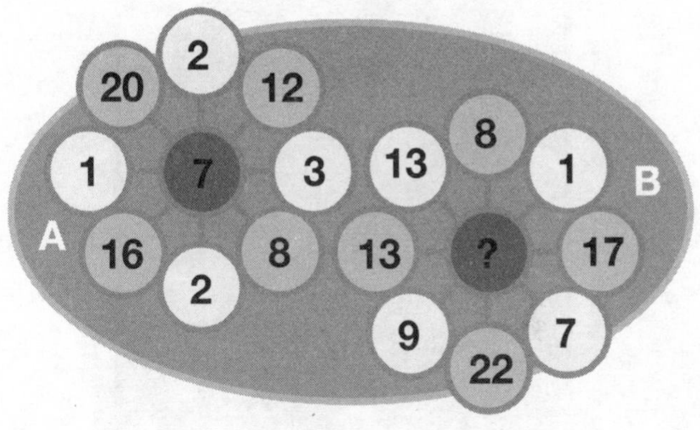


Answer on page 190

## LOOPLINK: Connect adjacent dots with either horizontal or vertical lines to create a continuous unbroken loop which never crosses over itself. Some, but not all of the boxes are numbered. The numbers in these boxes tell you how many sides of that box are used by your unbroken line.

| | | | | | |
|---|---|---|---|---|---|
| 1 | | 2 | | 2 | 2 |
| 2 | 2 | 3 | 2 | | 3 |
| | 0 | 3 | 2 | 2 | 2 |
| | 3 | | | 2 | |
| 1 | | 2 | 2 | 1 | 2 |
| 3 | 2 | 2 | 2 | | 3 |

Answer on page 190

## MAGIC SQUARES: Complete the square using nine consecutive numbers, so that all rows, columns and large diagonals add up to the same total.

Answer on page 191

## THE GREAT DIVIDE: Divide up the grid into four equal size, equally shaped parts, each containing one each of the four different symbols.

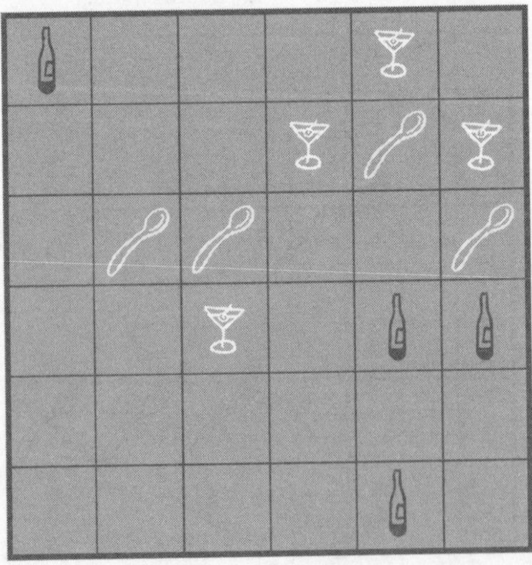

Answer on page 191

## SMALL LOGIC: Little Tom collects insects. Can you discover where he found these three, at what time of day, and what he put them in so he could take them home?

1) The spider was found in the evening, not in a field.
2) The butterfly was found in the forest, though not in the morning, and Tom didn't put it in a jar.
3) The creature found in a field was placed in a bottle.

| | Forest | Roadside | Field | Jar | Bottle | Matchbox | Morning | Afternoon | Evening |
|---|---|---|---|---|---|---|---|---|---|
| Beetle | | | | | | | | | |
| Spider | | | | | | | | | |
| Butterfly | | | | | | | | | |
| Morning | | | | | | | | | |
| Afternoon | | | | | | | | | |
| Evening | | | | | | | | | |
| Jar | | | | | | | | | |
| Bottle | | | | | | | | | |
| Matchbox | | | | | | | | | |

Answer on page 191

## SUDOKU: Complete the grid so that all rows and columns, and each outlined block of nine squares, contain the numbers 1, 2, 3, 4, 5, 6, 7, 8 and 9.

| | | | | | | | | |
|---|---|---|---|---|---|---|---|---|
| | | 6 | | 7 | | 5 | 3 | |
| 8 | | | 1 | 3 | | 2 | | |
| | | 9 | | | 2 | | | |
| 9 | | | | 5 | | | 4 | |
| | | 4 | | | 6 | | 8 | 5 |
| 2 | 8 | | 7 | 9 | | 6 | | |
| | 1 | | | 6 | | | | 9 |
| | 7 | | | | | 4 | 2 | 1 |
| 5 | | 8 | 4 | | | | 6 | |

Answer on page 191

**SUDOKU:** Fill in the numbers 1, 2, 3, 4, 5, 6, 7, 8, and 9 so they appear once only in each row, column and 9 x 9 grid

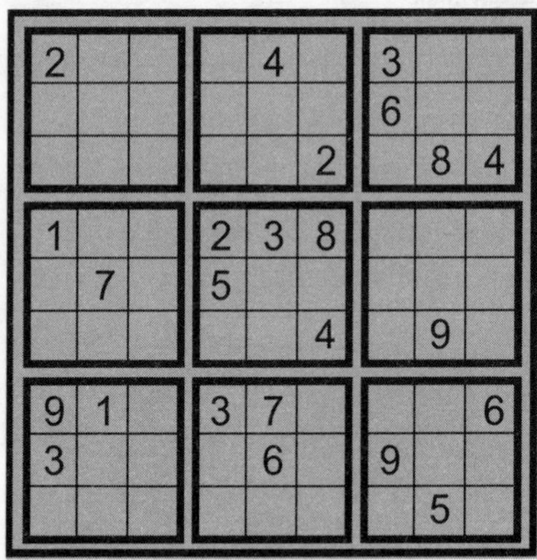

| | | | | | | | | |
|---|---|---|---|---|---|---|---|---|
| 2 | | | | 4 | | 3 | | |
| | | | | | | 6 | | |
| | | | | | 2 | | 8 | 4 |
| 1 | | | 2 | 3 | 8 | | | |
| | 7 | | 5 | | | | | |
| | | | | | 4 | | 9 | |
| 9 | 1 | | 3 | 7 | | | | 6 |
| 3 | | | | 6 | | 9 | | |
| | | | | | | | 5 | |

Answer on page 191

**THE RED CORNER:** Use the corners to make the central number the same way in all three cases. What number should replace the question mark?

Answer on page 191

# CODOKU SIX:

Complete the first grid so that every row and column contain all the letters ABJKY and Z. Do the same with grid 2 and the numbers 12345 and 6. To decode the finished grid, add the numbers in the shaded squares to the letters in the matching squares in the second (ie: A + 3 = D, Y + 4 = C) to get six new letters which can be arranged to spell the name of a famous composer.

| | | | | | |
|---|---|---|---|---|---|
| Z | | A | | | |
| | | Y | | Z | |
| | | | A | J | |
| Y | J | | | | |
| | B | | | | Y |
| J | | K | | A | |

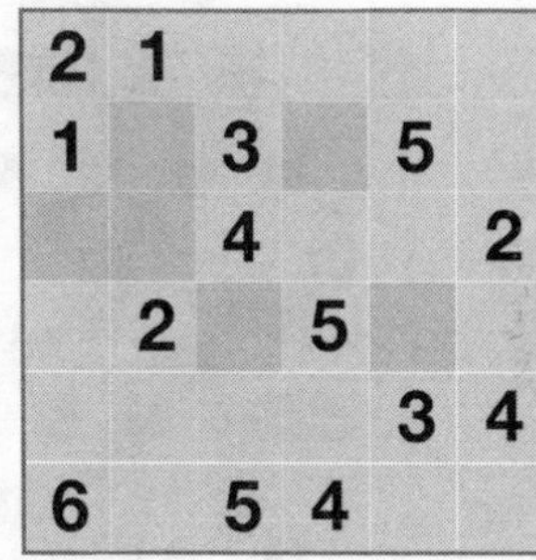

| | | | | | |
|---|---|---|---|---|---|
| 2 | 1 | | | | |
| 1 | | 3 | | 5 | |
| | | 4 | | | 2 |
| | 2 | | 5 | | |
| | | | | 3 | 4 |
| 6 | | 5 | 4 | | |

Answer on page 191

# NUMBER MOUNTAIN:

Replace the question marks with numbers so that each pair of blocks adds up to the block directly above them.

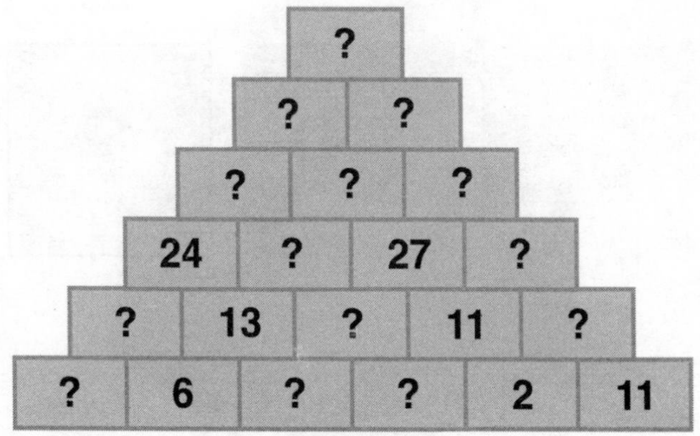


Answer on page 191

**SYMMETRY:** This picture, when finished, is symmetrical along a vertical line up the middle. Can you colour in the missing squares and work out what the picture is of?

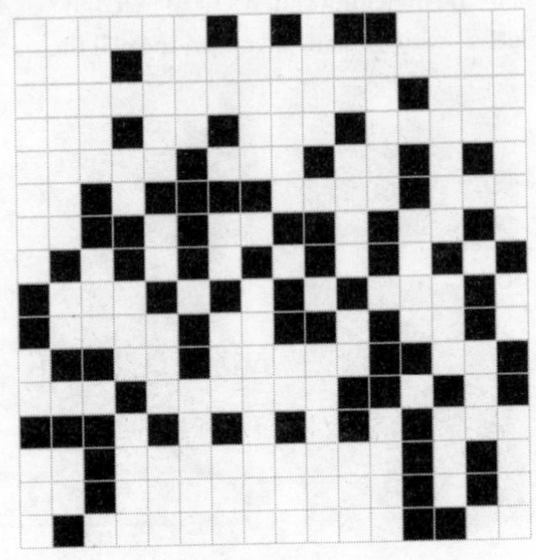

Answer on page 192

**CUBE VOLUME:** These little cubes originally made a big 5 x 5 x 5 cube measuring 15 cm x 15 cm x 15 cm. Now some of the little cubes have been removed, can you work out what volume the remaining cubes have? Assume all hidden cubes are present.

Answer on page 192

# DICE PUZZLE:

Which of these dice is not like the other three?

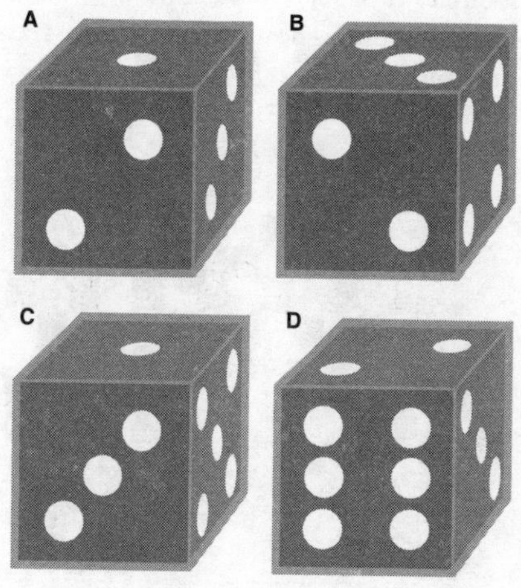


Answer on page 192

# KILLER SIX:

Complete the grid so that all rows and columns contain the numbers 1, 2, 3, 4, 5 and 6. Areas with a dotted outline contain numbers that add up to the total shown.

| | | | | | |
|---|---|---|---|---|---|
| 15 | 4 | 11 | | 5 | |
| | | | 11 | | 6 |
| | 7 | | **1** | 6 | |
| 6 | **6** | 9 | | | 11 |
| | 9 | | 9 | **4** | |
| | | | | 6 | |

Answer on page 192

# MASYU:

Draw a single continuous line around the grid that passes through all the circles. The line must enter and leave each box in the centre of one of its four sides. **Black Circle:** Turn left or right in the box, and the line must pass straight through the next and previous boxes. **White Circle:** Travel straight through the box, and the line must turn in the next and/or previous box.

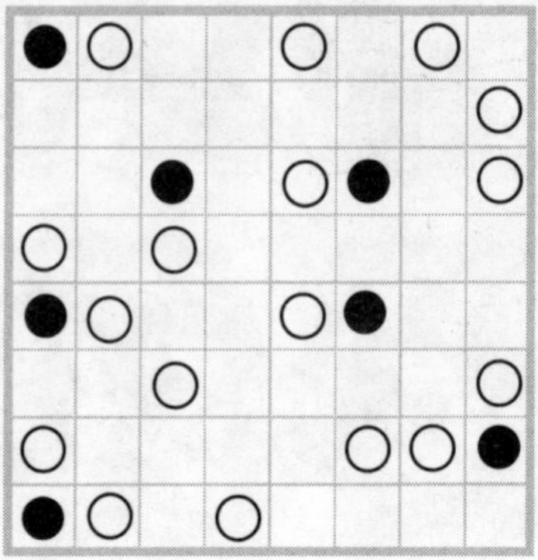

Answer on page 192

# MINI NONOGRAM:

The numbers by each row and column describe black squares and groups of black squares that are adjoining. Colour in all the black squares and a six number combination will be revealed.

| | | | | | | | | | | | | | | | |
|---|---|---|---|---|---|---|---|---|---|---|---|---|---|---|---|
| | | | | | | | | | | 1 | | | | | |
| | | | | | | 1 | | | 3 | 1 | 5 | | | 5 | |
| | | | | | 3 | 5 | 5 | | 5 | 1 | 5 | | 1 | 1 | 5 |
| 1 | 1 | 1 | 1 | 1 | | | | | | | | | | | |
| 1 | 1 | 1 | 1 | 1 | | | | | | | | | | | |
| | | 3 | 3 | 1 | | | | | | | | | | | |
| | | 1 | 1 | 1 | | | | | | | | | | | |
| | | 1 | 1 | 1 | | | | | | | | | | | |
| | | | | | | | | | | | | | | | |
| | | 1 | 3 | 3 | | | | | | | | | | | |
| | 1 | 1 | 1 | 1 | | | | | | | | | | | |
| | 1 | 1 | 1 | 1 | | | | | | | | | | | |
| | 1 | 1 | 1 | 1 | | | | | | | | | | | |
| | | 1 | 3 | 1 | | | | | | | | | | | |

Answer on page 192

## NUMBER CHUNKS: Divide up the grid into four equal size, equally shaped parts, each containing numbers that add up to 35.

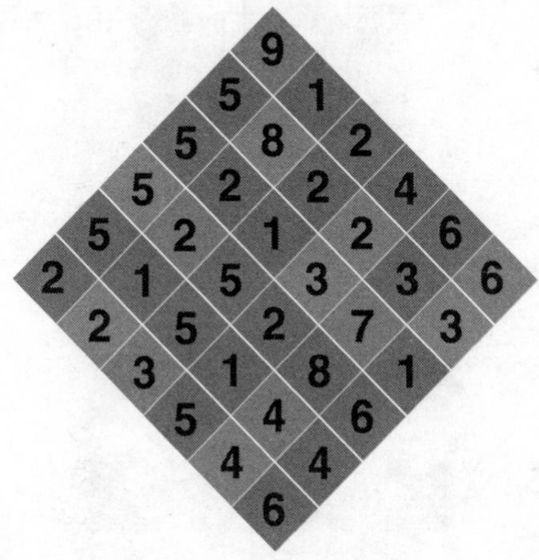

Answer on page 192

## FLOOR FILLERS: Below is a marked out floor waiting to be tiled, together with some pre-assembled groups of tiles... Can you fit them together so that they fill the floor?

Answer on page 192

## JIGSAW: Which four of the pieces below can complete the jigsaw and make a perfect square?

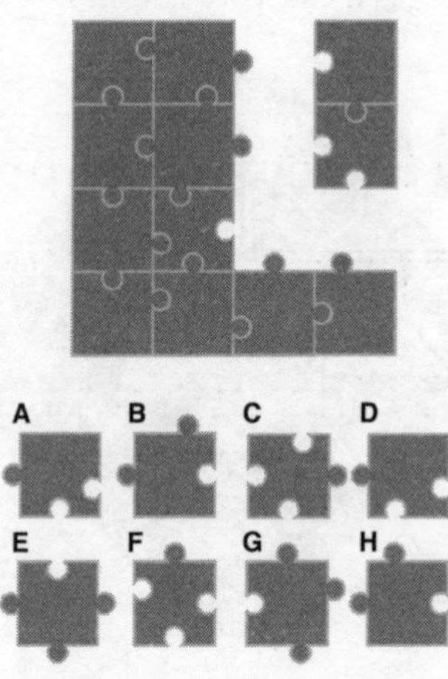


Answer on page 193

## LOGIC SEQUENCE: The balls below have been rearrange. Can you work out a new sequence of the balls from the clues given below?

The 2 ball isn't touching the 5 or the 4.
The 4 ball is touching the 10 but not the 6.
The 8 ball is immediately to the left of the 6.
The bottom row totals 16.

Answer on page 193

**SCALES:** The arms of these scales are divided into sections - a weight two sections away from the middle will be twice as heavy as a weight one section away. Can you arranged the supplied weights in such a way as to balance the whole scale?

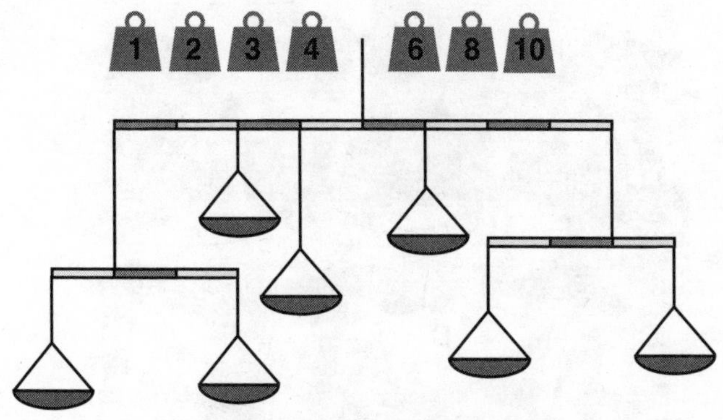


Answer on page 193

**NUMBER MOUNTAIN:** Replace the question marks with numbers so that each pair of blocks adds up to the block directly above them.

Answer on page 193

# MIRROR IMAGE:

Only one of these pictures is an exact mirror image of the first one. Can you spot it?

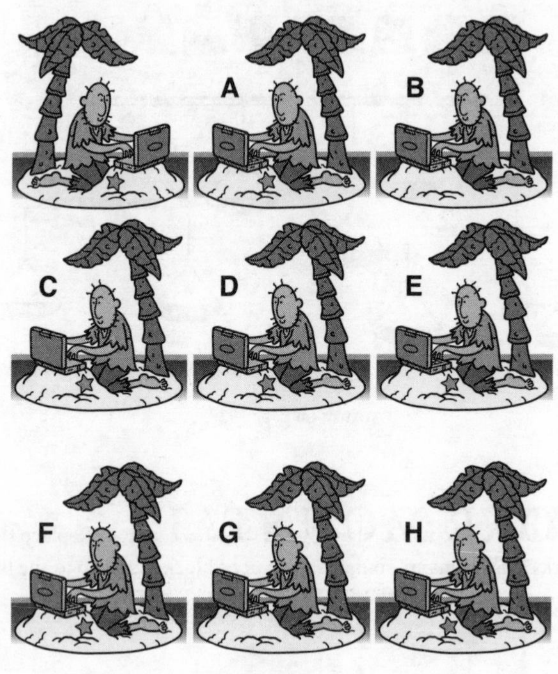


Answer on page 193

## WRINKLY QUOTE

"I think I've discovered the secret of life – you just hang around until you get used to it."

CHARLES SCHULZ

# LOOPLINK: 

Connect adjacent dots with either horizontal or vertical lines to create a continuous unbroken loop which never crosses over itself. Some, but not all of the boxes are numbered. The numbers in these boxes tell you how many sides of that box are used by your unbroken line.

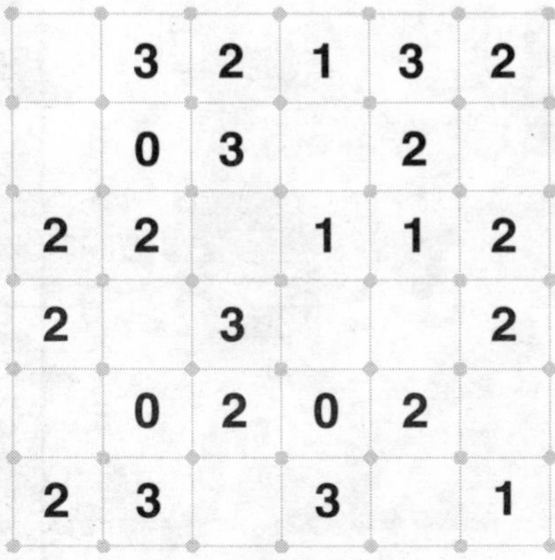

| | | | | | |
|---|---|---|---|---|---|
| | 3 | 2 | 1 | 3 | 2 |
| | 0 | 3 | | 2 | |
| 2 | 2 | | 1 | 1 | 2 |
| 2 | | 3 | | | 2 |
| | 0 | 2 | 0 | 2 | |
| 2 | 3 | | 3 | | 1 |

Answer on page 193

# SUDOKU: 

Complete the grid so that all rows and columns, and each outlined block of nine squares, contain the numbers 1, 2, 3, 4, 5, 6, 7, 8 and 9.

| | | | | | | | | |
|---|---|---|---|---|---|---|---|---|
| | 8 | 1 | 2 | 3 | | 5 | | 4 |
| 3 | | | 4 | | | | | 8 |
| | 4 | 6 | | | 5 | | | |
| | 6 | | | 2 | | 3 | | 5 |
| 1 | | 4 | | | | | | 7 |
| | | | 7 | | | 9 | | |
| | | 3 | | | | | 8 | |
| 7 | 2 | | | 9 | | 1 | | |
| | | | 8 | | 3 | 6 | | 2 |

Answer on page 193

## MATRIX: Which of the four boxed figures completes the set?

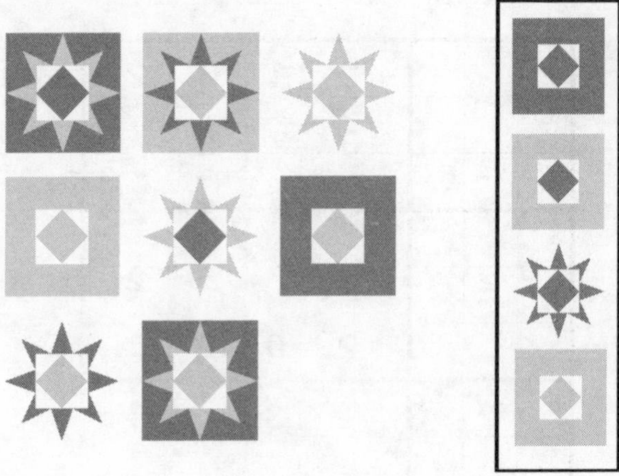

Answer on page 194

## THINK OF A NUMBER: Yellowbeard the pirate had 27 crew under him on his ship, the Blue Goose. He had less prisoners than that in the hold. One night, half of them escaped, leaving the ship exactly 15 percent less occupied than it was before. How many prisoners escaped?

Answer on page 194

# KILLER SUDOKU:

Complete the grid so that all rows and columns, and each outlined block of nine squares, contain the numbers 1, 2, 3, 4, 5, 6, 7, 8 and 9. Areas with a dotted outline contain numbers that add up to the total shown.

| | | | | | | | | |
|---|---|---|---|---|---|---|---|---|
| 14 | | | 6 | | | 17 | | |
| 17 | | | 19 | 25 | | 11 | | 9 |
| 5 | 13 | | | | **2** | | 17 | |
| | 9 | | | 21 | | | | 9 |
| 14 | | **9** | 14 | **5** | 21 | | | |
| | 15 | | | 10 | | | | 20 |
| | 4 | | | | | 16 | 12 | |
| 16 | 7 | **4** | 15 | | | | | |
| | | 23 | | | | 6 | | |

Answer on page 194

# HUB SIGNS:

What number should appear in the hub of the second wheel?

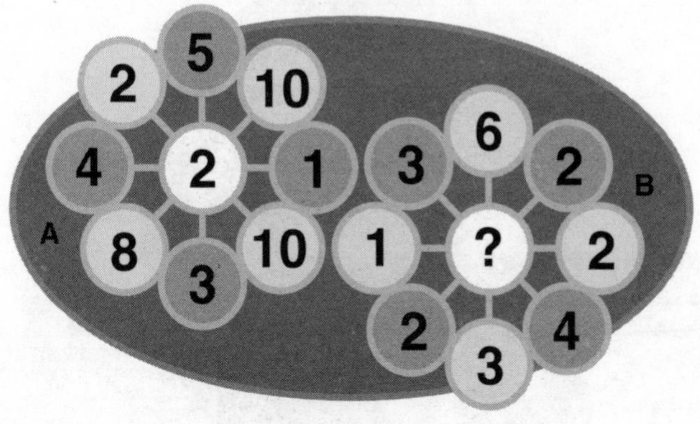


Answer on page 194

# SMALL LOGIC: Jack's garage has seen some fancy cars this week. From the clues below, can you work out when he worked on each car, what colour each was, and what jobs he had to do?

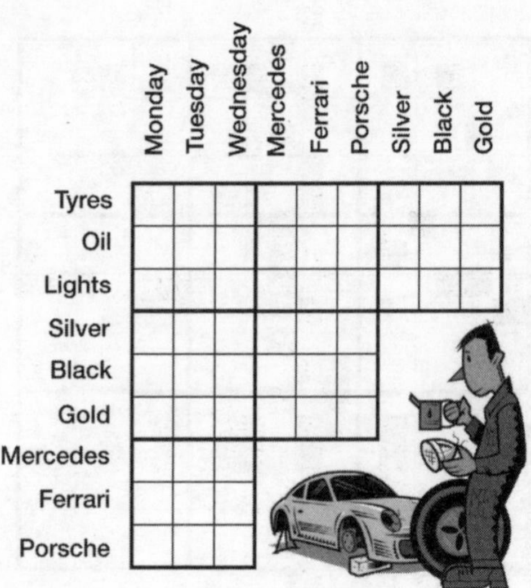


1) The Porsche was black, and didn't need an oil change
2) Jack changed tyres on Monday, but not on the Ferrari
3) The Ferrari was done before the lights but after the silver car

Answer on page 194

## Wrinkly Quote

"Experience is that marvellous thing that enables you to recognise a mistake when you make it again."

F P JONES

# SYMMETRY:

This picture, when finished, is symmetrical along a vertical line up the middle. Can you shade in the missing squares and work out what the picture is of?

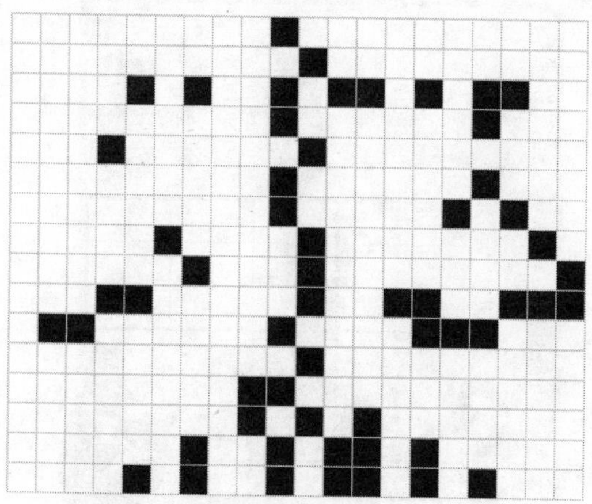

Answer on page 195

# LATIN SQUARE:

Complete the grid so that every row and column, and every outlined area, contains the letters A, B, C, D, E and F.

| | | | | | |
|---|---|---|---|---|---|
| | | | | A | |
| | | | B | | |
| | C | | | | |
| | | | | D | |
| F | | E | | | |
| | | | | | |

Answer on page 195

## MAGIC SQUARES: Complete the square using nine consecutive numbers, so that all rows, columns and large diagonals add up to the same total.

Answer on page 195

## REVOLUTIONS: Cog A has 8 teeth, cog B has 9, cog C has 10 and cog D has 18. How many revolutions must cog A turn through to get all the cogs into an upright position?

Answer on page 195

## Wrinkly Quote

"Once you finally have the brains, the body is gone or going."

RUBY WAX

**MASYU:** Draw a single continuous line around the grid that passes through all the circles. The line must enter and leave each box in the centre of one of its four sides. **Black Circle:** Turn left or right in the box, and the line must pass straight through the next and previous boxes. **White Circle:** Travel straight through the box, and the line must turn in the next and/or previous box.

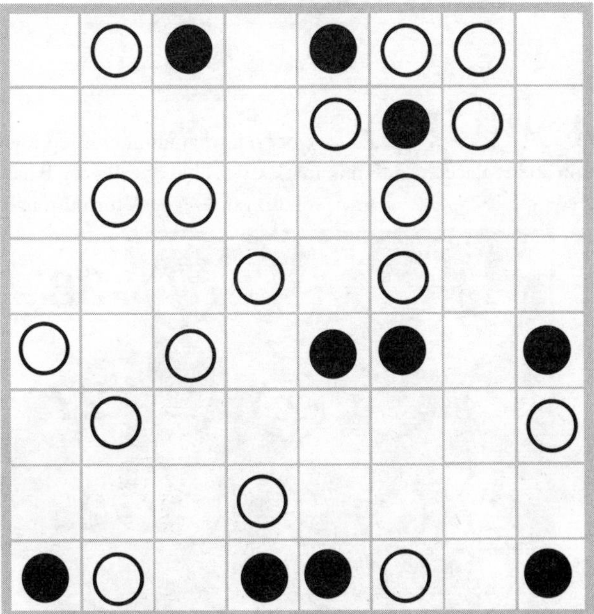

Answer on page 195

## ROULETTE:

The roulette ball is dropped into the wheel at the 0 section. When the ball falls into a number 15 seconds later, it has travelled at an average speed of 3 metres per second clockwise, while the wheel has travelled at an average 1 metre per second in the other direction. The ball starts rolling 50 centimetres away from the wheel's centre. Where does it land? Take pi as having a value of exactly 3.2.

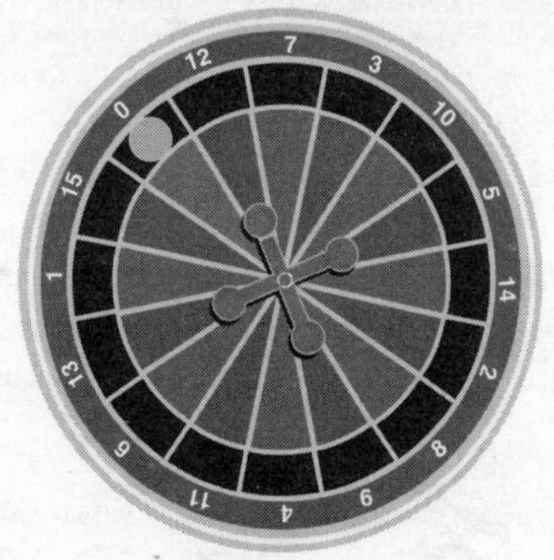

Answer on page 195

## SUM PEOPLE:

Work out what number is represented by which person and replace the question mark.

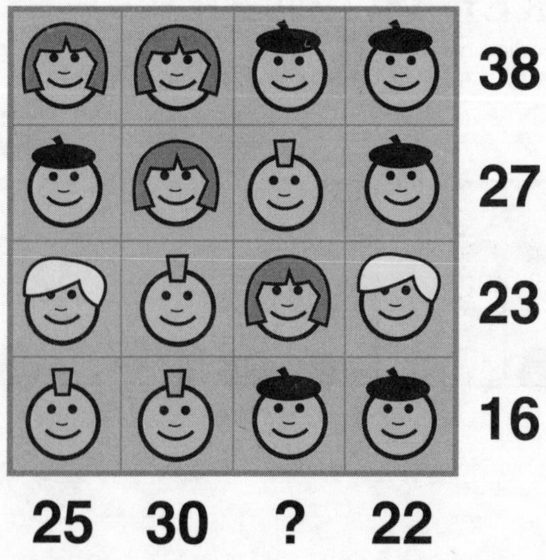


Answer on page 196

# SHUFFLE:

Fill up the shuffle box so that each row, column and long diagonal contains a Jack, Queen, King and Ace of each suit.

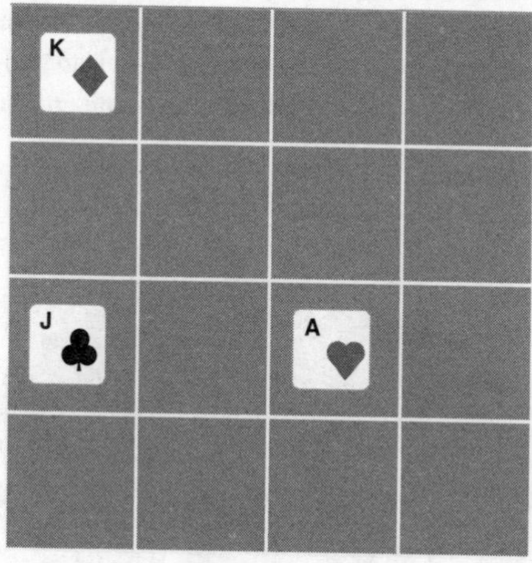


Answer on page 196

# THE RED CORNER:

Use the corners to make the central number the same way in all three cases. What number should replace the question mark?

Answer on page 196

**RIDDLE:** At the rocket scientists' canteen, two boffins were chatting in the queue. "How many kids do you have?" asked Professor Numero. "Three" replied Doctor Egghead. "Oh yeah? How old?" said Professor Numero. "Ah," said Dr Egghead, "Well, their ages add up to 13 and multiply to 36, and two of them are twins". "Hmm…" said the Professor. "My eldest is a girl," said Dr Egghead. "Aha! That makes all the difference," said Professor Numero, and promptly told the good Doctor the ages of all his children.
How did that last piece of information help, and how old are the Doctor's kids?

Answer on page 196

WRINKLY QUOTE

"Youth would be an ideal state if it came a little later in life."

HERBERT ASQUITH

# MINESWEEPER:

The numbers in some squares in the grid indicate the exact number of black squares that should surround it. Shade these squares until all the numbers are surrounded by the correct number of black squares.

| | 2 | 1 | 1 | | 3 | | 2 |
|---|---|---|---|---|---|---|---|
| 4 | | 3 | | 1 | | | |
| | | | | 1 | | 1 | 1 |
| 4 | | 4 | | 2 | | 0 | |
| | 2 | 2 | | | 3 | 3 | |
| 2 | | 2 | 4 | | | | |
| | 3 | | | | | 6 | 3 |
| 2 | | | 3 | 4 | | 3 | |

Answer on page 196

# MORE OR LESS:

The arrows indicate whether a number in a box is greater or smaller than an adjacent number. Complete the grid so that all rows and columns contain the numbers 1 to 6.

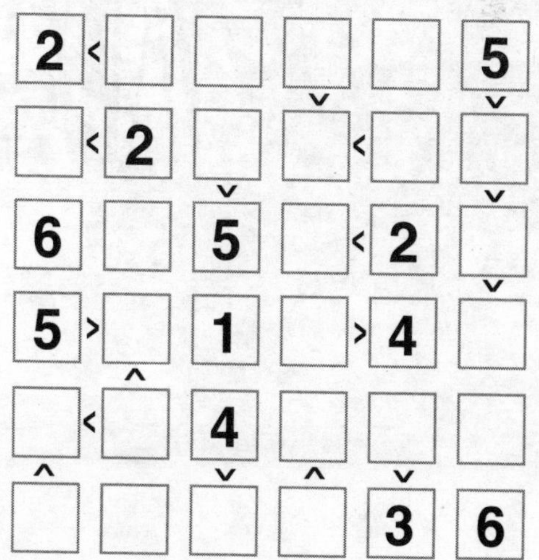


Answer on page 196

## SIGNPOST: Can you crack the logical secret behind the numbers by these footballers' names, and work out what number Fabregas might be?

Answer on page 197

## SUM PEOPLE: Work out what number is represented by which person and replace the question mark.

Answer on page 197

**SCALES:** The arms of these scales are divided into sections – a weight two sections away from the middle will be twice as heavy as a weight one section away. Can you arrange the supplied weights in such a way as to balance the whole scale?

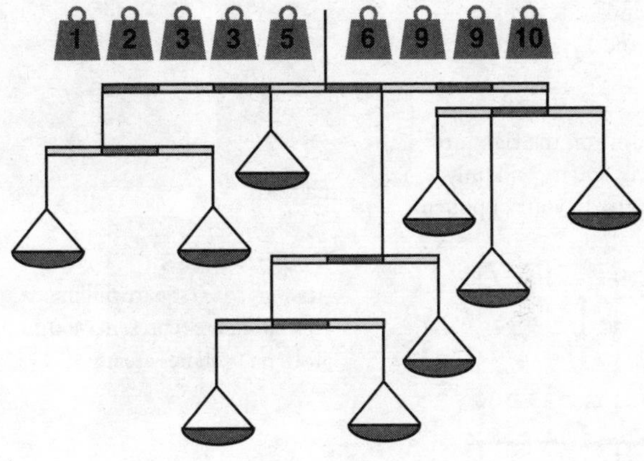


Answer on page 197

**SAFECRACKER:** To open the safe, all the buttons must be pressed in the correct order before the "open"button is pressed. What is the first button pressed in your sequence?

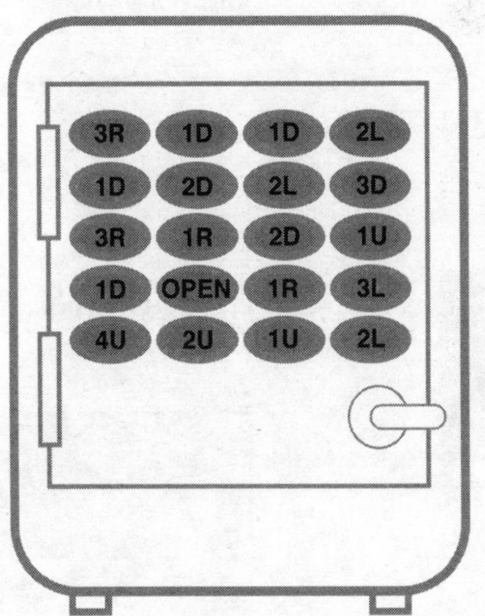


Answer on page 197

ANSWERS

**Page 13**

**BITS AND PIECES**
Answer: A and G, B and D, C and H, E and F

**BOXES**
Solution: A line on the right or bottom of this square will only give up one box to your opponent

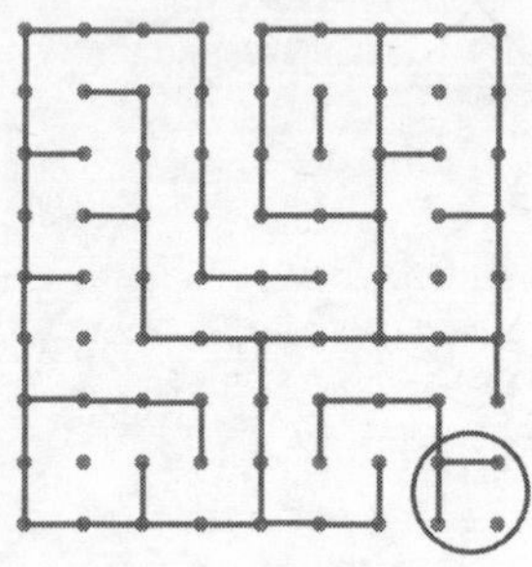

**Page 14**

**CUT AND FOLD**
Answer A

**GAME OF TWO HALVES**
Solution: C and D

**Page 15**

**DOUBLE DRAT**

**Page 16**

**IN THE AREA**
Answer: 5,000 square millimetres. Each 20 x 20 square represents 400 $mm^2$. 12 and a half squares are used

**JIGSAW**
Answer: A, C and E

**Page 17**

**SUM PEOPLE**
Answer 6

**SHAPE SHIFTING**

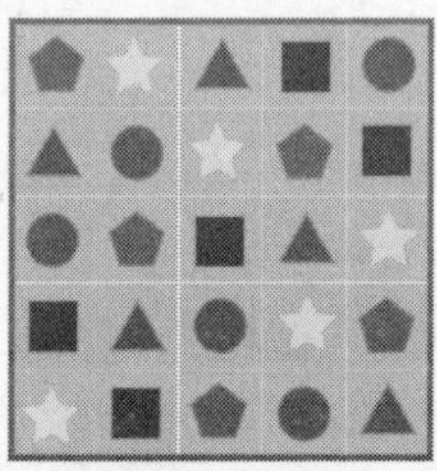

**Page 18**

## POTS OF DOTS

Solution: 13

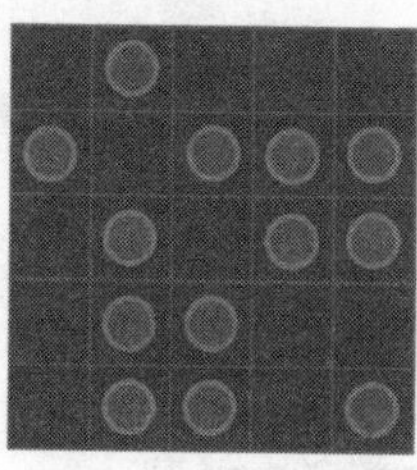

## PICTURE PARTS

Answer: A

**Page 19**

## ODD CLOCKS

Answer: 1.55 am on Wednesday in Singapore and 2.55 pm on Tuesday in Buenos Aires

## MASYU

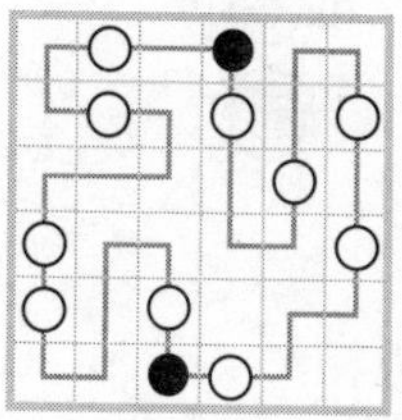

**Page 20**

## MATRIX

Solution:

Each horizontal and vertical line contains a clear star, a shaded star and a circled star. Each line contains a halved circle that has been turned through 0 degrees, 90 degrees and 180 degrees. The missing image should contain a clear star, and a circle that has been turned through 90 degrees

## FACE IN THE CROWD

Answer: The 5th face down in the third column

**Page 21**

## SUDOKU

| 8 | 3 | 4 | 1 | 7 | 5 | 2 | 6 | 9 |
|---|---|---|---|---|---|---|---|---|
| 1 | 7 | 9 | 2 | 8 | 6 | 4 | 3 | 5 |
| 2 | 5 | 6 | 9 | 3 | 4 | 1 | 7 | 8 |
| 4 | 1 | 3 | 8 | 2 | 7 | 5 | 9 | 6 |
| 7 | 2 | 5 | 3 | 6 | 9 | 8 | 1 | 4 |
| 9 | 6 | 8 | 4 | 5 | 1 | 7 | 2 | 3 |
| 6 | 4 | 1 | 7 | 9 | 8 | 3 | 5 | 2 |
| 3 | 9 | 7 | 5 | 4 | 2 | 6 | 8 | 1 |
| 5 | 8 | 2 | 6 | 1 | 3 | 9 | 4 | 7 |

## RIDDLE

Answer: 7 elephants and 8 emus

**Page 22**

BITS AND PIECES
Answer: A and F, B and H, C and E, D and G

CUT AND FOLD
Answer: C

**Page 23**

MIRROR IMAGE
Answer: D

NUMBER JIGSAW

**Page 24**

MISSING LINK
Answer: A square containing a white circle and a black number 2. Each row and column contains two white circles and numbers that add up to five

PICTURE PARTS
Answer: A

**Page 25**

SUM PEOPLE
Solution: 10

1 

2 

3

5 

USUAL SUSPECTS
Answer: Officer Lassiter is policeman F

**Page 26**

WHERE'S THE PAIR?
Answer: F and G are the pair

ODD CLOCKS
Answer: 7.15 am on Saturday in Melbourne
11.15 pm on Friday in Madrid

**Page 27**

WHERE'S THE PAIR?
Answer: D and E are the pair

**Page 28**

WHERE'S THE PAIR?
Answer: E and I are the pair

**Page 29**

MAGIC SQUARES
Solution:

| | | |
|---|---|---|
| 4 | 9 | 2 |
| 3 | 5 | 7 |
| 8 | 1 | 6 |

DEEP SEA DRESSER
Answer: F, D, H, C, B, E, G, A

**Page 30**

GAME OF TWO HALVES
Solution: B and F

HUB SIGNS
Answer:
A) 8 – subtract the numbers opposite each other
B) 18 – add the opposite numbers

**Page 31**

PAINT BY NUMBERS
Solution:

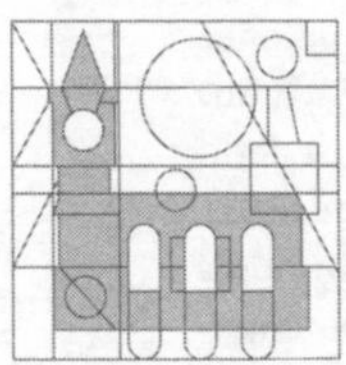

**Page 32**
RIDDLE
Answer: Six. He ate two on Monday and two more on Tuesday

CATS AND COGS
Answer: Down

**Page 33**

CHECKERS

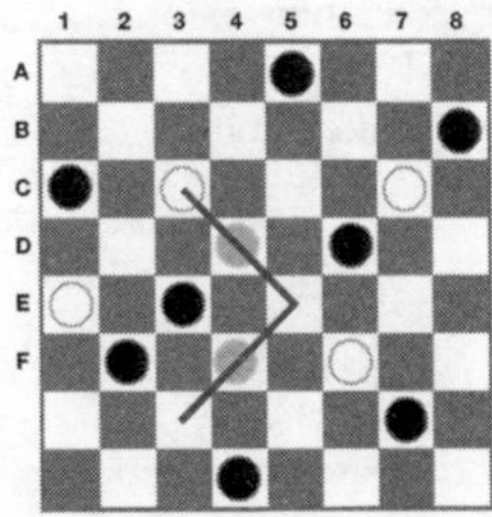


IN THE AREA
Answer: 3400 square millimetres. Each 20 x 20 square represents 400 mm$^2$. 5 squares (2000 mm$^2$) and 7 half-square triangles (1400 mm$^2$) form the bird

**Page 34**

### MATRIX

Answer: D. Each horizontal and vertical line contains two airships with dark-shaded fins, and one with light-shaded fins. Each line contains two airships with dark-shaded gondolas underneath, and one with a light-shaded gondola. Each line contains two airships facing left and one facing right. Each line contains two airships with four lights on the balloon, and one with three lights. The missing image has light-shaded fins, a light-shaded gondola, faces left and has four lights on the balloon:

### MISSING LINK

Answer: A square containing a dot. All the rows and columns should contain two white stars and one dot

**Page 35**

### SUM TOTAL

Solution: 16 + 2 ÷ 3 x 1 = 6

### MORE OR LESS

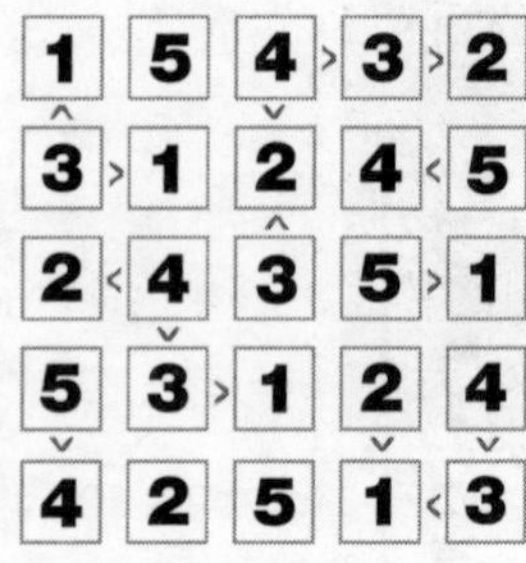


**Page 36**

### RIDDLE

Answer: Just 4.

### BOXES

Solution: A line on the top or bottom of this square will only give up one box to your opponent

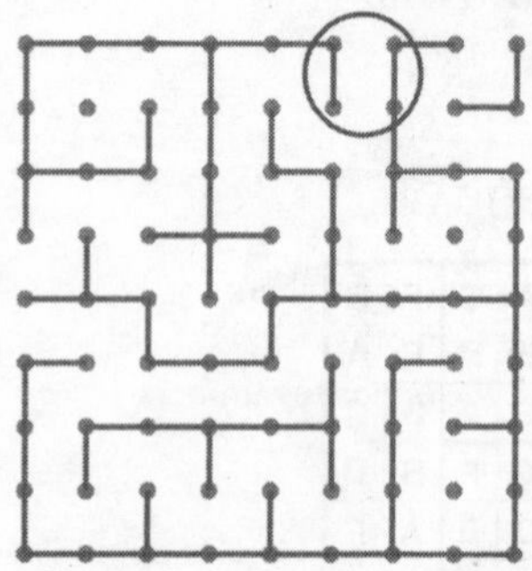

**Page 37**

DOUBLE DRAT
Answer: 19

BOATS AND BUOYS

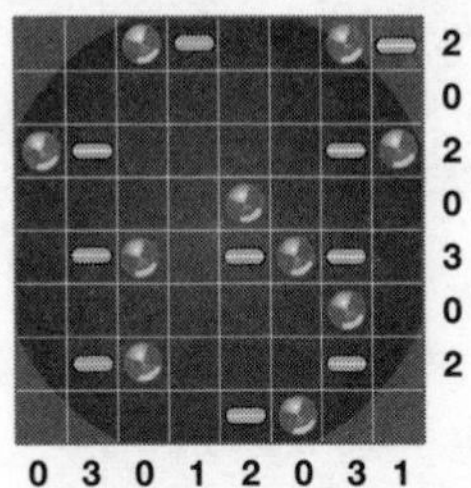


**Page 38**

RIDDLE
Answer: Tony has 5 bags, Tina has 7

CUBISM
Answer: 3

**Page 39**

CUT AND FOLD
Answer: B

LATIN SQUARE

| | | | | | |
|---|---|---|---|---|---|
| E | D | A | C | F | B |
| D | C | F | B | E | A |
| B | F | E | A | D | C |
| A | E | C | F | B | D |
| C | B | D | E | A | F |
| F | A | B | D | C | E |

**Page 40**

RIDDLE
Answer: The head and tail are 9 centimetres long, the middle is 27 centimetres long

**Page 41**

BITS AND PIECES
Answer: A and G, B and H, C and F, D and E

MATRIX
Solution: Each horizontal or vertical line contains a group of 4 black dots, a group of 4 white dots and a single white dot. Each line contains a light grey symbol, a dark grey symbol and a black symbol. The missing picture must be a black symbol with 4 black (and therefore invisible) dots

**Page 42**

**NEXT!**
Answer: D. The colours on the ball are alternating, while the number on it is increasing, by 1, then 2, then 3 etc

**NEXT!**
Answer: C. The star and circle are swapping places each time. The smallest shape is taking the shade of the previous background square. The background square is taking the shade of the previous medium-sized shape, and the medium-sized shape is taking the shade of theprevious smallest shape

**Page 43**

**BLOCK PARTY**
Answer: 76

**PICTURE PARTS**
Answer: C

**Page 44**

**POTS OF DOTS**
Solution: 18

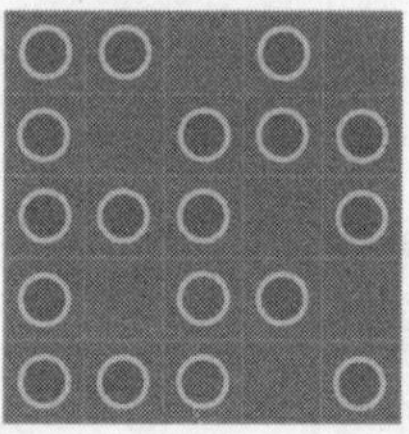

**SUM TOTAL**
Solution: 9 × 2 × 3 ÷ 9 = 6

**Page 45**

**RIDDLE**
Answer: $305 dollars. Three of each denomination and one more $50 bill

**BLOCK PARTY**
Answer: 24

**Page 46**

**BOXES**
Solution: A line on either side of this square will only give up one box to your opponent

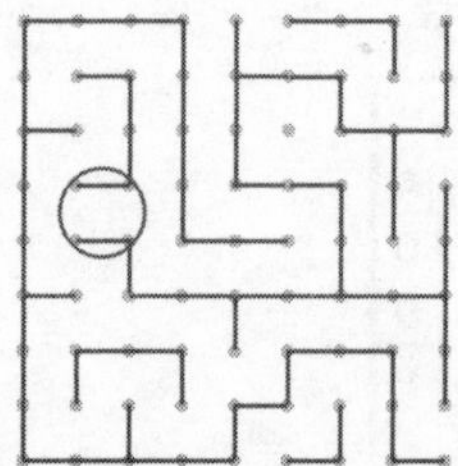

**DOUBLE DRAT**
Answer: A

**Page 47**

**CHECKERS**

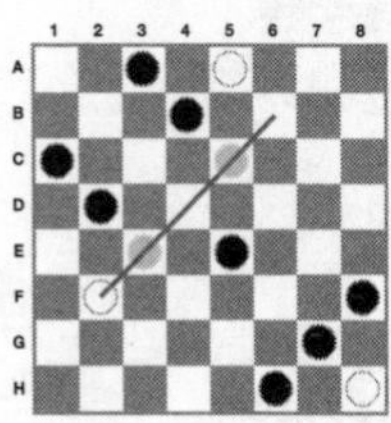


**BOXES**
Solution: A line on either side of this square will only give up one box to your opponent

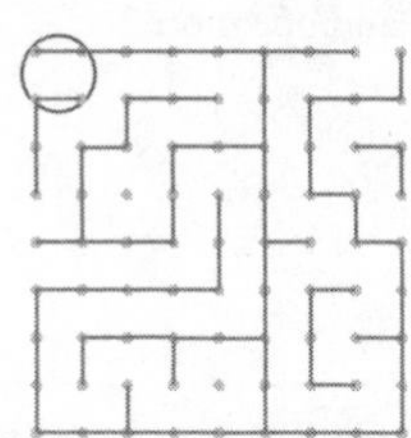

**Page 48**

**DRESSING SNOWMAN**
Answer: G, B, F, E, D, H, A, C

**Page 49**

**RIDDLE**
Answer: Bread A and B go under the grill. One minute later, Gordon tuns bread A over and swaps bread B for Bread C. One minute later he removes bread A, turns over bread C and puts B back under for a further minute

**X AND O**

| 1 | 2 | 4 | 4 | 3 | 2 |
|---|---|---|---|---|---|
| 6 | X | O | X | X | 4 |
| 3 | X | O | O | X | 4 |
| 2 | O | X | O | O | 3 |
| 2 | O | O | X | O | 1 |
| 2 | 3 | 2 | 2 | 5 | 1 |

**Page 50**

**IN THE AREA**
Answer: 5400 square millimetres. Each 20 × 20 square represents $400mm^2$. 11 squares ($4400mm^2$) and 5 half-square triangles ($1000mm^2$) form the Q

**THINK OF A NUMBER**
Answer: 70 percent. Total number of doughnuts - 40, becomes 100 when multiplied by 2.5. Multiply the other numbers by 2.5 to get percentages

**Page 51**

MIRROR IMAGE
Answer: B

**Page 52**
MATRIX

Solution: Each horizontal and vertical line contains 1 circle, 1 square and 1 triangle. Each line contains a yellow star, a white star and one picture without a star. Each line contains an orange symbol, a red symbol and a yellow symbol. The missing picture must be a yellow circle containing a yellow star

SYMMETRY
Solution below

**Page 53**

NUMBER MOUNTAIN

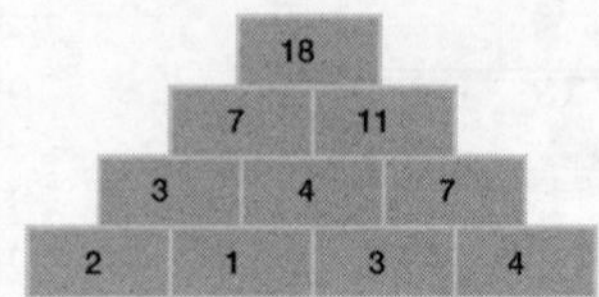


ODD CLOCKS
Answer: 3.50 am on Sunday in Karachi, 11.50 pm on Saturday in Paris

**Page 54**

PICTURE PARTS
Answer: B

SUM TOTAL
Solution: $4 \times 8 - 7 \div 5 = 5$

**Page 55**

PICTURE PARTS
Answer: A

**Page 56**

**SCALES**

**SUM PEOPLE**
Solution: 11

1 

3 

4 

7 

**Page 57**

**PAINT BY NUMBERS**
Solution: 2 Chess pieces

**Page 58**
**SUDOKU SIXPACK**

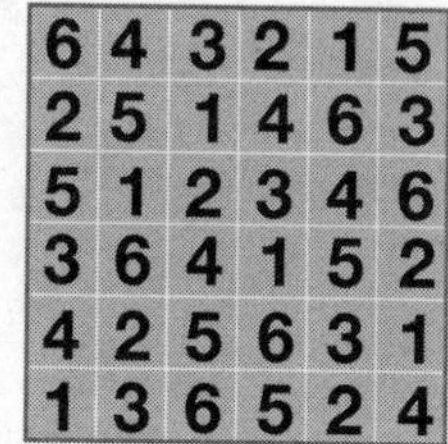

| | | | | | |
|---|---|---|---|---|---|
| 6 | 4 | 3 | 2 | 1 | 5 |
| 2 | 5 | 1 | 4 | 6 | 3 |
| 5 | 1 | 2 | 3 | 4 | 6 |
| 3 | 6 | 4 | 1 | 5 | 2 |
| 4 | 2 | 5 | 6 | 3 | 1 |
| 1 | 3 | 6 | 5 | 2 | 4 |

**SHUFFLE**
Solution: 146

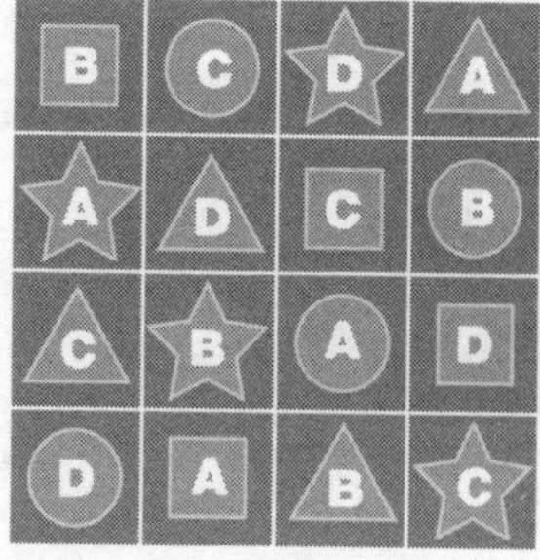


**Page 59**

**SHUFFLE**

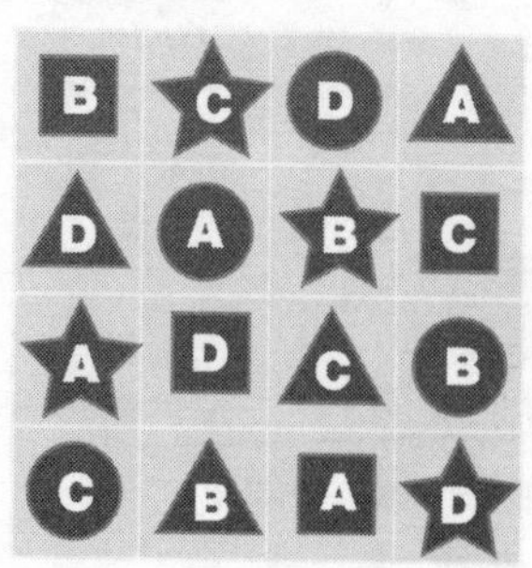

**Page 59**

SHAPE STACKER
Answer: 48.
The numbers represent the number of sides in the shape they occupy. when shapes overlap, the numbers are multiplied. 3 × 4 × 4 = 48

**Page 60**

SHAPE SHIFTING

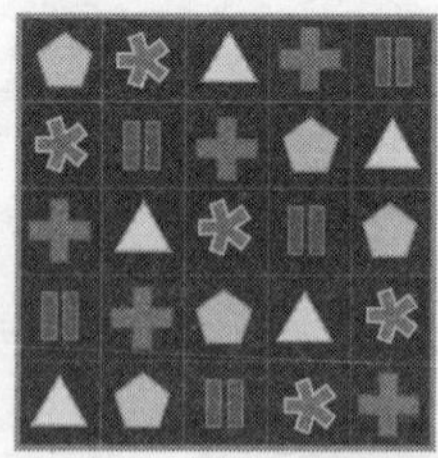

**Page 61**

RIDDLE
Answer: 4 hamsters and 3 cages

SIGNPOST
Answer: 6. Score three for each consonant and two for a vowel. Subtract the vowel total from the consonant total. 12 - 6 = 6

**Page 63**

BOXES

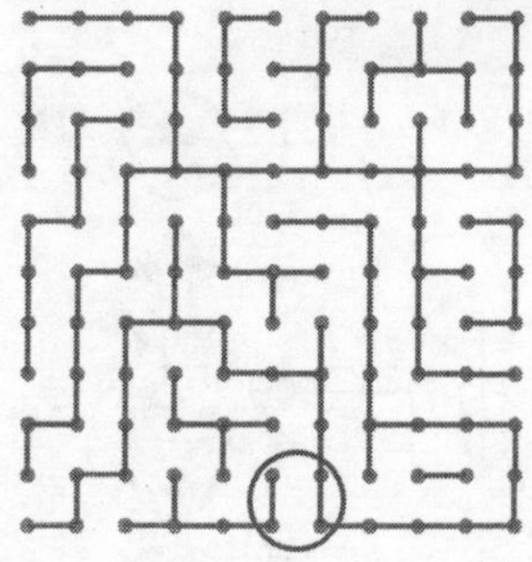

CUT AND FOLD
Answer: A

**Page 64**

MAGIC SQUARES

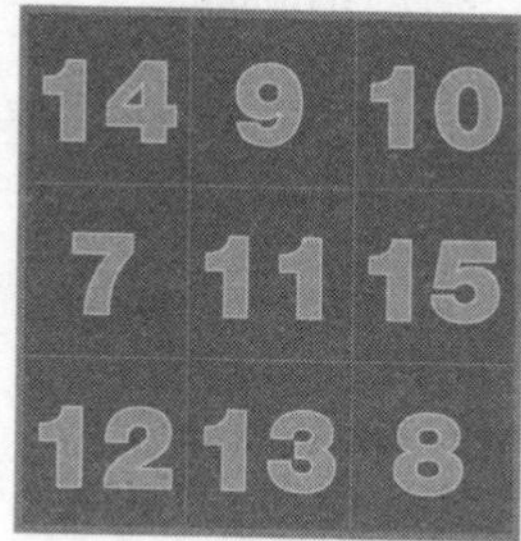


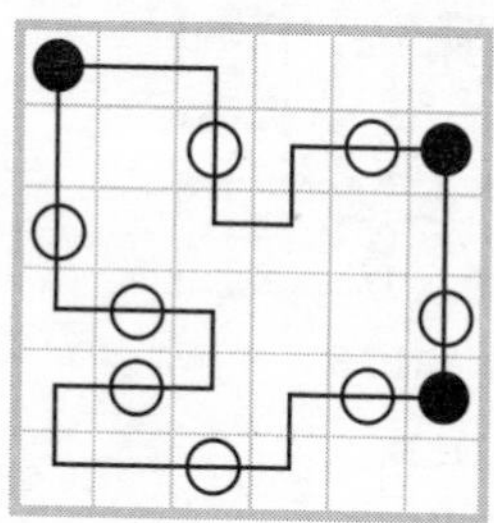

**Page 65**

RIDDLE

Answer: 10. On the 10th jump he makes it!

THINK OF A NUMBER

Answer: Two thirds and one third. 351 divided by 3 is 117 (39 + 78) 117 × 2 = 234 (203 + 31)

**Page 66**

THINK OF A NUMBER

Solution: 16

2

3

4

5

TENTS AND TREES

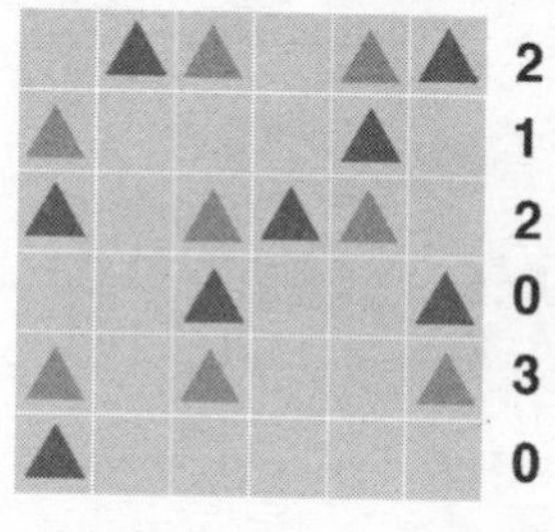


2 0 3 0 2 1

**Page 67**

SIGNPOST

Answer: 42

Score one for a consonant and two for a vowel, then multiply the totals together.

6 × 7 = 42

BLOCK PARTY

Answer: 68

## Page 68

### WHERE'S THE PAIR

Answer: B and H are the pair

### DOUBLE DRAT

## Page 69

### MORE OR LESS

| | | | | | | | | |
|---|---|---|---|---|---|---|---|---|
| 2 | < | 3 | | 1 | | 5 | > | 4 |
| | | | | ^ | | | | |
| 5 | | 1 | | 4 | | 3 | | 2 |
| | | | | | | v | | ^ |
| 4 | < | 5 | | 2 | | 1 | | 3 |
| v | | | | | | | | |
| 3 | > | 2 | | 5 | | 4 | | 1 |
| | | ^ | | v | | | | ^ |
| 1 | < | 4 | | 3 | > | 2 | | 5 |

## Page 70

### PERCENTAGE POINT

44% is darker, 56% is lighter. 11 out of 25 squares in the grid are darker, 14 are lighter. Multiply both numbers by 4 and you see a percentage

### RIDDLE

Answer: Thursday. The goat is lying!

## Page 71

### BOX IT

### BOXES

## Page 72

### TENTS AND TREES

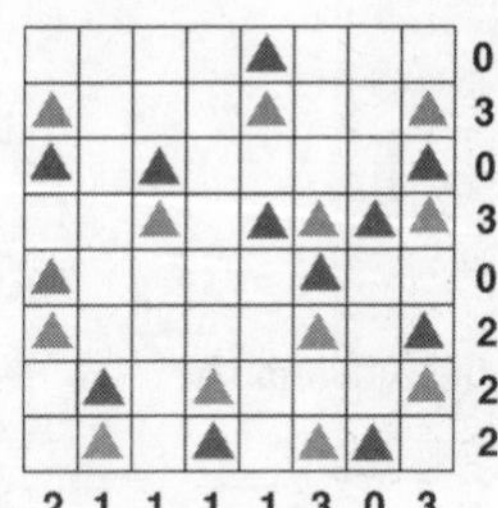

## CHECKERS

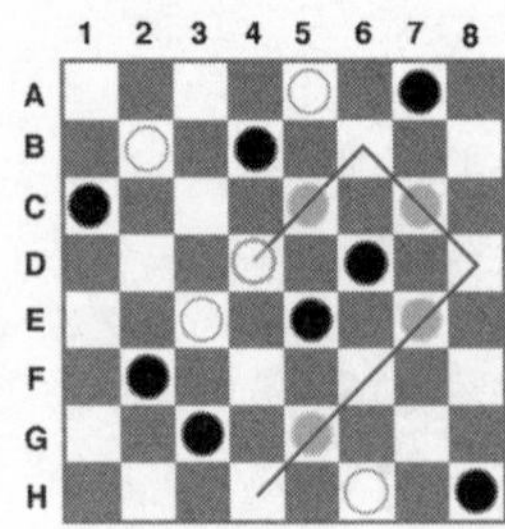


## Page 73

### DICE PUZZLE

Answer: 4. Subtract the right face from the front face and multiply by the top one

### FIGURE IT OUT

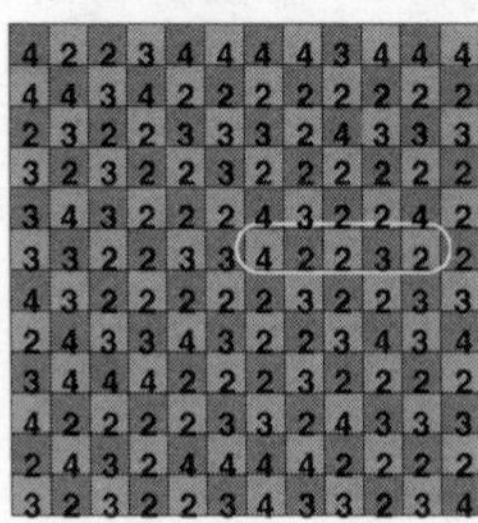

## Page 74

### GAME OF THREE HALVES

Solution:
A, B, and D

### LATIN SQUARE

| E | C | A | D | F | B |
|---|---|---|---|---|---|
| A | B | C | E | D | F |
| D | F | E | B | C | A |
| C | D | F | A | B | E |
| B | E | D | F | A | C |
| F | A | B | C | E | D |

## Page 75

### LOOPLINK

| 3 |  | 2 |  | 3 |
|---|---|---|---|---|
|  | 2 |  | 3 |  |
| 2 |  | 2 |  | 2 |
|  | 1 |  | 3 | 2 |
| 3 | 2 |  | 2 |  |

### MASYU

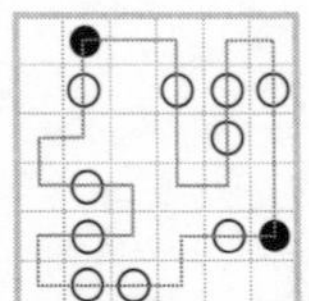

## Page 76

### MORE OR LESS

| | | | | | |
|---|---|---|---|---|---|
| 4 | 5 | 3 | 6 | 2 | 1 |
| 6 | 3 | 2 | 1 | 5 | 4 |
| 1 | 2 | 6 | 3 | 4 | 5 |
| 2 | 6 | 4 | 5 | 1 | 3 |
| 5 | 4 | 1 | 2 | 3 | 6 |
| 3 | 1 | 5 | 4 | 6 | 2 |

## Page 77

### POTS OF DOTS

Solution: 25

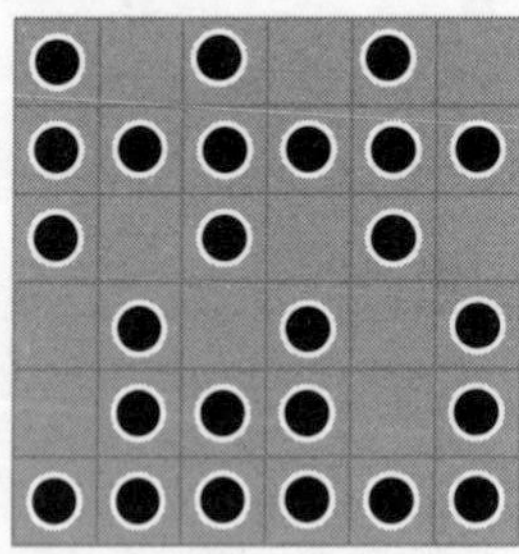

### RIDDLE

Answer: The game was on the 24th day of the month

## Page 78

### SAFECRACKER

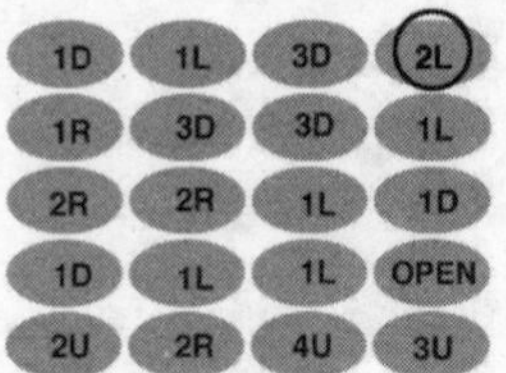


### SCALES

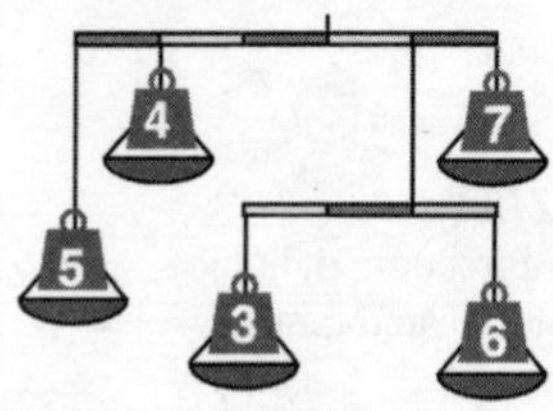


## Page 79

### SHAPE SHIFTING

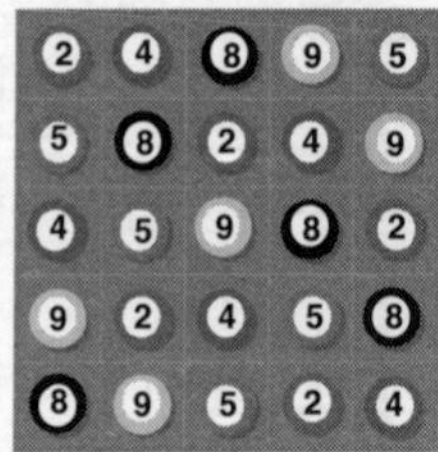


### SIGNPOST

Answer: 92

Multiply the alphabetical position of the first letter of each city by 5, then subtract the alphabetical position of the last letter 22 x 5 = 110 – 18 = 92

**Page 80**

## SUDOKU SIXPACK

| 2 | 6 | 5 | 3 | 1 | 4 |
|---|---|---|---|---|---|
| 6 | 4 | 1 | 5 | 3 | 2 |
| 4 | 1 | 3 | 2 | 5 | 6 |
| 5 | 2 | 6 | 1 | 4 | 3 |
| 3 | 5 | 2 | 4 | 6 | 1 |
| 1 | 3 | 4 | 6 | 2 | 5 |

## SUM PEOPLE

Solution: 20

**Page 81**

## SUDOKU

| 9 | 8 | 2 | 3 | 1 | 7 | 4 | 5 | 6 |
|---|---|---|---|---|---|---|---|---|
| 6 | 5 | 1 | 2 | 9 | 4 | 7 | 3 | 8 |
| 7 | 4 | 3 | 5 | 6 | 8 | 2 | 1 | 9 |
| 8 | 6 | 7 | 9 | 2 | 1 | 3 | 4 | 5 |
| 3 | 2 | 5 | 4 | 8 | 6 | 9 | 7 | 1 |
| 1 | 9 | 4 | 7 | 3 | 5 | 6 | 8 | 2 |
| 5 | 1 | 9 | 6 | 4 | 3 | 8 | 2 | 7 |
| 4 | 7 | 6 | 8 | 5 | 2 | 1 | 9 | 3 |
| 2 | 3 | 8 | 1 | 7 | 9 | 5 | 6 | 4 |

**Page 82**

## THINK OF A NUMBER

Answer: Kaplutski 56 percent, Wojowitz 44 percent. The total number is 25. Multiply this number, and the others, by 4 to get percentages

## VENN DIAGRAMS

Answer: J and D

**Page 83**

## BITS AND PIECES

Answer: Tom Cruise

**Page 84**

## FINDING NEMO

| N | O | M | N | M | M | M | M | O | M | M | M |
|---|---|---|---|---|---|---|---|---|---|---|---|
| E | N | E | M | N | O | E | E | E | N | N | N |
| M | E | N | E | E | E | N | O | M | E | E | E |
| N | M | O | O | O | M | O | E | E | M | M | M |
| E | N | M | E | M | E | E | N | N | N | N | N |
| O | E | E | M | E | O | M | E | E | E | M | E |
| M | O | O | E | M | N | E | O | M | M | N | O |
| E | M | N | O | E | E | N | E | E | N | M | M |
| O | E | E | N | O | M | O | N | N | E | E | E |
| M | N | M | E | M | E | E | M | O | M | O | M |
| E | E | N | M | E | N | M | E | E | N | M | E |
| O | O | O | E | M | M | O | N | M | O | N | O |

## MAGIC SQUARES

| 7 | 12 | 11 |
|---|---|---|
| 14 | 10 | 6 |
| 9 | 8 | 13 |

**Page 85**

## MATRIX

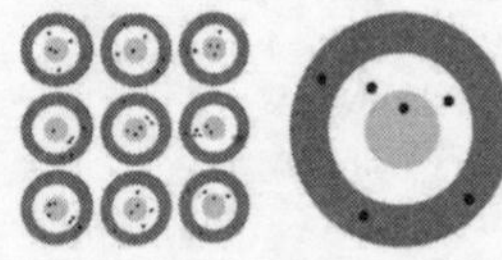

Solution: Each line contains one target with three holes in the bullseye, two holes in the middle and one hole in the outside. Each line contains one target with three holes in the middle, two holes in the bullseye and one hole in the outside. Each line contains one target with three holes in the outside, two holes in the middle and one hole in the bullseye. The missing picture must have three holes in the outside, two holes in the middle and one in the bullseye.

## ODD CLOCKS

Answer:
1.15 pm on Saturday in Miami
6.15 am on Sunday in Auckland

**Page 86**

## RIDDLE

Answer: Monday the 8th

## SAFECRACKER

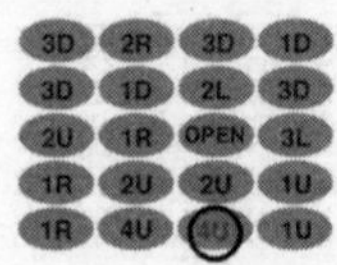


**Page 87**

## LOGIC SEQUENCE

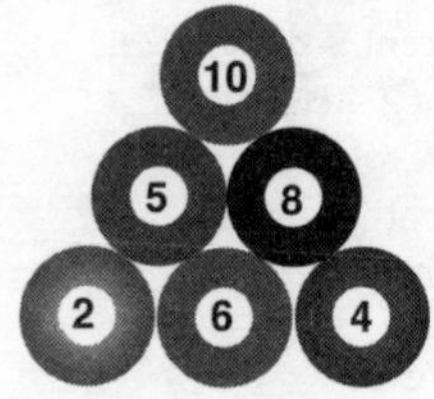


## BOXES

Solution: A line on the left or right of this square will only give up one box to your opponent

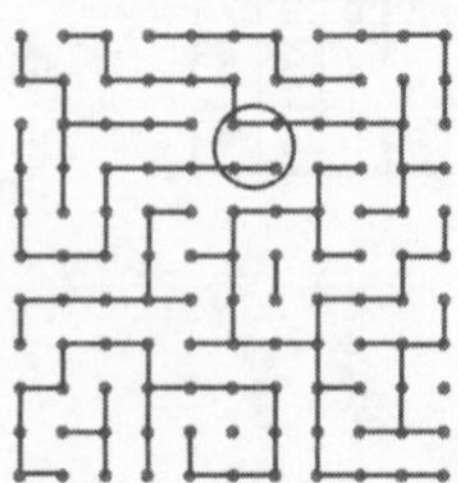

**Page 88**

## X AND O

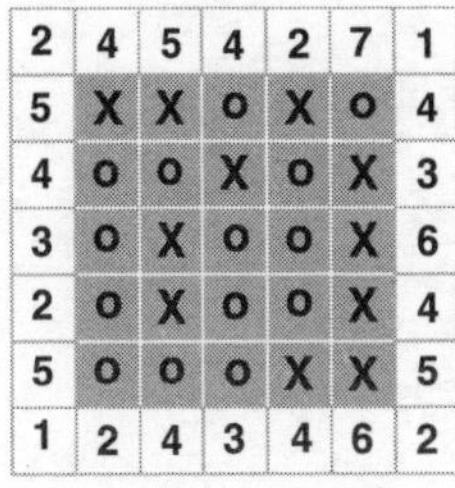

2 4 5 4 2 7 1
5 X X o X o 4
4 o o X o X 3
3 o X o o X 6
2 o X o o X 4
5 o o o X X 5
1 2 4 3 4 6 2


**Page 89**

## PERCENTAGE POINT

Answer: 48% percent is darker, 52% is lighter. 12 out of 25 triangles that make up the shape are darker, 13 are lighter. Multiply both numbers by 4 and you see a percentage

## POTS OF DOTS

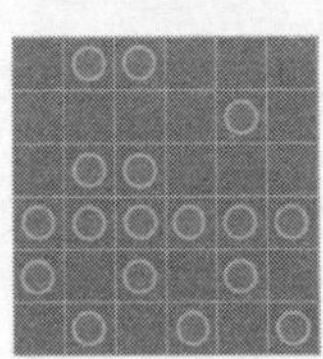

**Page 90**

## CHECKERS

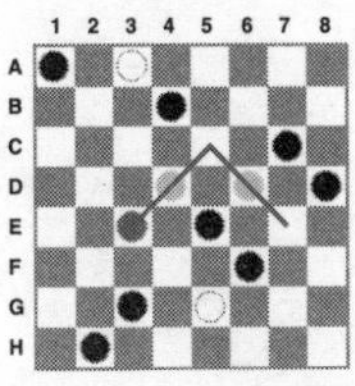


## LATIN SQUARE

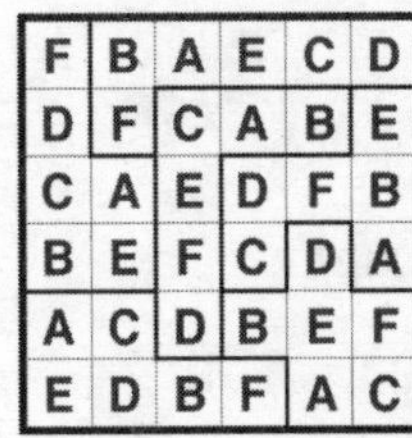


**Page 91**

## NUMBER MOUNTAIN

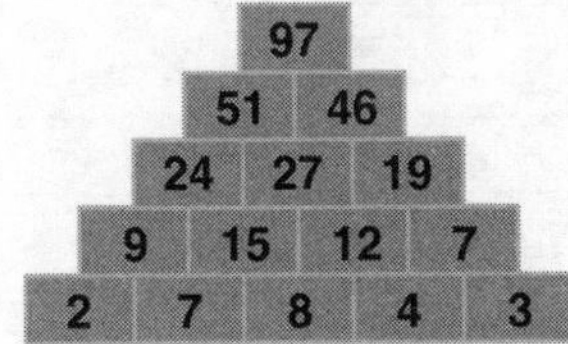


## PICTURE PARTS

Answer: B

**Page 92**

THINK OF A NUMBER
Answer: Bobby. There are 290 sweets in the jar

**Page 93**

SUM PEOPLE
Solution: 22

THINK OF A NUMBER
Answer: 50.
22 red, 11 yellow and 17 orange

**Page 94**

SHUFFLE

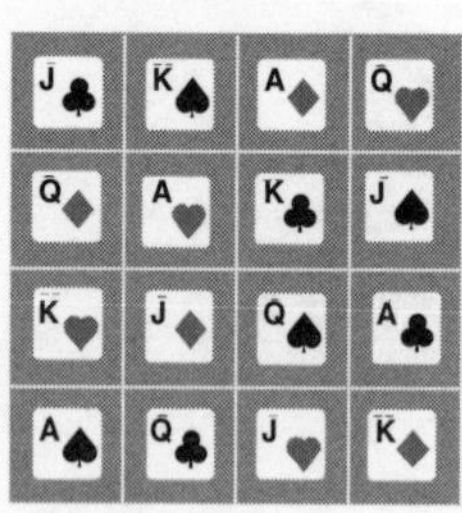


**Page 95**

DOUBLE DRAT

WHERE'S THE PAIR?
Answer: A and F are the pair

**Page 96**

THE RED CORNER
Answer: Add the top two corners, then add the bottom two. Then multiply the two totals
3 + 1 = 4
8 + 2 = 10
4 x 10 = 40

HUB SIGNS
Answers:
A) 24 - multiply the opposite numbers
B) 5 - divide the opposite numbers

**Page 97**

## BOX IT

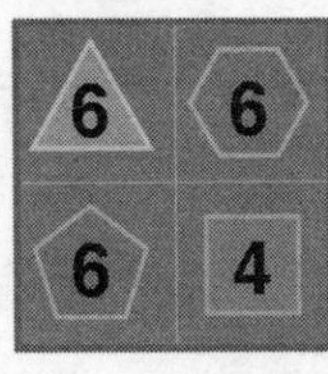

## REVOLUTIONS

Answer: 28 revolutions of cog A, which will make exactly 35 revolutions of cog B and 20 revolutions of cog C

**Page 98**

## THINK OF A NUMBER

Answer: £100

## WHERE'S THE PAIR?

Answer: A and I are the pair

**Page 99**

## CATS AND COGS

Answer: Up

## CUT AND FOLD

Answer: C

**Page 100**

## MORE OR LESS

| 4 | > | 2 | | 1 | | 3 | | 5 | | 6 |
|---|---|---|---|---|---|---|---|---|---|---|
| | | | | ^ | | | | v | | |
| 2 | < | 5 | > | 3 | | 6 | > | 4 | | 1 |
| | | ^ | | | | v | | | | |
| 3 | | 6 | | 2 | | 4 | | 1 | | 5 |
| | | | | | | | | ^ | | v |
| 6 | > | 4 | | 5 | | 1 | | 2 | | 3 |
| | | v | | v | | | | | | |
| 1 | | 3 | | 4 | | 5 | < | 6 | | 2 |
| | | | | ^ | | | | | | ^ |
| 5 | | 1 | | 6 | | 2 | < | 3 | | 4 |

## RIDDLE

Answer: Stick the signpost back up. If the sign to Aystown is pointing the way they have just come, then the rest of the signs will be pointing the right way

**Page 101**

## SHAPE SHIFTING

| 0 | ÷ | × | − | + | = |
|---|---|---|---|---|---|
| ÷ | = | + | × | − | 0 |
| = | + | − | 0 | × | ÷ |
| × | 0 | ÷ | + | = | − |
| − | × | 0 | = | ÷ | + |
| + | − | = | ÷ | 0 | × |

## BLOCK PARTY
Answer: 49

**Page 102**

## DOUBLE MAZE

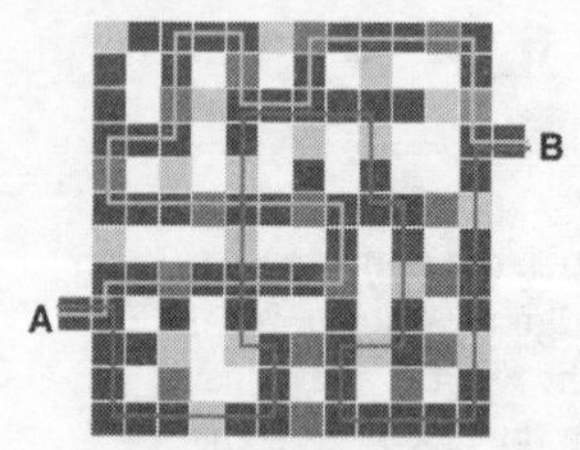


## RADAR

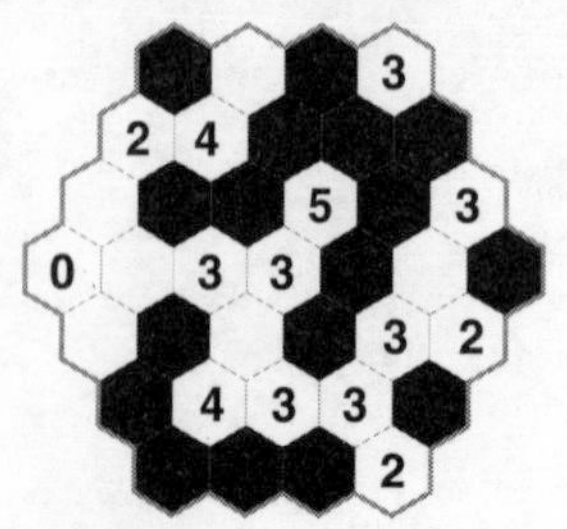


**Page 103**

## SHUFFLE

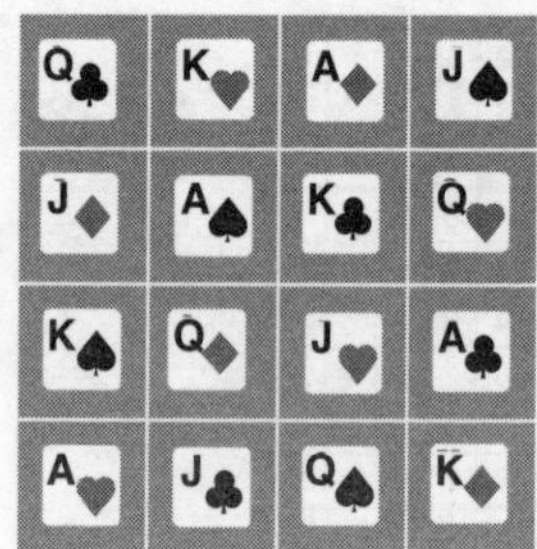


## SILHOUETTE
Answer: F

**Page 104**

## SYMBOL SUMS
Answer:
white 1
lightly-shaded 2
dark shaded 3
black 4

## IN THE AREA
Answer: 3650 square millimetres.
Each 20 × 20 square represents 400 mm$^2$.
4 squares, 6 half–squares,
2 half–square triangles,
3 quarter–squares and
3 8th of a square triangles
are used

**Page 105**

## SUDOKU

| | | | | | | | | |
|---|---|---|---|---|---|---|---|---|
| 5 | 1 | 6 | 7 | 2 | 3 | 4 | 9 | 8 |
| 4 | 3 | 9 | 1 | 8 | 6 | 2 | 7 | 5 |
| 2 | 8 | 7 | 9 | 5 | 4 | 6 | 1 | 3 |
| 6 | 7 | 3 | 2 | 1 | 9 | 5 | 8 | 4 |
| 1 | 4 | 5 | 6 | 7 | 8 | 9 | 3 | 2 |
| 9 | 2 | 8 | 3 | 4 | 5 | 1 | 6 | 7 |
| 3 | 5 | 1 | 8 | 6 | 2 | 7 | 4 | 9 |
| 7 | 9 | 2 | 4 | 3 | 1 | 8 | 5 | 6 |
| 8 | 6 | 4 | 5 | 9 | 7 | 3 | 2 | 1 |

**Page 106**

## SUDOKU SIXPACK

| | | | | | |
|---|---|---|---|---|---|
| 2 | 5 | 1 | 6 | 4 | 3 |
| 4 | 6 | 3 | 2 | 1 | 5 |
| 6 | 3 | 5 | 4 | 2 | 1 |
| 3 | 4 | 6 | 1 | 5 | 2 |
| 1 | 2 | 4 | 5 | 3 | 6 |
| 5 | 1 | 2 | 3 | 6 | 4 |

## FLOOR FILLERS

**Page 107**

## TENTS AND TREES

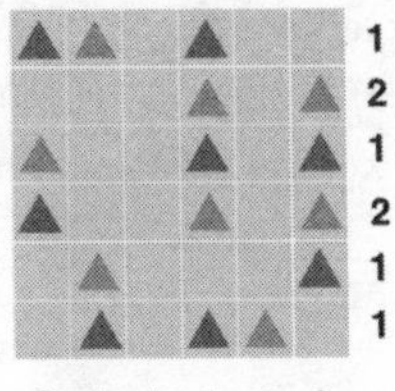


## LOOPLINK

| | | | | |
|---|---|---|---|---|
| 3 | 2 | 2 | 2 | 3 |
| 3 | 1 | 1 | 2 | 2 |
| 3 | 0 | 2 | 2 | 2 |
| 3 | 2 | 3 | 2 | 3 |
| 3 | 1 | 2 | 2 | 2 |

**Page 108**

## MAGIC SQUARES

| | | |
|---|---|---|
| 23 | 18 | 19 |
| 16 | 20 | 24 |
| 21 | 22 | 17 |

## SHAPE STACKER

Answer: 720

The numbers represent the number of sides in the shape they occupy. When shapes overlap, the numbers are multiplied

3 x 3 x 4 x 4 x 5 = 720

**Page 109**

**ODD CLOCKS**
Answer:
3.25 am on Thursday in Karachi.
7.25 pm on Wednesday in Rio

**SCALES**

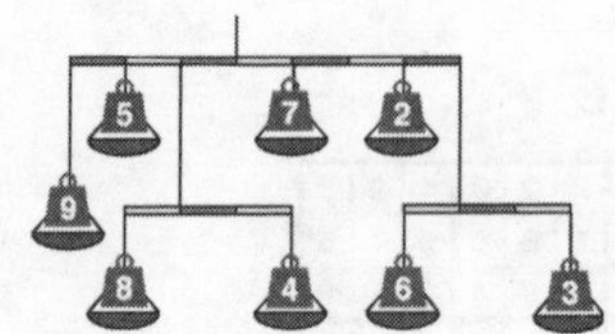

**Page 110**

**SIGNPOST**
Answer: 16
Multiply the alphabetical position of the first letter of each name by the number of vowels it contains. H = 8 and Hong Kong contains 2 vowels. 8 x 2 = 16

**MIRROR IMAGE**
Answer: H

**Page 111**

**NUMBER SWEEP**

**Page 113**

**MINESWEEPER**

**WHERE'S THE PAIR?**
Answer: B and G are the pair

**Page 114**

**MASYU**

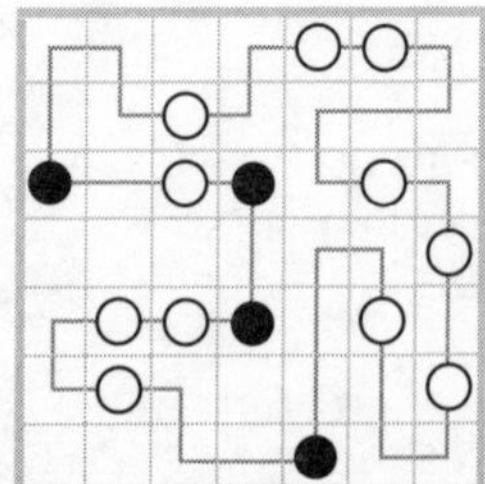

## TENTS AND TREES

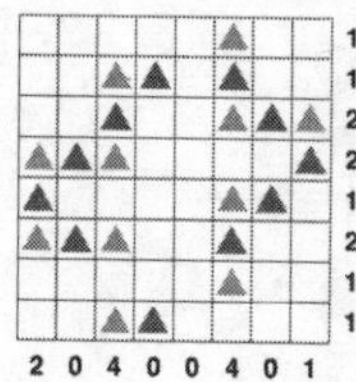

**Page 115**

## CODOKU SIX

| | | | | | |
|---|---|---|---|---|---|
| C | M | W | B | I | U |
| I | C | M | U | B | W |
| B | U | I | C | W | M |
| U | I | B | W | M | C |
| W | B | U | M | C | I |
| M | W | C | I | U | B |

| | | | | | |
|---|---|---|---|---|---|
| 6 | 1 | 2 | 3 | 5 | 4 |
| 3 | 6 | 4 | 5 | 1 | 2 |
| 5 | 4 | 1 | 6 | 2 | 3 |
| 4 | 5 | 3 | 2 | 6 | 1 |
| 2 | 3 | 5 | 1 | 4 | 6 |
| 1 | 2 | 6 | 4 | 3 | 5 |

C + 1 = D  1 + 5 = N
B + 3 = E  W + 2 = Y
U + 4 = Y  M + 5 = S

Answer: SYDNEY

## CUBE VOLUME

Answer: 6,144 cubic centimetres. Each little cube measures 4 x 4 x 4 cm, or 64 cubic centimetres, and there are 96 little cubes left. 64 x 96 = 6,144

**Page 116**

## WHERE'S THE PAIR?

Answer: B and F are the pair

**Page 117**

## PERCENTAGE POINT

Answer: There are 25 honeycomb cells and 8 bees. Multiply both figures by 4 and we get an occupation percentage of 32%. 6 out of 8 bees, or three-quarters, or 75%, are awake.

## MINESWEEPER

**Page 118**

## LOGIC SEQUENCE

## A PIECE OF PIE

Answer: 12. The inner numbers are made up of the two outer numbers of the opposite segment multiplied. 4 x 3 = 12

## Page 119

### FIVE-POINT PROBLEM

Solution: Each pentagon contains numbers that add up to 20, with the sides nearest adjoining pentagons adding up to 10

### THE GREAT DIVIDE

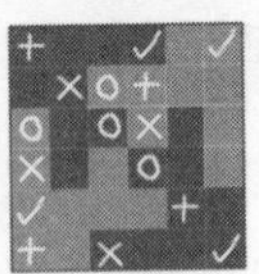

## Page 120

### KILLER SIX

| | | | | | |
|---|---|---|---|---|---|
| 5 | 1 | 4 | 6 | 2 | 3 |
| 6 | 4 | 5 | 3 | 1 | 2 |
| 4 | 2 | 3 | 1 | 6 | 5 |
| 3 | 6 | 2 | 4 | 5 | 1 |
| 2 | 3 | 1 | 5 | 4 | 6 |
| 1 | 5 | 6 | 2 | 3 | 4 |

### LOOPLINK

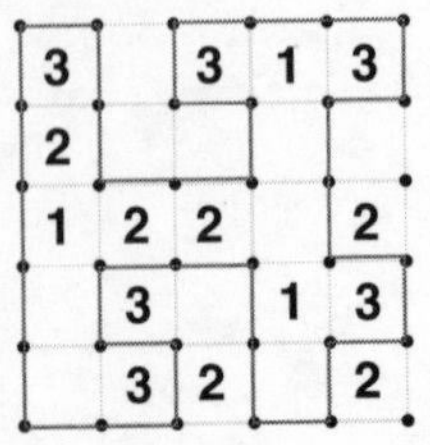

## Page 121

### MASYU

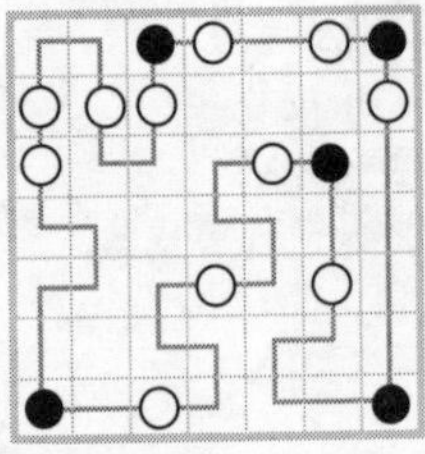

### MINI NONOGRAM

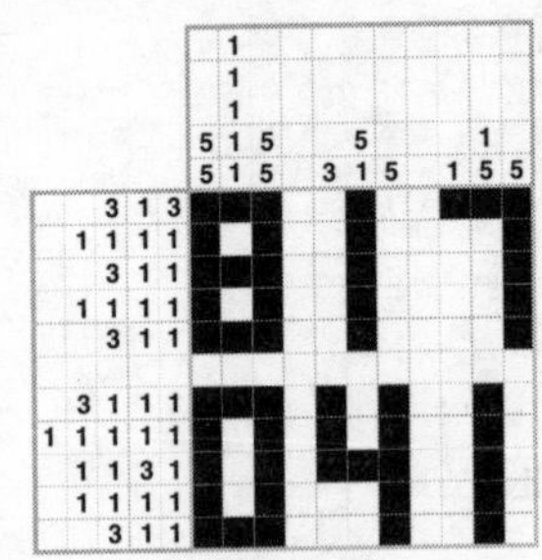

## Page 122

### MIRROR IMAGE

Answer: E

**Page 123**

### SHAPE STACKER
Answer: 2520
The numbers represent the number of sides in the shape they occupy. When shapes overlap, the numbers are added together

A: 6 + 4 + 4 = 14
B: 10 + 4 + 4 = 18
C: 5 + 4 + 1 = 10

14 x 18 x 10 = 2520

### SILHOUETTE
Answer: D

**Page 124**

### SUM PEOPLE
Solution: 25

4

5

6

9

**Page 125**

### SUM PEOPLE
Solution: 55

1

5

10

20

### WHERE'S THE PAIR?
Answer: C and H are the pair

**Page 126**

### CAN YOU CUT IT?

### DICE PUZZLE
Answer: D. The number six is turned 90 degrees compared to the other dice

**Page 127**

## FLOOR FILLERS

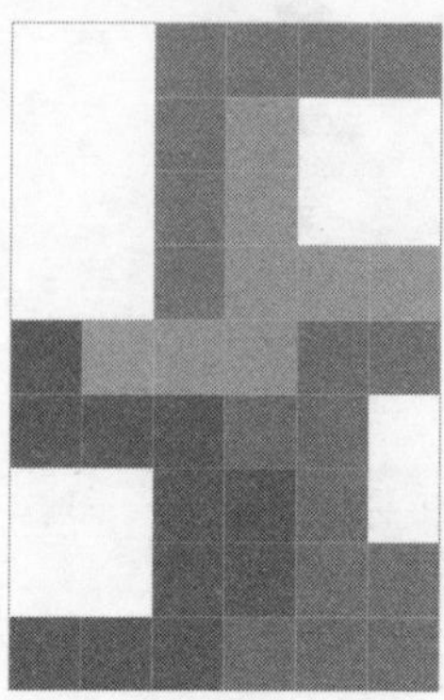

## HUB SIGNS

Answer: 6. Subtract the total of the numbers in the darker circles from the total of the numbers in the lighter circles in both cases

**Page 128**

## JIGSAW

Answer: A, C, E and F

## LATIN SQUARE

| | | | | | |
|---|---|---|---|---|---|
| B | F | E | A | C | D |
| F | A | D | C | E | B |
| D | C | A | B | F | E |
| A | E | C | D | B | F |
| C | B | F | E | D | A |
| E | D | B | F | A | C |

**Page 129**

## LOGIC SEQUENCE

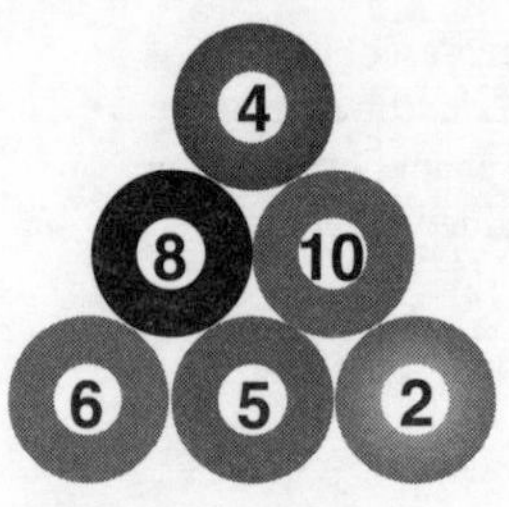


## MINESWEEPER

| | | | | | | | |
|---|---|---|---|---|---|---|---|
| ■ | ■ | ■ | 2 | | 0 | 2 | ■ |
| 3 | 4 | 4 | ■ | | | | ■ |
| 1 | ■ | | 2 | ■ | 3 | 4 | ■ |
| | 1 | | 1 | 3 | ■ | ■ | 2 |
| 1 | 2 | | 3 | 4 | ■ | 3 | |
| 2 | ■ | ■ | ■ | ■ | 3 | 2 | 1 |
| ■ | 4 | 5 | 5 | | 3 | ■ | |
| 2 | ■ | 2 | ■ | ■ | 2 | 1 | 1 |

**Page 130**

## BATTLESHIPS

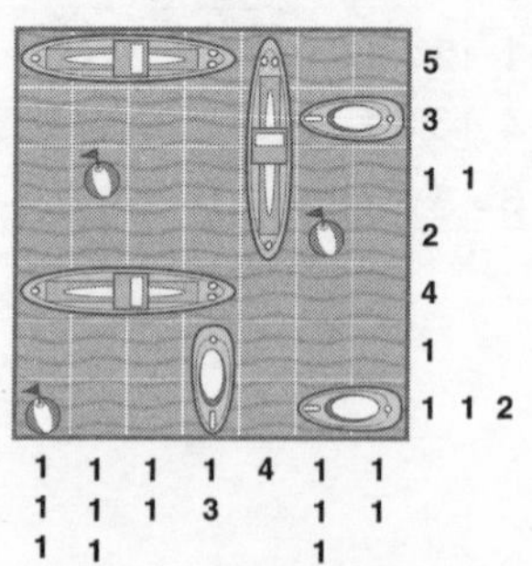

**Page 131**

## TENTS AND TREES

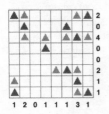

| | | | | | | | | |
|---|---|---|---|---|---|---|---|---|
| ▲ | ▲ | | | | | ▲ | ▲ | 2 |
| | ▲ | | | | ▲ | | | 0 |
| | ▲ | | ▲ | | ▲ | ▲ | ▲ | 4 |
| | | | ▲ | | | | | 0 |
| | | | | | | | | 0 |
| | | | | ▲ | ▲ | ▲ | | 2 |
| ▲ | | | | | | ▲ | | 1 |
| ▲ | | | | | | ▲ | ▲ | 1 |
| 1 | 2 | 0 | 1 | 1 | 1 | 3 | 1 | |

## LOOPLINK

| | | | | | |
|---|---|---|---|---|---|
| 3 | 1 | 2 | 2 | | 3 |
| 3 | | 2 | | 2 | 2 |
| 2 | 2 | | 2 | | |
| | 3 | 1 | 3 | 3 | 2 |
| 2 | | 2 | | 2 | |
| 2 | 2 | | 2 | | 2 |

**Page 132**

## MORE OR LESS

| | | | | | |
|---|---|---|---|---|---|
| 1 | 5 | 2 | 3 | 6 | 4 |
| 2 | 6 | 3 | 4 | 5 | 1 |
| 6 | 4 | 5 | 1 | 2 | 3 |
| 5 | 3 | 1 | 2 | 4 | 6 |
| 3 | 2 | 4 | 6 | 1 | 5 |
| 4 | 1 | 6 | 5 | 3 | 2 |

## NUMBER CHUNKS

| | | | | | |
|---|---|---|---|---|---|
| 8 | 2 | 1 | 2 | 2 | 4 |
| 6 | 3 | 1 | 1 | 6 | 3 |
| 4 | 9 | 9 | 9 | 3 | 5 |
| 5 | 7 | 1 | 5 | 5 | 5 |
| 2 | 7 | 3 | 1 | 6 | 4 |
| 9 | 7 | 3 | 2 | 3 | 7 |

**Page 133**

## SAFECRACKER

## SUDOKU

| | | | | | | | | |
|---|---|---|---|---|---|---|---|---|
| 5 | 2 | 9 | 1 | 6 | 8 | 3 | 4 | 7 |
| 1 | 3 | 7 | 9 | 2 | 4 | 6 | 8 | 5 |
| 4 | 6 | 8 | 7 | 3 | 5 | 1 | 9 | 2 |
| 6 | 7 | 1 | 4 | 5 | 9 | 2 | 3 | 8 |
| 3 | 9 | 4 | 2 | 8 | 1 | 5 | 7 | 6 |
| 2 | 8 | 5 | 6 | 7 | 3 | 4 | 1 | 9 |
| 7 | 1 | 6 | 8 | 4 | 2 | 9 | 5 | 3 |
| 8 | 4 | 3 | 5 | 9 | 6 | 7 | 2 | 1 |
| 9 | 5 | 2 | 3 | 1 | 7 | 8 | 6 | 4 |

## Page 134

### TENTS AND TREES

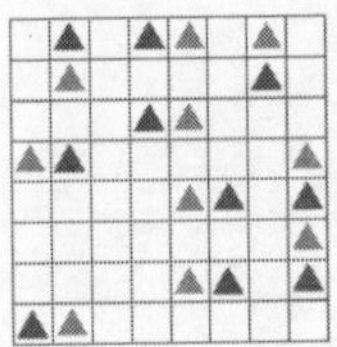

## Page 135

### CAN YOU CUT IT?

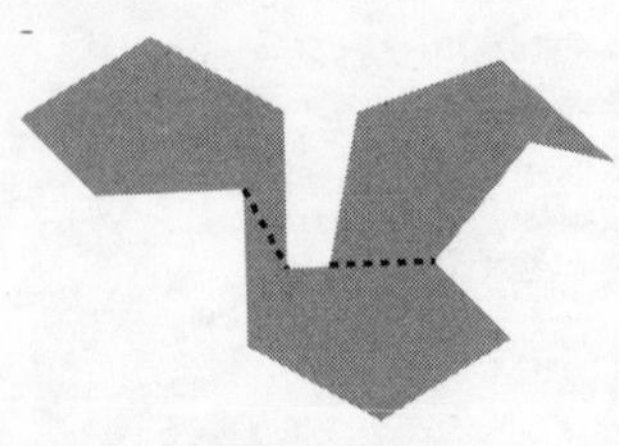

### FIVE POINT PROBLEM

Solution: Each pentagon contains numbers that add up to 24, with the sides facing each other on adjoining pentagons, when multiplied together, also making 24

## Page 136

### GRIDLOCK

Answer: A. Each row and column in the grid contains shapes whose sides total 12, two of which are light and one of which is dark

### KILLER SIX

| 3 | 1 | 4 | 5 | 2 | 6 |
|---|---|---|---|---|---|
| 5 | 6 | 1 | 2 | 3 | 4 |
| 1 | 5 | 6 | 3 | 4 | 2 |
| 2 | 4 | 3 | 1 | 6 | 5 |
| 4 | 3 | 2 | 6 | 5 | 1 |
| 6 | 2 | 5 | 4 | 1 | 3 |

## Page 137

### HUB SIGNS

Answer: 2. Divide the total of the numbers in the darker circles by the total of the numbers in the lighter circles in each case

### LOOPLINK

| 1 |  | 2 |  | 2 | 2 |
|---|---|---|---|---|---|
| 2 | 2 | 3 | 2 |  | 3 |
|  | 0 | 3 | 2 | 2 | 2 |
|  | 3 |  |  | 2 |  |
| 1 |  | 2 | 2 | 1 | 2 |
| 3 | 2 | 2 | 2 |  | 3 |

## Page 138

### MAGIC SQUARES

| | | |
|---|---|---|
| 5 | 10 | 9 |
| 12 | 8 | 4 |
| 7 | 6 | 11 |

### THE GREAT DIVIDE

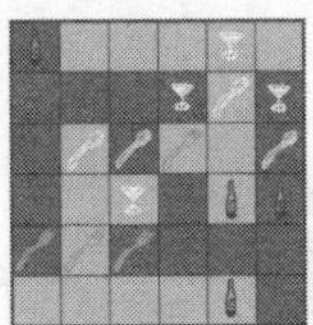

## Page 139

### SMALL LOGIC

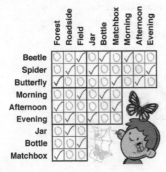

| | Forest | Roadside | Field | Jar | Bottle | Matchbox | Morning | Afternoon | Evening |
|---|---|---|---|---|---|---|---|---|---|
| Beetle | O | O | ✓ | O | ✓ | O | ✓ | O | O |
| Spider | O | ✓ | O | ✓ | O | O | O | O | ✓ |
| Butterfly | ✓ | O | O | O | O | ✓ | O | ✓ | O |
| Morning | O | O | ✓ | O | ✓ | O | | | |
| Afternoon | ✓ | O | O | O | O | ✓ | | | |
| Evening | O | ✓ | O | ✓ | O | O | | | |
| Jar | O | ✓ | O | | | | | | |
| Bottle | O | O | ✓ | | | | | | |
| Matchbox | ✓ | O | O | | | | | | |

### SUDOKU

| | | | | | | | | |
|---|---|---|---|---|---|---|---|---|
| 1 | 2 | 6 | 9 | 7 | 8 | 5 | 3 | 4 |
| 8 | 4 | 7 | 1 | 3 | 5 | 2 | 9 | 6 |
| 3 | 5 | 9 | 6 | 4 | 2 | 1 | 7 | 8 |
| 9 | 6 | 1 | 8 | 5 | 3 | 7 | 4 | 2 |
| 7 | 3 | 4 | 2 | 1 | 6 | 9 | 8 | 5 |
| 2 | 8 | 5 | 7 | 9 | 4 | 6 | 1 | 3 |
| 4 | 1 | 2 | 3 | 6 | 7 | 8 | 5 | 9 |
| 6 | 7 | 3 | 5 | 8 | 9 | 4 | 2 | 1 |
| 5 | 9 | 8 | 4 | 2 | 1 | 3 | 6 | 7 |

## Page 140

### SUDOKU

| | | | | | | | | |
|---|---|---|---|---|---|---|---|---|
| 2 | 8 | 9 | 6 | 4 | 7 | 3 | 1 | 5 |
| 4 | 5 | 7 | 1 | 8 | 3 | 6 | 2 | 9 |
| 6 | 3 | 1 | 9 | 5 | 2 | 7 | 8 | 4 |
| 1 | 9 | 4 | 2 | 3 | 8 | 5 | 6 | 7 |
| 8 | 7 | 2 | 5 | 9 | 6 | 4 | 3 | 1 |
| 5 | 6 | 3 | 7 | 1 | 4 | 8 | 9 | 2 |
| 9 | 1 | 8 | 3 | 7 | 5 | 2 | 4 | 6 |
| 3 | 2 | 4 | 4 | 6 | 1 | 9 | 7 | 8 |
| 7 | 4 | 6 | 8 | 2 | 9 | 1 | 5 | 3 |

### THE RED CORNER

Answer: 36. Add all the red corners and multiply the total by two. 3 + 3 + 7 + 5 = 18 x 2 = 36

## Page 141

### CODOKU SIX

| | | | | | |
|---|---|---|---|---|---|
| Z | K | A | B | Y | J |
| B | A | Y | J | Z | K |
| K | Y | B | A | J | Z |
| Y | J | Z | K | B | A |
| A | B | J | Z | K | Y |
| J | Z | K | Y | A | B |

| | | | | | |
|---|---|---|---|---|---|
| 2 | 1 | 6 | 3 | 4 | 5 |
| 1 | 4 | 3 | 2 | 5 | 6 |
| 3 | 5 | 4 | 6 | 1 | 2 |
| 4 | 2 | 1 | 5 | 6 | 3 |
| 5 | 6 | 2 | 1 | 3 | 4 |
| 6 | 3 | 5 | 4 | 2 | 1 |

B+6=H Z+1=A
K+3=N Y+5=D
A+4=E J+2=L
Answer: HANDEL

### NUMBER MOUNTAIN

216
109 107
53 56 51
24 29 27 24
11 13 16 11 13
5 6 7 9 2 11

## Page 142

### SYMMETRY

### CUBE VOLUME

Answer: 2484 cubic centimetres. Each little cube measures 3 x 3 x 3 cm, or 27 cubic centimetres, and there are 92 little cubes left. 27 x 92 = 2484

## Page 143

### DICE PUZZLE

Answer: B. The right hand side should be showing a six

### KILLER SIX

| 5 | 1 | 6 | 4 | 2 | 3 |
|---|---|---|---|---|---|
| 4 | 3 | 1 | 5 | 6 | 2 |
| 6 | 2 | 5 | 1 | 3 | 4 |
| 3 | 6 | 4 | 2 | 1 | 5 |
| 1 | 5 | 2 | 3 | 4 | 6 |
| 2 | 4 | 3 | 6 | 5 | 1 |

## Page 144

### MASYU

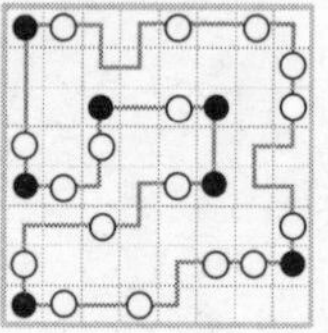

### MINI NONOGRAM

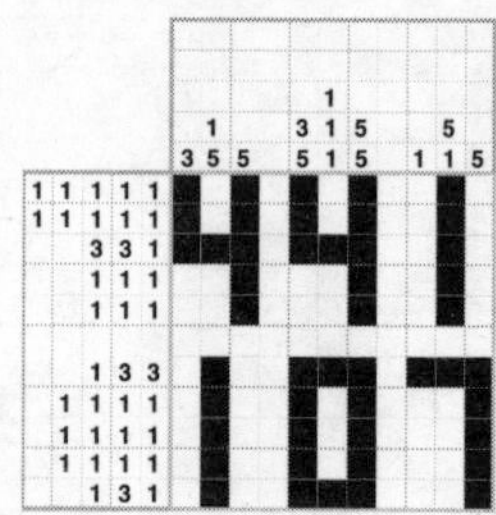

## Page 145

### NUMBER CHUNKS

### FLOOR FILLERS

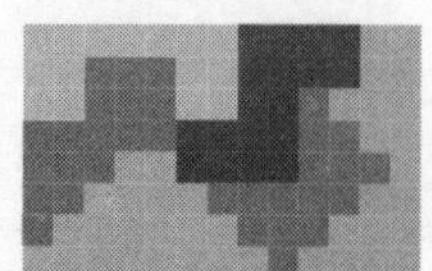

**Page 146**

JIGSAW
Answer: A, C, E and H

LOGIC SEQUENCE

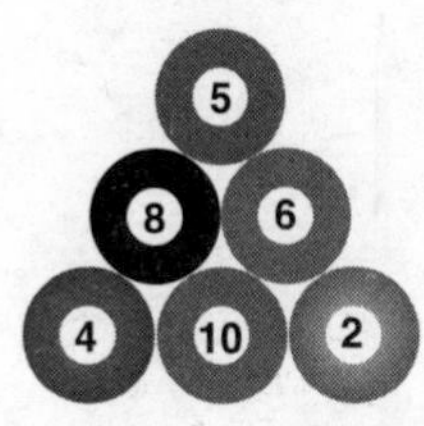


**Page 147**

SCALES

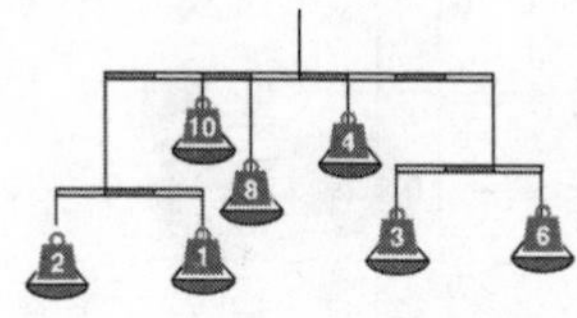


NUMBER MOUNTAIN

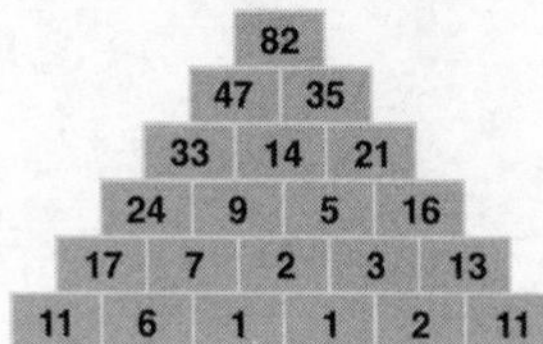


**Page 148**

MIRROR IMAGE
Answer: D

**Page 149**

LOOPLINK

| | | | | | |
|---|---|---|---|---|---|
| 2 | 3 | 2 | 1 | 3 | 2 |
| 3 | 0 | 3 | 1 | 2 | 2 |
| 2 | 2 | 2 | 1 | 1 | 2 |
| 2 | 2 | 3 | 3 | 3 | 2 |
| 3 | 0 | 2 | 0 | 2 | 2 |
| 2 | 3 | 3 | 3 | 2 | 1 |

SUDOKU

| | | | | | | | | |
|---|---|---|---|---|---|---|---|---|
| 9 | 8 | 1 | 2 | 3 | 7 | 5 | 6 | 4 |
| 3 | 7 | 5 | 4 | 6 | 1 | 2 | 9 | 8 |
| 2 | 4 | 6 | 9 | 8 | 5 | 7 | 3 | 1 |
| 8 | 6 | 7 | 1 | 2 | 9 | 3 | 4 | 5 |
| 1 | 9 | 4 | 3 | 5 | 6 | 8 | 2 | 7 |
| 5 | 3 | 2 | 7 | 4 | 8 | 9 | 1 | 6 |
| 6 | 1 | 3 | 5 | 7 | 2 | 4 | 8 | 9 |
| 7 | 2 | 8 | 6 | 9 | 4 | 1 | 5 | 3 |
| 4 | 5 | 9 | 8 | 1 | 3 | 6 | 7 | 2 |

## Page 150

### MATRIX

Every vertical and horizontal line contains one darker, one lighter and one white outer box. Each line also contains one darker inner diamond and two lighter ones. Finally each line contains one darker star and two lighter ones. The missing image should be a lighter outer box with a darker inner diamond and a lighter star.

### THINK OF A NUMBER

Solution: 6. There were 12 prisoners in the hold before the escape, making 40 people in all on the ship, and 15 percent of 40 is 6

## Page 151

### KILLER SUDOKU

| | | | | | | | | |
|---|---|---|---|---|---|---|---|---|
| 2 | 9 | 3 | 5 | 1 | 8 | 4 | 6 | 7 |
| 8 | 4 | 5 | 3 | 6 | 7 | 2 | 9 | 1 |
| 1 | 7 | 6 | 9 | 4 | 2 | 3 | 5 | 8 |
| 4 | 6 | 2 | 7 | 8 | 9 | 1 | 3 | 5 |
| 3 | 1 | 9 | 2 | 5 | 6 | 8 | 7 | 4 |
| 5 | 8 | 7 | 4 | 3 | 1 | 6 | 2 | 9 |
| 6 | 3 | 1 | 8 | 7 | 5 | 9 | 4 | 2 |
| 9 | 5 | 4 | 1 | 2 | 3 | 7 | 8 | 6 |
| 7 | 2 | 8 | 6 | 9 | 4 | 5 | 1 | 3 |

### HUB SIGNS

Answer: 4. Multiply all the numbers in darker circles and add all the numbers in lighter circles. Divide the darker total by the lighter one.

3 x 2 x 4 x 2 = 48

1 + 6 + 2 + 3 = 12

48 divided by 12 is 4

## Page 152

### SMALL LOGIC

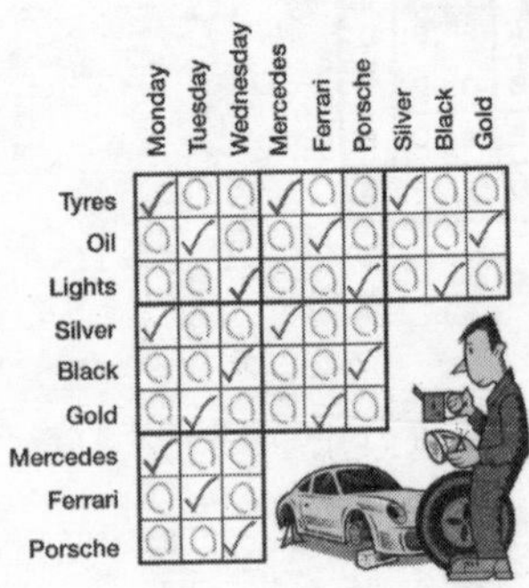

**Page 153**

SYMMETRY

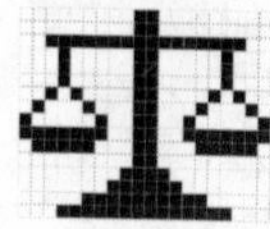

LATIN SQUARE

| | | | | | |
|---|---|---|---|---|---|
| B | F | C | D | A | E |
| D | A | F | B | E | C |
| E | C | A | F | B | D |
| A | E | B | C | D | F |
| F | D | E | A | C | B |
| C | B | D | E | F | A |

**Page 154**

MAGIC SQUARES

| | | |
|---|---|---|
| 10 | 9 | 14 |
| 15 | 11 | 7 |
| 8 | 13 | 12 |

REVOLUTIONS
Answer: 22 and a half revolutions of cog A, which will make exactly 20 revolutions of cog B, 18 revolutions of cog C and 10 revolutions of cog D

**Page 155**

MASYU

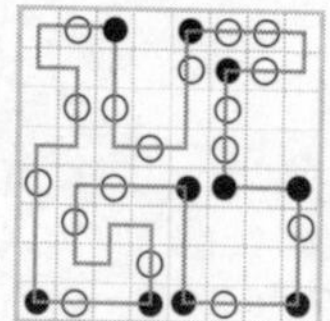

**Page 156**

ROULETTE
Answer: In the number 6 space. The ball travels at a speed of 4 metres per second (relative to the wheel) for 15 seconds, making a distance of 6000 centimetres in a clockwise direction. The circumference of the wheel is 320 centimetres (2 x pi (3.2) x radius (50cm)). The ball must then travel 18.75 laps of the wheel, placing it three quarters of the way around the wheel in a clockwise direction, in the 6 space

**Page 156**

SUM PEOPLE:
Solution: 27

**Page 157**

SHUFFLE

THE RED CORNER
Answer: 50. Multiply the two largest red corners, then multiply the two smallest corners. Subtract the smaller total from the larger.
8 x 7 = 56
6 x 1 = 6
56 – 6 = 50

**Page 158**

RIDDLE
Answer: 9, 2 and 2. Before he knew that the twins were younger than the single child, the Professor could have come up with the answer 6, 6 and 1

**Page 159**

MINESWEEPER

MORE OR LESS

| | | | | | |
|---|---|---|---|---|---|
| 2 < | 6 | 3 | 4 | 1 | 5 |
| 1 < | 2 | 6 | 3 < | 5 | 4 |
| 6 | 4 | 5 | 1 < | 2 | 3 |
| 5 > | 3 | 1 | 6 > | 4 | 2 |
| 3 < | 5 | 4 | 2 | 6 | 1 |
| 4 | 1 | 2 | 5 | 3 | 6 |

**Page 160**

SIGNPOST

Answer: 66. Score one for a consonant and two for a vowel, then multiply the total by the alphabetical position of the first letter. 5 + 6 = 11, 11 x 6 = 66

SUM PEOPLE

Answer: 18

**Page 161**

SCALES

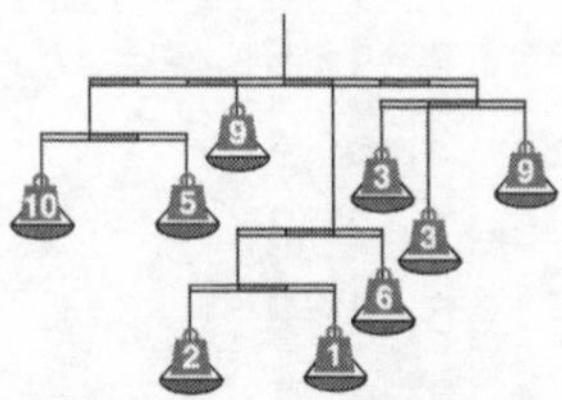


SAFECRACKER

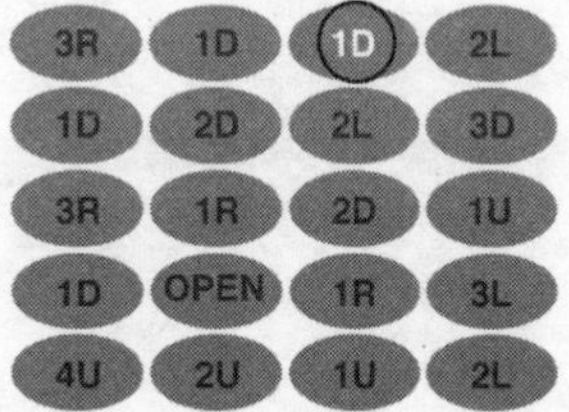

## WRINKLY QUOTE

"People say that age is just a state of mind. I say it's more about the state of your body."

GEOFFREY PARFITT

# EASY PUZZLES

**MASYU:** Draw a single unbroken line around the grid that passes through all the circles. The line must enter and leave each box in the centre of one of its four sides.
Black Circle: Turn left or right in the box, and the line must pass straight through the next and previous boxes.
White Circle: Travel straight through the box, and the line must turn in the next and/or previous box.

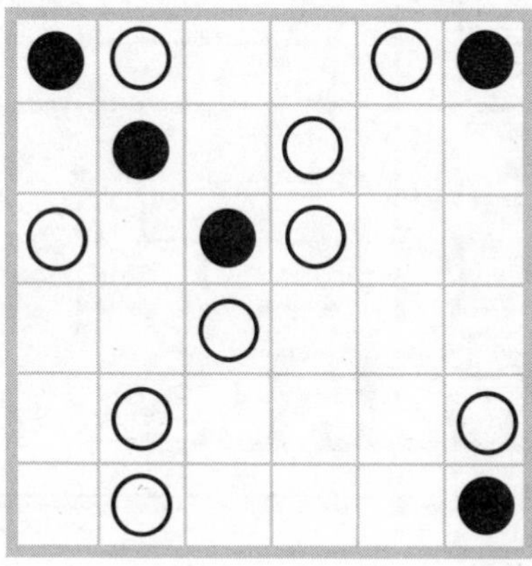

Answer on page 348

**BITS AND PIECES:** Can you match the four halves of broken plate?

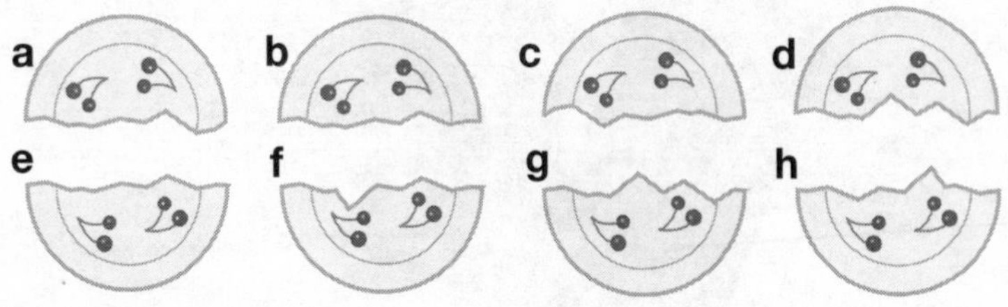


Answer on page 348

**BOXES:** Playing the game of boxes, each player takes it in turns to join two adjacent dots with a line. If a player's line completes a box, the player wins the box and has another go. It's your turn in the game below. To avoid giving your opponent a lot of boxes, what's your best move?

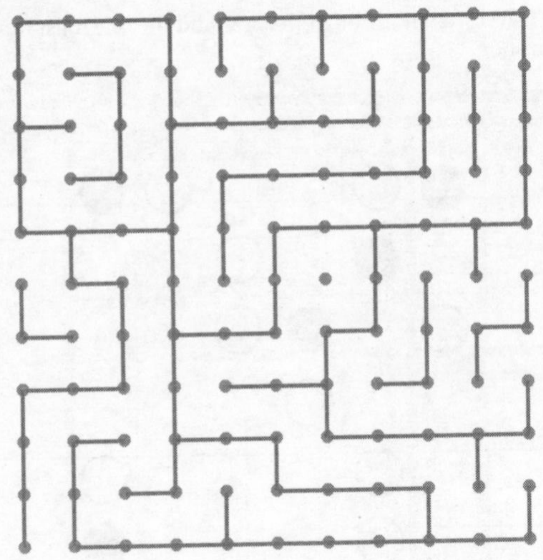

Answer on page 348

**CAN YOU CUT IT?:** Cut a straight line through this shape to create two shapes that are identical.

Answer on page 348

**SUDOKU:** Complete the grid so that the numbers 1, 2, 3, 4, 5, 6, 7, 8 and 9 appear once only in each row, column and 9x9 square.

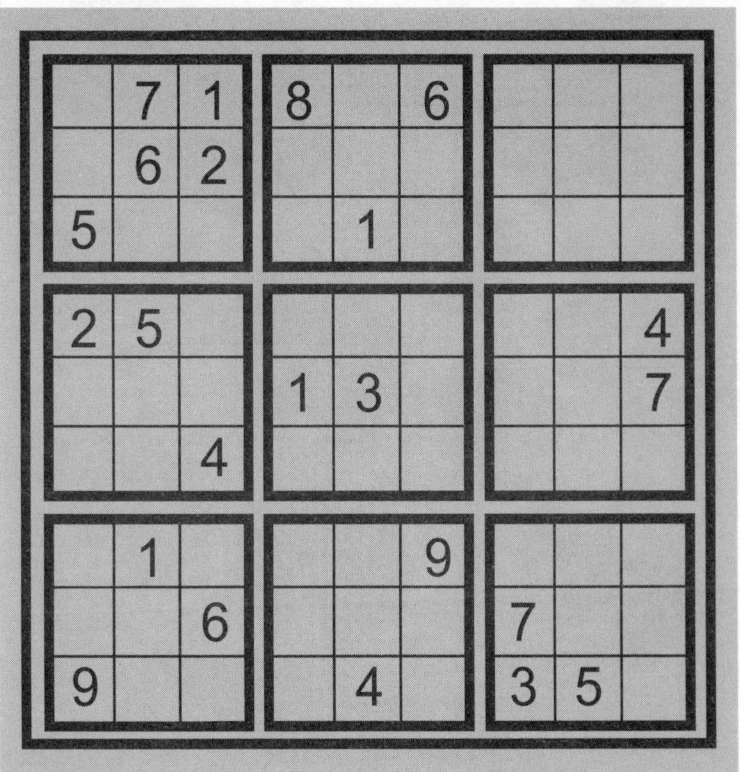

| | | | | | | | | |
|---|---|---|---|---|---|---|---|---|
| | 7 | 1 | 8 | | 6 | | | |
| | 6 | 2 | | | | | | |
| 5 | | | | 1 | | | | |
| 2 | 5 | | | | | | | 4 |
| | | | 1 | 3 | | | | 7 |
| | | 4 | | | | | | |
| | 1 | | | | 9 | | | |
| | | 6 | | | | 7 | | |
| 9 | | | | 4 | | 3 | 5 | |

Answer on page 348

# WHERE'S THE PAIR?:

Only two of the shapes below are exactly the same, can you find the matching pair?

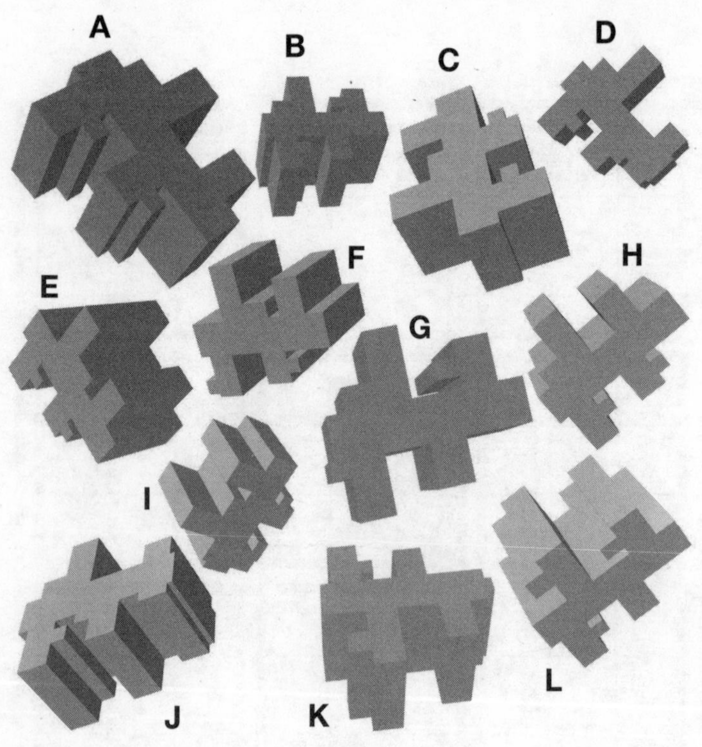


Answer on page 348

## WRINKLY QUOTE

"The best angle for looking through bifocals is when you lean way back and look through the lens bottoms, thus affording the public a spectacular panoramic view of your nasal passages."

DAVE BARRY

**RIDDLE:** On this island in the middle of a lake, there is a tractor, used in summer to give tourists rides around the place. The tractor didn't get there by boat or by air, and it wasn't built there either... so how did it get there?

Answer on page 348

**ODD CLOCKS:** Buenos Aires is 13 hours behind Melbourne, which is 9 hours ahead of London. It is 12.35 pm on Wednesday in Melbourne – what time is it in the other two cities?

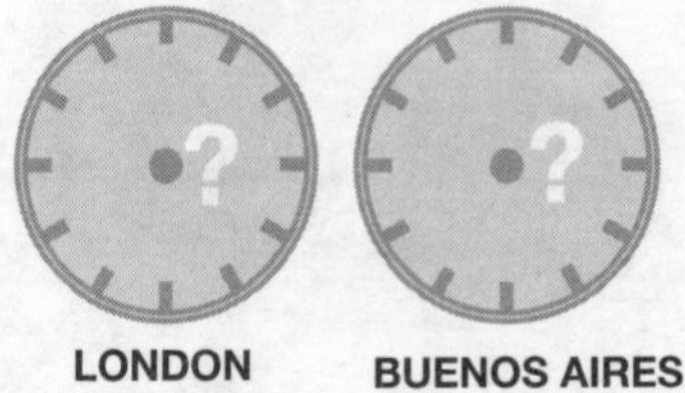


Answer on page 348

**SUM TOTAL:** Replace the question marks with mathematical symbols (+, –, × or ÷, inserting brackets where necessary) to make a working sum.

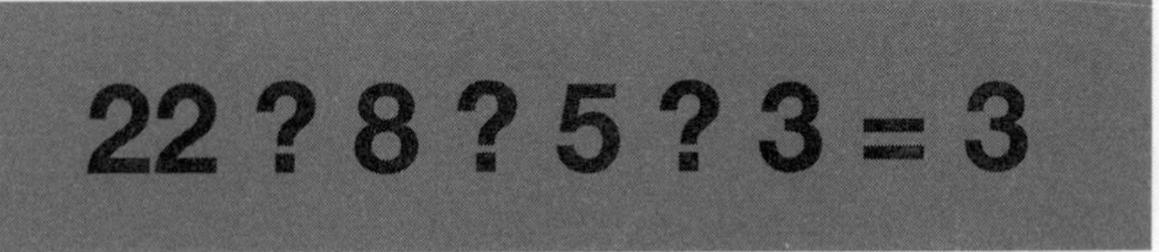


Answer on page 348

# CHECKERS:

Make a move for white so that eight black pieces are left, none of which are in the same column or row.

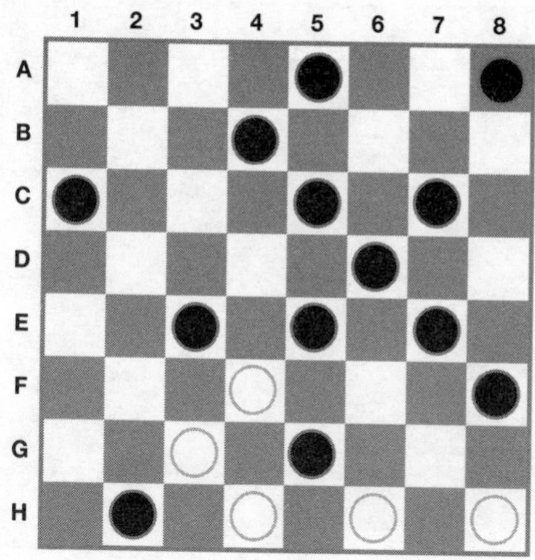


Answer on page 349

# CUT AND FOLD:

Which of the Patterns below is created by this fold and cut?

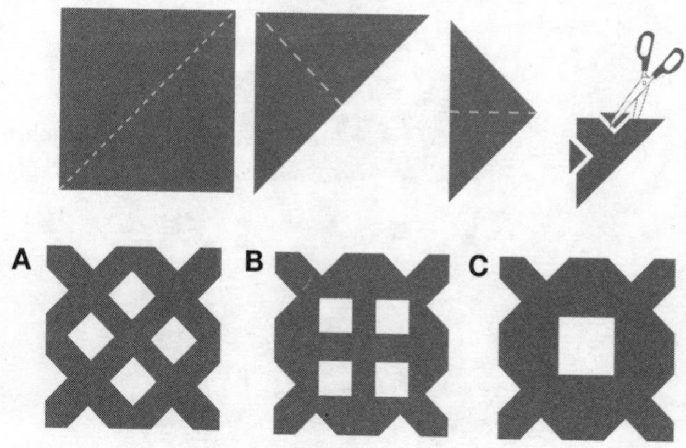


Answer on page 349

## DOUBLE DRAT: All these shapes appear twice in the box except one. Can you spot the singleton?

Answer on page 349

## GAME OF TWO HALVES: Which two shapes below will pair up to create the top shape?

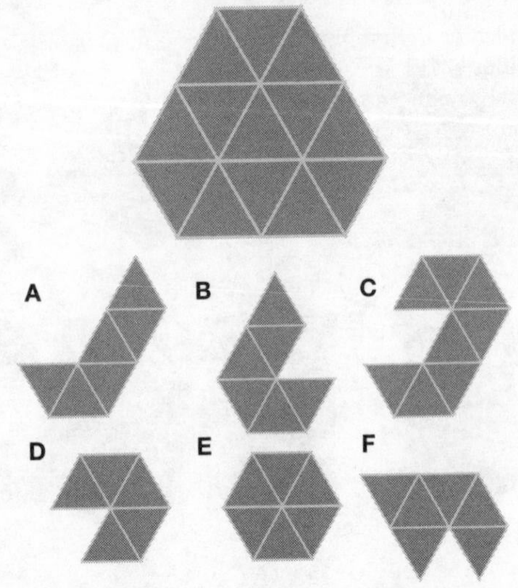


Answer on page 349

# GRIDLOCK: Which square correctly completes the grid?

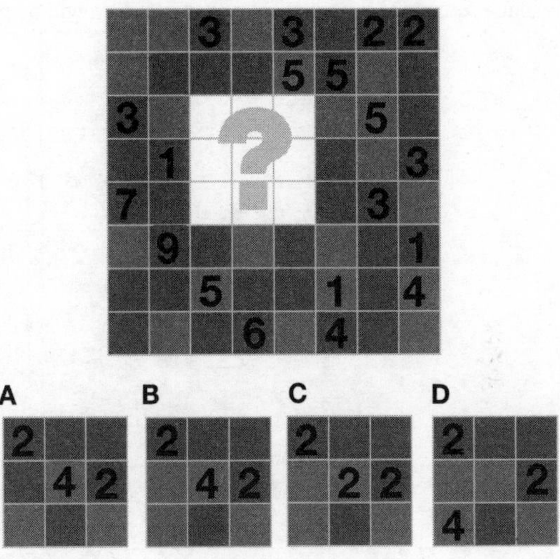


Answer on page 349

# MASYU: Draw a single unbroken line around the grid that passes through all the circles. The line must enter and leave each box in the centre of one of its four sides.

Black Circle: Turn left or right in the box, and the line must pass straight through the next and previous boxes.

White Circle: Travel straight through the box, and the line must turn in the next and/or previous box.

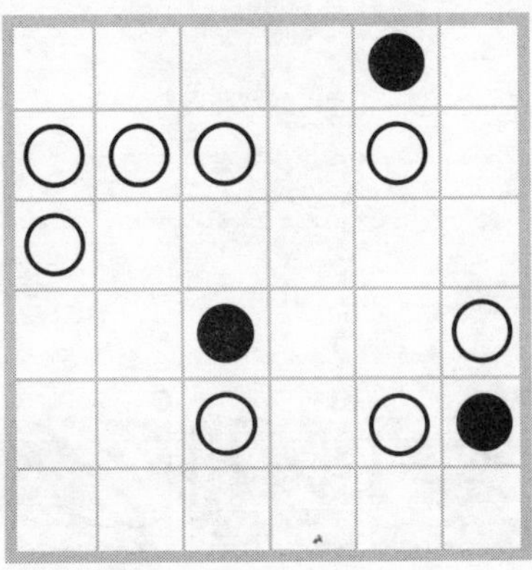

Answer on page 349

# MINI NONOGRAM:

The numbers by each row and column describe black squares and groups of black squares that are adjoining. Colour in all the black squares and a six number combination will be revealed.

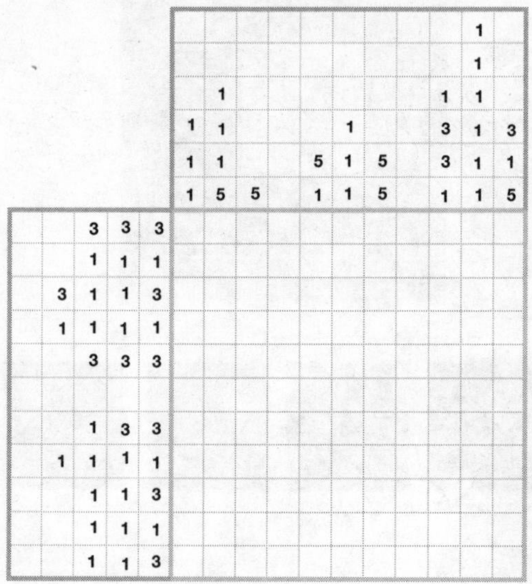

Answer on page 349

# PICTURE PARTS:

Which box contains exactly the right bits to make the pic?

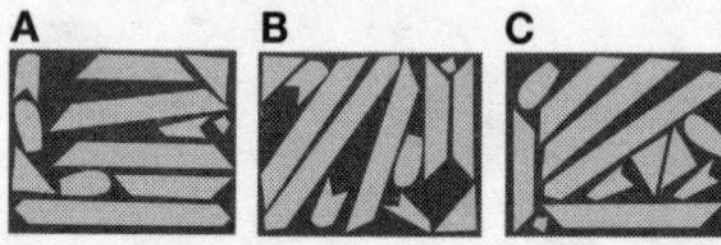


Answer on page 349

# MIRROR IMAGE: Only one of these pictures is an exact mirror image of the first one? Can you spot it?

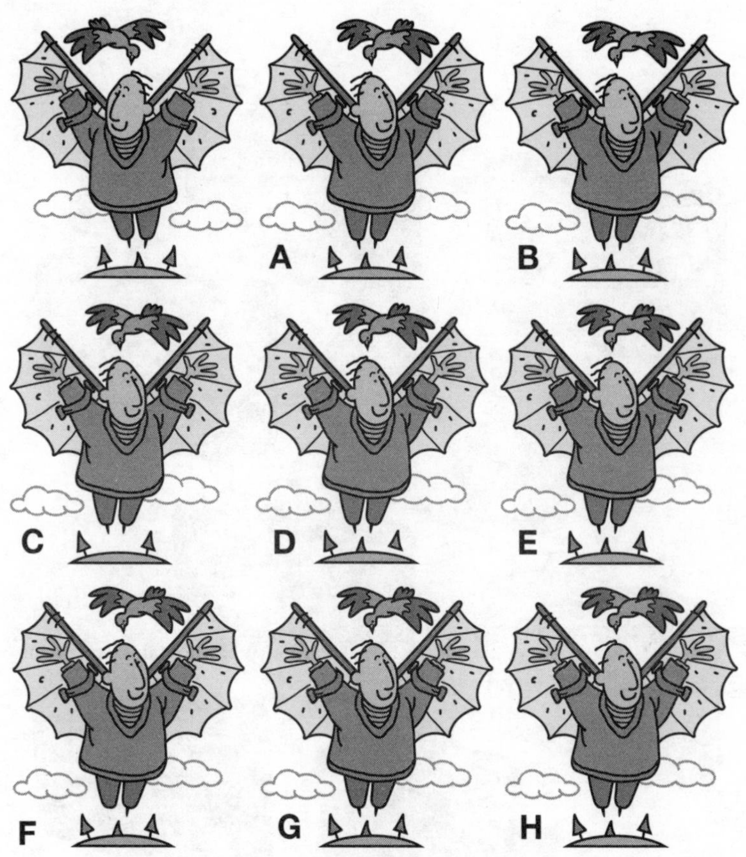


Answer on page 349

# WHERE'S THE PAIR?: Only two of these pictures are exactly the same. Can you spot the matching pair?

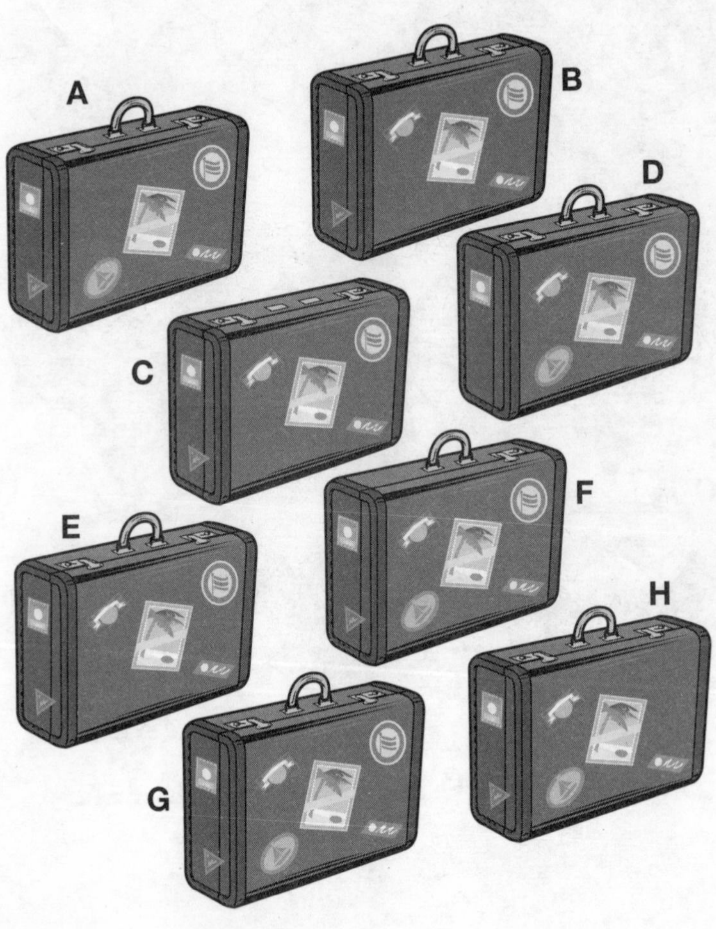


Answer on page 350

**SUM PEOPLE:** Work out what number is represented by which person and replace the question mark.

Answer on page 350

**SUDOKU:** Complete the grid so that the numbers 1, 2, 3, 4, 5, 6, 7, 8 and 9 appear once only in each row, column and 9x9 square.

| | | | | | | | | |
|---|---|---|---|---|---|---|---|---|
| 7 | | | | 1 | | | | |
| | | | 6 | | 4 | 8 | | |
| | 8 | 5 | | | | | | 3 |
| | 7 | | | 6 | | | | |
| | 9 | | | | | 4 | 6 | |
| | | 3 | 5 | 7 | 1 | | | |
| 4 | | | 8 | | | | | |
| | | 7 | | | 5 | | 1 | |
| | | | | 3 | | | | |

Answer on page 350

## SHAPE SHIFTING: Fill in the empty squares so that each row, column and long diagonal contains five different symbols

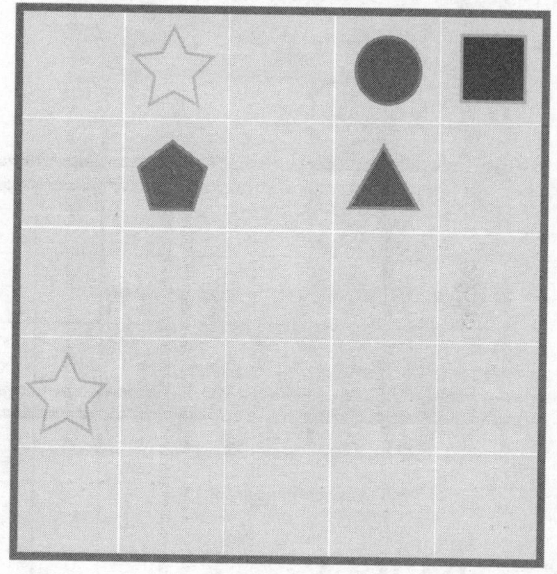

Answer on page 350

## NUMBER MOUNTAIN: Replace the question marks with numbers so that each pair of blocks adds up to the block directly above them.

Answer on page 350

**POTS OF DOTS:** How many dots should there be in the hole in this pattern?

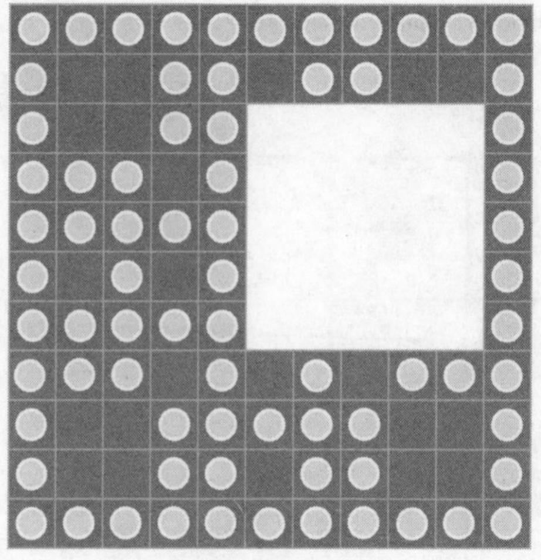

Answer on page 350

**BLOCK PARTY:** Assuming all blocks that are not visible from this angle are present, how many blocks have been removed from this 5 × 5 × 5 cube?

Answer on page 350

**BOXES:** Playing the game of boxes, each player takes it in turns to join two adjacent dots with a line. If a player's line completes a box, the player wins the box and has another go. It's your turn in the game below. To avoid giving your opponent a lot of boxes, what's your best move?

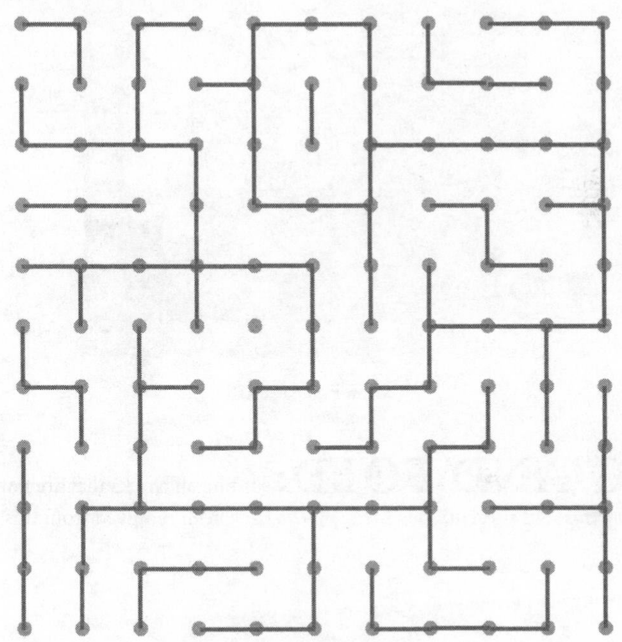

Answer on page 351

## Wrinkly Quote

"There is a trade off – as you grow older you gain wisdom but you lose spontaneity."

KENNY ROGERS

## CATS AND COGS: Turn the handle in the indicated direction... Does the cat go up or down?

Answer on page 351

## CUT AND FOLD: Which of the patterns below is created by this fold and cut?

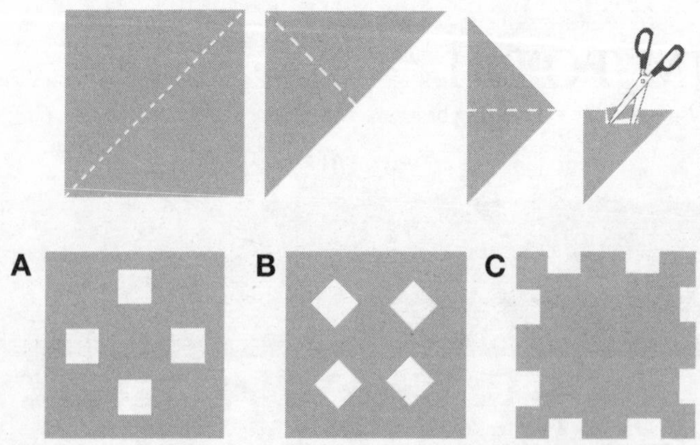


Answer on page 351

## RIDDLE: When the new hospital was built, Big Dave was hired to paint the numbers 1 to 100 on the rooms. How many times will Dave be painting the number 9?

Answer on page 351

## SUM TOTAL: Replace the question marks with mathematical symbols (+, –, × or ÷, inserting brackets where necessary) to make a working sum.

Answer on page 351

**ODD CLOCKS:** Karachi is 4 hours ahead of Paris, which is 8 hours behind Tokyo. It is 9.05 pm on Thursday in Paris – what time is it in the other two cities?

Answer on page 351

**POTS OF DOTS:** How many dots should there be in the hole in this pattern?

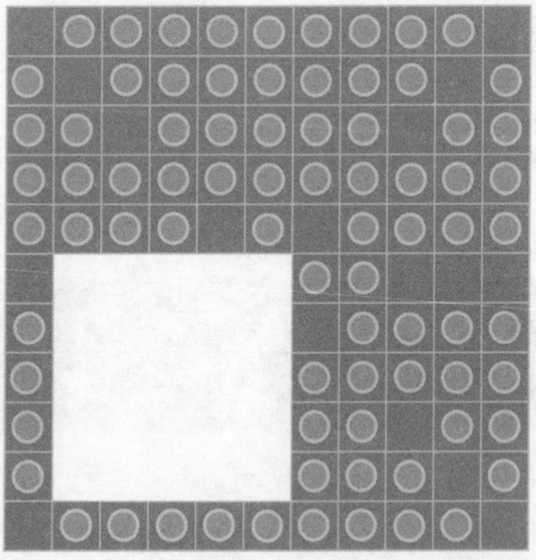

Answer on page 351

**RIDDLE:** At the auction house, George and Jenna were browsing through the items before the sale began. George had his eye on a ceremonial sword, inscribed to "Captain Beswick Alistair Campbell, for Exceptional Valour in the Field, Belgium, November 12th 1917, WWI". Jenna told him not to be daft, it was forgery! How did she know?

Answer on page 351

WRINKLY QUOTE

"Maturity is the time of life when, if you had the time, you'd have the time of your life."

ANON

## GAME OF TWO HALVES: Which two shapes below will pair up to create the top shape?

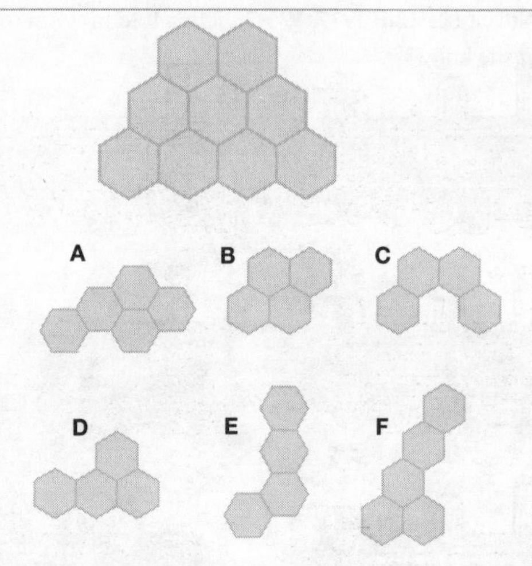


Answer on page 352

## MATRIX: Which of the boxed figures completes the set?

Answer on page 352

**WHERE'S THE PAIR?:** Only two of these pictures are exactly the same. Can you spot the matching pair?

Answer on page 352

WRINKLY QUOTE

"You can be young without money but you can't be old without it."

TENNESSEE WILLIAMS

## BITS AND PIECES: Can you match four pieces twice to make two letters of the alphabet?

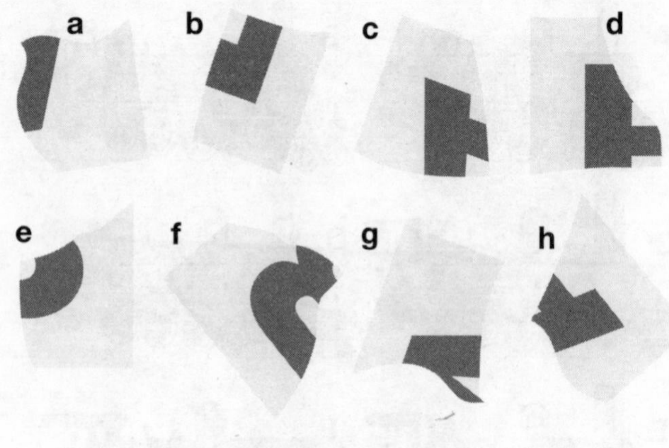


Answer on page 352

## BLOCK PARTY: Assuming all blocks that are not visible from this angle are present, how many blocks have been removed from this 5 × 5 × 5 cube?

Answer on page 352

**RIDDLE-ME-TEA:** Discovering a fly in my tea, I asked the waiter if he could get me another cup, one without a fly. He came back with my new tea, I tasted it and guess what? The cheeky chancer had given me the same cup of tea back! But how did I know?

Answer on page 352

### WRINKLY QUOTE

There are three periods in life: youth, middle age and "how well you look".

NELSON A ROCKEFELLER

# WHERE'S THE PAIR?: Only two of the shapes below are exactly the same – can you find the matching pair?

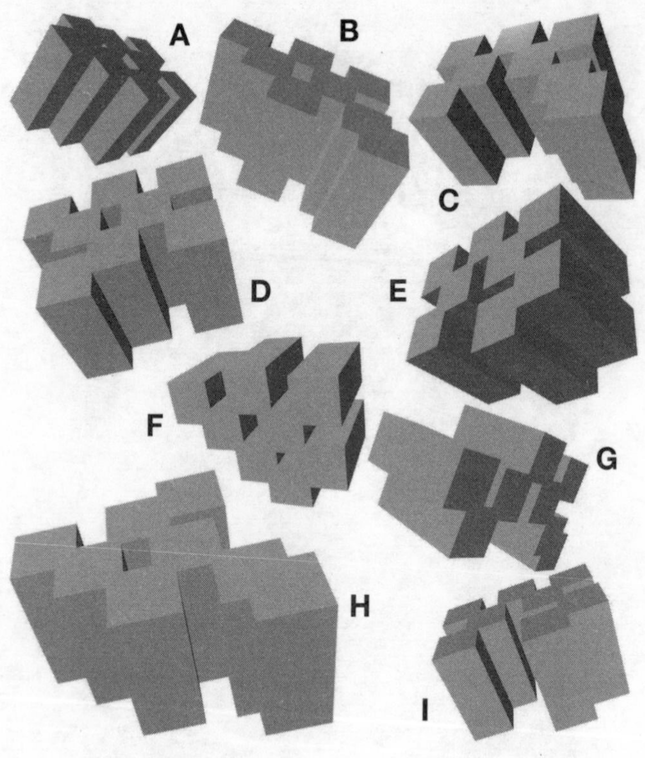


Answer on page 352

## WRINKLY QUOTE

"There's an old story about the person who wished his computer were as easy to use as his telephone. That wish has come true, since I no longer know how to use my telephone."

STROUSTRUP

**MIRROR IMAGE:** Only one of these pictures is an exact mirror image of the first one? Can you spot it?

Answer on page 352

**SUM TOTAL:** Replace the question marks with mathematical symbols (+, –, × or ÷, including brackets if necessary) to make a working sum.

10 ? 2 ? 4 ? 7 = 13

Answer on page 352

# WHERE'S THE PAIR?: Only two of these pictures are exactly the same. Can you spot the matching pair?

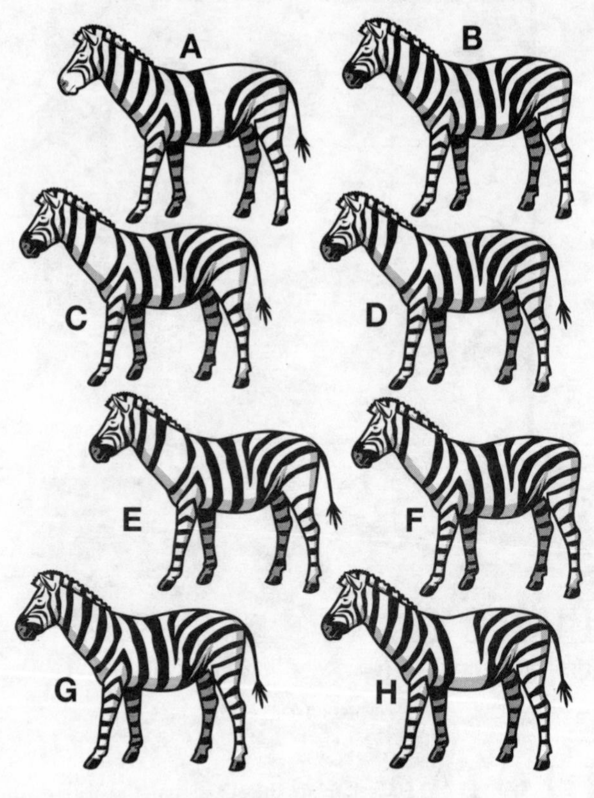


Answer on page 352

## MAGIC SQUARES: Complete the square using nine consecutive numbers, so that all rows, columns and large diagonals add up to the same total.

Answer on page 353

## PICTURE PARTS: Which box does NOT contain exactly the right bits to make the pic?

Answer on page 353

## MAGIC SQUARES: Complete the square using nine consecutive numbers, so that all rows, columns and large diagonals add up to the same total.

| | | |
|---|---|---|
| | | 6 |
| | | |
| | | 10 |

Answer on page 353

## PICTURE PARTS: Which box has exactly the right bits to make the pic?

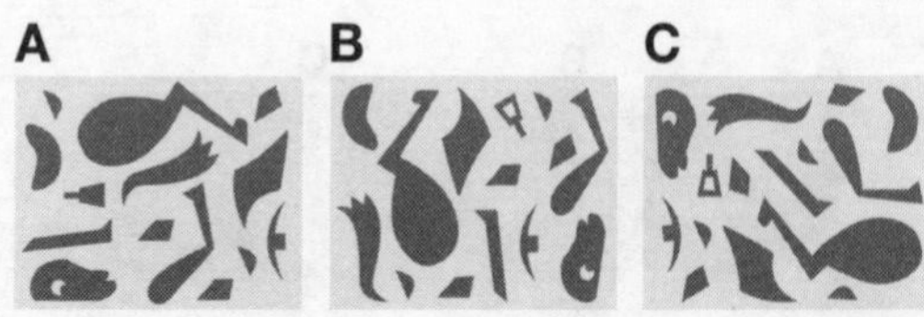


Answer on page 353

# WHERE'S THE PAIR?: Only two of these pictures are exactly the same – can you spot the matching pair?

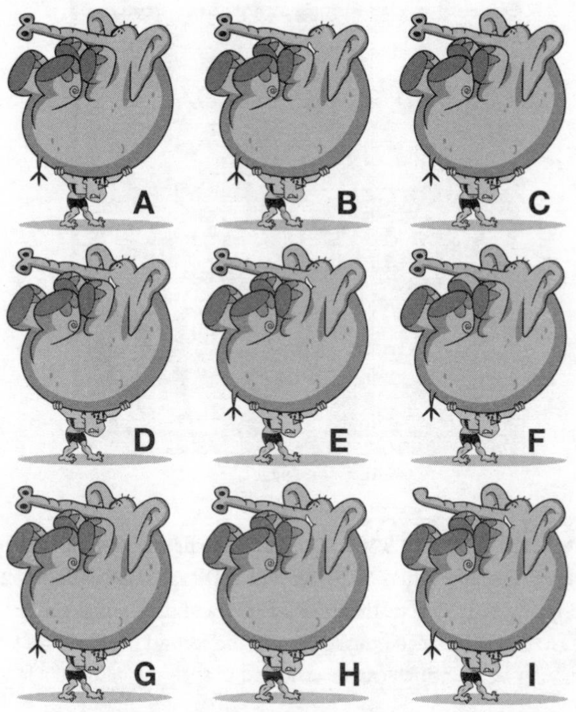


Answer on page 353

WRINKLY QUOTE

"Another way to live to be 100 is to reach 99, and then live very carefully."

ANON

**BOX IT:** The value of each shape is the number of sides each shape has, multiplied by the number within it. Thus a square containing the number 4 has a value of 16. Find a block of four squares (two squares wide by two squares high) with a total value of exactly 50.

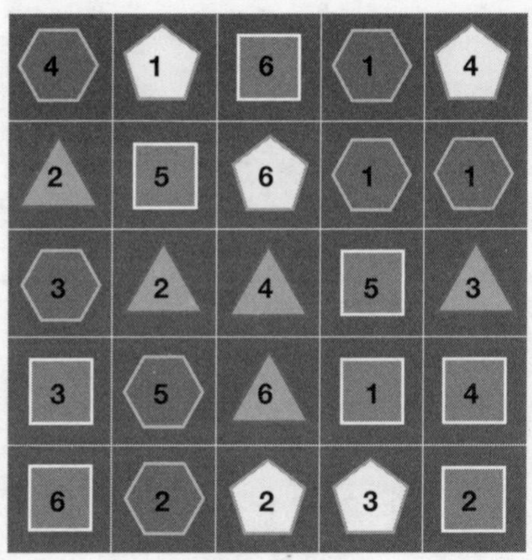


Answer on page 353

**SUDOKU SIX:** Complete the first grid so that every row and column contain all the letters GLMRW and Y. Do the same with grid 2 and the numbers 12345 and 6. To decode the finished grid, add the numbers in the shaded squares to the letters in the matching squares in the second (ie: A + 3 = D, Y + 4 = C) to get six new letters which can be arranged to spell the name of a famous composer.

| | | | | | |
|---|---|---|---|---|---|
| 4 | | | 1 | 3 | |
| | 1 | 6 | | | 4 |
| | 4 | | | 2 | |
| 6 | | 1 | | 4 | |
| | | | 3 | | 6 |
| 1 | 3 | 5 | | | 2 |

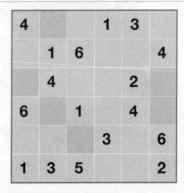

Answer on page 353

**BOXES:** Playing the game of boxes, each player takes it in turns to join two adjacent dots with a line. If a player's line completes a box, the player wins the box and has another go. It's your turn in the game below. To avoid giving your opponent a lot of boxes, what's your best move?

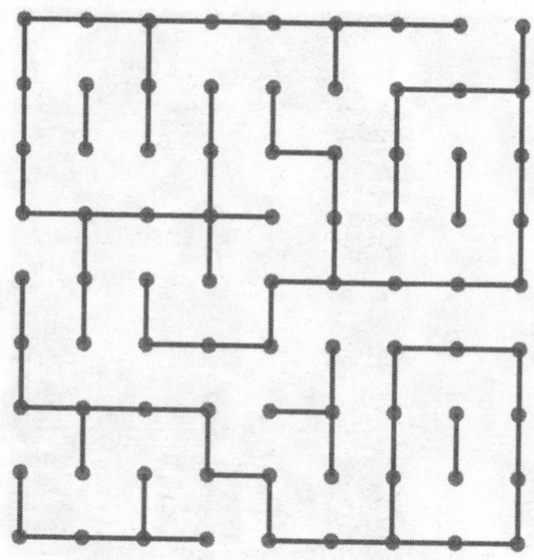

Answer on page 353

**REVOLUTIONS:** Cog A has 12 teeth, cog B has 8 and cog C has 10. How many revolutions must cog A turn through to bring all three cogs back to these exact positions?

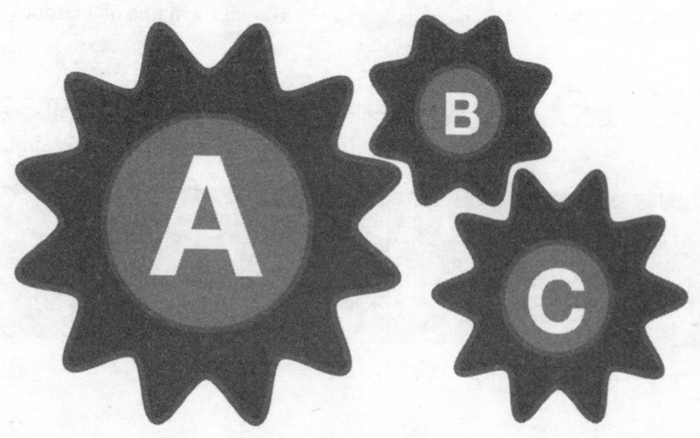


Answer on page 353

**CHECKERS:** Make a move for white so that eight black pieces are left, none of which are in the same column or row.

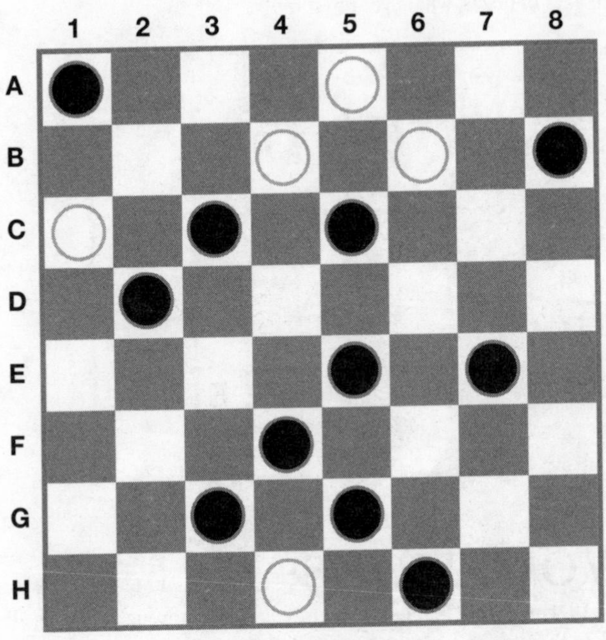


Answer on page 354

**SUM TOTAL:** Replace the question marks with mathematical symbols (+, –, ×, or ÷, including brackets if necessary) to make a working sum.

Answer on page 354

**WHERE'S THE PAIR?:** Only two of the shapes below are exactly the same – can you find the matching pair?

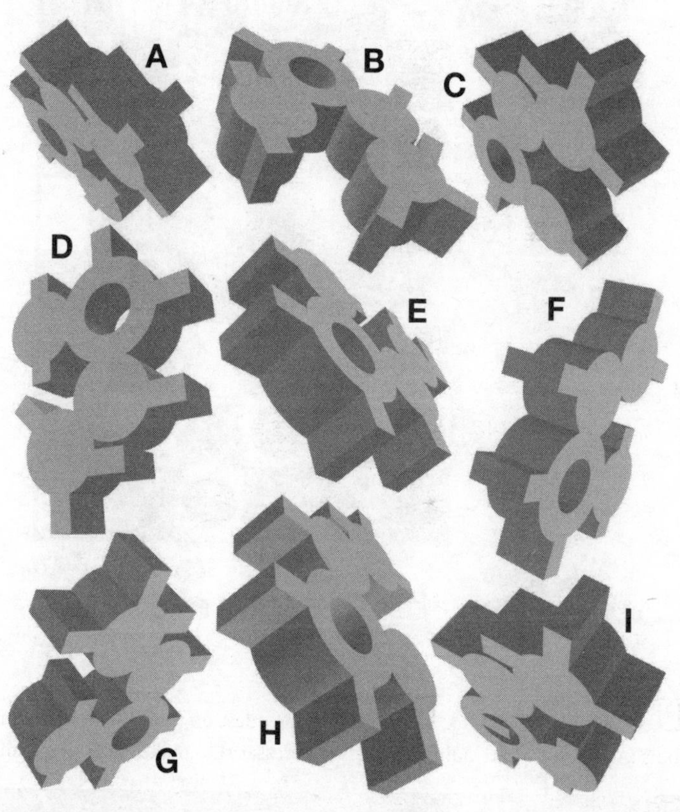


Answer on page 354

# WHERE'S THE PAIR?: Only two of these pictures are exactly the same. Can you spot the matching pair?

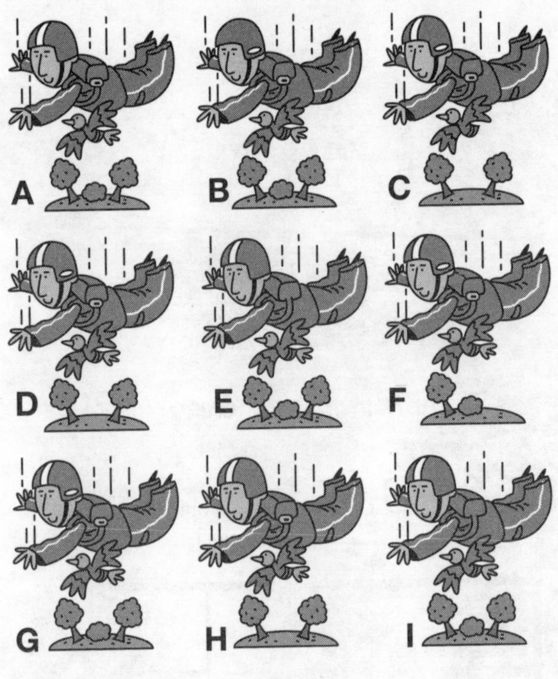


Answer on page 354

## WRINKLY QUOTE

"I never drink coffee at lunch. I find it keeps me awake for the afternoon."

RONALD REAGAN

## ODD CLOCKS:

Cairo is 7 hours ahead of Mexico City, which is 5 hours behind Reykjavik. It is 10.30pm on Monday in Mexico City – What time is it in the other two cities?

MEXICO CITY

REYKJAVIK CAIRO

Answer on page 354

## LATIN SQUARE:

Complete the grid so that every row and column, and every outlined area, contains the letters A, B, C, D, E and F.

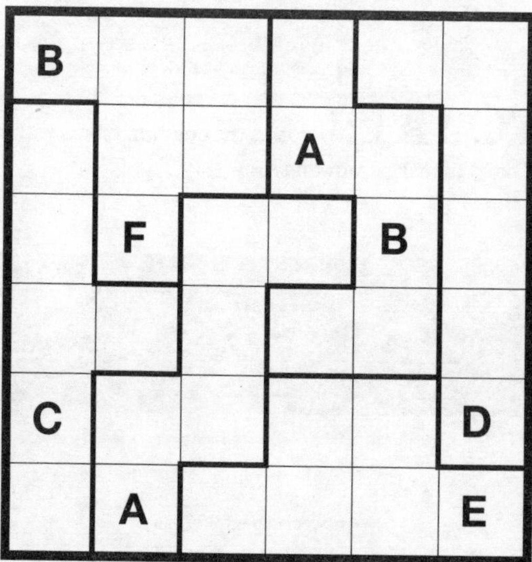


Answer on page 354

**SAFECRACKER:** To open the safe, all the buttons must be pressed in the correct order before the "open" button is pressed. What is the first button pressed in your sequence?

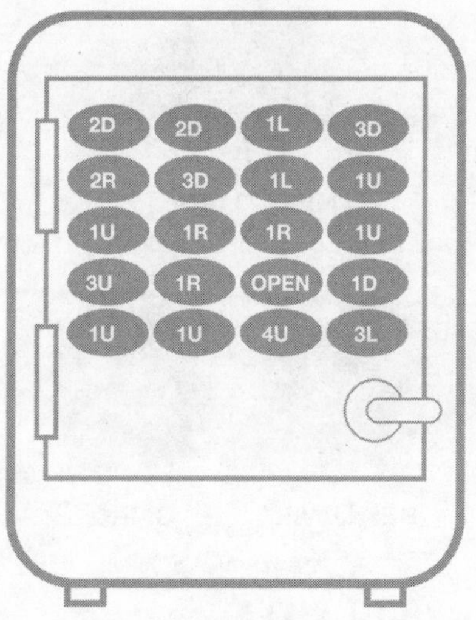


Answer on page 354

**SUM TOTAL:** Replace the question marks with mathematical symbols (+, –, × or ÷) to make a working sum.

Answer on page 354

## HUB SIGNS: What numbers should appear in the hubs of these number wheels?

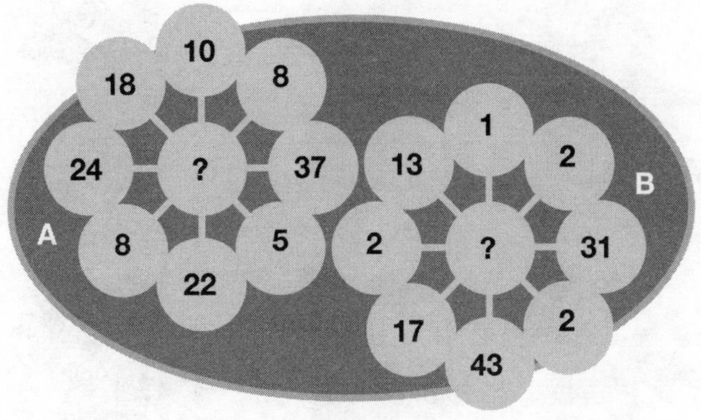


Answer on page 355

## CUT AND FOLD: Which of the patterns below is created by this fold and cut?

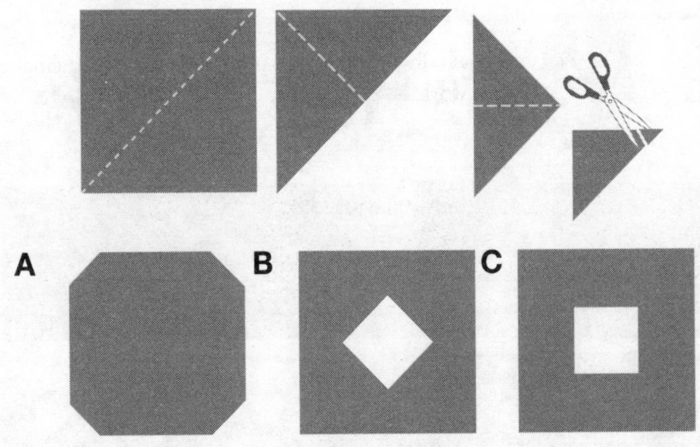


Answer on page 355

# WHERE'S THE PAIR?:

Only two of these pictures are exactly the same. Can you spot the matching pair?

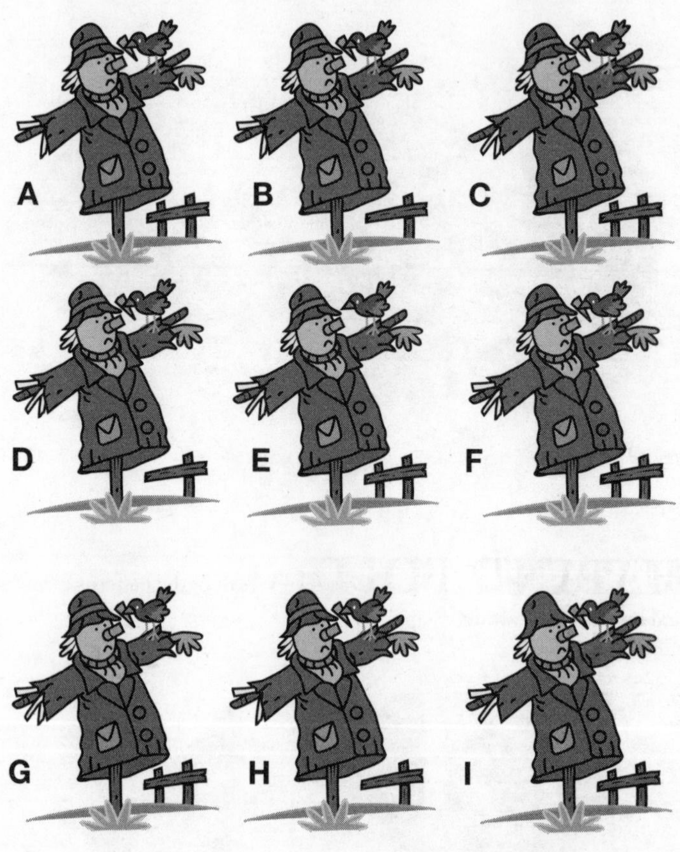


Answer on page 355

## WRINKLY QUOTE

"The older I get the better I used to be.."

LEE TREVINO

**POTS OF DOTS:** How many dots should there be in the hole in this pattern?

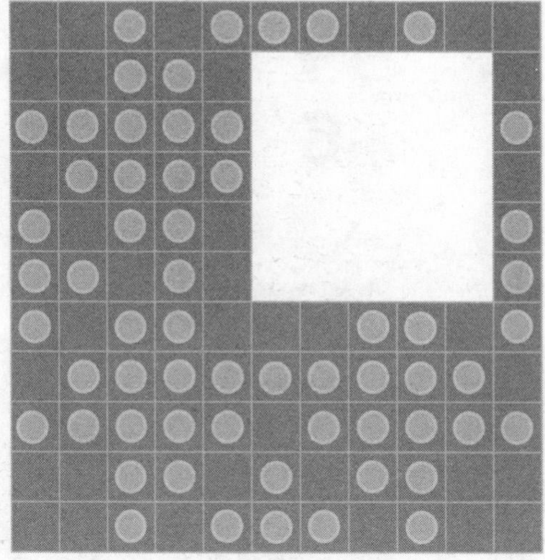

Answer on page 355

**SHAPE STACKER:** Can you work out the logic behind the numbers in these shapes, and suggest a number to replace the A and B?

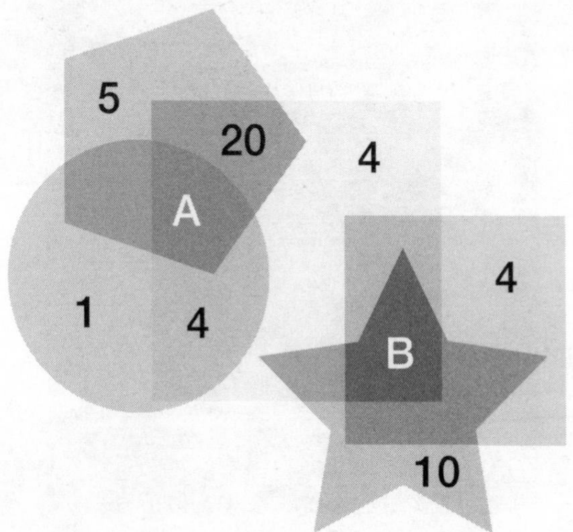


Answer on page 355

## SUDOKU SIXPACK: Complete the grid so that every row, column and long diagonal contains the numbers 1, 2, 3, 4, 5 and 6

| 2 |   | 4 |   | 5 | 6 |
|---|---|---|---|---|---|
|   |   | 6 |   | 3 | 5 |
| 3 |   |   | 1 |   |   |
|   |   |   |   |   | 1 |
| 6 | 5 |   |   |   | 2 |
|   | 2 | 1 |   |   |   |

Answer on page 355

## DOUBLE DRAT: All these shapes appear twice in the box except one. Can you spot the singleton?

Answer on page 355

**CUBISM:** The shape below can be folded to make a cube. Which of the four cubes pictured below could it make?

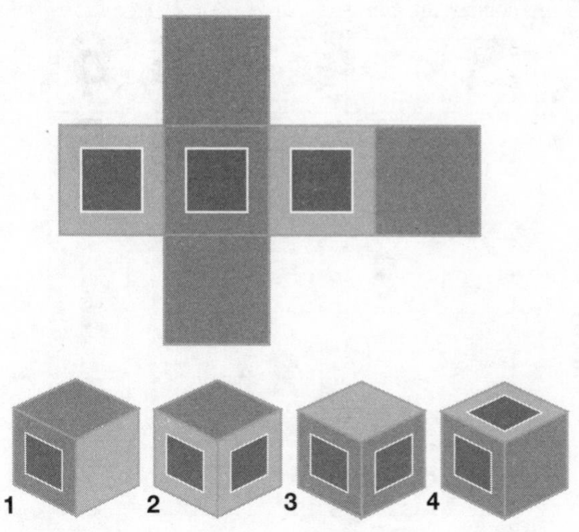


Answer on page 355

**GAME OF TWO HALVES:** Which two shapes below will pair up to create the top shape?

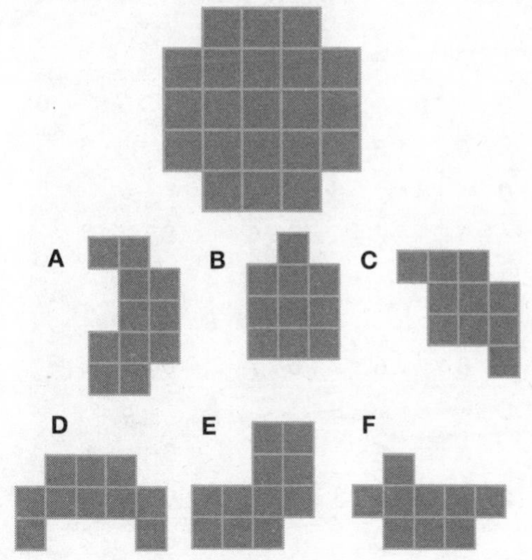


Answer on page 355

# MORE OR LESS:

The arrows indicate whether a number in a box is greater or smaller than an adjacent number. Complete the grid so that all rows and columns contain the numbers 1 to 5.

Answer on page 356

# NUMBER SWEEP:

The numbers in some squares in the grid indicate the exact number of shaded squares that should surround it. Colour in the squares until all the numbers are surrounded by the correct number of shaded squares, and a number will be revealed!

| | 0 | | 0 | | 3 | | | 5 | | 2 | |
|---|---|---|---|---|---|---|---|---|---|---|---|
| 0 | | 0 | | 3 | | | 8 | | 5 | | 0 |
| | 0 | | 3 | | 7 | | | 8 | | 3 | |
| 0 | | 3 | | 6 | | | 8 | | 5 | | 0 |
| | 3 | | 6 | | 6 | 6 | | 8 | | 3 | |
| 3 | | | | 3 | | | 8 | | | | |
| | | | | 4 | | | 8 | | | | |
| | 8 | | 6 | | 6 | 7 | | 8 | | 6 | |
| 5 | | 8 | | 8 | | | 8 | | 8 | | 5 |
| | 5 | | 5 | | | | | 8 | | 6 | |
| 2 | | 3 | | 3 | | | 8 | | 6 | | 2 |
| | 0 | | 0 | | | | | 5 | | 2 | |

Answer on page 356

# MIRROR IMAGE: Only one of these pictures is an exact mirror image of the first one? Can you spot it?

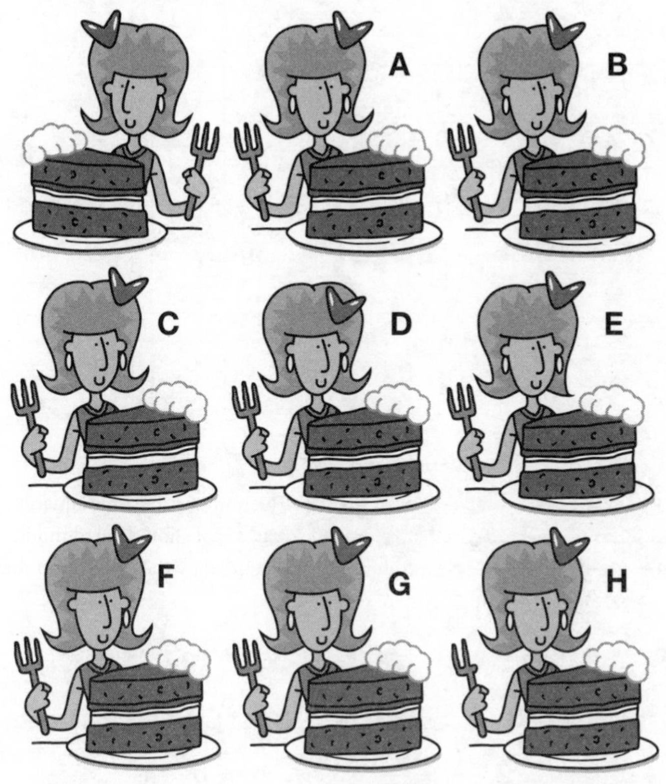


Answer on page 356

## WRINKLY QUOTE

"It is hard enough to remember my opinions, without also remembering my reasons for them!"

FRIEDRICH NIETZSCHE

# PAINT BY NUMBERS: Colour in the odd numbers to reveal... What?

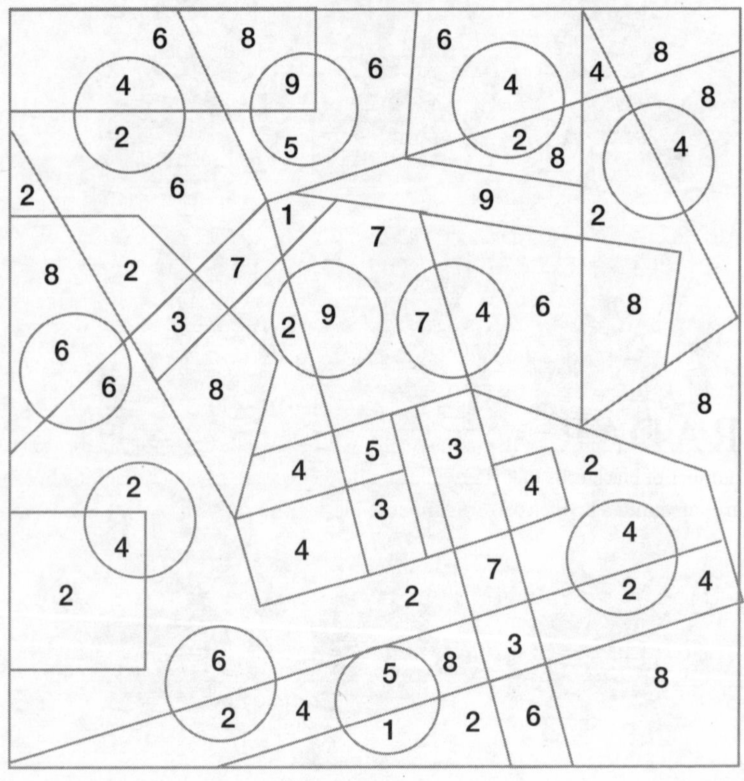

Answer on page 356

## PICTURE PARTS: Which box contains exactly the right bits to make the pic?

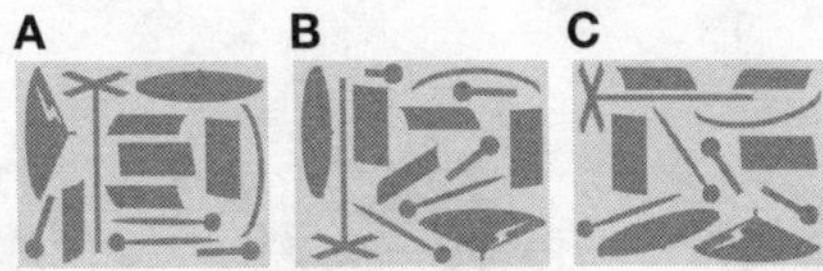


Answer on page 356

## RADAR: The numbers in some cells in the grid indicate the exact number of black cells that should border it. Shade these black, until all the numbers are surrounded by the correct number of black cells.

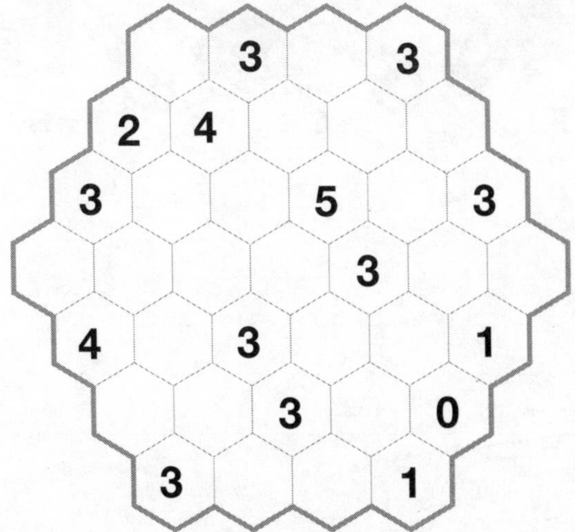


Answer on page 356

**SILHOUETTE:** Which of the coloured-in pics matches our silhouette?

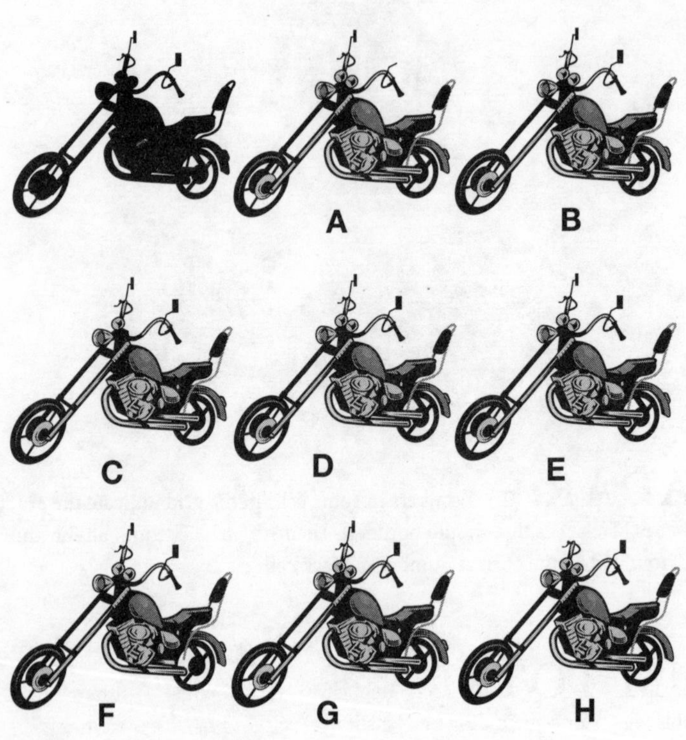


Answer on page 356

# PICTURE PARTS: Which box has exactly the right bits to make the pic?

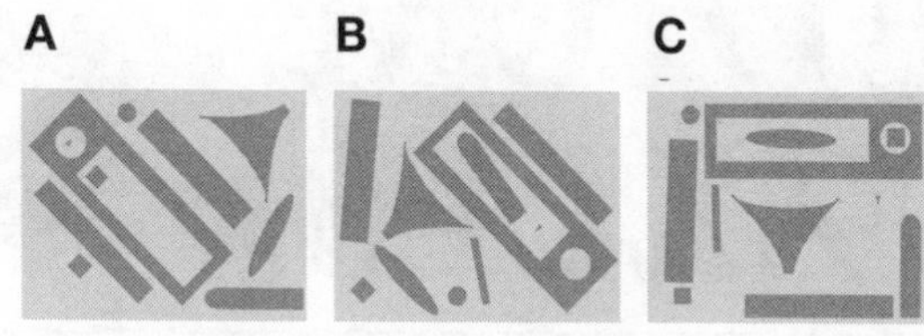


Answer on page 356

# SUM TOTAL: Replace the question marks with mathematical symbols (+, -, x or ÷, including brackets if necessary) to make a working sum.

35 ? 7 ? 4 ? 4 = 3

Answer on page 356

# MEDIUM PUZZLES

**FOLLOW THAT:** The sequence below follows a logical pattern. Can you work out what letter follows, and which way up it should be?

Answer on page 356

**FRACTION ACTION:** Can you determine what fraction of this tiling job remains unfinished?

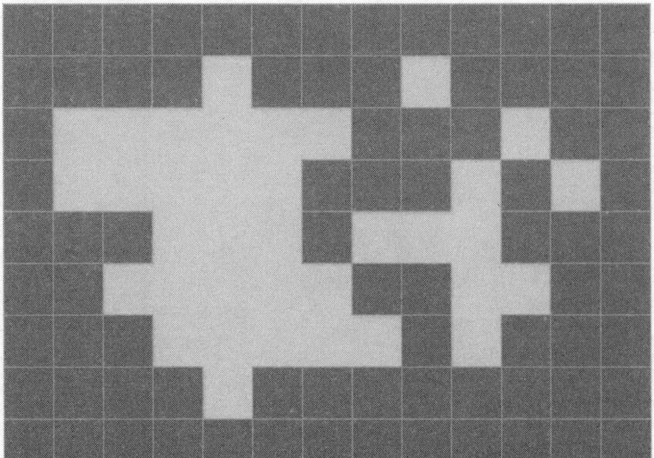

Answer on page 356

## MASYU: Draw a single continuous line around the grid that passes through all the circles. The line must enter and leave each box in the centre of one of its four sides.

Black Circle: Turn left or right in the box, and the line must pass straight through the next and previous boxes.

White Circle: Travel straight through the box, and the line must turn in the next and/or previous box.

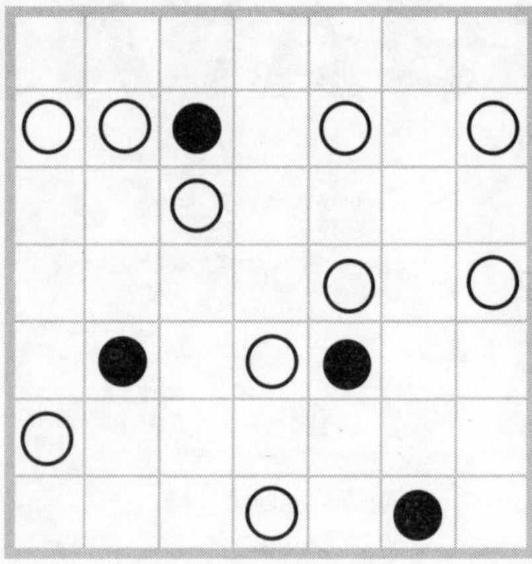

Answer on page 357

## MATRIX: Which of the boxed figures completes the set?

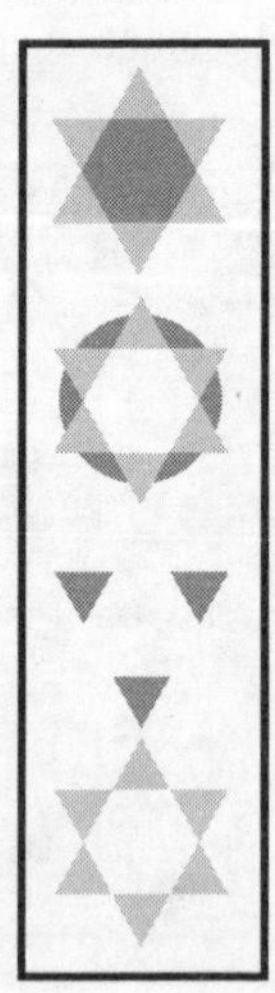

Answer on page 357

**MINESWEEPER:** The numbers in some squares in the grid indicate the exact number of black squares that should surround it. Shade these squares until all the numbers are surrounded by the correct number of black squares.

|   | 2 |   |   |   | 2 |   | 1 |
|---|---|---|---|---|---|---|---|
| 2 |   | 3 |   | 2 | 3 |   | 3 |
|   | 3 |   | 3 | 3 |   |   |   |
| 3 |   | 2 |   |   | 6 |   | 5 |
|   |   |   | 4 |   |   |   |   |
| 2 |   | 3 |   | 5 |   | 5 | 2 |
| 3 | 4 |   |   | 3 |   |   | 2 |
|   |   | 2 | 1 |   | 2 |   |   |

Answer on page 357

**MORE OR LESS:** The arrows indicate whether a number in a box is greater or smaller than an adjacent number. Complete the grid so that all rows and columns contain the numbers 1 to 5.

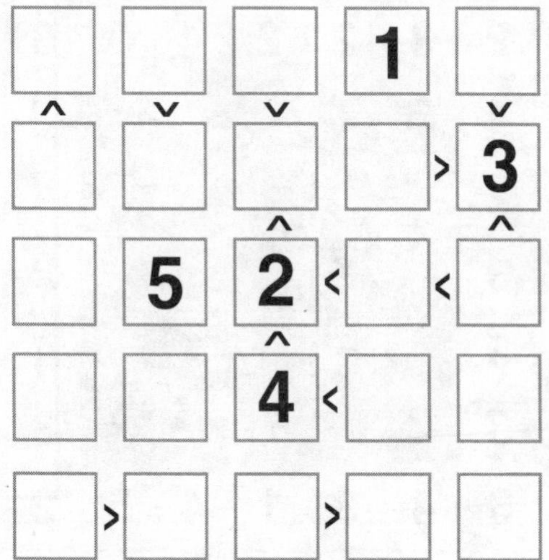

Answer on page 357

## A PIECE OF PIE: Can you crack the pie code and work out what number belongs where the question mark is?

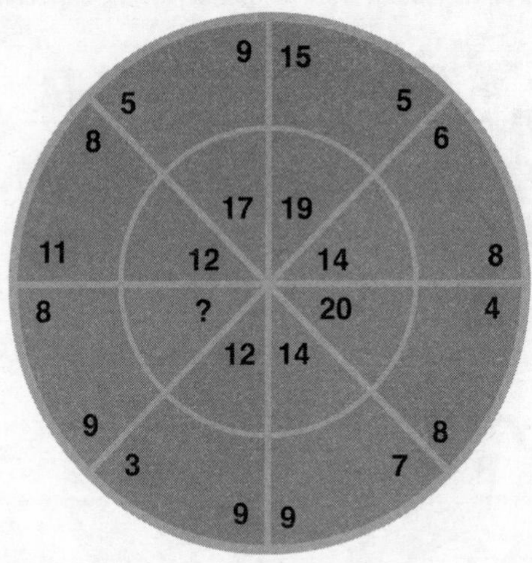


Answer on page 357

## X AND O: The numbers around the edge of the grid describe the number of X's in the vertical, horizontal and diagonal lines connecting with that square. Complete the grid so that there is an X or O in every square.

| 2 | 3 | 2 | 2 | 4 | 3 | 3 |
|---|---|---|---|---|---|---|
| 4 | O | | | | X | 3 |
| 2 | | | | | | 4 |
| 3 | | X | | | | 2 |
| 3 | | | | X | | 4 |
| 3 | X | | | | X | 3 |
| 3 | 4 | 3 | 1 | 4 | 5 | 2 |

Answer on page 357

**WHERE'S THE PAIR?:** Only two of these pictures are exactly the same. Can you spot the matching pair?

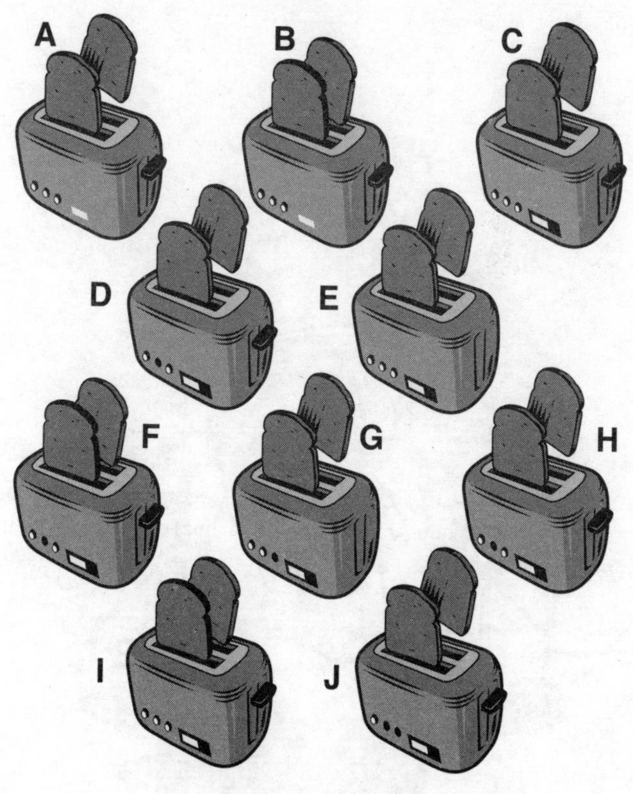


Answer on page 358

**RIDDLE:** Chef Gordon Ramsfoot was challenged one day to perfectly soft boil a goose egg, so that the white was all set and the yolk left perfectly runny. A goose egg, he discovers, takes exactly nine minutes to boil this way, but Gordon only has two egg timers – the old fashioned glass and sand type. One timer is for 4 minutes and the other for 7. Using the two timers, how can Gordon perfectly time his 9 minute egg?

Answer on page 358

**SUM PEOPLE:** Work out what number is represented by which person and replace the question mark.

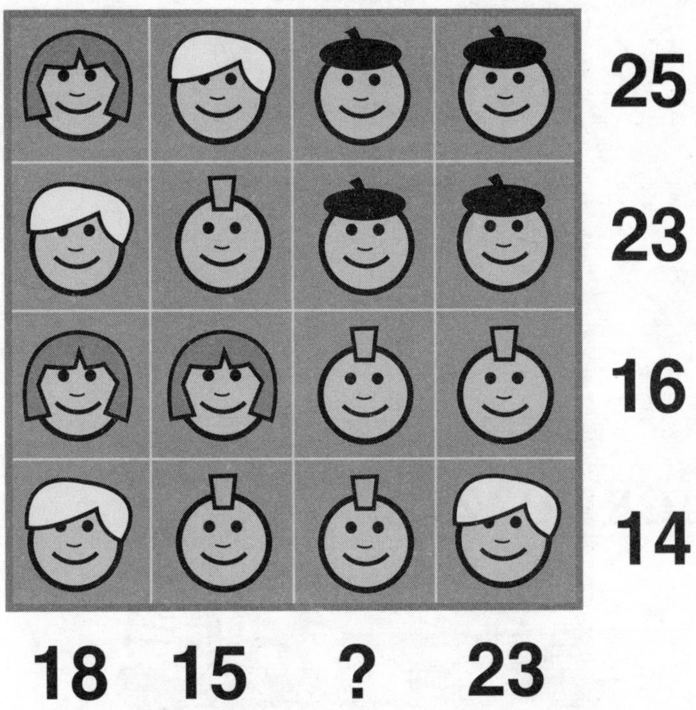


Answer on page 358

WRINKLY QUOTE

"Happiness is good health and a bad memory."

INGRID BERGMAN

## SAFECRACKER: To open the safe, all the buttons must be pressed in the correct order before the "open" button is pressed. What is the first button pressed in your sequence?

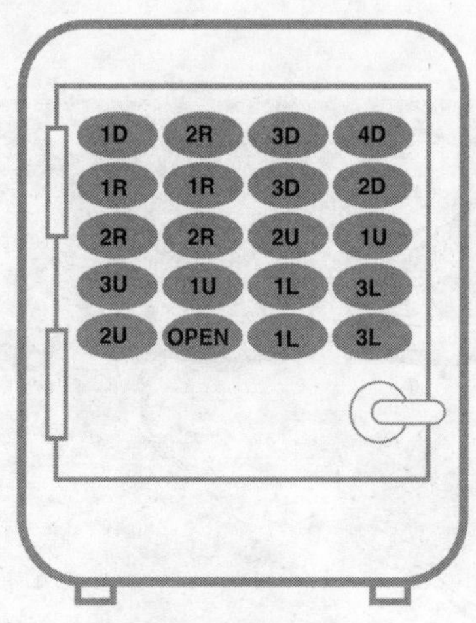


Answer on page 358

## DICE PUZZLE: What's the missing number?

Answer on page 358

# MIRROR IMAGE: Only one of these pictures is an exact mirror image of the first one? Can you spot it?

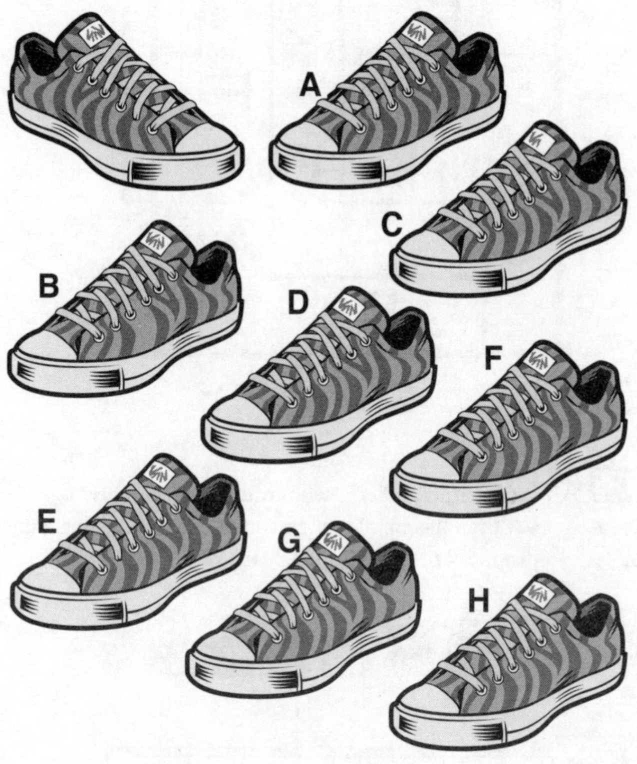


Answer on page 358

# LATIN SQUARE:

Complete the grid so that every row and column, and every outlined area, contains the letters A, B, C, D, E and F.

Answer on page 358

# SCALES:

The arms of these scales are divided into sections – a weight two sections away from the middle will be twice as heavy as a weight one section away. Can you arranged the supplied weights in such a way as to balance the whole scale?

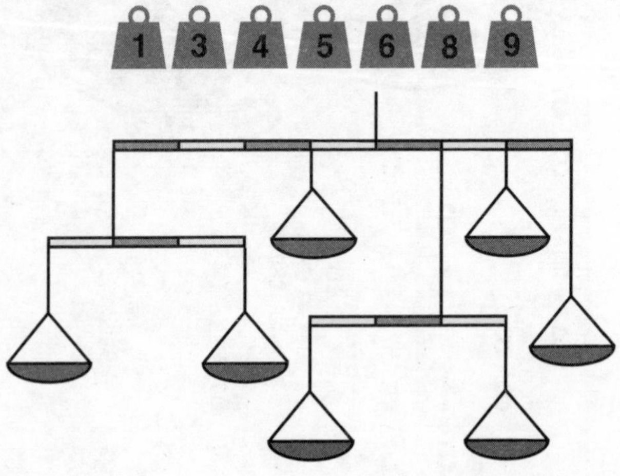


Answer on page 358

**SIGNATURES:** Can you crack the logical secret behind the numbers next to theses famous composers, and work out what number might be next to Mozart?

**Beethoven 60**

**Tchaikovsky 72**

**Mozart ?**

**Schubert 36**

**Brahms 15**

Answer on page 359

**SUDOKU:** Complete the grid so that all rows and columns, and each outlined block of nine squares, contain the numbers 1, 2, 3, 4, 5, 6, 7, 8, and 9.

| | | | | | | | | |
|---|---|---|---|---|---|---|---|---|
| 8 | | | 7 | 1 | | 5 | | 4 |
| | 3 | | | | 2 | | | 7 |
| 5 | | | | | | 1 | | |
| 9 | | | 6 | 7 | | 4 | | 5 |
| | | 8 | | | | | | |
| | | | | 9 | 5 | 6 | | |
| 3 | 8 | | | | 7 | | | 1 |
| | 6 | 1 | 5 | | | 2 | | |
| | | 5 | 3 | | 1 | | 6 | |

Answer on page 359

# WHERE'S THE PAIR?: Only two of the shapes below are exactly the same – can you find the matching pair?

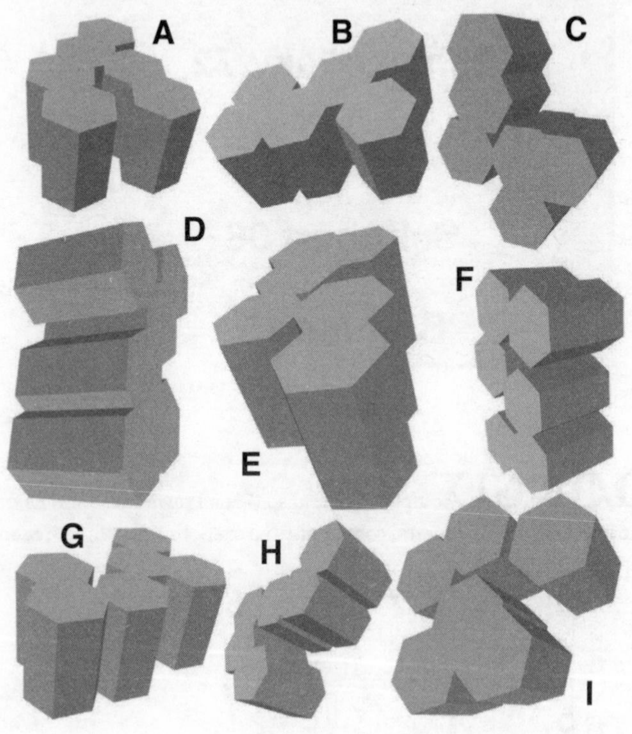


Answer on page 359

## WRINKLY QUOTE

"When I was younger, I could remember anything, whether it happened or not."

MARK TWAIN

# FLOOR FILLERS:

Below is a plan of a living room, showing fitted units that cannot be moved. Can you tile the whole floor using only the shape of tile shown? The tiles are not reversible!

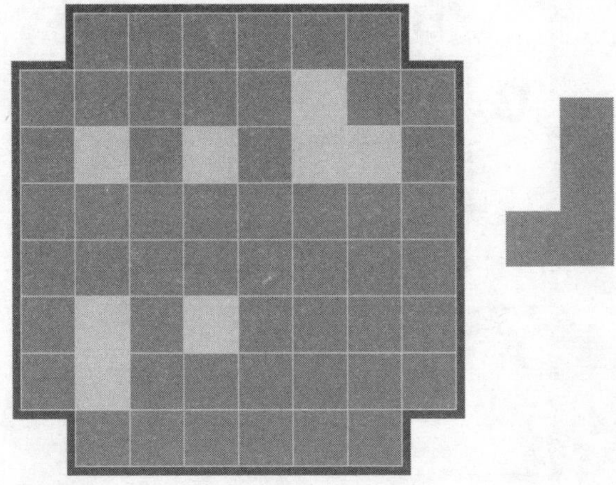

Answer on page 359

# KILLER SIX:

Complete the grid so that all rows and columns contain the numbers 1, 2, 3, 4, 5 and 6. Areas with a dotted outline contain numbers that add up to the total shown.

| 9 | 6 | | | 11 | |
|---|---|---|---|---|---|
| | 1 | 12 | | | 15 |
| 9 | 7 | | 1 | | |
| | 12 | | 11 | 9 | |
| 3 | | 2 | | | 5 |
| | 13 | | | | |

Answer on page 359

# LATIN SQUARE:

Complete the grid so that every row and column, and every outlined area, contains the letters A, B, C, D, E and F.

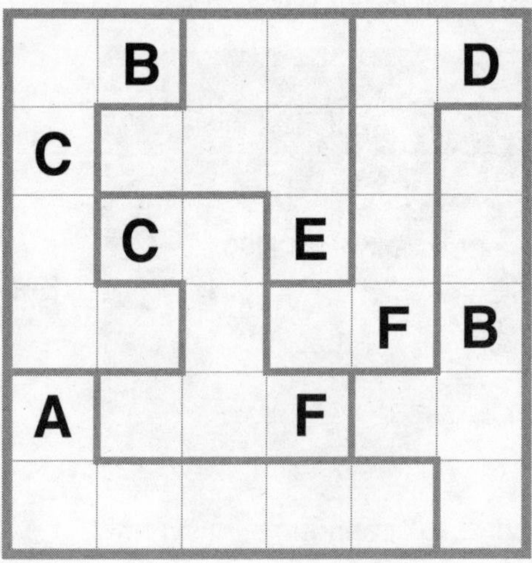

Answer on page 359

# MASYU:

Draw a single continuous line around the grid that passes through all the circles. The line must enter and leave each box in the centre of one of its four sides.

Black Circle: Turn left or right in the box, and the line must pass straight through the next and previous boxes.

White Circle: Travel straight through the box, and the line must turn in the next and/or previous box.

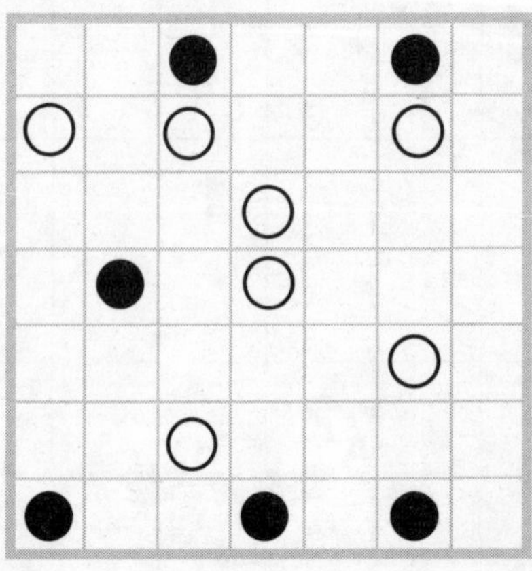

Answer on page 359

**ODD CLOCKS:** Sydney is 8 hours ahead of Cairo, which is 1 hour ahead of London. It is 8.20 pm on Saturday in Cairo – what time is it in the other two cities?

Answer on page 360

**SHUFFLE:** Fill up the shuffle box so that each row, column and long diagonal contains a Jack, Queen, King and Ace of each suit.

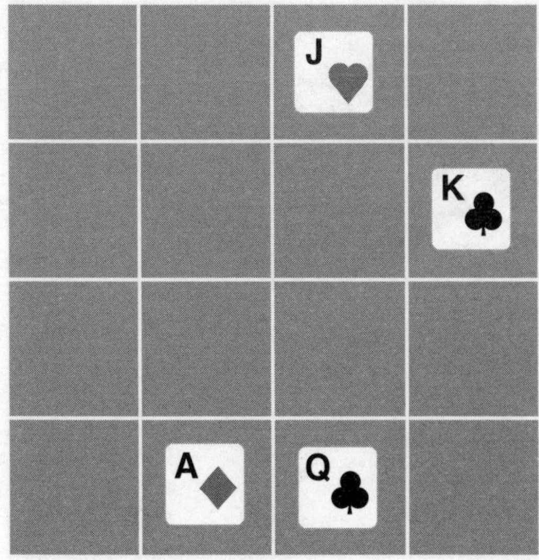


Answer on page 360

**RIDDLE:** Charlie is organizing his music collection. He manages to sort out a box of Jazz records and a box of Soul records before he has to rush off to give his nephew a guitar lesson. He puts the rest of the Jazz and Soul records into a third box. He quickly writes labels for all three boxes – Jazz, Soul and J&S. Unfortunately, in his haste, he puts the wrong labels on all three boxes. When he returns, how can he re-label his boxes correctly by listening to just one record?

Answer on page 360

# SUDOKU:

Complete the grid so that all rows and columns, and each outlined block of nine squares, contain the numbers 1, 2, 3, 4, 5, 6, 7, 8 and 9.

| | | | | | | | | |
|---|---|---|---|---|---|---|---|---|
| 8 | | 9 | 6 | 1 | 4 | | | 3 |
| | 2 | | | | 9 | 6 | 7 | |
| 5 | | 3 | 7 | | | | 4 | |
| | | 6 | 9 | | 7 | 4 | 8 | 5 |
| 4 | 3 | | | | | | | |
| 7 | | | 8 | | 6 | 3 | | |
| 9 | | 1 | 2 | | | 8 | | 6 |
| 6 | | 7 | | | 3 | | 2 | |
| | 5 | | 4 | | 8 | 7 | | 1 |

Answer on page 360

## WRINKLY QUOTE

"If you want to test your memory, try to recall what you were worrying about one year ago today."

E. JOSEPH COSSMAN

## SUM PEOPLE: Work out what number is represented by which person and fill in the question mark.

Answer on page 360

# WHERE'S THE PAIR?: Only two of these pictures are exactly the same. Can you spot the matching pair?

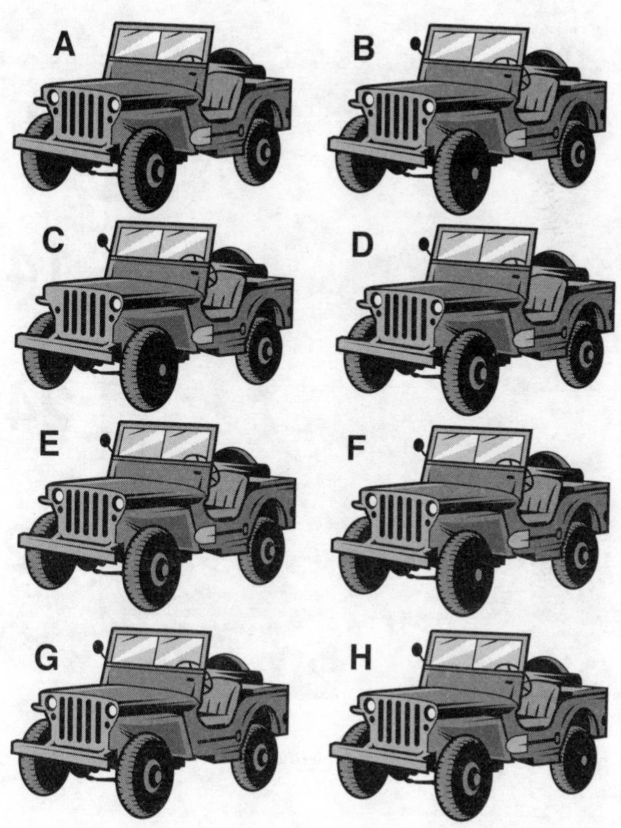


Answer on page 360

# WHERE'S THE PAIR?: Only two of the shapes below are exactly the same, can you find the matching pair?

Answer on page 360

WRINKLY QUOTE

"Old minds are like old horses; you must exercise them if you wish to keep them in working order."

JOHN QUINCY ADAMS

**BOX IT:** The value of each shape is the number of sides each shape has, multiplied by the number within it. Thus a square containing the number 4 has a value of 16. Find a block of four squares (two squares wide by two squares high) with a total value of exactly 60.

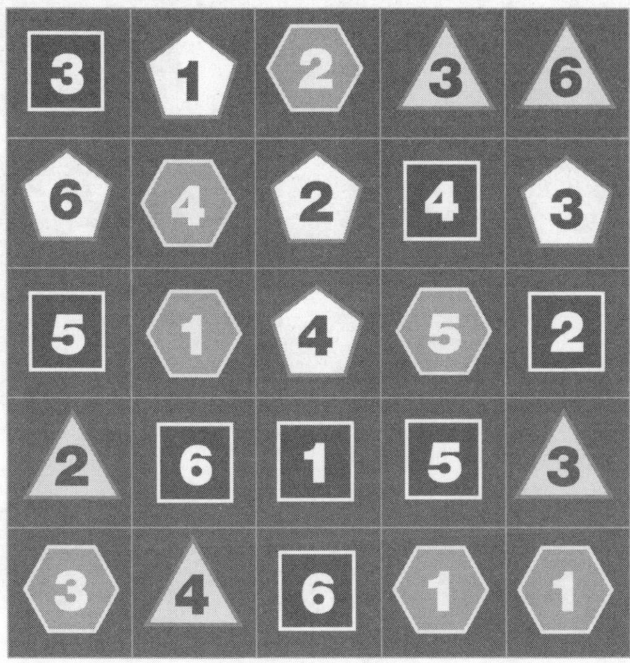

Answer on page 360

# KILLER SIX:

Complete the grid so that all rows and columns contain the numbers 1, 2, 3, 4, 5 and 6. Areas with a dotted outline contain numbers that add up to the total shown.

| | | | | | |
|---|---|---|---|---|---|
| 5 | 15 | | 7 | 7 | |
| | | | | 2 | 18 |
| 11 | 1 | 8 | | | |
| | 6 | | 7 | | |
| 5 | | 11 | | 7 | 5 |
| | 9 | | 2 | | |

Answer on page 361

# MORE OR LESS:

The arrows indicate whether a number in a box is greater or smaller than an adjacent number. Complete the grid so that all rows and columns contain the numbers 1 to 6.

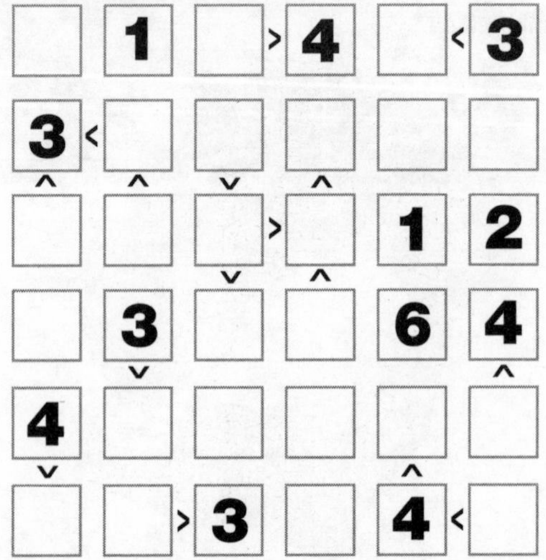

Answer on page 361

## SUDOKU: 

Couplet the grid so that all rows and columns, and each outlined block of nine squares, contain the numbers 1, 2, 3, 4, 5, 6, 7, 8 and 9.

| | | | | | | | | |
|---|---|---|---|---|---|---|---|---|
| 9 | | 4 | | 6 | 8 | 5 | | 3 |
| 1 | 3 | | 9 | | | | 8 | |
| | 6 | | | 4 | 5 | 1 | | 2 |
| | | 6 | 2 | 5 | | 7 | 4 | |
| | 5 | | | | 3 | | | 6 |
| 4 | 7 | | | 1 | | 2 | | |
| | 4 | 3 | | 9 | 1 | | | 7 |
| | 8 | | | 3 | | 4 | 6 | 9 |
| 7 | | 2 | 6 | 8 | | | 5 | 1 |

Answer on page 361

## THINK OF A NUMBER: 

Yellowbeard the pirate had a treasure chest containing 720 gold coins following his latest raid. He took a third himself, his navigator and first mate took one eighth each and the rest of the crew split the rest equally. Tom the cabin boy got 20 coins, How many people were on the boat altogether?

Answer on page 361

# MINI NONOGRAM:

The numbers by each row and column describe black squares and groups of black squares that are adjoining. Colour in all the black squares and a six number combination will be revealed.

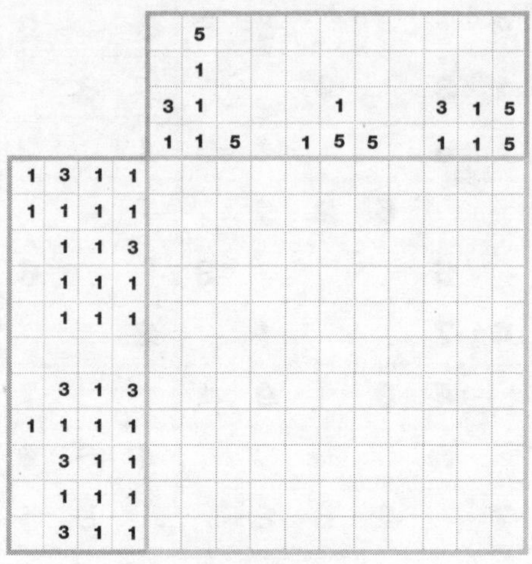


Answer on page 361

# MORE OR LESS:

The arrows indicate whether a number in a box is greater or smaller than an adjacent number. Complete the grid so that all rows and columns contain the numbers 1 to 6.

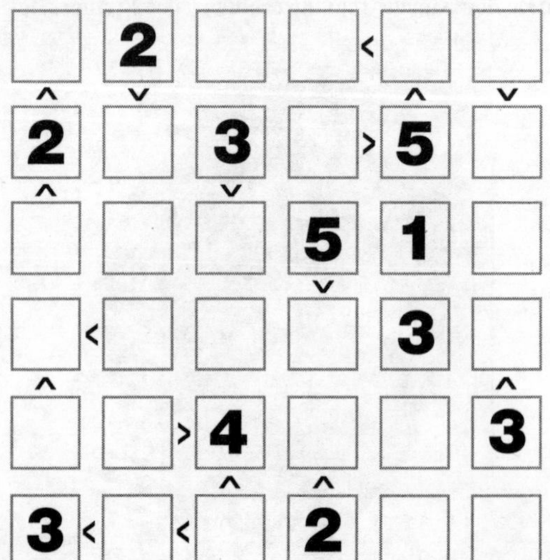


Answer on page 361

**ARROWS:** Complete the grid by drawing an arrow in each box that points in any one of the eight compass directions (N, E, S, W, NE, NW, SE, SW). The numbers in the outside boxes in the finished puzzle will reflect the number of arrows pointing in their direction.

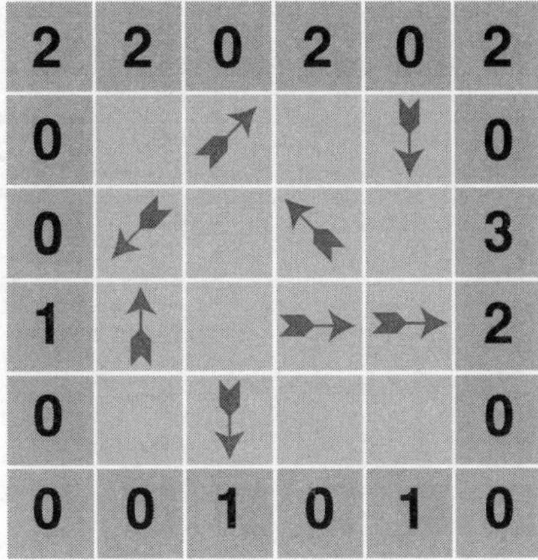


Answer on page 361

**BATTLESHIPS:** The numbers on the side and bottom of the grid indicate occupied squares or groups of consecutive occupied squares in each row or column. Can you finish the grid so that it contains three Cruisers, three Launches and three Buoys and the numbers tally?

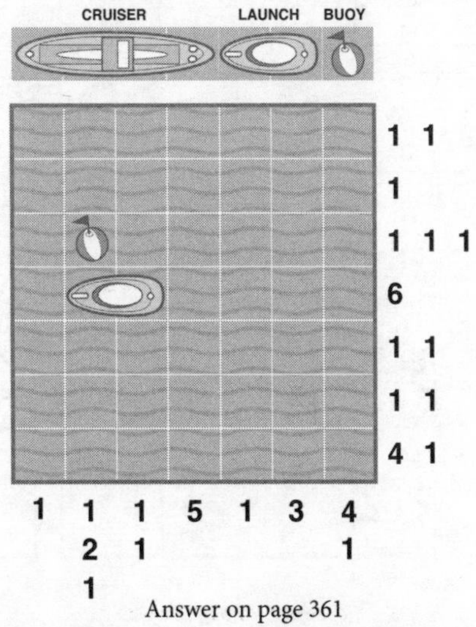


Answer on page 361

## BOXES:

Playing the game of boxes, each player takes it in turns to join two adjacent dots with a line. If a player's line completes a box, the player wins the box and has another go. It's your turn in the game below. To avoid giving your opponent a lot of boxes, what's your best move?

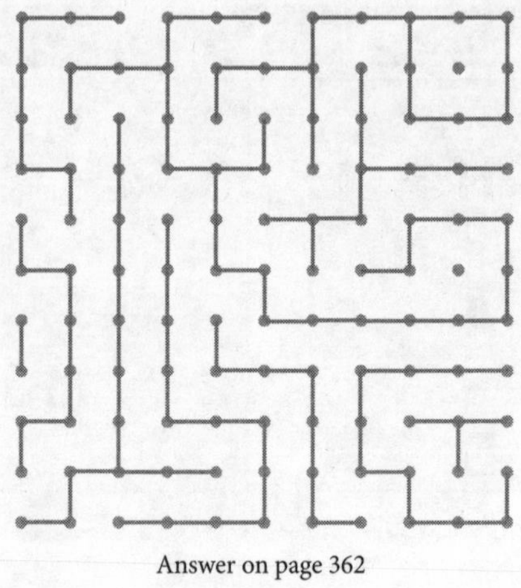

Answer on page 362

## MORE OR LESS:

The arrows indicate whether a number in a box is greater or smaller than an adjacent number. Complete the grid so that all rows and columns contain the numbers 1 to 5.

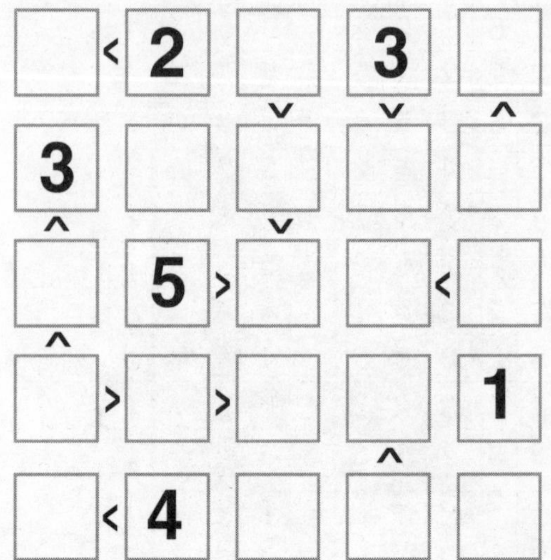

Answer on page 362

# SUDOKU SIX: 

Complete the first grid so that every row and column contains all the letters ACDHI and N. Do the same with grid 2 and the numbers 12345 and 6. To decode the finished grid, add the numbers in the yellow squares to the letters in the matching squares in the second (ie: A + 3 = D, Y + 4 = C) to get six new letters which can be arranged to spell the name of a city.

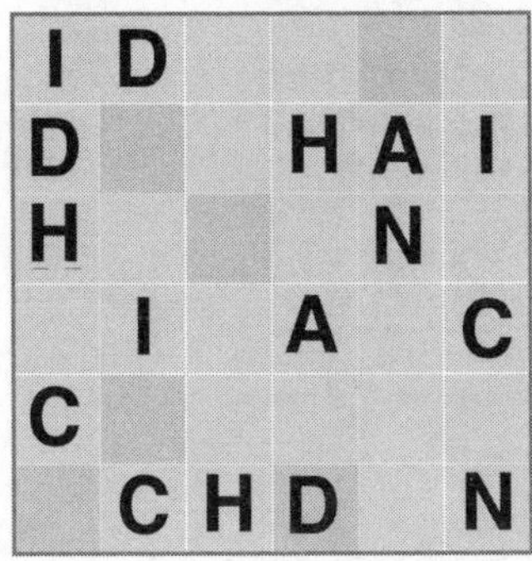

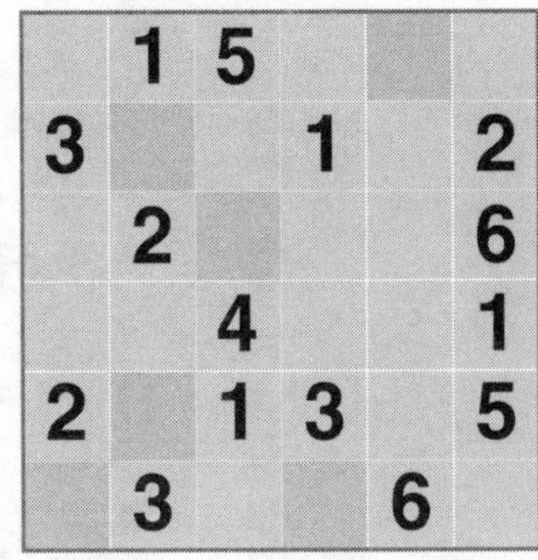

Answer on page 362

# FIGURE IT OUT: 

The sequence 12345 can be found once in the grid, reading up, down, backwards, forwards or diagonally. Can you pick it out?

| 1 | 5 | 1 | 2 | 4 | 1 | 2 | 5 | 2 | 1 | 2 | 3 |
|---|---|---|---|---|---|---|---|---|---|---|---|
| 2 | 2 | 2 | 1 | 5 | 2 | 2 | 2 | 4 | 2 | 3 | 2 |
| 3 | 5 | 3 | 5 | 4 | 2 | 3 | 3 | 3 | 3 | 1 | 1 |
| 5 | 3 | 4 | 5 | 2 | 3 | 3 | 2 | 4 | 4 | 2 | 3 |
| 4 | 3 | 3 | 1 | 3 | 4 | 4 | 1 | 2 | 2 | 5 | 2 |
| 3 | 1 | 2 | 5 | 2 | 5 | 5 | 3 | 5 | 3 | 4 | 3 |
| 3 | 2 | 3 | 4 | 1 | 3 | 4 | 4 | 4 | 3 | 4 | 5 |
| 5 | 2 | 3 | 3 | 5 | 3 | 4 | 5 | 3 | 3 | 3 | 5 |
| 1 | 4 | 3 | 2 | 2 | 4 | 2 | 3 | 5 | 2 | 2 | 1 |
| 3 | 3 | 7 | 1 | 5 | 2 | 3 | 5 | 2 | 5 | 1 | 3 |
| 1 | 2 | 3 | 4 | 3 | 5 | 4 | 4 | 4 | 1 | 3 | 2 |
| 5 | 1 | 5 | 2 | 5 | 3 | 5 | 3 | 4 | 3 | 2 | 1 |

Answer on page 362

**LOOPLINK:** Connect adjacent dots with either horizontal or vertical lines to create a continuous unbroken loop which never crosses over itself. Some, but not all of the boxes are numbered. The numbers in these boxes tell you how many sides of that box are used by your unbroken line.

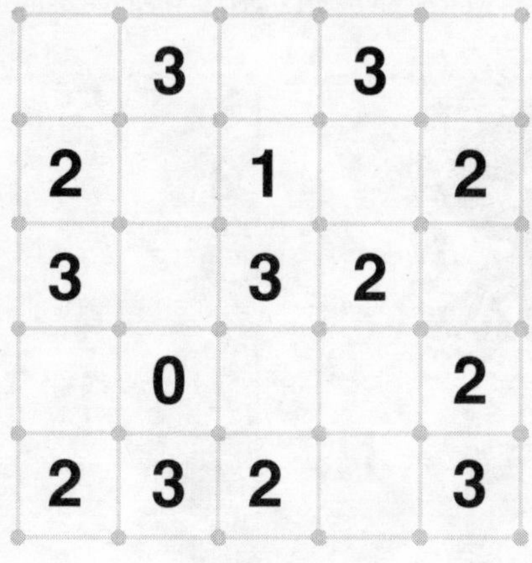

| | | | | |
|---|---|---|---|---|
| | 3 | | 3 | |
| 2 | | 1 | | 2 |
| 3 | | 3 | 2 | |
| | 0 | | | 2 |
| 2 | 3 | 2 | | 3 |

Answer on page 362

**SHAPE STACKER:** Can you work out the logic behind the numbers in these shapes, and the total of A x B x C?

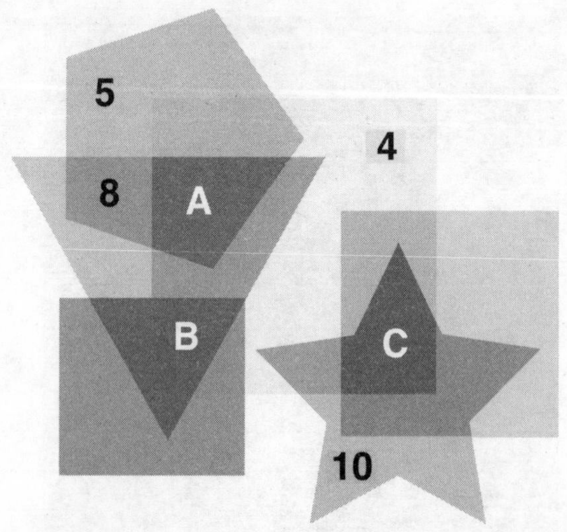


Answer on page 362

**SILHOUETTE:** Which of the coloured-in pics matches our silhouette?

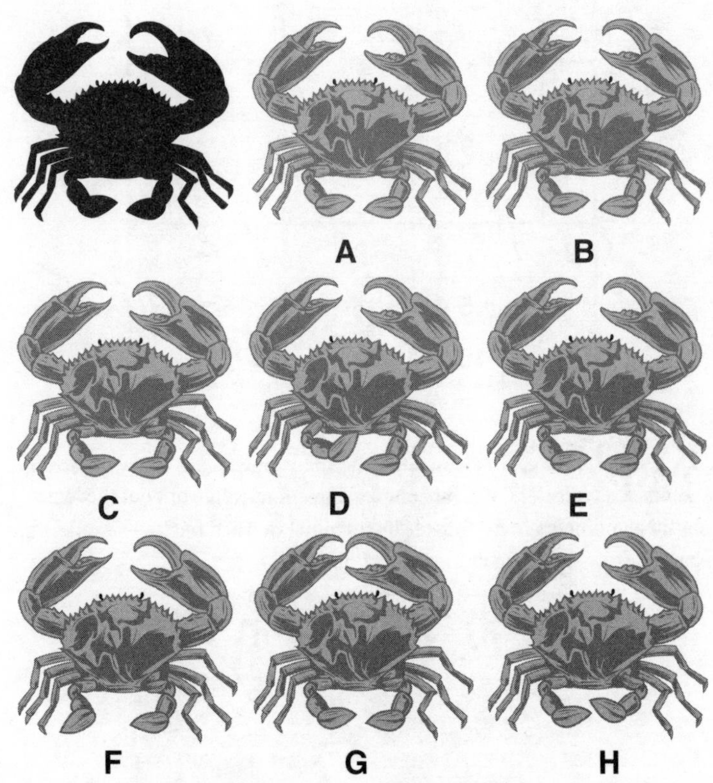


Answer on page 362

# SUDOKU: Complete the grid so that all rows and columns, and each outlined block of nine squares, contain the numbers 1, 2, 3, 4, 5, 6, 7, 8 and 9.

| | | | | | | | | |
|---|---|---|---|---|---|---|---|---|
| 7 | | | | | | | 3 | |
| 1 | | 4 | | 2 | | 5 | | 9 |
| 8 | | | 9 | | 6 | | 7 | |
| 6 | 1 | | 2 | 5 | | | | |
| | | 9 | | | | | | 6 |
| | | | 6 | | | 9 | | |
| 9 | 7 | | | 8 | | 4 | | 3 |
| | | 5 | | | 1 | | | 7 |
| 2 | | 6 | 4 | 9 | | 8 | | 1 |

Answer on page 363

# ARROWS: Complete the grid by drawing an arrow in each box that points in any one of the eight compass directions (N, E, S, W, NE, NW, SE, SW). The numbers in the outside boxes in the finished puzzle will reflect the number of arrows pointing in their direction.

| | | | | | |
|---|---|---|---|---|---|
| 0 | 0 | 1 | 0 | 0 | 1 |
| 0 | | ↘ | | | 0 |
| 1 | ← | | ↓ | ↓ | 3 |
| 0 | → | | → | | 2 |
| 0 | | | | | 1 |
| 0 | 3 | 0 | 1 | 1 | 2 |

Answer on page 363

**BOXES:** Playing the game of boxes, each player takes it in turns to join two adjacent dots with a line. If a player's line completes a box, the player wins the box and has another go. It's your turn in the game below. To avoid giving your opponent a lot of boxes, what's your best move?

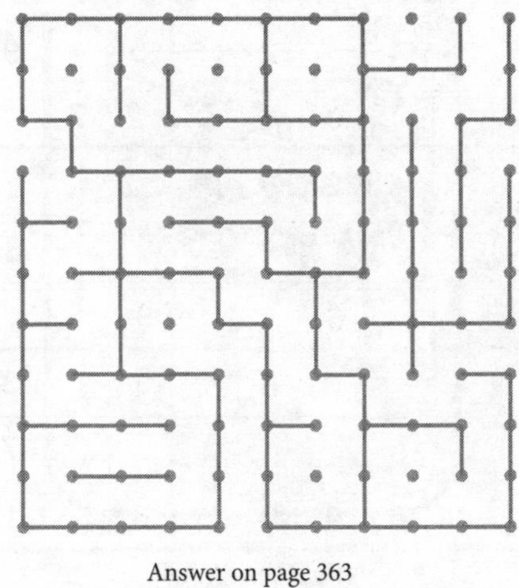

Answer on page 363

**FIVE POINT PROBLEM:** Discover the pattern behind the numbers on these pentagons and fill in the blanks to complete the puzzle.

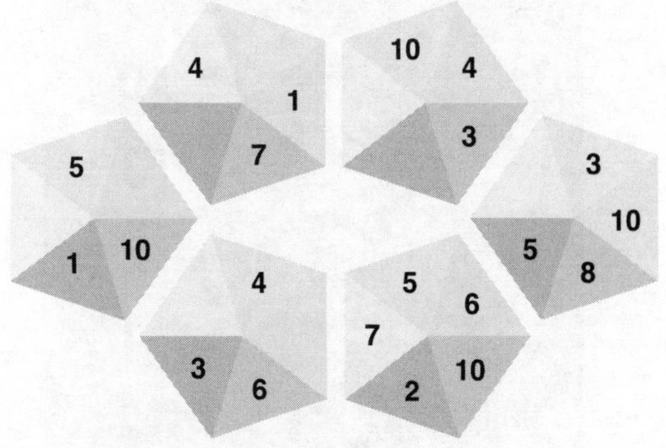


Answer on page 363

## SAFECRACKER: To open the safe, all the buttons must be pressed in the correct order before the "open" button is pressed. What is the first button pressed in your sequence?

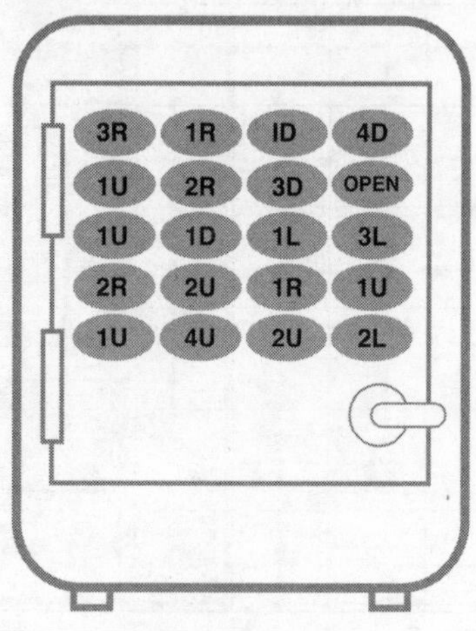


Answer on page 364

## THE GREAT DIVIDE: Divide the grid into four equal sized, equally shaped parts, each containing the numbers 1, 2, 3 and 4.

| | | | | | |
|---|---|---|---|---|---|
| 4 | | | | | 3 |
| | 1 | | 1 | 3 | |
| | 2 | 2 | | 2 | 4 |
| | | | | | |
| 3 | 4 | 3 | | 1 | 2 |
| | | 4 | | | 1 |

Answer on page 364

## KILLER SIX: Complete the grid so that all rows and columns contain the numbers 1, 2, 3, 4, 5 and 6. Areas with a dotted outline contain numbers that add up to the total shown.

| | | | | | |
|---|---|---|---|---|---|
| 3 | | 11 | 10 | 14 | |
| 7 | | | | | 2 |
| 15 | 6 | | | 3 | |
| | 6 | | 8 | 4 | 12 |
| | 3 | 5 | | | |
| 7 | | | 4 | | 6 |

Answer on page 364

## BEES AND BLOOMS: Every bloom has at least one bee found horizontally or vertically adjacent to it. No bee can be in an adjacent square to another bee (even diagonally). The numbers by each row and column tell you how many bees are there. Can you locate all the bees?

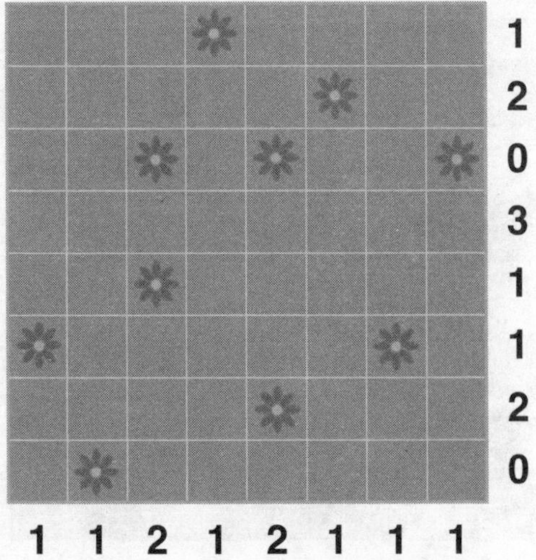


Answer on page 364

**BOXES:** Playing the game of boxes, each player takes it in turns to join two adjacent dots with a line. If a player's line completes a box, the player wins the box and has another go. It's your turn in the game below. To avoid giving your opponent a lot of boxes, what's your best move?

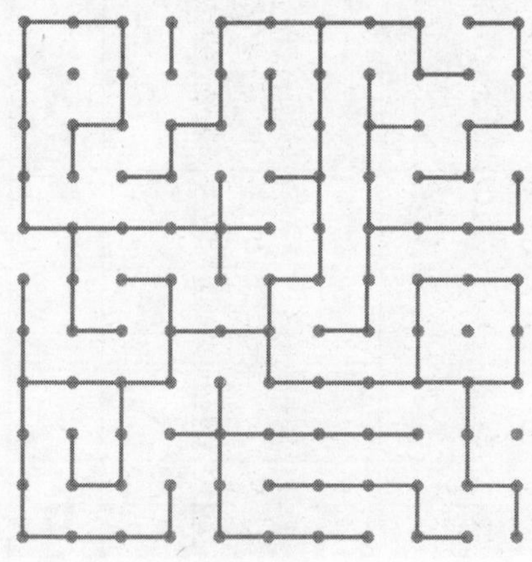

Answer on page 364

**CHECKERS:** Make a move for white so that eight black pieces are left, none of which are in the same column or row.

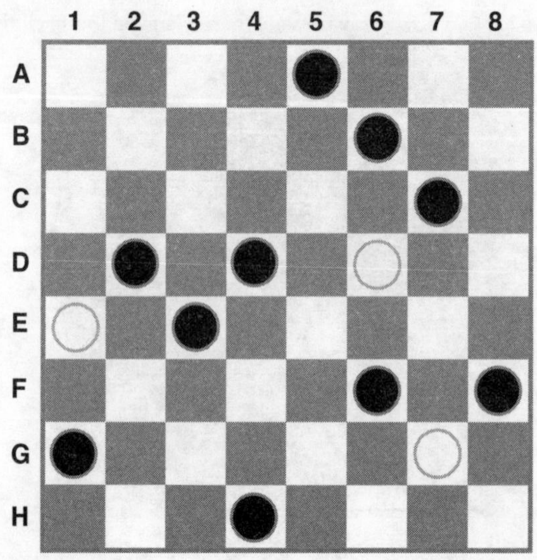


Answer on page 364

## HIDDEN PARIS: The word PARIS can be found once in the grid, reading up, down, backwards, forwards, or diagonally. Can you pick it out?

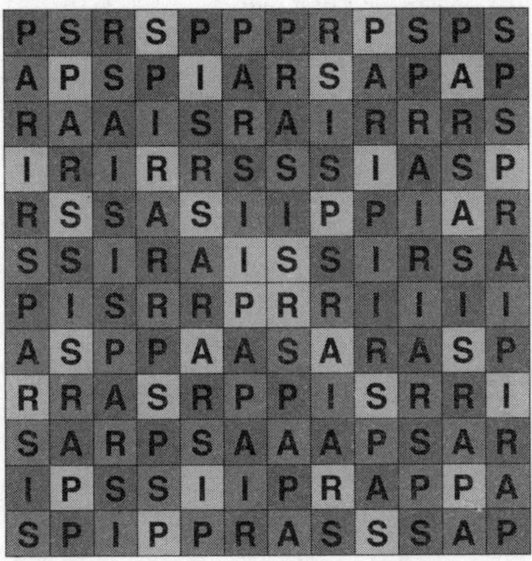


Answer on page 364

## IN THE AREA: Can you work out the approximate area that this crab is occupying?

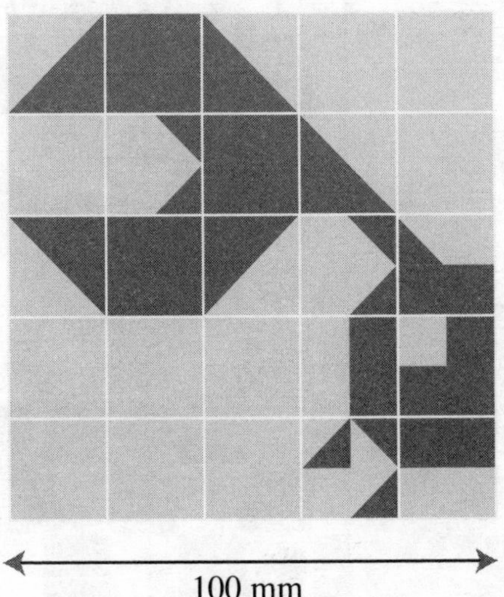


Answer on page 364

## X AND O:

The numbers around the edge of the grid describe the number of X's in the vertical, horizontal and diagonal lines connecting with that square. Complete the grid so that there is an X or O in every square.

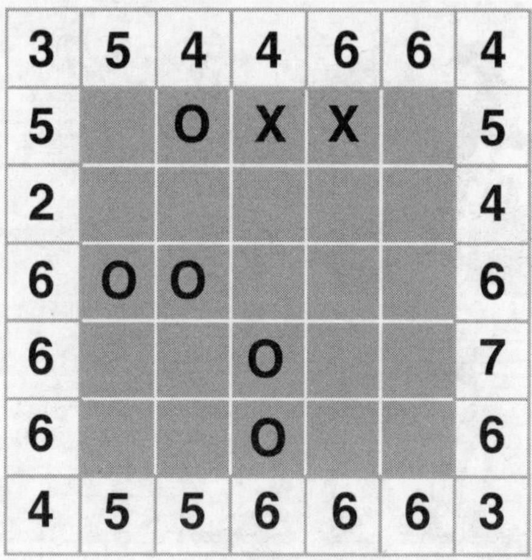


Answer on page 365

## SUDOKU:

Complete the grid so that all rows and columns, and each outlined block of nine squares, contain the numbers 1, 2, 3, 4, 5, 6, 7, 8 and 9.

| | | | | | | | | |
|---|---|---|---|---|---|---|---|---|
| | | 1 | | 3 | | | | 4 |
| | | | 4 | 6 | | | 9 | |
| 2 | | | | | 5 | 7 | | |
| | | | | 2 | | 3 | | 5 |
| 1 | | | | | | 8 | | |
| 5 | 3 | | | 4 | | | 1 | 6 |
| 6 | | 3 | 5 | | 2 | | | 9 |
| | | 8 | | 9 | | | 5 | |
| 4 | | | | 1 | | | 7 | 2 |

Answer on page 365

# SILHOUETTE: Which of the coloured-in pics matches our silhouette?

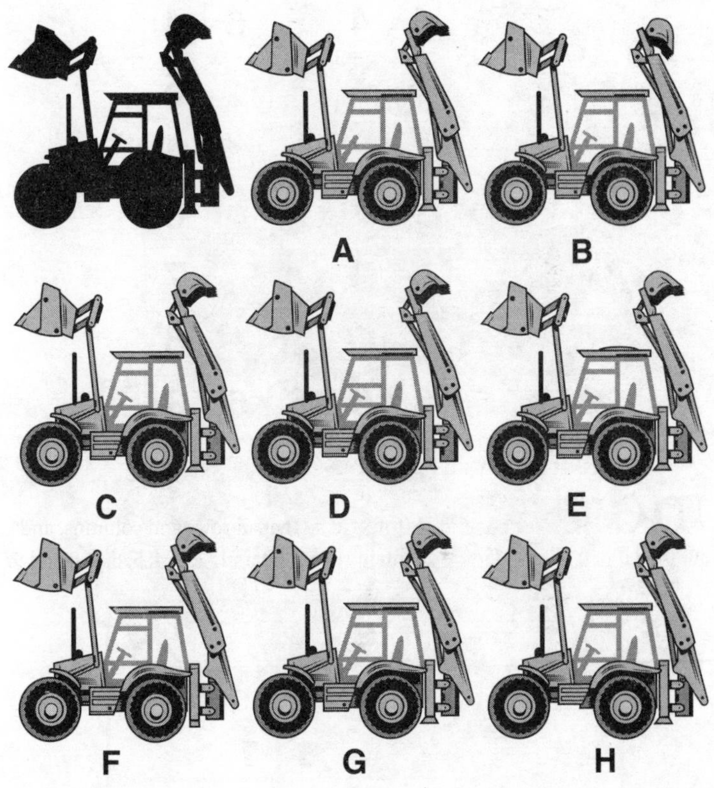


Answer on page 365

## Wrinkly Quote

"Human beings, who are almost unique in having the ability to learn from the experience of others, are also remarkable for their apparent disinclination to do so."

DOUGLAS ADAMS

**RIDDLE:** Geoff the farmer has to boat across the river with his dog, a chicken and a bag of grain. There is only room for Geoff and one passenger in the boat, and he can't leave the dog alone with the chicken, or the chicken alone with the grain... What can he do?

Answer on page 365

## SHAPE STACKER: Can you work out the logic behind the numbers in these shapes, and replace the question mark with a number?

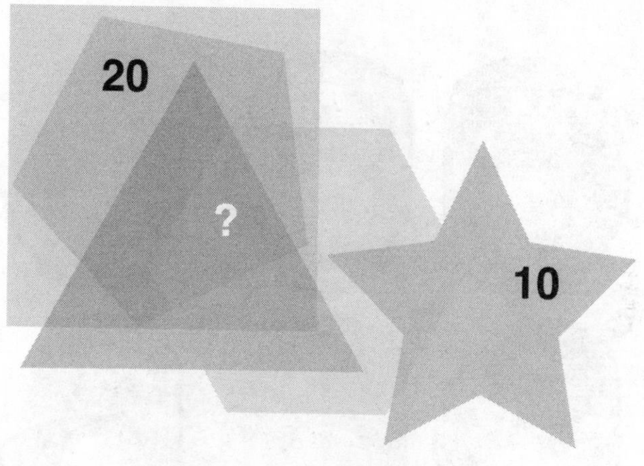


Answer on page 365

## SIGNPOST: Can you crack the logical secret behind the distances to these great cities, and work out how far it is to Melbourne?

Answer on page 365

# MIRROR IMAGE:

Only one of these pictures is an exact mirror image of the first one? Can you spot it?

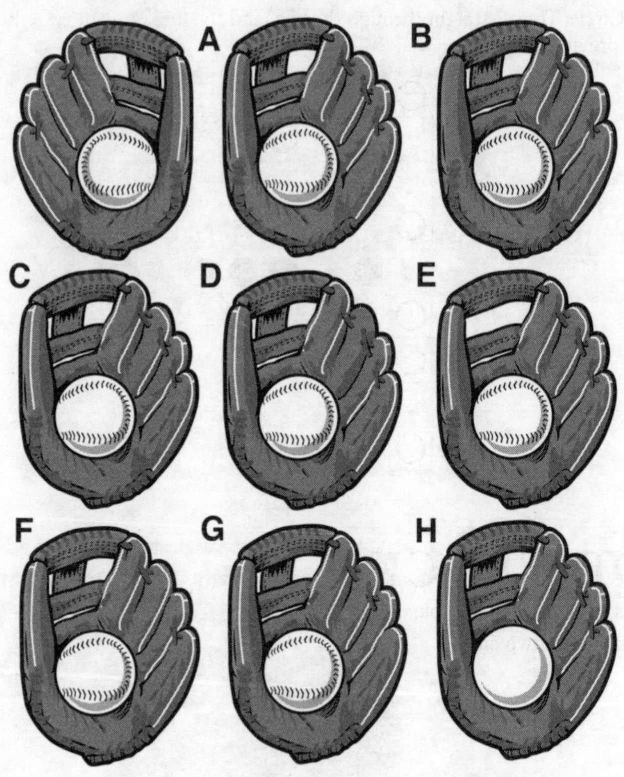


Answer on page 365

# MASYU:

Draw a single continuous line around the grid that passes through all the circles. The line must enter and leave each box in the centre of one of its four sides.

Black Circle: Turn left or right in the box, and the line must pass straight through the next and previous boxes.

White Circle: Travel straight through the box, and the line must turn in the next and/or previous box.

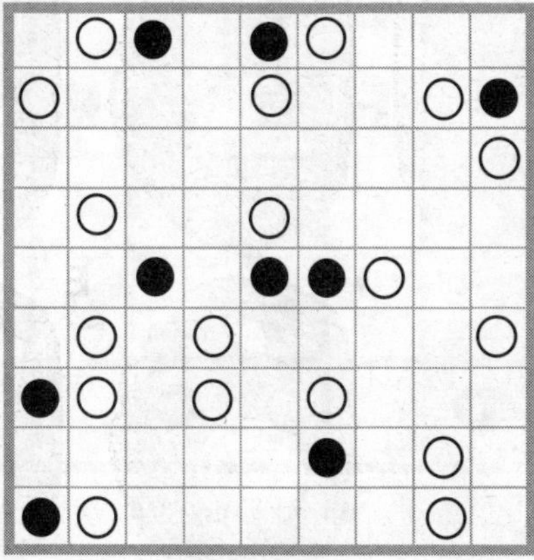

Answer on page 365

# ODD CLOCKS:

Singapore is 12 hours ahead of Miami, which is 13 hours behind Tokyo. It is 11.05 pm on Wednesday in Miami – what time is it in the other two cities?

MIAMI

TOKYO SINGAPORE

Answer on page 365

# LATIN SQUARE:

Complete the grid so that every row and column, and every outlined area, contains the letters A, B, C, D, E and F

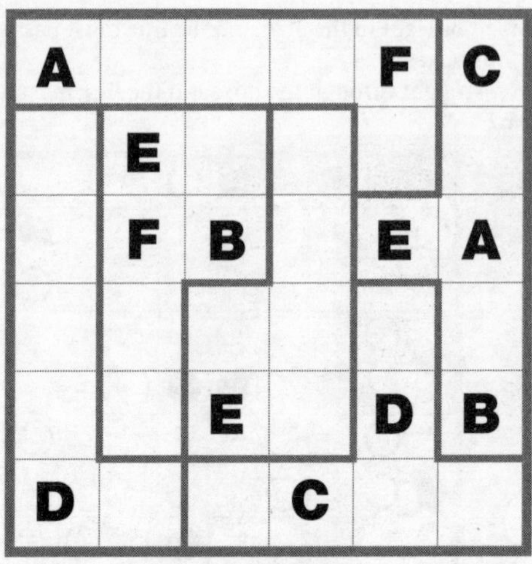

Answer on page 366

# MAGIC SQUARES:

Complete the square using nine consecutive numbers, so that all rows, columns and large diagonals add up to the same total.

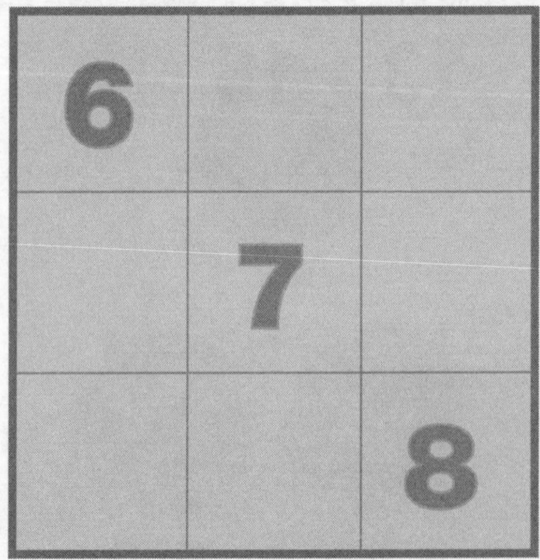

Answer on page 366

## SUM PEOPLE: Work out what number is represented by which person and replace the question mark.

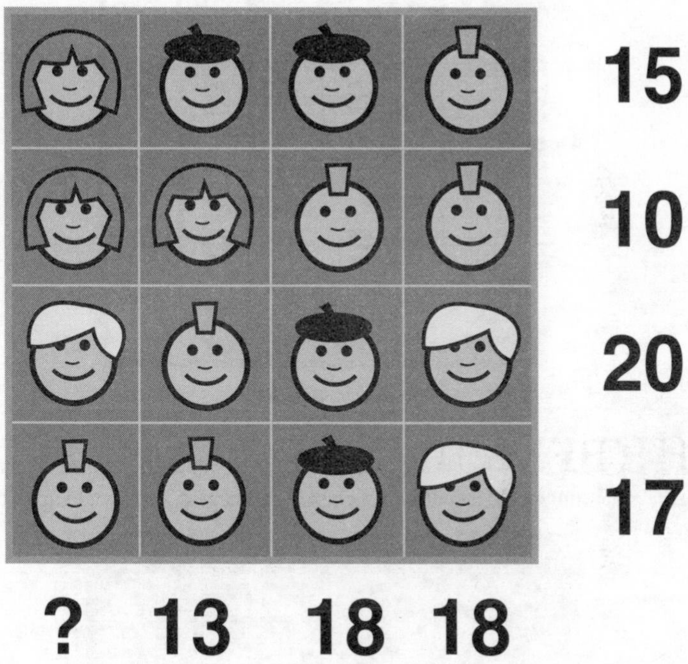


Answer on page 366

### WRINKLY QUOTE

"Experience is that marvellous thing that enables you to recognize a mistake when you make it again."

F. P. JONES

**SCALES:** The arms of these scales are divided into sections – a weight two sections away from the middle will be twice as heavy as a weight one section away. Can you arranged the supplied weights in such a way as to balance the whole scale?

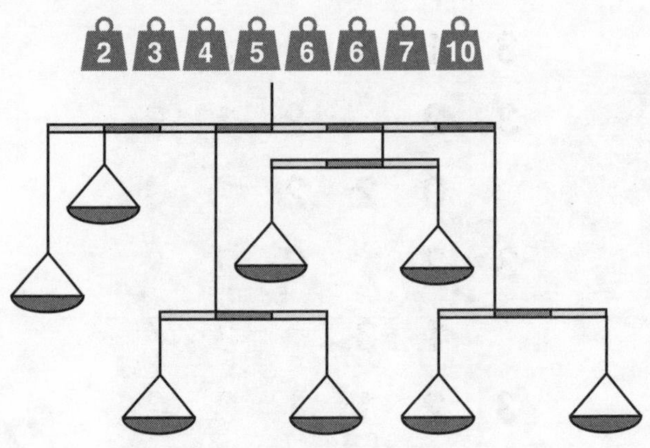


Answer on page 366

**SHUFFLE:** Fill up the shuffle box so that each row, column and long diagonal contains a Jack, Queen, King and Ace of each suit.

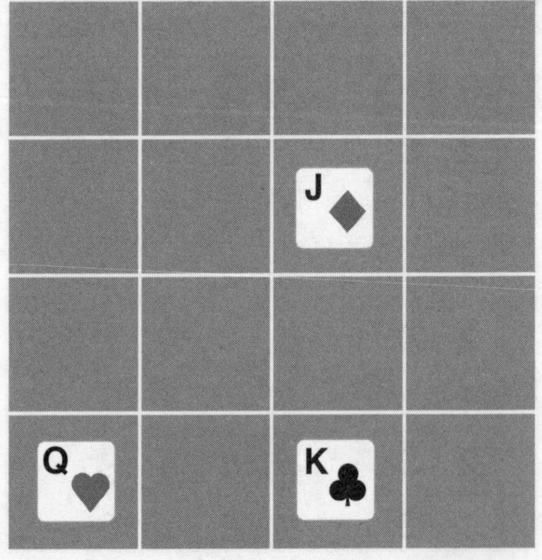


Answer on page 366

# LOOPLINK:

Connect adjacent dots with either horizontal or vertical lines to create a continuous unbroken loop which never crosses over itself. Some, but not all of the boxes are numbered. The numbers in these boxes tell you how many sides of that box are used by your unbroken line.

| | | | | | |
|---|---|---|---|---|---|
| 3 | 1 | 3 | 2 | 3 | 2 |
| 3 | 2 | | 2 | 1 | 3 |
| | 0 | 2 | 2 | | 3 |
| 3 | 2 | | 2 | 2 | 2 |
| | 1 | 3 | | 3 | |
| 3 | 2 | 1 | 1 | 3 | 2 |

Answer on page 366

# MINESWEEPER:

The numbers in some squares in the grid indicate the exact number of black squares that should surround it. Shade these squares until all the numbers are surrounded by the correct number of black squares.

| | | | | | | | |
|---|---|---|---|---|---|---|---|
| 0 | 1 | | 2 | 3 | | | 2 |
| 2 | 3 | 3 | | 3 | | 5 | |
| | | 4 | 2 | 4 | 2 | 4 | |
| 3 | | 4 | | 2 | | 3 | 2 |
| 2 | 4 | | 5 | 4 | 4 | | 3 |
| 1 | | | | | 4 | | |
| 2 | 5 | | 6 | 4 | 4 | | 4 |
| | 3 | | | 2 | | 3 | |

Answer on page 366

# MINI NONOGRAM:

The numbers by each row and column describe black squares and groups of black squares that are adjoining. Colour in all the black squares and a six number combination will be revealed.

| Col 1 | Col 2 | Col 3 | Col 4 | Col 5 | Col 6 | Col 7 | Col 8 | Col 9 | Col 10 | Col 11 |
|---|---|---|---|---|---|---|---|---|---|---|
| | 1 | | | | 1 | | | | | |
| | 1 | | | | 1 | | | | 1 | |
| 1 | 1 | 3 | | 1 | 1 | 3 | | | 1 | |
| 3 | 1 | 1 | | 3 | 1 | 1 | | | 1 | |
| 5 | 1 | 5 | | 5 | 1 | 5 | | 5 | 5 | 5 |

Row clues (top to bottom):

| Row | Clues |
|---|---|
| 1 | 3 3 3 |
| 2 | 1 1 1 1 |
| 3 | 3 3 3 |
| 4 | 1 1 1 1 |
| 5 | 3 3 3 |
| 6 | |
| 7 | 3 3 1 |
| 8 | 1 1 1 1 1 |
| 9 | 1 1 1 1 1 |
| 10 | 1 1 1 1 1 |
| 11 | 3 3 1 |

Answer on page 367

# SMALL LOGIC:

Three lucky ladies received flowers this morning. Using the clues below, can you work out who got which flowers, in which colour, and for what occasion?

1) The surprise flowers were roses, but not red ones.
2) Marianna received tulips, but it isn't her birthday.
3) Natasha's flowers were white, and she knew they would be.

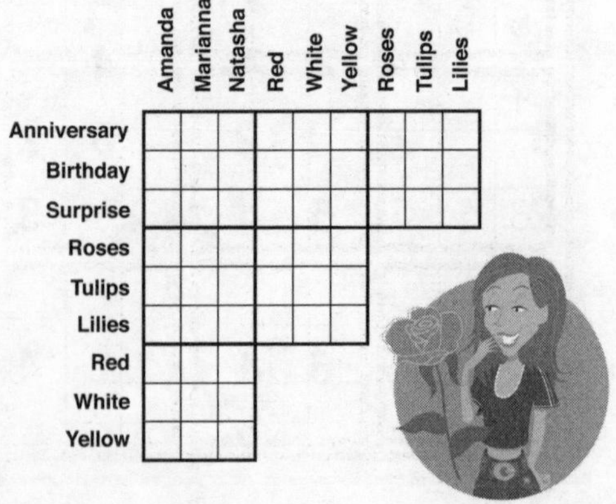


Answer on page 367

## FLOOR FILLERS: 

Below is a plan of the entrance pathway to a theatre, complete with spaces either side for plant pots. Below are some oddly shaped pieces of red carpet... Can you fill the floor with them?

Answer on page 367

## SUDOKU: 

Fill in each row, column and 9x9 box with the numbers 1, 2, 3, 4, 5, 6, 7, 8, 9 once only.

| | | | | | | | | |
|---|---|---|---|---|---|---|---|---|
| 4 | | | 1 | 3 | | | | 8 |
| | | | | | 7 | | | |
| 5 | 9 | | | | | | 4 | |
| 1 | | | 9 | 8 | | | | |
| | | | | 7 | | 3 | | |
| 8 | | | | | 1 | 6 | | |
| 9 | | | 3 | | | | | |
| | | | 7 | | 2 | | | 5 |
| | | | | 4 | 5 | | 2 | |

Answer on page 367

# JIGSAW:

Which four of the pieces below can complete the jigsaw and make a perfect square?

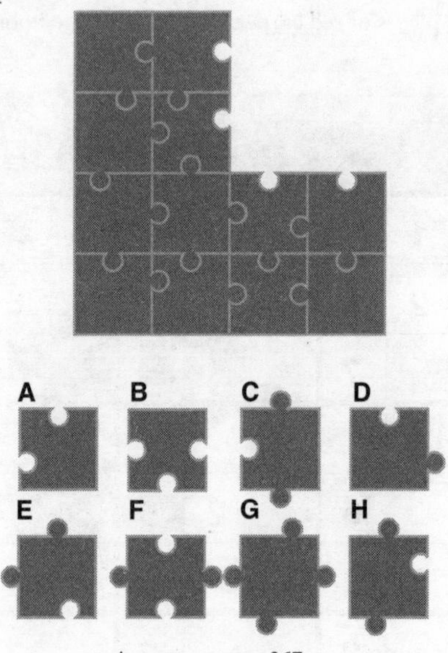


Answer on page 367

# RADAR:

The numbers in some cells in the grid indicate the exact number of black cells that should border it. Shade these black, until all the numbers are surrounded by the correct number of black cells.

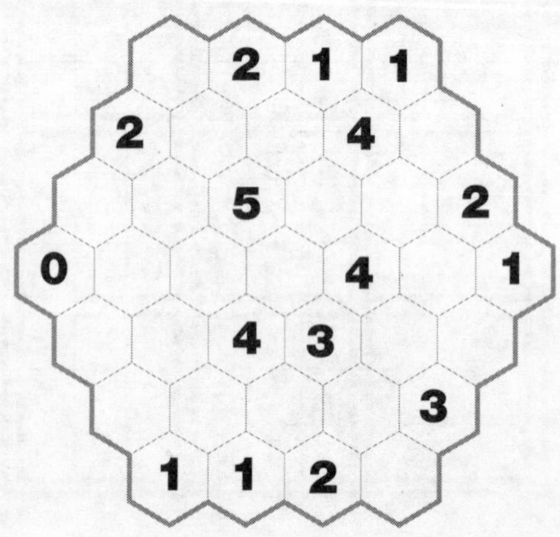


Answer on page 367

# SUDOKU:

Complete the grid so that all rows and columns, and each outlined block of nine squares, contain the numbers 1, 2, 3, 4, 5, 6, 7, 8, 9..

| | | | | | | | | |
|---|---|---|---|---|---|---|---|---|
| | 1 | | | 3 | 6 | | 2 | 9 |
| 9 | 2 | 8 | | | 7 | 3 | 6 | |
| | | 7 | | | | | 4 | 8 |
| | 5 | | 3 | | 1 | 4 | | 6 |
| 8 | | 6 | | 2 | 9 | 5 | 1 | 7 |
| | 7 | 4 | | | 8 | | | 3 |
| 5 | | 3 | | | 2 | | 7 | |
| | | 2 | 7 | 8 | | 9 | 5 | 1 |
| | 9 | | 5 | | 4 | | | |

Answer on page 368

## Wrinkly Quote

"You take all of the experience and judgment of men over 50 out of the world and there wouldn't be enough left to run it."

HENRY FORD

# HARD PUZZLES

## WHERE'S THE PAIR?: Only two of the shapes below are exactly the same – can you find the matching pair?

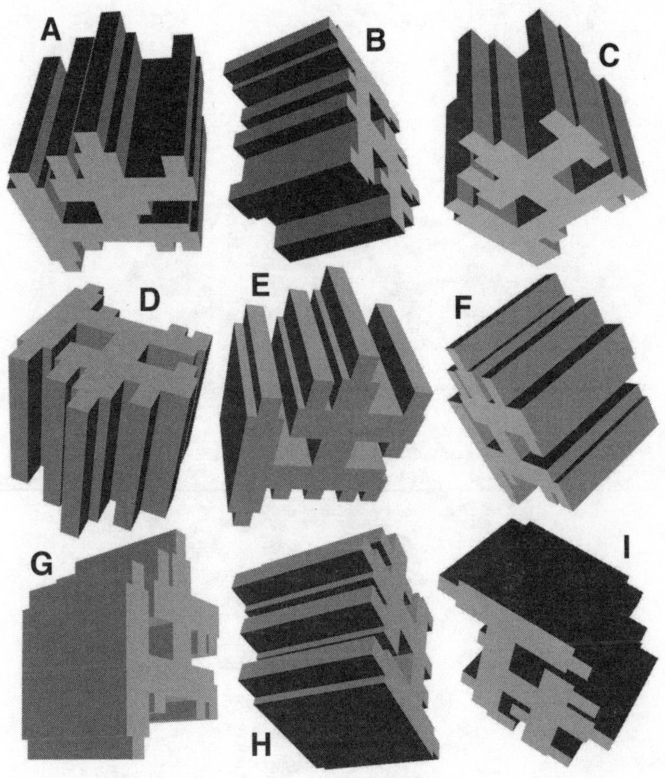


Answer on page 368

WRINKLY QUOTE

"If you're 48 and you haven't seen people in 30 years, don't do it. They're 48. They look like parents."

BILL CROSBY

**RIDDLE:** Pete goes back to visit the farm he lived on as a boy. From the town exit, he drives 3 miles east, then turns left and drives 4 miles north. Then he finds out there is a new road that leads directly from the town exit to the farm! How many miles would he have saved had he known that before?

Answer on page 368

**MASYU:** Draw a single continuous line around the grid that passes through all the circles. The line must enter and leave each box in the centre of one of its four sides.
Black Circle: Turn left or right in the box, and the line must pass straight through the next and previous boxes.
White Circle: Travel straight through the box, and the line must turn in the next and/or previous box.

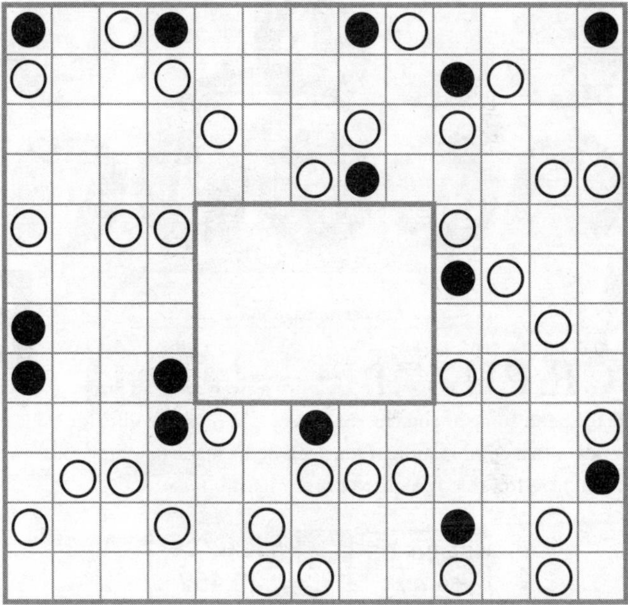

Answer on page 368

WRINKLY QUOTE

"My memory's starting to go. The only thing I still retain is water."

ALEX COLE

## LOGIC SEQUENCE: The balls below have been rearranged. Can you work out the new sequence of the balls from the clues given below?

There are two balls between the X and the triangle.
There are two balls between the star and the circle.
There is one ball between the star and the square.
The circle is immediately to the left of the X.

Answer on page 368

## PRICE PUZZLE: At a swanky Bond Street jewellers, you decide to spend some of your recent lottery win on some gifts for some of your closest friends. What combination of fourteen items made up of the four shown could you purchase for exactly a quarter of a million?

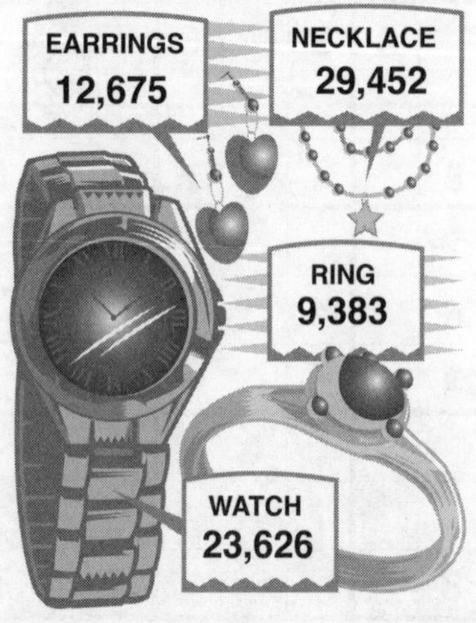


Answer on page 368

# MINESWEEPER: The numbers in some squares in the grid indicate the exact number of black squares that should surround it. Shade these squares until all the numbers are surrounded by the correct number of black squares.

| | | | | | | | |
|---|---|---|---|---|---|---|---|
| 3 | | 2 | 1 | | 2 | | |
| | | | 2 | | | 3 | 1 |
| 3 | 3 | 1 | 2 | | | | 0 |
| | 2 | | | 3 | | 2 | 0 |
| | | 1 | 1 | 3 | 2 | | 1 |
| | 2 | 1 | | 3 | | 3 | |
| 2 | | | 3 | | 4 | | 3 |
| | 1 | 1 | | 3 | | 3 | |

Answer on page 368

# MORE OR LESS SUDOKU: Complete the grid so that all rows and columns, and each outlined block of nine squares, contain the numbers 1, 2, 3, 4, 5, 6, 7, 8 and 9. The numbers in the arrowed squares are bigger than the numbers in the squares the arrows are pointing at.

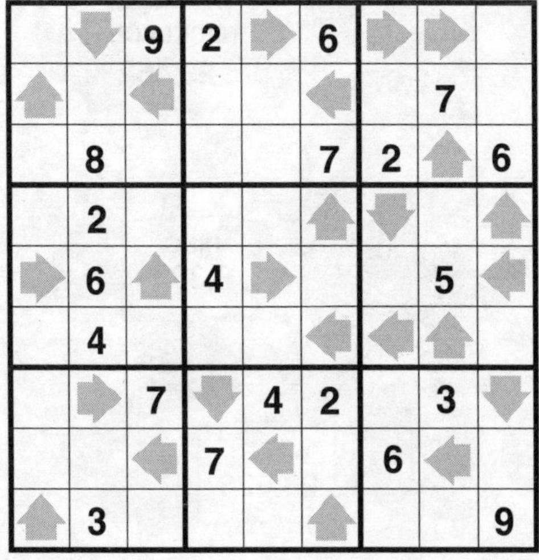


Answer on page 368

## NUMBER CHUNKS: Divide up the grid into four equal size, equally shaped parts, each containing numbers that add up to 40.

Answer on page 369

## WHERE'S THE PAIR?: Only two of these pictures are exactly the same. Can you spot the matching pair?

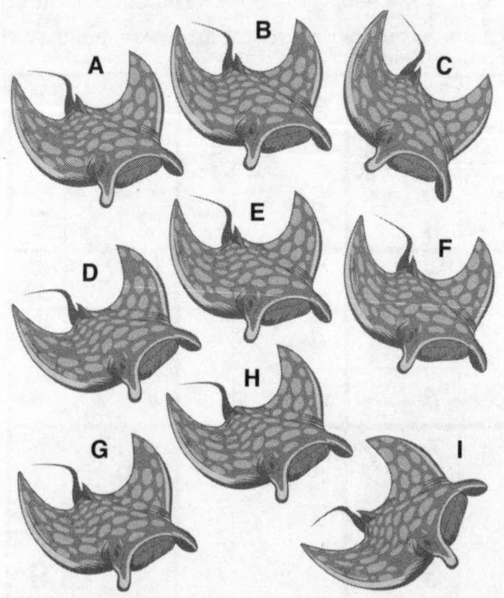


Answer on page 369

# SUM PEOPLE:

Work out what number is represented by which person and replace the question mark.

Answer on page 369

## WRINKLY QUOTE

"Experience is a great advantage. The problem is that when you get the experience, you're too damned old to do anything about it."

JIMMY CONNORS

# SILHOUETTE: Which of the coloured-in pics matches our silhouette?

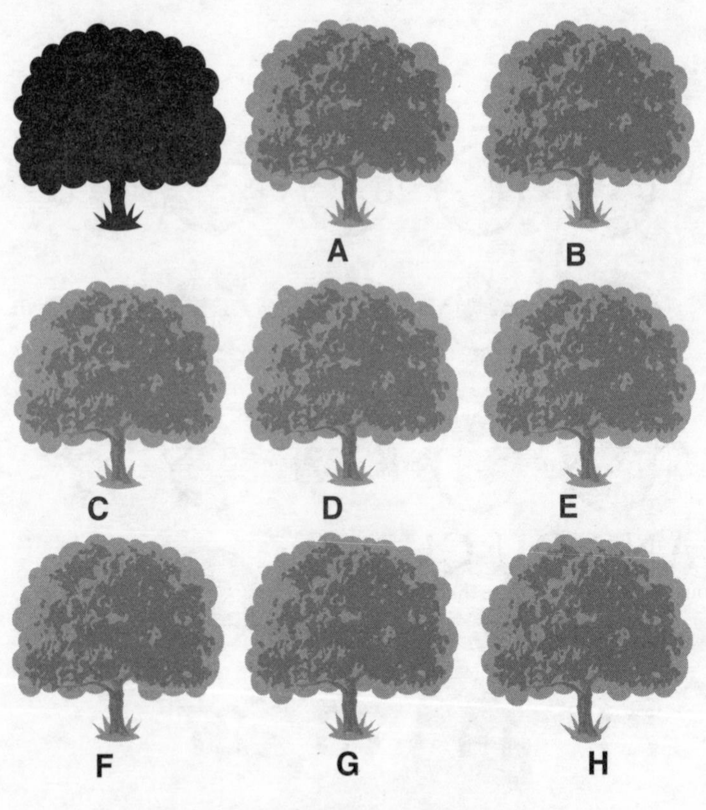


Answer on page 369

## Wrinkly Quote

"Advice in old age is foolish; for what can be more absurd than to increase our provisions for the road the nearer we approach to our journey's end."

MARCUS TULLIUS CICERO

**BITS AND PIECES:** These ten pieces can be arranged to spell out the name of a famous historical figure... but who?

Answer on page 369

**CAN YOU CUT IT?:** Cut two straight lines through this shape to create three shapes that are identical.

Answer on page 369

## FIVE POINT PROBLEM: Discover the pattern behind the numbers on these pentagons and fill in the blanks to complete the puzzle.

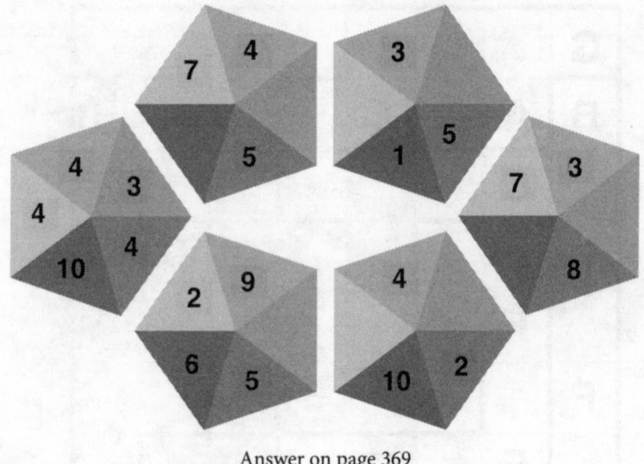


Answer on page 369

## KILLER SIX: Complete the grid so that all rows and columns contain the numbers 1, 2, 3, 4, 5 and 6. Areas with a dotted outline contain numbers that add up to the total shown.

| | | | | | |
|---|---|---|---|---|---|
| 11 | 1 | 12 | | | 8 |
| | 9 | 10 | 3 | | |
| | | | 10 | 8 | |
| 5 | 11 | | | 9 | |
| | | 8 | 5 | | |
| 5 | | | 5 | | 6 |

Answer on page 369

# LATIN SQUARE: Complete the grid so that every row and column, and every outlined area, contains the letters A to H.

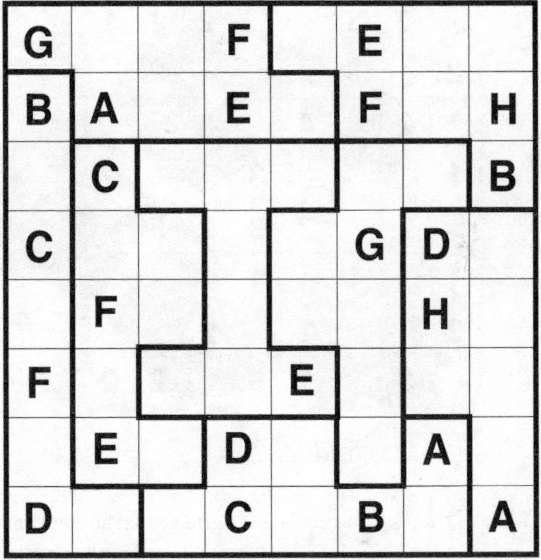

Answer on page 370

WRINKLY QUOTE

"They say that after the age of 20 you lose 50,000 brain cells a day. I don't believe it. I think it's much more."

NED SHERRIN

## MINESWEEPER: The numbers in some squares in the grid indicate the exact number of black squares that should surround it. Shade these squares until all the numbers are surrounded by the correct number of black squares.

<table>
<tr><td></td><td>2</td><td>3</td><td></td><td></td><td>2</td><td>1</td><td>1</td></tr>
<tr><td>2</td><td></td><td>3</td><td></td><td></td><td></td><td>2</td><td></td></tr>
<tr><td></td><td>2</td><td></td><td>4</td><td></td><td>3</td><td></td><td></td></tr>
<tr><td>1</td><td></td><td>3</td><td></td><td>3</td><td></td><td>4</td><td></td></tr>
<tr><td></td><td>2</td><td></td><td>3</td><td>3</td><td>2</td><td>5</td><td></td></tr>
<tr><td>1</td><td></td><td>4</td><td></td><td>1</td><td></td><td></td><td></td></tr>
<tr><td>2</td><td></td><td></td><td>2</td><td></td><td>2</td><td></td><td></td></tr>
<tr><td></td><td>3</td><td></td><td>1</td><td>0</td><td></td><td>2</td><td>2</td></tr>
</table>

Answer on page 370

## PRICE PUZZLE: Taking your wife, parents and kids to High Tea at a swish hotel in Bournemouth, you picked up the bill. The seven of you had two cakes each and a big pot of tea cost you 4.95. The bill was exactly twenty pounds. How many eclairs did your family eat?

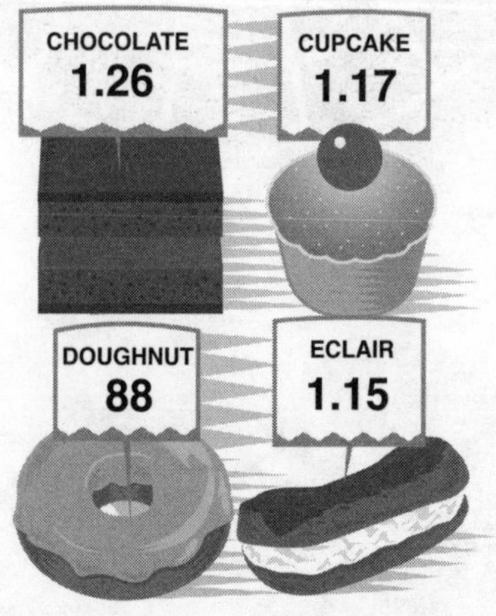


Answer on page 370

# ROULETTE:

The roulette ball is dropped into the wheel at the the 0 section. When the ball falls into a number 16 seconds later, it has travelled at an average speed of 3 metres per second clockwise, while the wheel has travelled at an average 2 metre per second in the other direction. The ball starts rolling 50 centimetres away from the wheel's centre. Where does it land? Take pi as having a value of exactly 3.2.

Answer on page 370

# SHAPE STACKER: Can you work out the logic behind the numbers in these shapes, and the total of A × B × C?

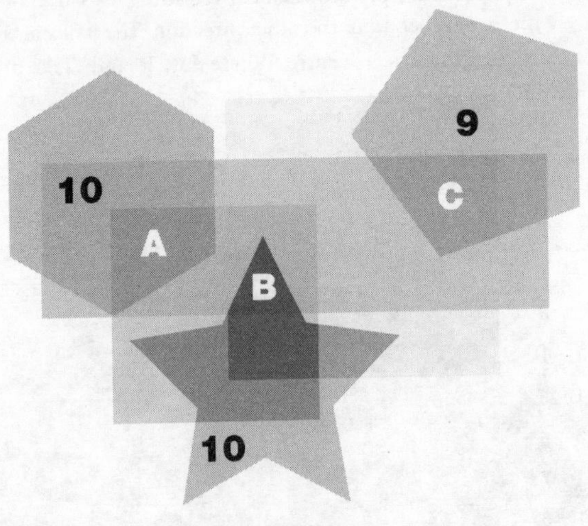


Answer on page 370

# SUDOKU: Complete the grid so that all rows and columns, and each outlined block of nine squares, contain the numbers 1, 2, 3, 4, 5, 6, 7, 8 and 9.

| | 7 | | | | 5 | | 4 | |
|---|---|---|---|---|---|---|---|---|
| | | | 1 | | 6 | | | |
| 2 | | | 3 | | | 1 | | 8 |
| | | 5 | | | | 3 | | |
| | | | 4 | 1 | | | | |
| 3 | | 9 | | | 7 | | | 6 |
| 7 | | | 8 | | 4 | | 3 | |
| | | 2 | | 9 | | 5 | | |
| | 5 | | 6 | | | | 8 | 1 |

Answer on page 370

# MINI NONOGRAM:

The numbers by each row and column describe black squares and groups of black squares that are adjoining. Colour in all the squares and a picture will be revealed.

| | | | | | | | | | | | | | | | | | | |
|---|---|---|---|---|---|---|---|---|---|---|---|---|---|---|---|---|---|---|
| | | | | | 1 | 1 | | 1 | 1 | | | | | | | | | |
| | | | | | 1 | 1 | | 1 | 1 | | | | 4 | | 4 | | | |
| | | | | | 1 | 1 | | 1 | 1 | | 1 | | 1 | | 1 | | 1 | |
| | | | | 1 | 2 | 3 | 15 | 4 | 4 | 4 | 4 | 11 | 5 | 13 | 5 | 11 | 4 | 3 |
| | | | 1 | | | | | | | | | | | | | | | |
| | | | 3 | | | | | | | | | | | | | | | |
| 1 | 1 | 1 | 1 | | | | | | | | | | | | | | | |
| | | 1 | 3 | | | | | | | | | | | | | | | |
| | | 3 | 5 | | | | | | | | | | | | | | | |
| 1 | 1 | 1 | 7 | | | | | | | | | | | | | | | |
| | | 1 | 5 | | | | | | | | | | | | | | | |
| 3 | 1 | 1 | 1 | | | | | | | | | | | | | | | |
| 1 | 1 | 1 | 5 | | | | | | | | | | | | | | | |
| 1 | 1 | 1 | 1 | | | | | | | | | | | | | | | |
| | | 1 | 5 | | | | | | | | | | | | | | | |
| | | | 11 | | | | | | | | | | | | | | | |
| | | | 13 | | | | | | | | | | | | | | | |
| | | | 14 | | | | | | | | | | | | | | | |
| | | | 15 | | | | | | | | | | | | | | | |

Answer on page 371

## WRINKLY QUOTE

"To know how to grow old is the master-work of wisdom, and one of the most difficult chapters in the great art of living."

HENRI FREDERIC AMIEL

## SMALL LOGIC:

After the bank robbery, Tex, Sixgun and Hoss split up and headed for their hideouts. Can you name each bandit, the horse he rode, and where he escaped to?

1) Hoss rode Blanco to a town ending in the letter 'O'
2) Six-Gun MacGee didn't ride Sunset, or to Dodge
3) Williams, who wasn't called Tex, didn't ride to Reno

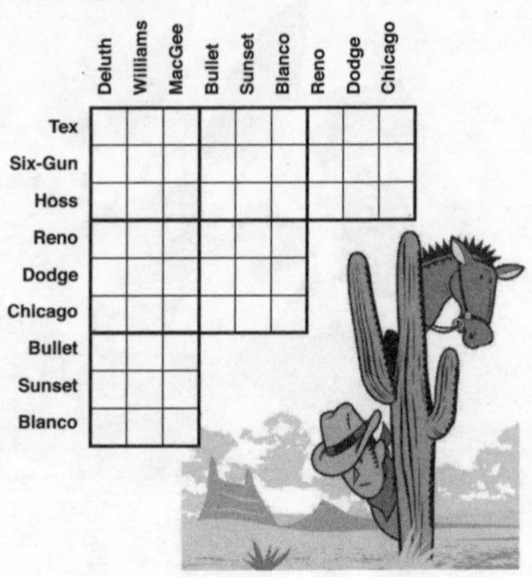


Answer on page 371

## BATTLESHIPS:

The numbers on the side and bottom of the grid indicate occupied squares or groups of consecutive occupied squares in each row or column. Can you finish the grid so that it contains four Cruisers, four Launches and four Buoys and the numbers tally?

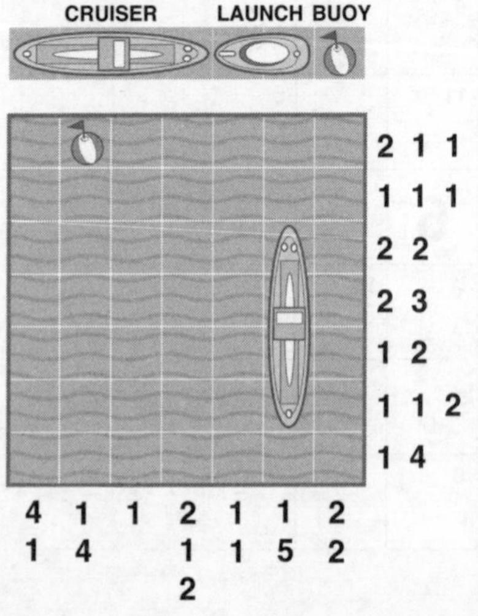


Answer on page 371

# BITS AND PIECES:

These pieces can be assembled to spell the name of a city... Which?

Answer on page 371

# KILLER SIX:

Complete the grid so that all rows and columns contain the numbers 1, 2, 3, 4, 5 and 6. Areas with a dotted outline contain numbers that add up to the total shown.

| | | | | | |
|---|---|---|---|---|---|
| 3 | | 6 | 7 | | 11 |
| 11 | | 8 | 3 | | |
| 6 | | | 11 | 4 | |
| 6 | 12 | | | 3 | |
| | | 3 | 6 | 8 | |
| 8 | | | | 10 | |

Answer on page 371

**CUBE VOLUME:** These little cubes originally made a big cube measuring 12cm x 12cm x 12cm. Now some of the little cubes have been removed, can you work out what volume the remaining cubes have now? Assume all invisible cubes are present.

Answer on page 371

**DICE PUZZLE:** What's the missing number?

Answer on page 371

# KILLER SIX:

Complete the grid so that all rows and columns contain the numbers 1, 2, 3, 4, 5 and 6. Areas with a dotted outline contain numbers that add up to the total shown.

| | | | | | |
|---|---|---|---|---|---|
| 15 | 6 | 9 | | | 7 |
| | | 1 | 10 | | |
| | | 8 | 8 | 12 | |
| 4 | 10 | | | 6 | |
| | | 9 | 4 | | |
| 7 | | | | 10 | |

Answer on page 372

# MATRIX:

Which of the four boxed figures completes the set?

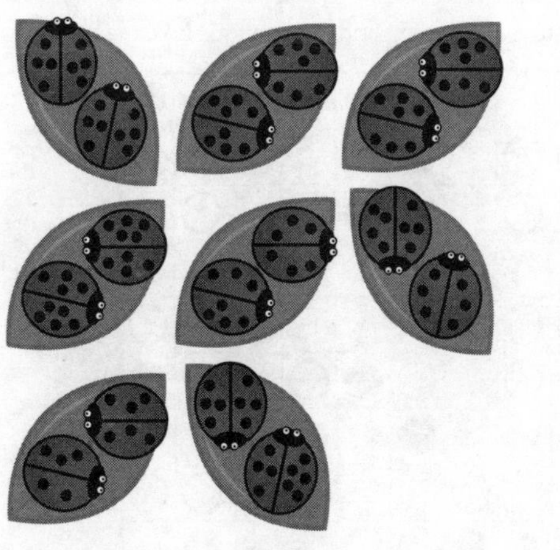

Answer on page 372

# KILLER SUDOKU:

Complete the grid so that all rows and columns, and each outlined block of nine squares, contain the numbers 1, 2, 3, 4, 5, 6, 7, 8 and 9. Areas with a dotted outline contain numbers that add up to the total shown.

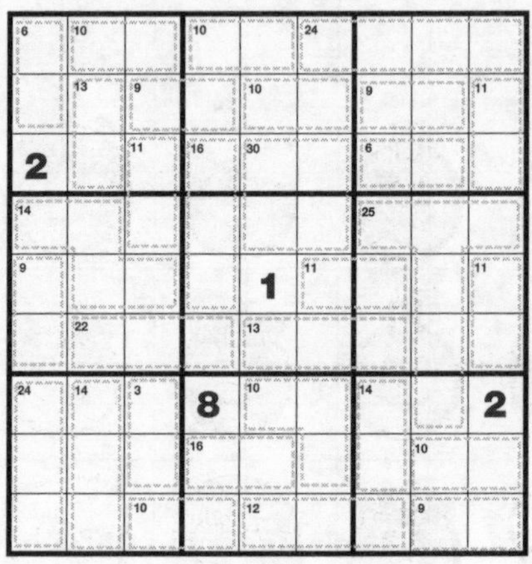

Answer on page 372

# MASYU:

Draw a single continuous line around the grid that passes through all the circles. The line must enter and leave each box in the centre of one of its four sides. Black Circle: Turn left or right in the box, and the line must pass straight through the next and previous boxes. White Circle: Travel straight through the box, and the line must turn in the next and/or previous box.

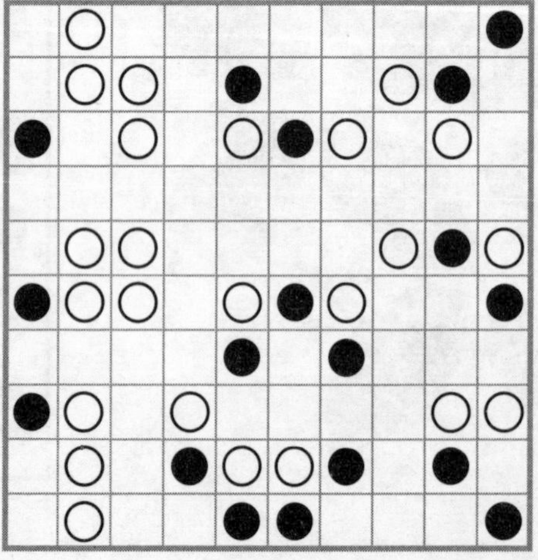

Answer on page 372

# SUM PEOPLE: Work out which number is represented by which person and fill in the question mark

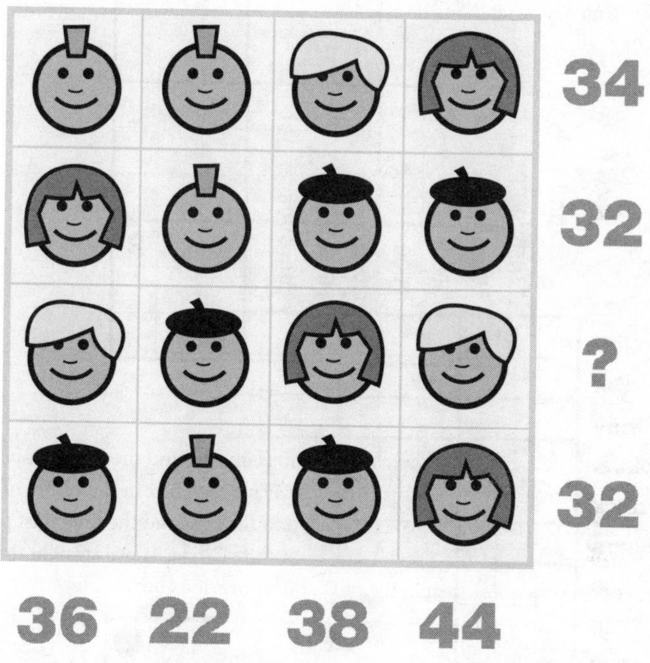


Answer on page 372

## WRINKLY QUOTE

"Only two things are infinite – the universe and human stupidity, and I'm not so sure about the universe."

STEPHEN FRY

# SMALL LOGIC:

Jeff, Tony and Bill all won poker tournaments in Las Vegas. Can you match up the first and last names with each player's poker nickname, and work out how much each player won?

1) Bill Sear's nickname isn't "Lucky".
2) Tony "The Diamond" isn't called Hopkins and won more than $500.
3) "Lucky" won a thousand dollars.

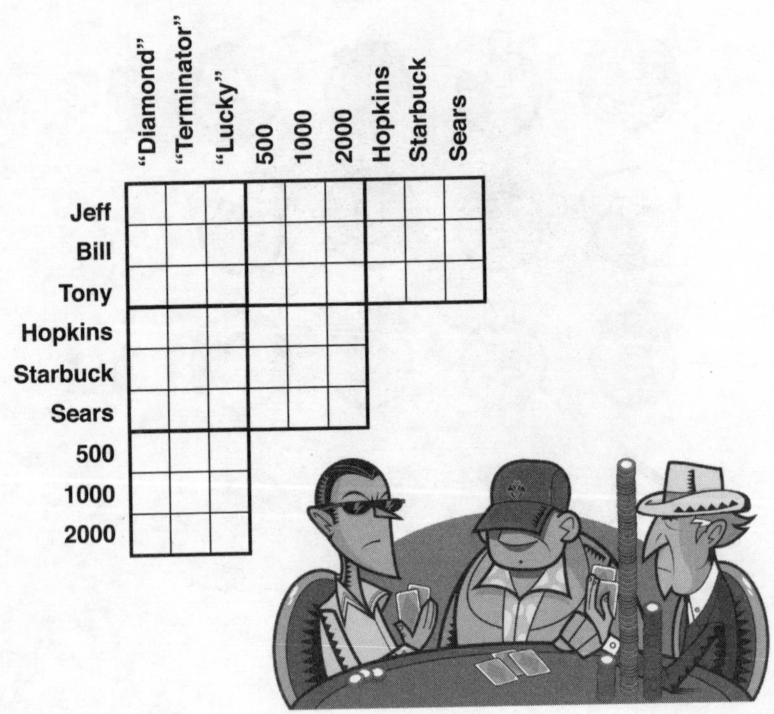


Answer on page 372

**RIDDLE:** Your four greedy nieces are paying you a visit. You had saved a slice of pizza for lunch but when you open the fridge, you discover that one of the little darlings has already eaten it!
Katy says "Holly ate it!"
Holly says "Amy ate it!"
Amy says "Holly's lying!"
Poppy says "Well, it wasn't me!"
If just ONE of the girls' statements is true – who ate the pizza?

Answer on page 372

**BITS AND PIECES:** These pieces can be assembled to spell the name of a giant of literature... Who?

Answer on page 372

**CAN YOU CUT IT?:** Turn this shape into three shapes that are identical in size and shape by making one continuous cut.

Answer on page 372

# MASYU:

Draw a single continuous line around the grid that passes through all the circles. The line must enter and leave each box in the centre of one of its four sides.
Black Circle: Turn left or right in the box, and the line must pass straight through the next and previous boxes.
White Circle: Travel straight through the box, and the line must turn in the next and/or previous box.

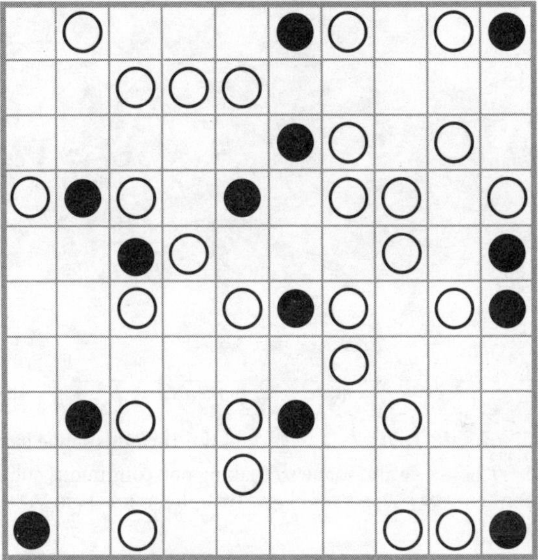

Answer on page 373

## WRINKLY QUOTE

"A 'senior moment' is a euphemism to indicate a temporary loss of marbles to anyone over 50."

ANON

## NUMBER MOUNTAIN: Replace the question marks with numbers so that each pair of blocks adds up to the block directly above them.

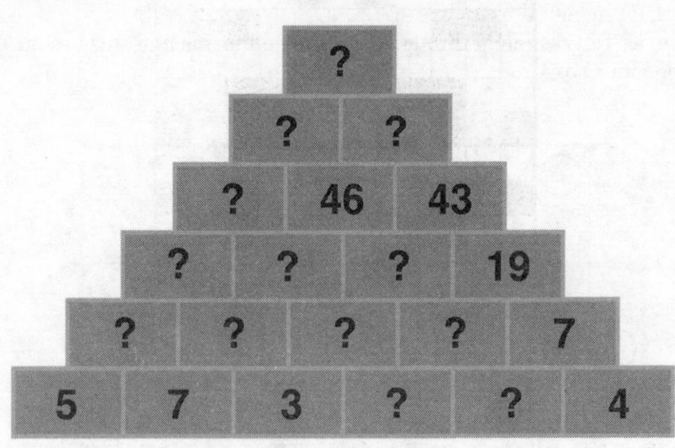


Answer on page 373

## MORE OR LESS SUDOKU: Complete the grid so that all rows and columns, and each outlined block of nine squares, contain the numbers 1, 2, 3, 4, 5, 6, 7, 8 and 9.

The numbers in the arrowed squares are bigger than the numbers in the squares the arrows are pointing at.

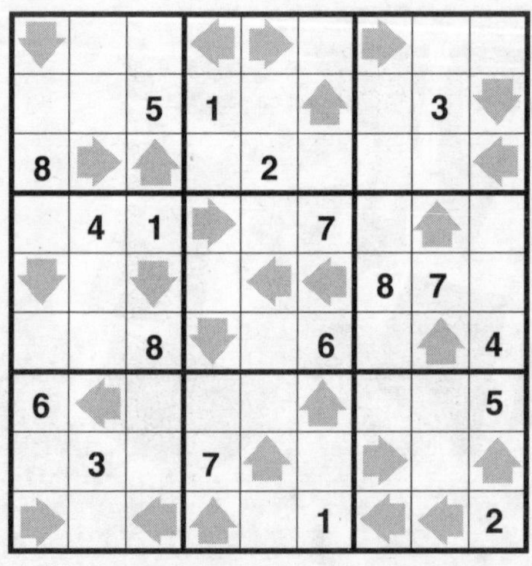


Answer on page 373

# NUMBER FILL-IN: Find homes for all the listed numbers to complete the grid.

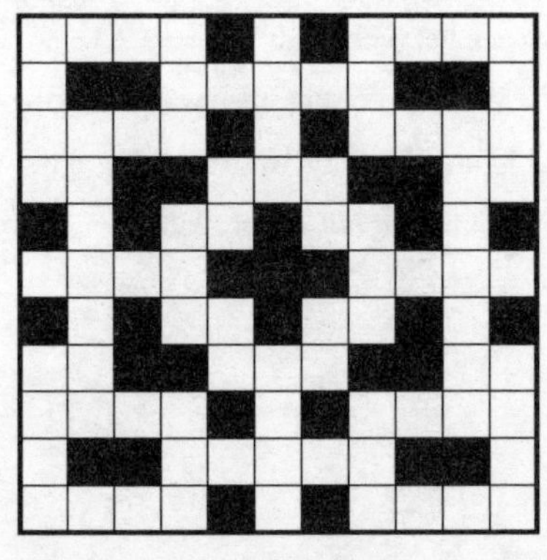

| | | | | | | | |
|---|---|---|---|---|---|---|---|
| 51 | 354 | 4488 | 28 | 578 | 1990 | 82 | 9120 | 6780 |
| 96 | 225 | 7276 | 50 | 534 | 1095 | 25 | 8547 | 2450 |
| 99 | 560 | 4045 | 26 | 121 | 2725 | 62720 | 1114400 | |
| 55 | 408 | 1547 | 39 | 1605 | 9676 | 35532 | 4967424 | |
| 18 | 981 | 2264 | 45 | 4459 | 5442 | | | |

Answer on page 374

# BITS AND PIECES: These pieces can be assembled to spell the name of a famous painter... Who?

Answer on page 374

# SMALL LOGIC:

Three professors were each studying different space phenomena, located in different directions and near different planets. Can you work out exactly who was looking in which direction at what, and what planet was near to each heavenly body?

1) Saturn was toward the West. Professor Green wasn't looking there.

2) The asteroid was near Jupiter. Fujyama wasn't looking at it.

3) Fujyama looked in the south, but not at a black hole.

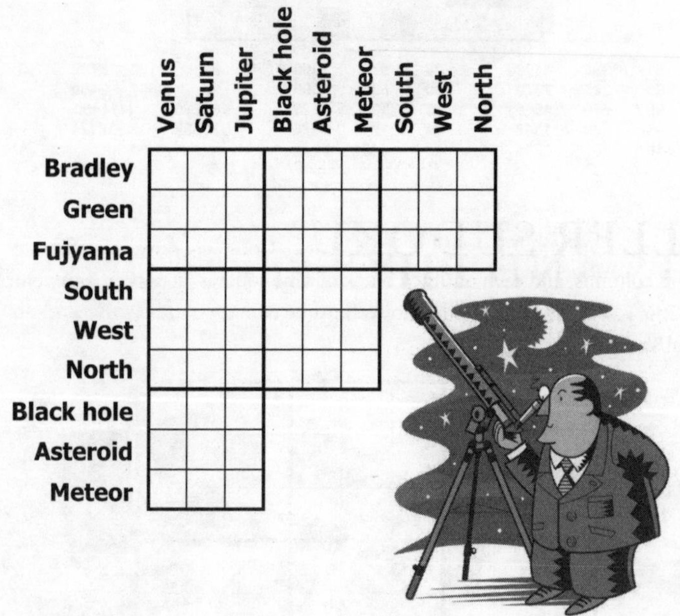


Answer on page 374

# CUBE VOLUME:

These little cubes originally made a big cube measuring 18 cm x 18 cm x 18 cm. Now some of the little cubes have been removed, can you work out what volume the remaining cubes have? Assume all invisible cubes are present.

Answer on page 374

# KILLER SUDOKU:

Complete the grid so that all rows and columns, and each outlined block of nine squares, contain the numbers 1, 2, 3, 4, 5, 6, 7, 8 and 9. Areas with a dotted outline contain numbers that add up to the total shown.

| 7 |  | 16 | 9 |  | 12 | 9 | 16 |  |
|---|---|---|---|---|---|---|---|---|
| 10 |  |  | 19 |  |  |  |  |  |
| 10 |  | **8** |  |  | 25 |  |  |  |
|  | 16 | 5 | 6 | 14 |  | 5 |  | 23 |
| 5 |  |  |  | 15 | 13 |  |  |  |
|  | 19 |  |  |  | 11 | 10 |  |  |
| 24 | 10 | 9 | 12 |  |  | 16 |  | 6 |
|  |  |  | 14 |  |  |  |  |  |
|  |  | 5 |  | 8 |  | **8** | 10 |  |

Answer on page 374

**SMALL LOGIC:** Phillipe, Luc and Bernard are ballooning in the mountains. From the clues below can you work out who travelled how far and landed in which country, and match each balloonist to their correct surname?

1) Phillipe travelled 50 miles, and he didn't land in Belgium.
2) Brunet (not Bernard), landed in Switzerland, more than 25 miles away from his take-off point.
3) The 25-mile flight landed in France, and wasn't piloted by Bernard or Dupont.

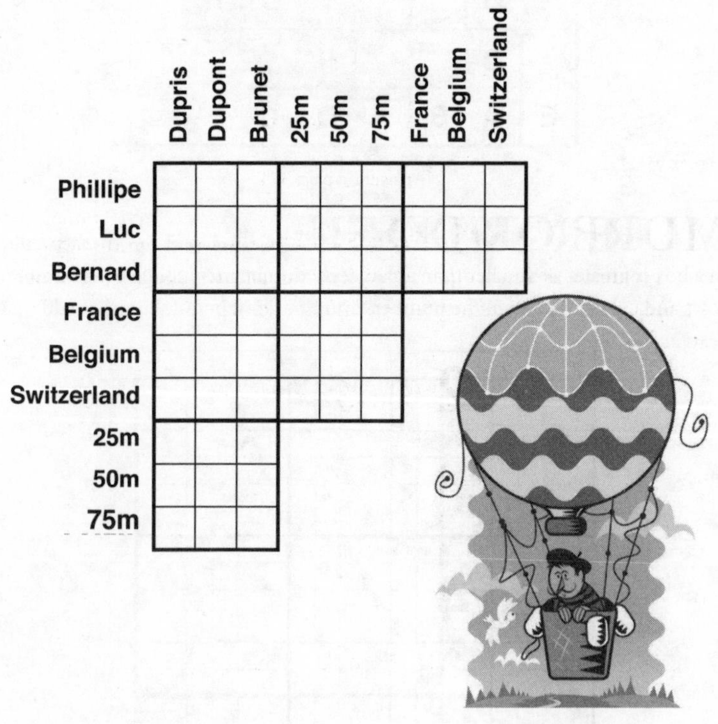


Answer on page 374

# LATIN SQUARE: Complete the grid so that every row and column, and every outlined area, contains the letters A to H.

| | | | | | | | |
|---|---|---|---|---|---|---|---|
| | | | | F | G | D | |
| | H | G | | E | | C | F |
| F | | A | | | | | |
| | | | | | E | | |
| | | | | | | A | |
| | B | | | | D | H | |
| | C | | | H | | | |
| E | A | B | | D | C | | |

Answer on page 374

# MORE OR LESS: The arrows indicate whether a number in a box is greater or smaller than an adjacent number. Complete the grid so that all rows and columns contain the numbers 1 to 5.

Answer on page 374

# MINI NONOGRAM:

The numbers by each row and column describe black squares and groups of black squares that are adjoining. Colour in all the black squares and a picture will be revealed.

| | | | | | | | | | | | | | | | | | | |
|---|---|---|---|---|---|---|---|---|---|---|---|---|---|---|---|---|---|---|
| | | | | | 1 | | | | | 2 | | | | | | | | |
| | | | | | 4 | | 4 | 4 | 3 | 2 | 1 | | | | | | | |
| | | | | | 1 | 5 | 2 | 2 | 1 | 1 | 2 | 3 | 1 | 10 | 9 | 8 | | 2 |
| | | | | 1 | 1 | 4 | 1 | 1 | 5 | 1 | 1 | 2 | 11 | 1 | 1 | 1 | 12 | 2 |
| | | 1 | 4 | | | | | | | | | | | | | | | |
| | | 5 | 3 | | | | | | | | | | | | | | | |
| | | 4 | 2 | | | | | | | | | | | | | | | |
| | | 4 | 4 | | | | | | | | | | | | | | | |
| | 3 | 1 | 5 | | | | | | | | | | | | | | | |
| | 2 | 1 | 7 | | | | | | | | | | | | | | | |
| | | 1 | 9 | | | | | | | | | | | | | | | |
| | | | 7 | | | | | | | | | | | | | | | |
| | | | 5 | | | | | | | | | | | | | | | |
| | | | 5 | | | | | | | | | | | | | | | |
| 1 | 1 | 2 | 2 | | | | | | | | | | | | | | | |
| | 5 | 1 | 1 | | | | | | | | | | | | | | | |
| | 4 | 1 | 1 | | | | | | | | | | | | | | | |
| 1 | 1 | 2 | 2 | | | | | | | | | | | | | | | |
| | | | 15 | | | | | | | | | | | | | | | |

Answer on page 375

## WRINKLY QUOTE

"Be yourself, be pleasant, play hard and have no regrets."

JIMMY BUFFETT

**SCALES:** The arms of these scales are divided into sections – a weight two sections away from the middle will be twice as heavy as a weight one section away. Can you arranged the supplied weights in such a way as to balance the whole scale?

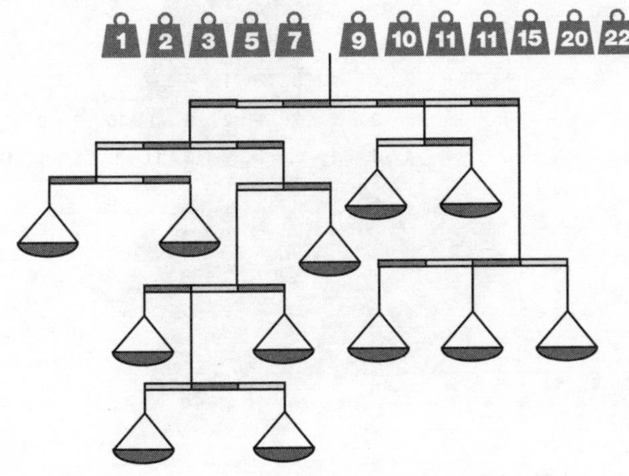


Answer on page 375

**SHAPE STACKER:** Can you work out the logic behind the numbers in these shapes, and whether A divided by B = C, D or E?

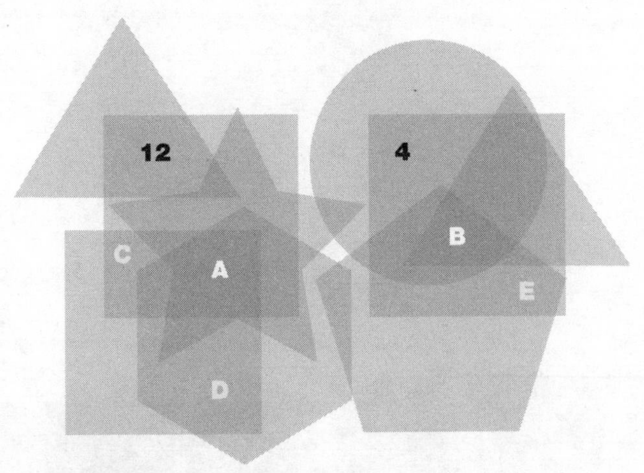


Answer on page 375

## CAN YOU CUT IT?: Turn this shape into three shapes that are identical in size and shape by making just two cuts.

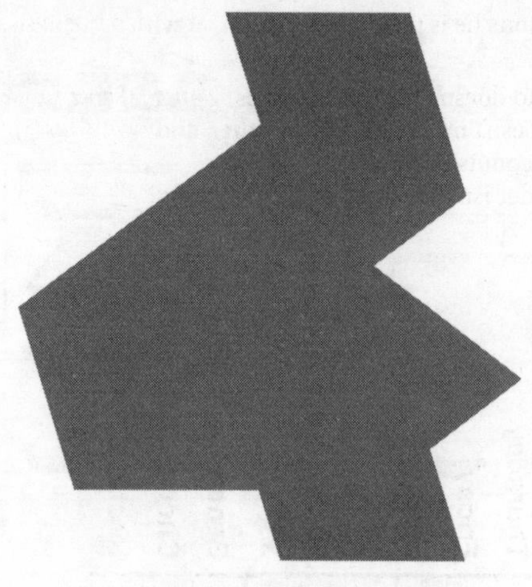

Answer on page 375

## CUBISM: The shape below can be folded to make a cube. Which of the four cubes pictured below could it make?

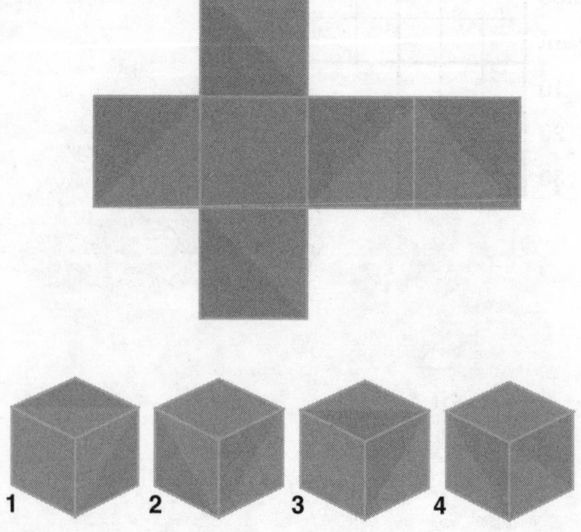


Answer on page 375

**SMALL LOGIC:** Swordfish Beach coconuts are in great demand on Marlin Island for their size and sweetness. Palm-climber Ray has a bunch to collect as the weekend approaches – can you work out from the clues below how many nuts he is picking for whom, at which business, and when he must deliver?

1) Arthur, who doesn't make chocolates, wants 30 coconuts.
2) Big Dan doesn't make chocolates either, and wants less than 20 coconuts on Saturday.
3) Friday's order isn't for Alice or the Beach Bar.

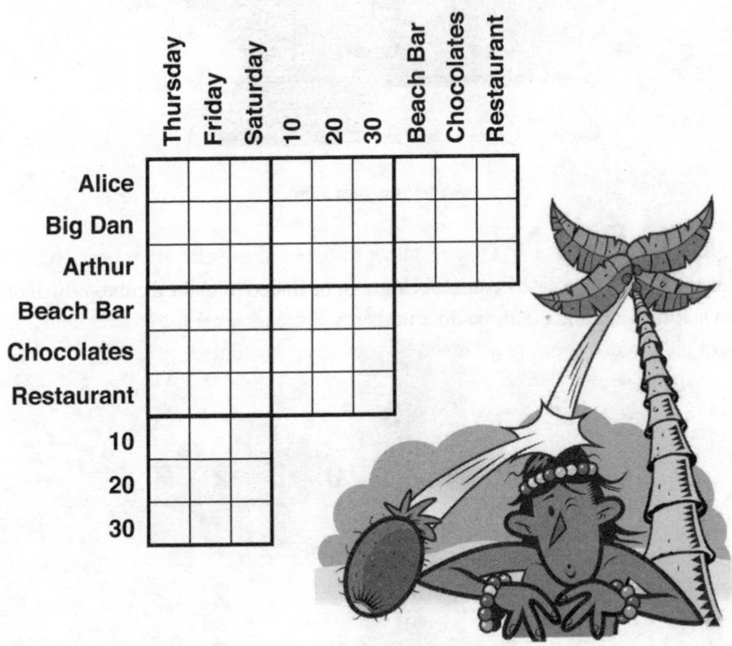


Answer on page 375

# SCALES:

The arms of these scales are divided into sections – a weight two sections away from the middle will be twice as heavy as a weight one section away. Can you arranged the supplied the weights in such a way as to balance the whole scale?

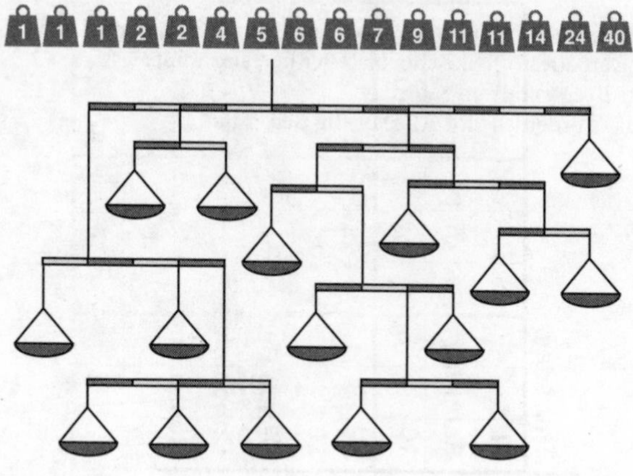


Answer on page 376

# LOOPLINK:

Connect adjacent dots with either horizontal or vertical lines to create a continuous unbroken loop which never crosses over itself. Some (but not all) of the boxes contain numbers revealing exactly how many sides of that box are occupied by your unbroken line.

| | | | | | | | |
|---|---|---|---|---|---|---|---|
| 2 | | 2 | 3 | | 2 | | 3 |
| 2 | 0 | 1 | | 0 | 3 | 2 | 2 |
| 3 | | 3 | 2 | | 2 | 1 | |
| 2 | 0 | 2 | 1 | 2 | | 2 | 2 |
| | 0 | | 2 | 3 | | 2 | 1 |
| 2 | 2 | | 1 | | 2 | | |
| | | 3 | 2 | | 2 | 3 | 2 |
| 3 | 1 | | 2 | 3 | 2 | | 2 |

Answer on page 376

# MORE OR LESS SUDOKU: Complete

the grid so that all rows and columns, and each outlined block of nine squares, contain the numbers 1, 2, 3, 4, 5, 6, 7, 8, and 9. The numbers in the arrowed squares are bigger than the numbers in the squares the arrows are pointing at.

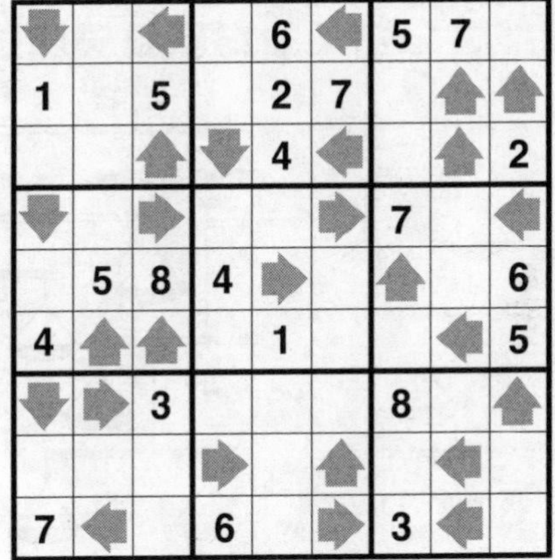

Answer on page 376

# NUMBER MOUNTAIN: Replace the

question marks with numbers so that each pair of blocks adds up to the number on the block directly above them.

Answer on page 376

# NUMBER CHUNKS: 

Divide up the grid into four equal sized, equally shaped parts, each containing numbers that add up to 50.

| 8 | 9 | 8 | 7 | 6 | 4 |
|---|---|---|---|---|---|
| 9 | 3 | 6 | 1 | 5 | 7 |
| 7 | 1 | 9 | 4 | 7 | 3 |
| 9 | 2 | 9 | 5 | 6 | 3 |
| 2 | 1 | 2 | 9 | 9 | 3 |
| 5 | 5 | 5 | 5 | 9 | 7 |

Answer on page 376

# SAFECRACKER: 

To open the safe, all the buttons must be pressed in the correct order before the "open" button is pressed. What is the first button pressed in your sequence?

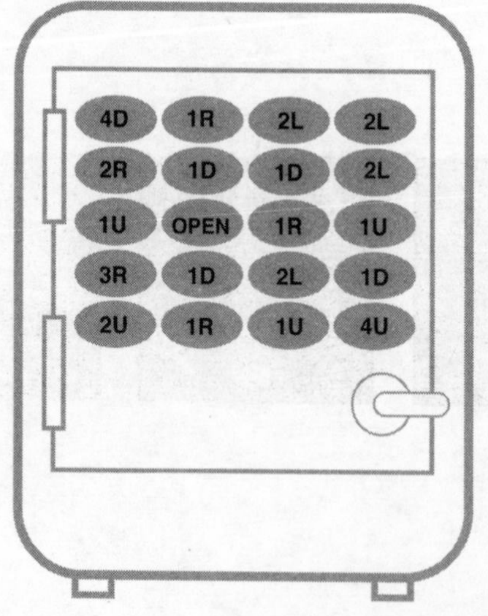


Answer on page 376

# PRICE PUZZLE:

Buying the prizes for your local school fete, you have been given a budget of 100 pounds, which you managed to spend exactly. If you bought 6 bears and 18 items altogether, how many dolls did you buy?

Answer on page 376

# CORNERED!:

Use the corner numbers to make the central number. What number should replace the question mark?

Answer on page 376

## SYMMETRY:

This picture, when finished, is symmetrical along a vertical line up the middle. Can you colour in the missing squares and work out what the picture is of?

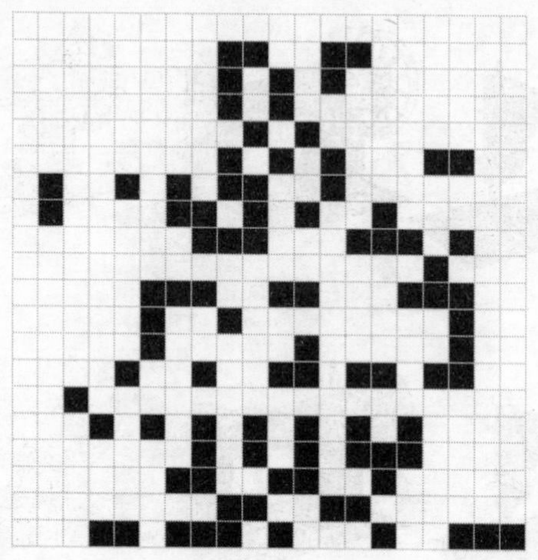

Answer on page 377

## SUDOKU:

Complete the grid so that all rows and columns, and each outlined block of nine squares, contain the numbers 1, 2, 3, 4, 5, 6, 7, 8 and 9.

| | | | | | | | | |
|---|---|---|---|---|---|---|---|---|
| | | | 6 | | | | 2 | |
| | 2 | | | | | 6 | | |
| 8 | 9 | | 4 | | 3 | 1 | | 7 |
| | 4 | 1 | | | | 5 | | |
| | | | | | | 8 | | 1 |
| | 7 | 8 | 5 | | 6 | | | |
| | | 2 | | 4 | | | | 5 |
| 1 | 3 | | | 5 | 2 | 9 | 8 | 6 |
| 9 | | | | | 1 | 3 | | |

Answer on page 377

# SILHOUETTE: Which of the coloured-in pics matches our silhouette?

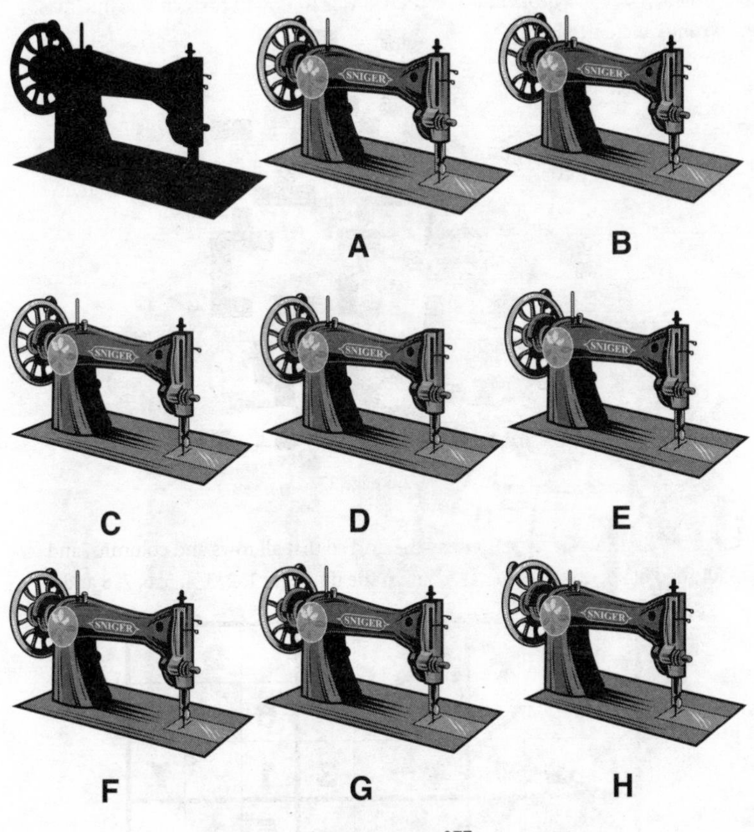


Answer on page 377

## WRINKLY QUOTE

"A good plan today is better than a perfect plan tomorrow."

ROBERT DE NIRO, *WAG THE DOG*

**RIDDLE:** Ten chocolate machines make truffles that weigh ten grams each. One day, one of the machines goes wrong and starts making truffles that only weigh 9.5 grams. If you weighed a truffle from each machine, you could find out which one has broken. But is there a way to find out which machine has gone wrong quicker than that?

Answer on page 377

## MINI NONOGRAM:

The numbers by each row and column describe black squares and groups of black squares that are adjoining. Colour in all the black squares and picture will be revealed.

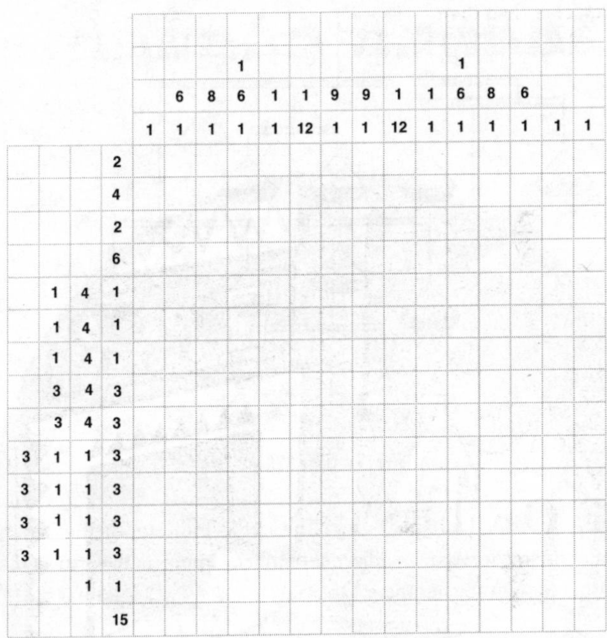


Answer on page 377

## DICE PUZZLE:

Which of these dice is not like the other three?

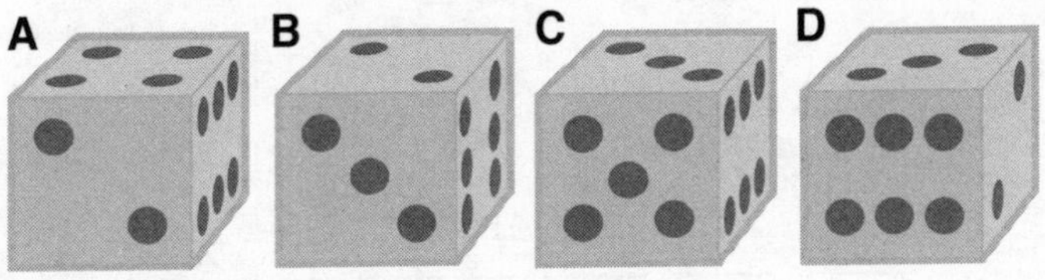


Answer on page 377

## SCALES:

The arms of these scales are divided into sections – a weight two sections away from the middle will be twice as heavy as a weight one section away. Can you arranged the supplied weights in such a way as to balance the whole scale?

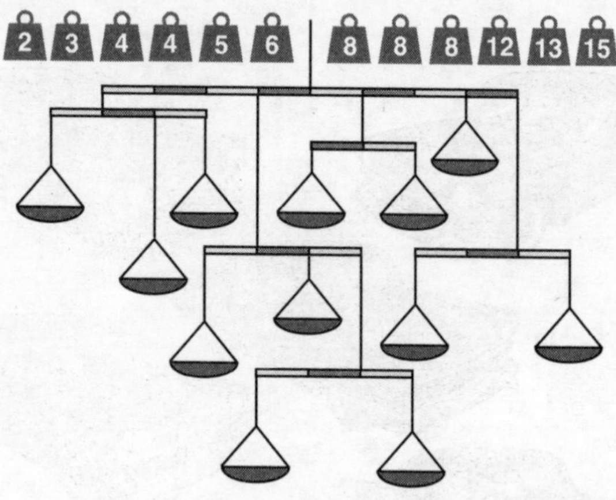


Answer on page 378

## MORE OR LESS:

The arrows indicate whether a number in a box is greater or smaller than an adjacent number. Complete the grid so that all rows and columns contain the numbers 1 to 6.

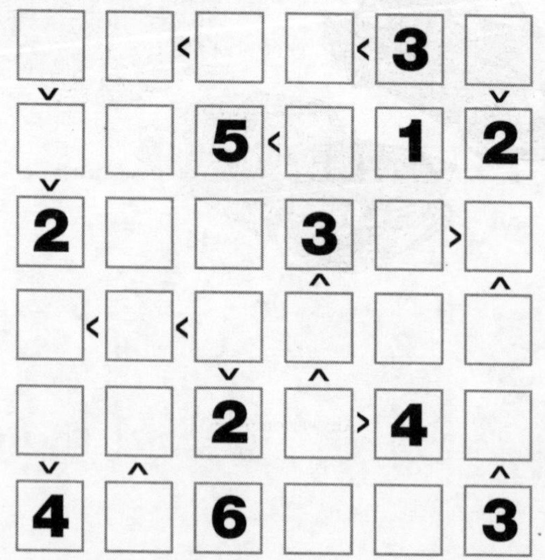


Answer on page 378

# MIRROR IMAGE: Only one of these pictures is an exact mirror image of the first one.Can you spot it?

Answer on page 378

# SUDOKU:

Complete the grid so that the numbers 1, 2, 3, 4, 5, 6, 7, 8 and 9 appear once only in each column, row and 9x9 box.

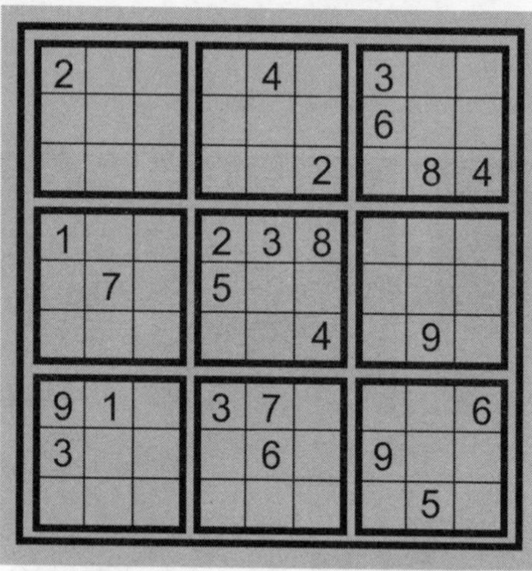

Answer on page 378

# LOOPLINK:

Connect adjacent dots with either horizontal or vertical lines to create a continuous unbroken loop which never crosses over itself. Some (but not all) of the boxes contain numbers revealing exactly how many sides of that box are occupied by your unbroken line.

| | | | | | | | |
|---|---|---|---|---|---|---|---|
| 2 | | 2 | 0 | | 2 | | 2 |
| 3 | 0 | 3 | | 3 | 0 | 1 | 3 |
| 3 | | | 1 | 3 | 2 | 3 | 2 |
| | 1 | 2 | 2 | | 1 | | 2 |
| 2 | | | | 1 | | 3 | |
| 2 | 2 | 3 | 2 | 2 | 3 | | 1 |
| | | 3 | | 1 | | 3 | |
| 2 | | 2 | 2 | 2 | 3 | 2 | 2 |

Answer on page 378

**CORNERED!:** Use the corner numbers to make the central number the same way in all three cases. What number should replace the question mark?

Answer on page 378

**REVOLUTIONS:** Cog A has 16 teeth, cog B has 8, cog C has 9, cog D has 10 and cog E has 18. How many revolutions must cog A turn through to get all the cogs back into their original position?

Answer on page 378

# ANSWERS

## Page 201

### MASYU

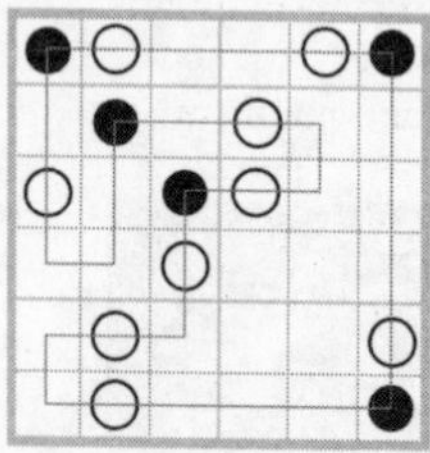

### BIT AND PIECES

Answer: A and C, B and E, H and F, D and G

## Page 202

### BOXES

Solution: A line on the top or bottom of this square will only give up one box to your opponent.

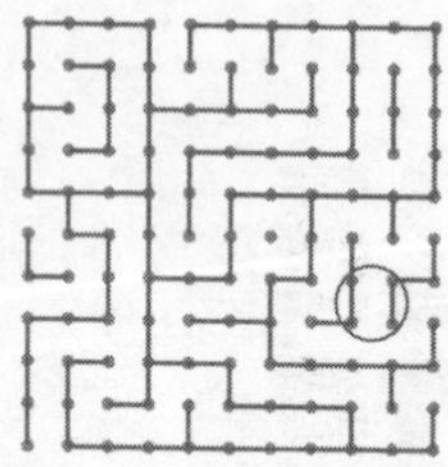

### CAN YOU CUT IT?

## Page 203

### SUDOKU

| | | | | | | | | |
|---|---|---|---|---|---|---|---|---|
| 4 | 7 | 1 | 8 | 5 | 6 | 2 | 9 | 3 |
| 8 | 6 | 2 | 7 | 9 | 3 | 4 | 1 | 5 |
| 5 | 9 | 3 | 4 | 1 | 2 | 8 | 7 | 6 |
| 2 | 5 | 7 | 9 | 6 | 8 | 1 | 3 | 4 |
| 6 | 8 | 9 | 1 | 3 | 4 | 5 | 2 | 7 |
| 1 | 3 | 4 | 2 | 7 | 5 | 9 | 6 | 8 |
| 7 | 1 | 5 | 3 | 8 | 9 | 6 | 4 | 2 |
| 3 | 4 | 6 | 5 | 2 | 1 | 7 | 8 | 9 |
| 9 | 2 | 8 | 6 | 4 | 7 | 3 | 5 | 1 |

## Page 204

### WHERE'S THE PAIR?

Answer: C and E are the pair

## Page 205

### RIDDLE

Answer: It was driven there in winter, when the lake was frozen.

## Page 206

### ODD CLOCKS

Answer: 3.35 am on Wednesday in London; 11.35 pm on Tuesday in Buenos Aires

### SUM TOTAL

Solution: $22 + 8 \div 5 - 3 = 3$

## Page 207

### CHECKERS

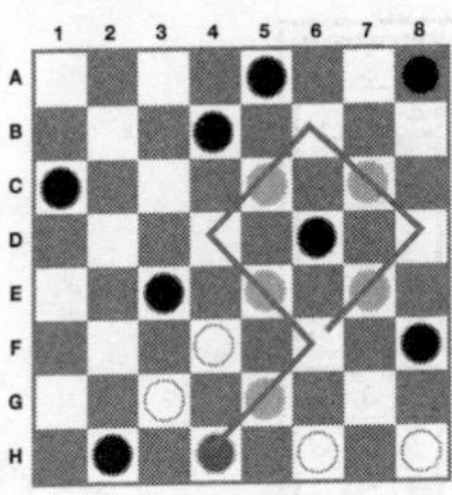

### CUT AND FOLD

Answer: A

## Page 208

### DOUBLE DRAT

### GAME OF TWO HALVES

Solution: C and D

## Page 209

### GRIDLOCK

Answer: B. Each row and column in the grid contains four dark and three light squares, and numbers that total 10

### MASYU

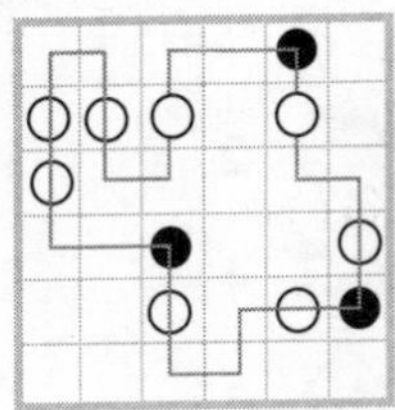

## Page 210

### MINI NONOGRAM

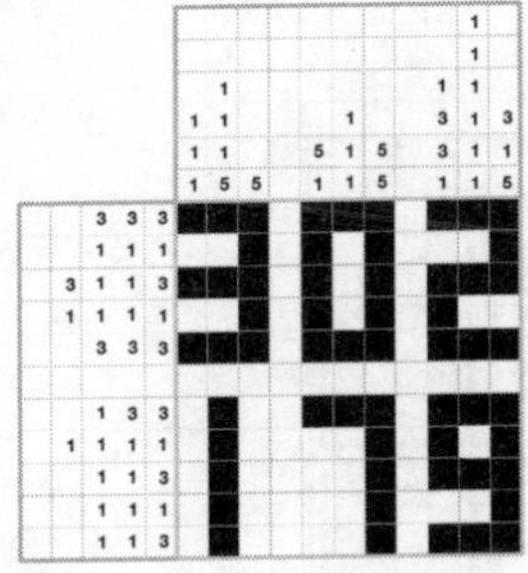

### PICTURE PARTS

Answer: A

## Page 211

### MIRROR IMAGE

Answer: G

**Page 212**

**WHERE'S THE PAIR?**
Answer: B and E are the pair

**Page 213**

**SUM PEOPLE**
Solution: 23

2

4

6

9

**Page 214**

**SUDOKU**

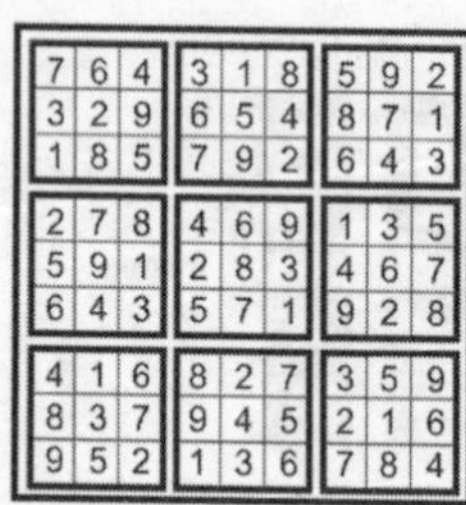

| | | | | | | | | |
|---|---|---|---|---|---|---|---|---|
| 7 | 6 | 4 | 3 | 1 | 8 | 5 | 9 | 2 |
| 3 | 2 | 9 | 6 | 5 | 4 | 8 | 7 | 1 |
| 1 | 8 | 5 | 7 | 9 | 2 | 6 | 4 | 3 |
| 2 | 7 | 8 | 4 | 6 | 9 | 1 | 3 | 5 |
| 5 | 9 | 1 | 2 | 8 | 3 | 4 | 6 | 7 |
| 6 | 4 | 3 | 5 | 7 | 1 | 9 | 2 | 8 |
| 4 | 1 | 6 | 8 | 2 | 7 | 3 | 5 | 9 |
| 8 | 3 | 7 | 9 | 4 | 5 | 2 | 1 | 6 |
| 9 | 5 | 2 | 1 | 3 | 6 | 7 | 8 | 4 |

**Page 215**

**SHAPE SHIFTING**

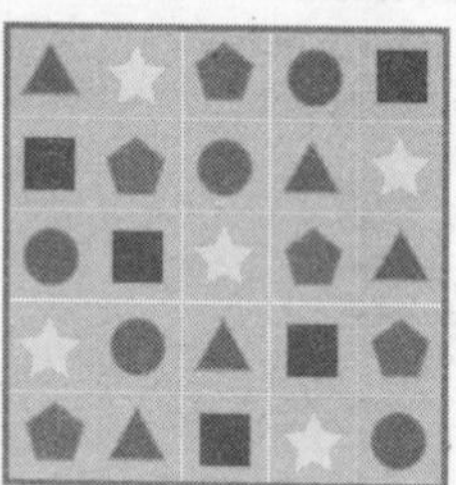

**NUMBER MOUNTAIN**

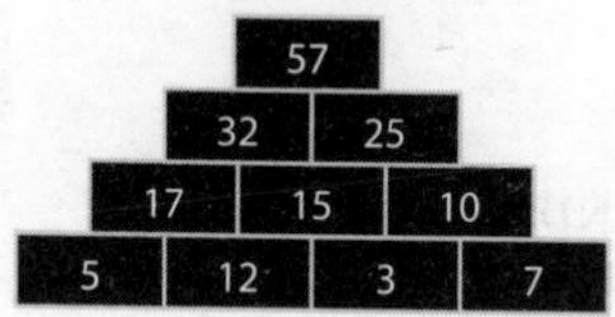


**Page 216**

**POTS OF DOTS**

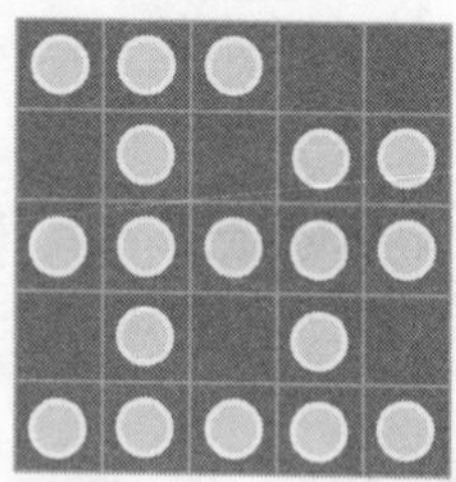

Answer: 18

**BOCK PARTY**
Answer: 37

**Page 217**

BOXES
Solution: A line on the left or bottom of this square will only give up one box to our opponent

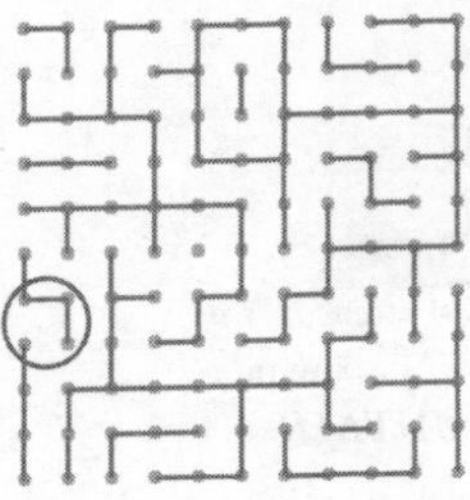

**Page 218**

CATS AND COGS
Answer: Down

CUT AND FOLD
Answer: A

**Page 219**

RIDDLE
Answer: 20 times. 9, 19, 29, 39, 49, 59, 69, 79, 89, 90, 91, 92, 93, 94, 95, 96, 97, 98 and twice in 99.

SUM TOTAL
Solution: $8 \times 3 \div 6 \times 2 = 8$

**Page 220**

ODD CLOCKS
Answer: 5.05 am on Friday in Tokyo
1.05 am on Friday in Karachi

POTS OF DOTS
Solution: 19

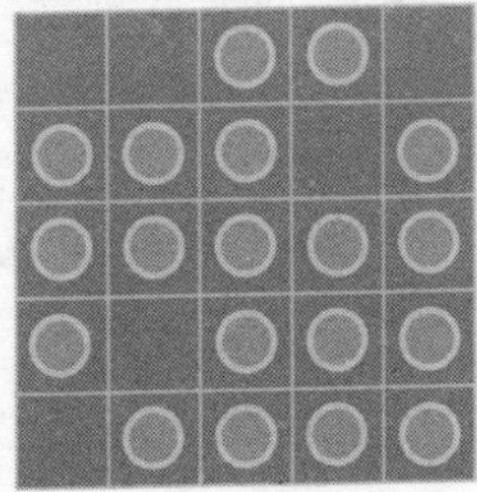

**Page 221**

RIDDLE
Answer: Because nobody knew it was World War One at the time

**Page 222**

**GAME OF TWO HALVES**
Solution: B and F

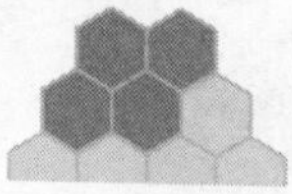

**MATRIX**
Solution: Each horizontal and vertical line contains one dog with a white ear.
Each line contains two dogs with a white patched eye.
Each line contains two dogs with their tongues out.
The missing image must have a white patched eye, no white ear, and the tongue out.

**Page 223**

**WHERE'S THE PAIR?**
Answer: D and H are the pair

**Page 224**

**BITS AND PIECES**
Answer: A, C, G and H, B, D, E and F (The letters are A and B)

**BLOCK PARTY**
Answer: 42

**Page 225**

**RIDDLE-ME-TEA**
Answer: I had put sugar in my tea, and the "new" cup, which should have been unsugared, was sweet!

**Page 226**

**WHERE'S THE PAIR?**
Answer: E and I are the pair

**Page 227**

**MIRROR IMAGE**
Answer: G

**SUM TOTAL**
Solution: $10 \div 2 \times 4 - 7 = 13$

**Page 228**

Answer: C and E are the pair.

**Page 229**

## MAGIC SQUARES

| 5 | 10 | 3 |
|---|---|---|
| 4 | 6 | 8 |
| 9 | 2 | 7 |

## PICTURE PARTS
Answer: B

**Page 230**

## MAGIC SQUARE

| 8 | 13 | 6 |
|---|---|---|
| 7 | 9 | 11 |
| 12 | 5 | 10 |

## PICTURE PARTS
Answer: B

**Page 231**

## WHERE'S THE PAIR?
Answer: C and G are the pair

**Page 232**

## BOX IT

## SUDOKU SIX
Solution: MOZART

| L | G | Y | W | R | M |
|---|---|---|---|---|---|
| Y | M | G | L | W | R |
| M | W | R | G | L | Y |
| W | R | M | Y | G | L |
| R | L | W | M | Y | G |
| G | Y | L | R | M | W |

| 4 | 6 | 2 | 1 | 3 | 5 |
|---|---|---|---|---|---|
| 3 | 1 | 6 | 2 | 5 | 4 |
| 5 | 4 | 3 | 6 | 2 | 1 |
| 6 | 2 | 1 | 5 | 4 | 3 |
| 2 | 5 | 4 | 3 | 1 | 6 |
| 1 | 3 | 5 | 4 | 6 | 2 |

**Page 233**

## BOXES
Solution: A line on the left or right of this square will only give up one box to your opponent

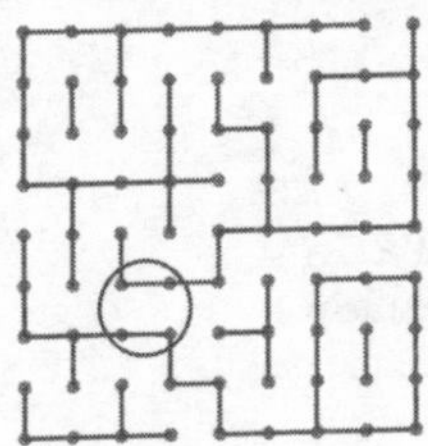

## REVOLUTIONS
Answer: 10 revolutions of cog A, which will make exactly 15 revolutions of cog B and 12 revolutions of cog C

**Page 234**

## CHECKERS

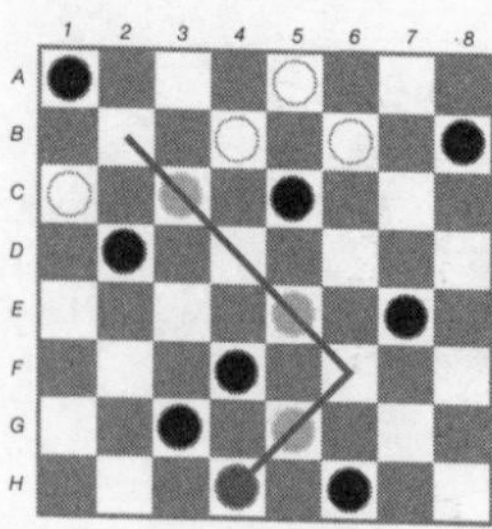


## SUM TOTAL

Answer:

A) 6 – Add opposite numbers and multiply the integers of the total

B) 12 – Multiply the opposite numbers, then multiply the integers of the total

**Page 235**

## WHERE'S THE PAIR?

Answer: A and G are the pair

**Page 236**

## WHERE'S THE PAIR?

Answer: E and I are the pair

**Page 237**

## ODD CLOCKS

Answer: 3.30 am on Tuesday in Reykjavic. 5.30 am on Tuesday in Cairo

## LATIN SQUARE

| B | D | A | C | E | F |
|---|---|---|---|---|---|
| D | C | E | A | F | B |
| E | F | C | D | B | A |
| A | B | F | E | D | C |
| C | E | B | F | A | D |
| F | A | D | B | C | E |

**Page 238**

## SAFECRACKER

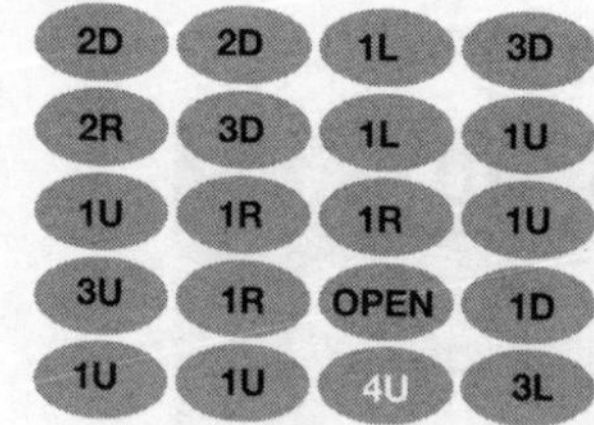


## SUM TOTAL

Solution: $14 \times 2 \div 7 + 1 = 5$

**Page 239**

## HUB SIGNS
Answer:
A) 6 – Add opposite numbers and multiply the integers of the total
B) 12 – Multiply the opposite numbers, then multiply the integers of the total

## CUT AND FOLD
Answer : B

**Page 240**

## WHERE'S THE PAIR?
Answer: B and H are the pair

**Page 241**

## POTS OF DOTS

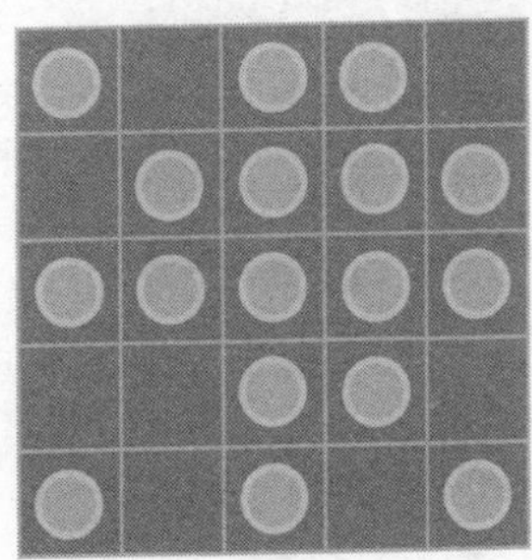

## SHAPE STACKER
Answer: A = 20 and B = 160
The numbers represent the number of sides in the shape they occupy. When shapes overlap, the numbers are multiplied. 5 x 4 x 1 = 20 and 4 x 4 x 10 = 160

**Page 242**

## SUDOKU SIXPACK

| | | | | | |
|---|---|---|---|---|---|
| 2 | 1 | 4 | 3 | 5 | 6 |
| 1 | 4 | 6 | 2 | 3 | 5 |
| 3 | 6 | 5 | 1 | 2 | 4 |
| 5 | 3 | 2 | 6 | 4 | 1 |
| 6 | 5 | 3 | 4 | 1 | 2 |
| 4 | 2 | 1 | 5 | 6 | 3 |

## DOUBLE DRAT

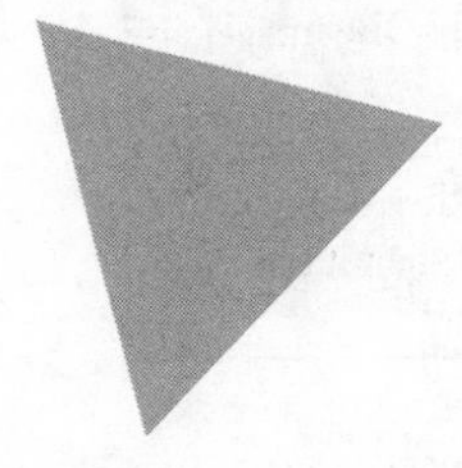

**Page 243**

## CUBISM
Answer: 4

## GAME OF TWO HALVES
Solution: C and E

## Page 244

### MORE OR LESS

| | | | | | | | | |
|---|---|---|---|---|---|---|---|---|
| 1 | | 2 | | 5 | > | 3 | | 4 |
| ^ | | ^ | | | | v | | ^ |
| 3 | | 4 | > | 1 | | 2 | | 5 |
| v | | | | | | | | |
| 2 | | 3 | < | 4 | | 5 | | 1 |
| | | | | | | v | | ^ |
| 5 | | 1 | | 2 | < | 4 | | 3 |
| | | | | ^ | | | | |
| 4 | < | 5 | | 3 | > | 1 | | 2 |

### NUMBER SWEEP

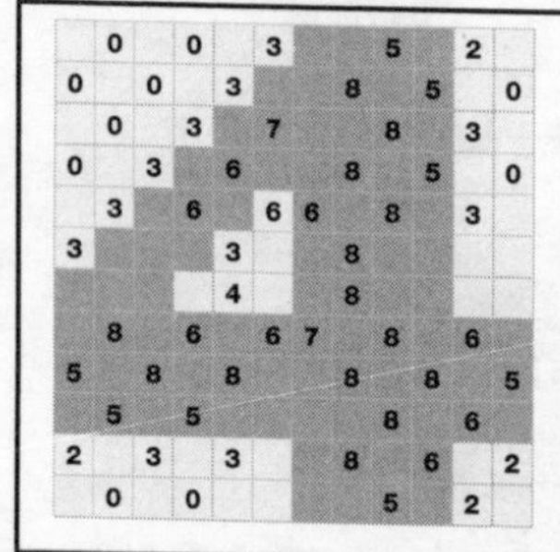

## Page 245

### MIRROR IMAGE
Answer: G

## Page 246

### PAINT BY NUMBERS
Solution: A Footballer

## Page 247

### PICTURE PARTS
Answer: C

### RADAR

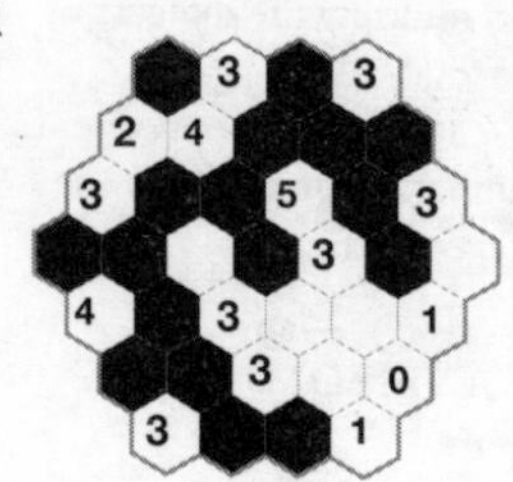

## Page 248

### SILHOUETTE
Answer: D

## Page 249

### PICTURE PARTS
Answer: C

### SUM TOTAL
Solution: 35 – 7 ÷ 4 – 4 = 3

## Page 251

### FOLLOW THAT
Answer: B, the right way up. Two letters the same are followed by a letter the right way up. Two letters the same way up are followed by a B

### FRACTION ACTION
Answer: There are 117 tiles in the finished job, 36 of which are missing. 117 divided by 9 is 13, and 36 divided by 9 is 4. So 4/13ths of the job remains unfinished

## Page 252

### MASYU

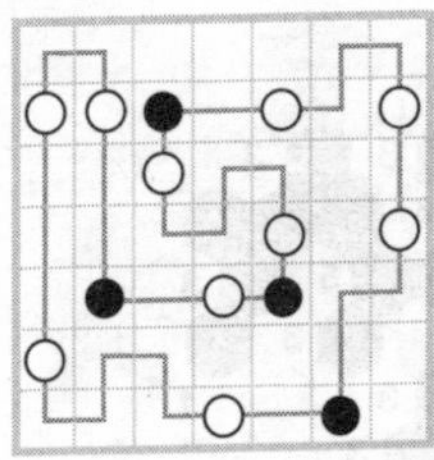

### MATRIX

Solution: Each vertical and horizontal line contains one light shaded, one dark shaded and one plain white circle. Each line also contains one light shaded, one dark shaded and one plain white hexagon. Each line contains right-side-up triangles in light shading, dark shading and plain white. Finally each line contains two inverted triangles in light shading and one in dark shading. The missing image should be of a plain white circle with a white hexagon and both triangles in light shading

## Page 253

### MINESWEEPER

### MORE OR LESS

| | | | | | | | | |
|---|---|---|---|---|---|---|---|---|
| 2 | | 4 | | 3 | | 1 | | 5 |
| ^ | | v | | v | | | | v |
| 5 | | 2 | | 1 | | 4 | > | 3 |
| | | | | ^ | | | | ^ |
| 1 | | 5 | | 2 | < | 3 | < | 4 |
| | | | | ^ | | | | |
| 3 | | 1 | | 4 | < | 5 | | 2 |
| 4 | > | 3 | | 5 | > | 2 | | 1 |

## Page 254

### A PIECE OF PIE

Answer: 16. The inner numbers are made up of the two outer numbers of the previous segment of the same colour. 9 + 7= 16

### X AND O

| | | | | | | |
|---|---|---|---|---|---|---|
| 2 | 3 | 2 | 2 | 4 | 3 | 3 |
| 4 | O | X | O | O | X | 3 |
| 2 | X | O | O | X | O | 4 |
| 3 | O | X | O | X | O | 2 |
| 3 | O | O | X | X | O | 4 |
| 3 | X | O | O | O | X | 3 |
| 3 | 4 | 3 | 1 | 4 | 5 | 2 |

## Page 255

### WHERE'S THE PAIR?

Answer: D and H are the pair

## Page 256

### RIDDLE

Answer: Gordon puts his egg in the water and starts both his timers at once.When the 4 minute timer is done, he flips it (4 minutes gone). When the 7 minute timer is done he flips it (7 minutes gone). At this point there is one minute to go on the 4 minute timer. When the 4 minute timer finishes (8 minutes gone) Gordon flips the 7 once more to let the 1 minute it has run go back the other way. 9 minutes.

## Page 257

### SUM PEOPLE

Solution: 22

## Page 258

### SAFECRACKER

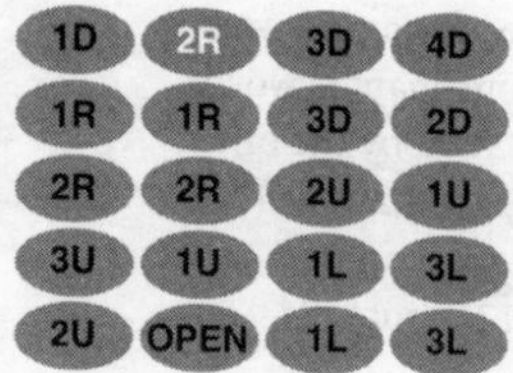


### DICE PUZZLE

Answer: F

## Page 259

### MIRROR IMAGE

Answer: E

## Page 260

### LATIN SQUARE

| B | A | E | D | C | F |
|---|---|---|---|---|---|
| F | E | A | C | D | B |
| E | B | D | A | F | C |
| D | F | C | E | B | A |
| C | D | F | B | A | E |
| A | C | B | F | E | D |

### SCALES

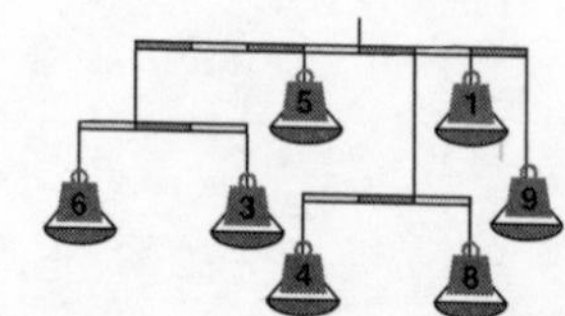

**Page 261**

## SIGNATURES

Answer: 24

Each vowel in each name is worth 1 point, each consonant is worth 3. Multiply one total by the other to make the number. 2 vowels (2) times
4 consonants (12) equals 24

## SUDOKU

| | | | | | | | | |
|---|---|---|---|---|---|---|---|---|
| 8 | 2 | 9 | 7 | 1 | 6 | 5 | 3 | 4 |
| 1 | 3 | 6 | 4 | 5 | 2 | 8 | 9 | 7 |
| 5 | 4 | 7 | 9 | 3 | 8 | 1 | 2 | 6 |
| 9 | 1 | 2 | 6 | 7 | 3 | 4 | 8 | 5 |
| 6 | 5 | 8 | 1 | 2 | 4 | 3 | 7 | 9 |
| 4 | 7 | 3 | 8 | 9 | 5 | 6 | 1 | 2 |
| 3 | 8 | 4 | 2 | 6 | 7 | 9 | 5 | 1 |
| 7 | 6 | 1 | 5 | 8 | 9 | 2 | 4 | 3 |
| 2 | 9 | 5 | 3 | 4 | 1 | 7 | 6 | 8 |

**Page 262**

## WHERE'S THE PAIR?

Answer: B and D are the pair.

**Page 263**

## FLOOR FILLERS

## KILLER SIX

| | | | | | |
|---|---|---|---|---|---|
| 4 | 3 | 1 | 2 | 6 | 5 |
| 5 | 1 | 6 | 4 | 2 | 3 |
| 3 | 2 | 5 | 1 | 4 | 6 |
| 6 | 4 | 3 | 5 | 1 | 2 |
| 1 | 5 | 2 | 6 | 3 | 4 |
| 2 | 6 | 4 | 3 | 5 | 1 |

**Page 264**

## LATIN SQUARE

| | | | | | |
|---|---|---|---|---|---|
| F | B | C | A | E | D |
| C | D | F | B | A | E |
| D | C | A | E | B | F |
| E | A | D | C | F | B |
| A | E | B | F | D | C |
| B | F | E | D | C | A |

## MASYU

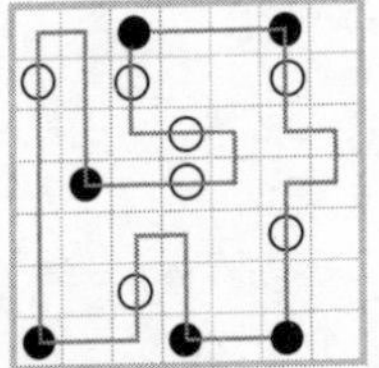

**Page 265**

**ODD CLOCKS**
Answer: 7.20 pm on Saturday in London, 4.20pm on Sunday in Sydney.

**SHUFFLE**

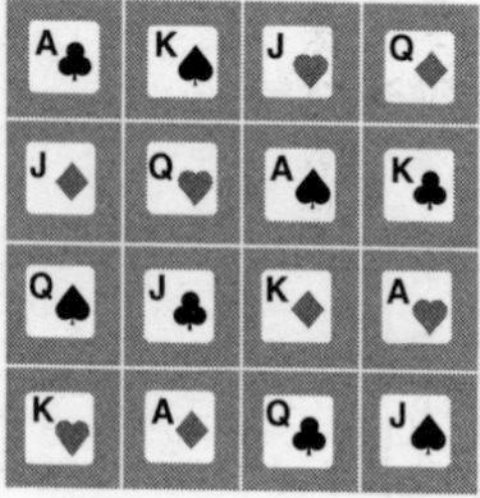


**Page 266**

**RIDDLE**
Answer: This is possible only if all the boxes are incorrectly labelled. Charlie takes one record from the box labelled J&S. If it's a Jazz record, then the (wrongly labelled) box it came from must be Jazz. If the (wrongly labelled) box marked Soul isn't Jazz, it can only be J&S. If he had taken out a Soul record then the box it came from must be Soul and the box marked Jazz must be J&S.

**Page 267**

**SUDOKU**

| | | | | | | | | |
|---|---|---|---|---|---|---|---|---|
| 8 | 7 | 9 | 6 | 1 | 4 | 2 | 5 | 3 |
| 1 | 2 | 4 | 3 | 5 | 9 | 6 | 7 | 8 |
| 5 | 6 | 3 | 7 | 8 | 2 | 1 | 4 | 9 |
| 2 | 1 | 6 | 9 | 3 | 7 | 4 | 8 | 5 |
| 4 | 3 | 8 | 5 | 2 | 1 | 9 | 6 | 7 |
| 7 | 9 | 5 | 8 | 4 | 6 | 3 | 1 | 2 |
| 9 | 4 | 1 | 2 | 7 | 5 | 8 | 3 | 6 |
| 6 | 8 | 7 | 1 | 9 | 3 | 5 | 2 | 4 |
| 3 | 5 | 2 | 4 | 6 | 8 | 7 | 9 | 1 |

**Page 268**

**SUM PEOPLE**
Solution: 16

**Page 269**

**WHERE'S THE PAIR?**
Answer: B and F are the pair

**Page 270**

**WHERE'S THE PAIR?**
Answer: B and G are the pair

**Page 271**

**BOX IT**

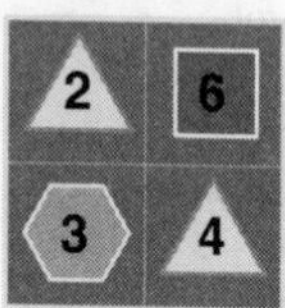

## Page 272

### KILLER SIX

| | | | | | |
|---|---|---|---|---|---|
| 1 | 6 | 4 | 3 | 5 | 2 |
| 4 | 5 | 3 | 1 | 2 | 6 |
| 5 | 1 | 2 | 6 | 4 | 3 |
| 6 | 2 | 1 | 4 | 3 | 5 |
| 2 | 3 | 6 | 5 | 1 | 4 |
| 3 | 4 | 5 | 2 | 6 | 1 |

### MORE OR LESS

| | | | | | |
|---|---|---|---|---|---|
| 6 | 1 | 5 > | 4 | 2 < | 3 |
| 3 < | 4 | 6 | 2 | 5 | 1 |
| 5 | 6 | 4 > | 3 | 1 | 2 |
| 1 | 3 | 2 | 5 | 6 | 4 |
| 4 | 2 | 1 | 6 | 3 | 5 |
| 2 | 5 > | 3 | 1 | 4 < | 6 |

## Page 273

### SUDOKU

| | | | | | | | | |
|---|---|---|---|---|---|---|---|---|
| 9 | 2 | 4 | 1 | 6 | 8 | 5 | 7 | 3 |
| 1 | 3 | 5 | 9 | 2 | 7 | 6 | 8 | 4 |
| 8 | 6 | 7 | 3 | 4 | 5 | 1 | 9 | 2 |
| 3 | 1 | 6 | 2 | 5 | 9 | 7 | 4 | 8 |
| 2 | 5 | 8 | 4 | 7 | 3 | 9 | 1 | 6 |
| 4 | 7 | 9 | 8 | 1 | 6 | 2 | 3 | 5 |
| 6 | 4 | 3 | 5 | 9 | 1 | 9 | 2 | 7 |
| 5 | 8 | 1 | 7 | 3 | 2 | 4 | 6 | 9 |
| 7 | 9 | 2 | 6 | 8 | 4 | 3 | 5 | 1 |

### THINK OF A NUMBER

Answer: 18. Yellowbeard got 240, the navigator and best mate got 180 between them leaving 300. If Tom got 20, there must be 15 crew

## Page 274

### MINI NONOGRAM

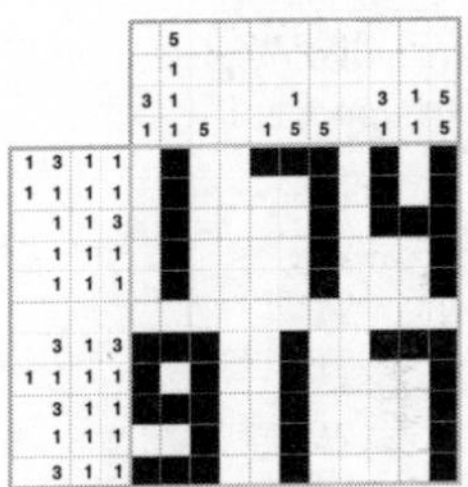

### MORE OR LESS

| | | | | | |
|---|---|---|---|---|---|
| 1 | 2 | 6 | 3 < | 4 | 5 |
| 2 | 1 | 3 | 6 > | 5 | 4 |
| 4 | 3 | 2 | 5 | 1 | 6 |
| 5 < | 6 | 1 | 4 | 3 | 2 |
| 6 | 5 > | 4 | 1 | 2 | 3 |
| 3 < | 4 < | 5 | 2 | 6 | 1 |

## Page 275

### ARROWS

| | | | | | |
|---|---|---|---|---|---|
| 2 | 2 | 0 | 2 | 0 | 2 |
| 0 | | | | | 0 |
| 0 | | | | | 3 |
| 1 | | | | | 2 |
| 0 | | | | | 0 |
| 0 | 0 | 1 | 0 | 1 | 0 |

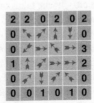

### BATTLESHIPS

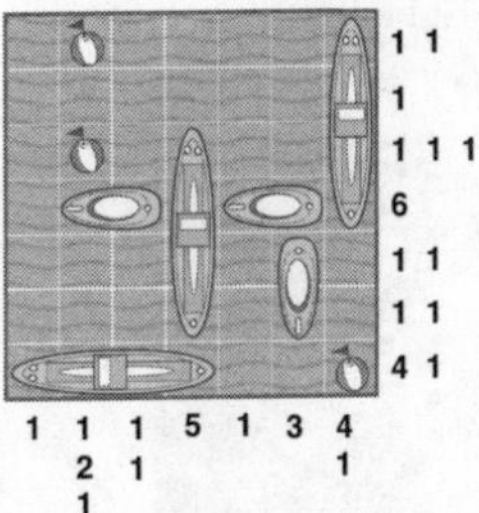

**Page 276**

**BOXES**

Solution: A line on the left or right of this square will only give up one box to your opponent

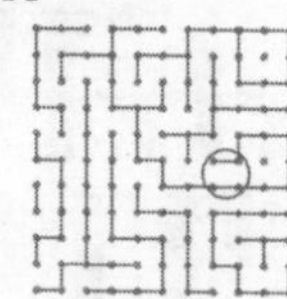

**MORE OR LESS**

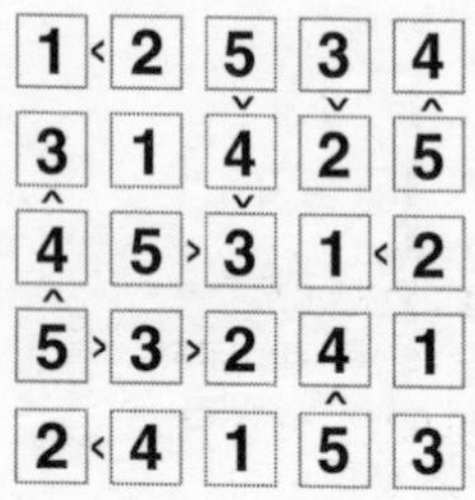


**Page 277**

**SUDOKU SIX**

A + 1 = B, C + 2 = E, N + 4 = R, I + 3 = L, D + 5 = I, H + 6 = N

Answer: BERLIN

**FIGURE IT OUT**

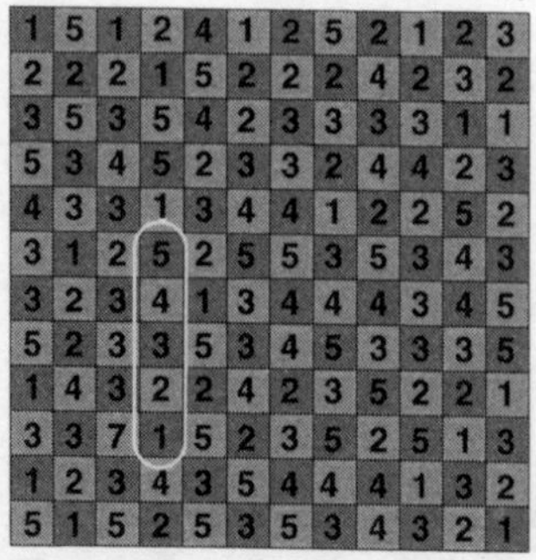


**Page 278**

**LOOPLINK**

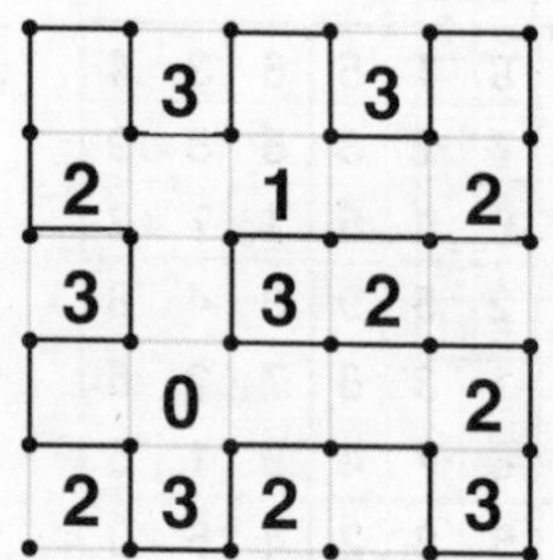


**SHAPE STACKER**

Answer: 2376

The numbers represent the number of sides in the shape they occupy. When shapes overlap, the numbers are added.

A: $3 + 4 + 5 = 12$

B: $4 + 4 + 3 = 11$,

C: $10 + 4 + 4 = 18$

$12 \times 11 \times 18 = 2376$

**Page 279**

**SILHOUETTE**

Answer: E

**Page 280**

SUDOKU

| | | | | | | | | |
|---|---|---|---|---|---|---|---|---|
| 7 | 9 | 2 | 8 | 1 | 5 | 6 | 3 | 4 |
| 1 | 6 | 4 | 7 | 2 | 3 | 5 | 8 | 9 |
| 8 | 5 | 3 | 9 | 4 | 6 | 1 | 7 | 2 |
| 6 | 1 | 7 | 2 | 5 | 9 | 3 | 4 | 8 |
| 5 | 4 | 9 | 1 | 3 | 8 | 7 | 2 | 6 |
| 3 | 2 | 8 | 6 | 7 | 4 | 9 | 1 | 5 |
| 9 | 7 | 1 | 5 | 8 | 2 | 4 | 6 | 3 |
| 4 | 8 | 5 | 3 | 6 | 1 | 2 | 9 | 7 |
| 2 | 3 | 6 | 4 | 9 | 7 | 8 | 5 | 1 |

ARROWS

| | | | | | |
|---|---|---|---|---|---|
| 0 | 0 | 1 | 0 | 0 | 1 |
| 0 | ↓ | ↘ | ↖ | ↘ | 0 |
| 1 | ← | ↘ | ↓ | ↓ | 3 |
| 0 | → | ↗ | → | ↗ | 2 |
| 0 | ↓ | ↙ | ↗ | ↘ | 1 |
| 0 | 3 | 0 | 1 | 1 | 2 |

**Page 281**

BOXES

Solution: A line on the top or right of this square wil only give up one box to your opponent

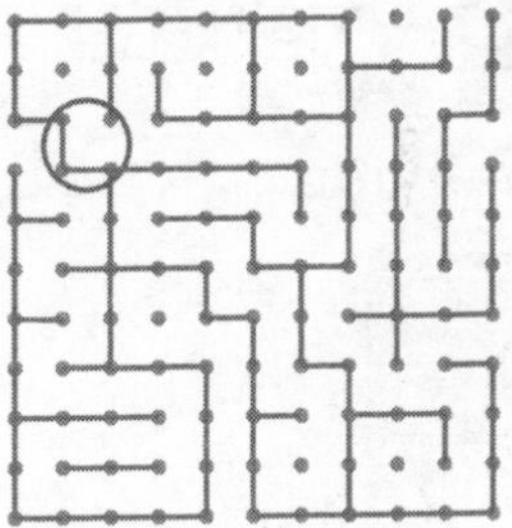

FIVE POINT PROBLEM

Solution: Each pentagon contains numbers that add up to 30, with the sides facing each other on adjoining pentagons showing the numbers 1 to 12 clockwise

## Page 282

### SAFECRACKER

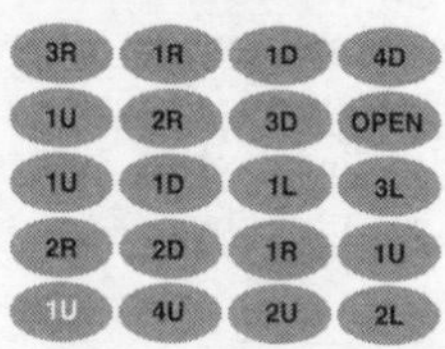


### THE GREAT DIVIDE

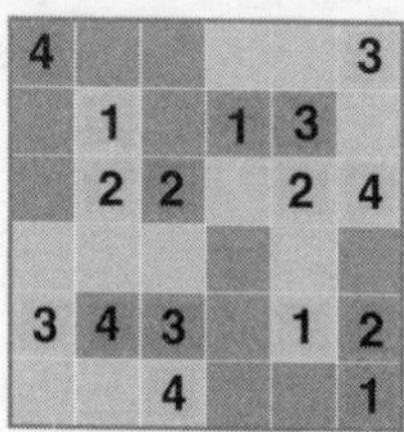

## Page 283

### KILLER SIX

| | | | | | |
|---|---|---|---|---|---|
| 1 | 2 | 6 | 4 | 3 | 5 |
| 3 | 4 | 5 | 1 | 6 | 2 |
| 4 | 6 | 3 | 5 | 2 | 1 |
| 5 | 1 | 2 | 6 | 4 | 3 |
| 6 | 3 | 1 | 2 | 5 | 4 |
| 2 | 5 | 4 | 3 | 1 | 6 |

### BEES AND BLOOMS

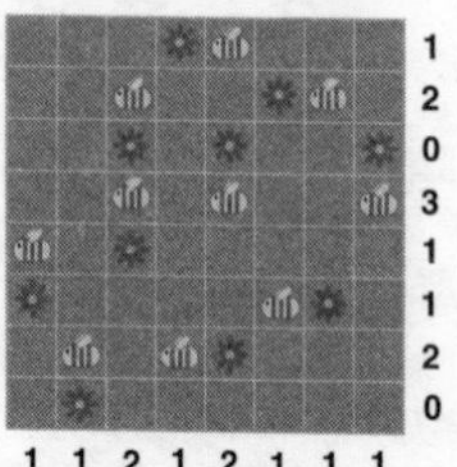

## Page 284

### BOXES

Solution: A line on the top or bottom of this square will only give up one box to your opponent

### CHECKERS

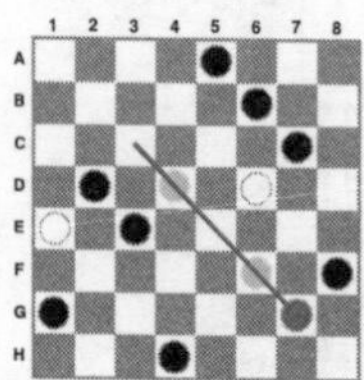

## Page 285

### HIDDEN PARIS

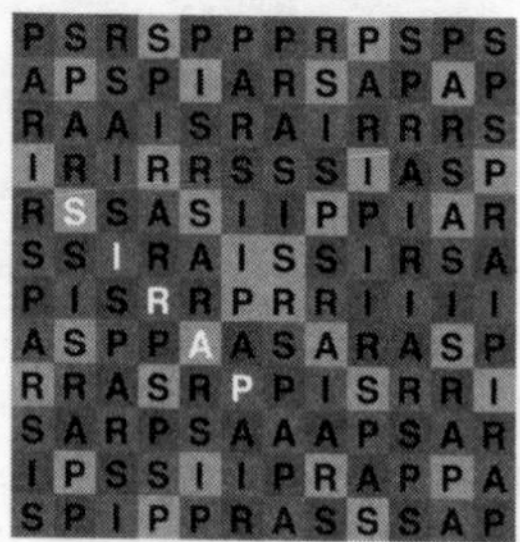


### IN THE AREA

Answer: 3500 square millimetres. Each 20 x 20 square represents 400 mm². 3 squares, 5 half-square triangles, 4 half-squares, 1 quarter square and 8 8th of a square triangles are used

**Page 286**

## X AND O

| 3 | 5 | 4 | 4 | 6 | 6 | 4 |
|---|---|---|---|---|---|---|
| 5 | O | O | X | X | X | 5 |
| 2 | X | O | O | O | O | 4 |
| 6 | O | O | X | X | X | 6 |
| 6 | X | X | O | X | X | 7 |
| 6 | X | X | O | X | X | 6 |
| 4 | 5 | 5 | 6 | 6 | 6 | 3 |

## SUDOKU

| 9 | 8 | 1 | 2 | 3 | 7 | 5 | 6 | 4 |
|---|---|---|---|---|---|---|---|---|
| 3 | 7 | 5 | 4 | 6 | 1 | 2 | 9 | 8 |
| 2 | 4 | 6 | 9 | 8 | 5 | 7 | 3 | 1 |
| 8 | 6 | 7 | 1 | 2 | 9 | 3 | 4 | 5 |
| 1 | 9 | 4 | 3 | 5 | 6 | 8 | 2 | 7 |
| 5 | 3 | 2 | 7 | 4 | 8 | 9 | 1 | 6 |
| 6 | 1 | 3 | 5 | 7 | 2 | 4 | 8 | 9 |
| 7 | 2 | 8 | 6 | 9 | 4 | 1 | 5 | 3 |
| 4 | 5 | 9 | 8 | 1 | 3 | 6 | 7 | 2 |

**Page 287**

## SILHOUETTE

Answer: G

**Page 288**

## RIDDLE

Answer: Geoff can take the chicken over and come back for the dog; then take the dog over, swap it for the chicken on the other side and come back for the grain. He leaves the chicken and takes the grain over, leaving it with the dog and finally returning for the chicken

**Page 289**

## SHAPE STACKER

Answer: 360.
The numbers represent the number of sides in the shape they occupy. Where shapes overlap, the numbers are multiplied 3 x 4 x 5 x 6 = 360

## SIGNPOST

Answer: 117
Take the alphabetical position of the first letter of the city, and multiply by the number of letters in the word 13 (M) × 9 = 117

**Page 290**

## MIRROR IMAGE

Answer: F

**Page 291**

## MASYU

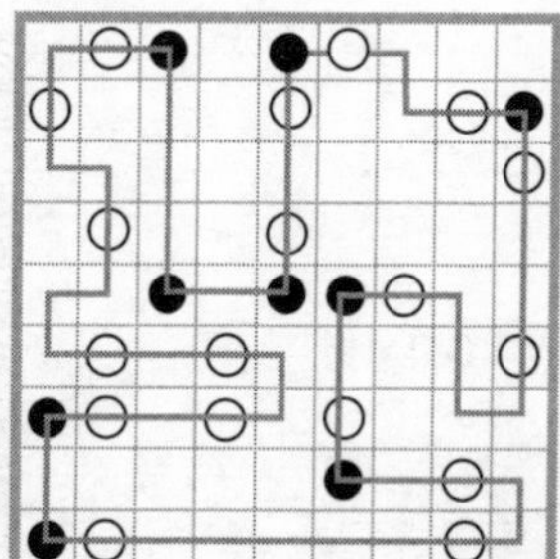

## ODD CLOCKS

Answer: 12.05 pm on Thursday in Tokyo;
11.05 am Thursday in Singapore

## Page 292

### LATIN SQUARE

| | | | | | |
|---|---|---|---|---|---|
| A | B | D | E | F | C |
| B | E | A | F | C | D |
| C | F | B | D | E | A |
| E | D | C | B | A | F |
| F | C | E | A | D | B |
| D | A | F | C | B | E |

### MAGIC SQUARES

| | | |
|---|---|---|
| 6 | 5 | 10 |
| 11 | 7 | 3 |
| 4 | 9 | 8 |

## Page 293

### SUM PEOPLE

Solution: 13

 5

 2

3

 6

## Page 294

### SCALES

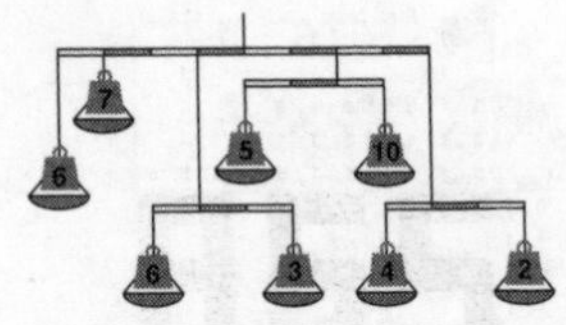


### SHUFFLE

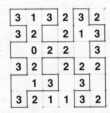

## Page 295

### LOOPLINK

| | | | | | |
|---|---|---|---|---|---|
| 3 | 1 | 3 | 2 | 3 | 2 |
| 3 | 2 | | 2 | 1 | 3 |
| | 0 | 2 | 2 | | 3 |
| 3 | 2 | | 2 | 2 | 2 |
| | 1 | 3 | | 3 | |
| 3 | 2 | 1 | 1 | 3 | 2 |

### MINESWEEPER

| | | | | | | | |
|---|---|---|---|---|---|---|---|
| 0 | 1 | | 2 | 3 | | | 2 |
| 2 | 3 | 3 | | 3 | | 5 | |
| | | 4 | 2 | 4 | 2 | 4 | |
| 3 | | 4 | | 2 | | 3 | 2 |
| 2 | 4 | | 5 | 4 | 4 | | 3 |
| 1 | | | | | 4 | | |
| 2 | 5 | | 6 | 4 | 4 | | 4 |
| | 3 | | | 2 | | 3 | |

## Page 296

### MINI NONOGRAM

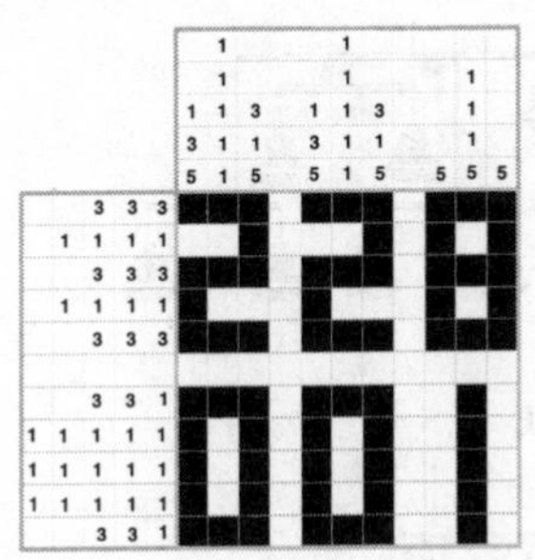

### SMALL LOGIC

| | Amanda | Marianna | Natasha | Red | White | Yellow | Roses | Tulips | Lilies |
|---|---|---|---|---|---|---|---|---|---|
| Anniversary | O | X | O | X | O | O | O | X | O |
| Birthday | O | O | X | O | X | O | O | O | X |
| Surprise | X | O | O | O | O | X | X | O | O |
| Roses | X | O | O | O | O | X | | | |
| Tulips | O | X | O | X | O | O | | | |
| Lilies | O | O | X | O | X | O | | | |
| Red | O | X | O | | | | | | |
| White | O | O | X | | | | | | |
| Yellow | X | O | O | | | | | | |

## Page 297

### FLOOR FILLERS

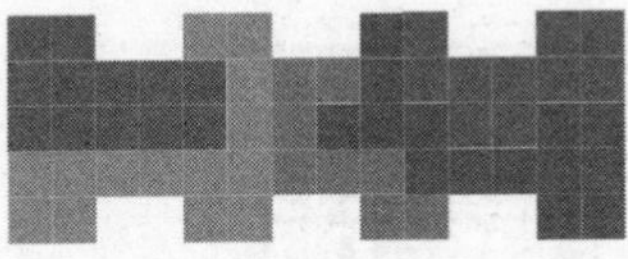

### SUDOKU

| | | | | | | | | |
|---|---|---|---|---|---|---|---|---|
| 4 | 7 | 2 | 1 | 3 | 9 | 5 | 6 | 8 |
| 3 | 8 | 6 | 4 | 5 | 7 | 2 | 1 | 9 |
| 5 | 9 | 1 | 2 | 6 | 8 | 7 | 4 | 3 |
| 1 | 6 | 7 | 9 | 8 | 3 | 4 | 5 | 2 |
| 2 | 5 | 9 | 6 | 7 | 4 | 3 | 8 | 1 |
| 8 | 3 | 4 | 5 | 2 | 1 | 6 | 9 | 7 |
| 9 | 2 | 5 | 3 | 1 | 6 | 8 | 7 | 4 |
| 6 | 4 | 8 | 7 | 9 | 2 | 1 | 3 | 5 |
| 7 | 1 | 3 | 8 | 4 | 5 | 9 | 2 | 6 |

## Page 298

### JIGSAW

Answer: A, C, G, and H

### RADAR

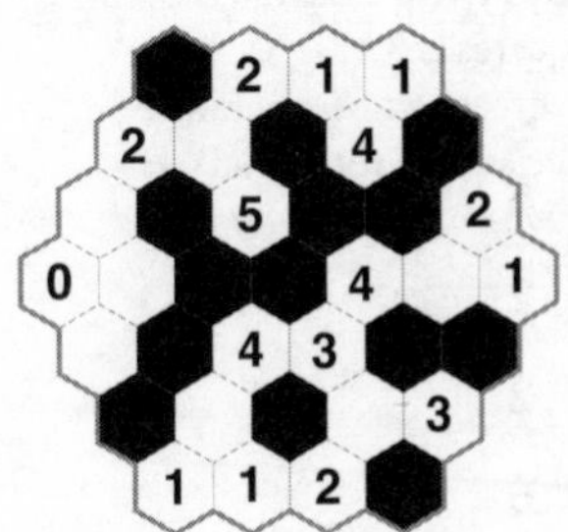

**Page 299**

## SUDOKU

| 4 | 1 | 5 | 8 | 3 | 6 | 7 | 2 | 9 |
|---|---|---|---|---|---|---|---|---|
| 9 | 2 | 8 | 1 | 4 | 7 | 3 | 6 | 5 |
| 3 | 6 | 7 | 2 | 9 | 5 | 1 | 4 | 8 |
| 2 | 5 | 9 | 3 | 7 | 1 | 4 | 8 | 6 |
| 8 | 3 | 6 | 4 | 2 | 9 | 5 | 1 | 7 |
| 1 | 7 | 4 | 6 | 5 | 8 | 2 | 9 | 3 |
| 5 | 8 | 3 | 9 | 1 | 2 | 6 | 7 | 4 |
| 6 | 4 | 2 | 7 | 8 | 3 | 9 | 5 | 1 |
| 7 | 9 | 1 | 5 | 6 | 4 | 8 | 3 | 2 |

**Page 301**

## WHERE'S THE PAIR?

Answer: B and H are the pair

**Page 302**

## RIDDLE

Answer: 2 miles. Pythagoras tells us the square of the hypotenuse on a right-angled triangle is equal to the sum of the squares of the other two sides. Pete's trip east and north are the two sides, so the sum of the squares is $3 \times 3 + 4 \times 4$, or 25. The direct route is therefore 5 miles (the square root of 25). His journey was 7 miles, so he would have saved 2

**Page 303**

## MASYU

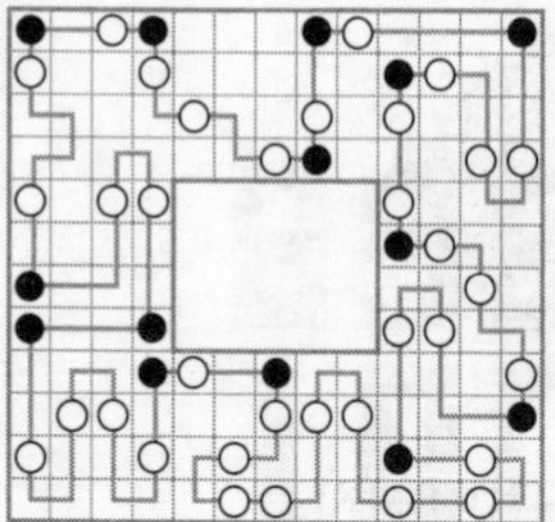

**Page 304**

## LOGIC SEQUENCE

## PRICE PUZZLE

Answer: 5 rings, 4 necklaces, 3 pairs of earrings and 2 watches
46,915 + 117,808 + 38,025 + 47,252 = 250,000

**Page 305**

## MINESWEEPER

## MORE OR LESS SUDOKU

| 1 | 7 | 9 | 2 | 8 | 6 | 5 | 4 | 3 |
|---|---|---|---|---|---|---|---|---|
| 2 | 5 | 6 | 9 | 3 | 4 | 8 | 7 | 1 |
| 4 | 8 | 3 | 1 | 5 | 7 | 2 | 9 | 6 |
| 7 | 2 | 5 | 3 | 6 | 9 | 4 | 1 | 8 |
| 9 | 6 | 8 | 4 | 2 | 1 | 3 | 5 | 7 |
| 3 | 4 | 1 | 5 | 7 | 8 | 9 | 6 | 2 |
| 6 | 9 | 7 | 8 | 4 | 2 | 1 | 3 | 5 |
| 5 | 1 | 2 | 7 | 9 | 3 | 6 | 8 | 4 |
| 8 | 3 | 4 | 6 | 1 | 5 | 7 | 2 | 9 |

## Page 306

### NUMBER CHUNKS

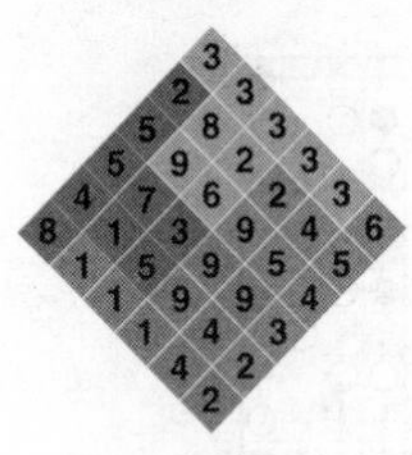

### WHERE'S THE PAIR?

Answer: B and G are the pair

## Page 307

### SUM PEOPLE

Solution: 22

3

4

5

9

## Page 308

### SILHOUETTE

Answer: B

## Page 309

### BITS AND PIECES

Cleopatra

### CAN YOU CUT IT?

## Page 310

### FIVE POINT PROBLEM

Solution: Starting at the bottom right each pentagon contains numbers that add up to 25, and sides facing each other on adjoining pentagons add 2

### KILLER SIX

| | | | | | |
|---|---|---|---|---|---|
| 5 | 1 | 2 | 4 | 6 | 3 |
| 6 | 3 | 4 | 1 | 2 | 5 |
| 4 | 2 | 6 | 3 | 5 | 1 |
| 3 | 5 | 1 | 6 | 4 | 2 |
| 2 | 6 | 3 | 5 | 1 | 4 |
| 1 | 4 | 5 | 2 | 3 | 6 |

## Page 311

### LATIN SQUARE

| | | | | | | | |
|---|---|---|---|---|---|---|---|
| G | B | H | F | A | E | C | D |
| B | A | D | E | C | F | G | H |
| A | C | F | G | D | H | E | B |
| C | H | A | B | F | G | D | E |
| E | F | G | A | B | D | H | C |
| F | D | C | H | E | A | B | G |
| H | E | B | D | G | C | A | F |
| D | G | E | C | H | B | F | A |

## Page 312

### MINESWEEPER

### PRICE PUZZLE

Answer: 20 – 4.95 (for the pot of tea) = 15.05
5 doughnuts (4.40) 4 cupcakes (4.68) 2 chocolate cakes (2.52) and 3 eclairs (3.45) make up the rest of the bill

## Page 313

### ROULETTE

Answer: In the 0 space.
The ball travels at a speed of 5 metres per second (relative to the wheel) for 16 seconds, making a distance of 8000 centimetres in a clockwise direction. The circumference of the wheel is 320 (well, 319.96!) centimetres (2 x pi (3.14) x radius (50.95 cm)). The ball must then travel exactly 25 laps of the wheel (8000 divided by 320 = 25), placing it back in the 0 space where it started.

## Page 314

### SHAPE STACKER

Answer: 4004.
The numbers represent the number of sides in the shape they occupy. When shapes overlap, the numbers are added together
A: 6 + 4 + 4 = 14
B: 10 + 4 + 4 + 4 = 22
C: 5 + 4 + 4 = 13
14 x 22 x 13 = 4004

### SUDOKU

| | | | | | | | | |
|---|---|---|---|---|---|---|---|---|
| 1 | 7 | 3 | 2 | 8 | 5 | 6 | 4 | 9 |
| 5 | 9 | 8 | 1 | 4 | 6 | 2 | 7 | 3 |
| 2 | 4 | 6 | 3 | 7 | 9 | 1 | 5 | 8 |
| 4 | 1 | 5 | 9 | 6 | 8 | 3 | 2 | 7 |
| 6 | 2 | 7 | 4 | 1 | 3 | 8 | 9 | 5 |
| 3 | 8 | 9 | 5 | 2 | 7 | 4 | 1 | 6 |
| 7 | 6 | 1 | 8 | 5 | 4 | 9 | 3 | 2 |
| 8 | 3 | 2 | 7 | 9 | 1 | 5 | 6 | 4 |
| 9 | 5 | 4 | 6 | 3 | 2 | 7 | 8 | 1 |

## Page 315

### MINI NONOGRAM

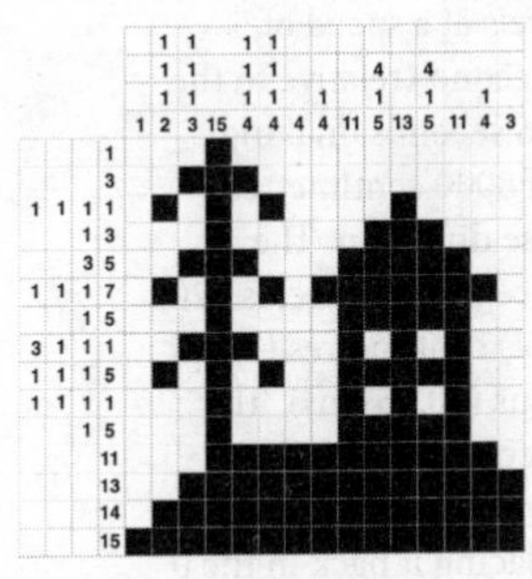


## Page 316

### SMALL LOGIC

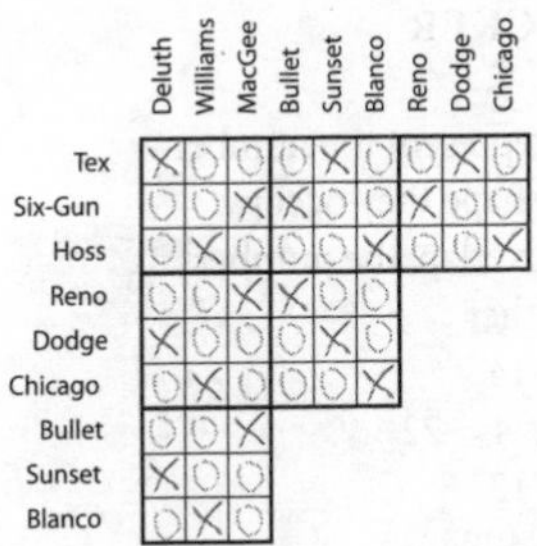


### BATTLESHIPS

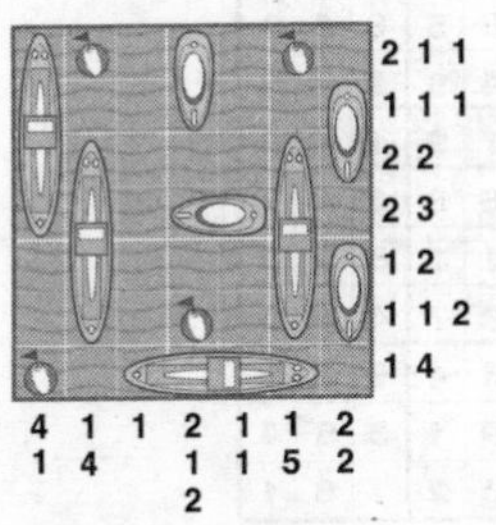


## Page 317

### BITS AND PIECES

### KILLER SIX

| | | | | | |
|---|---|---|---|---|---|
| 2 | 1 | 6 | 3 | 4 | 5 |
| 4 | 3 | 5 | 1 | 2 | 6 |
| 6 | 4 | 3 | 5 | 1 | 2 |
| 5 | 2 | 4 | 6 | 3 | 1 |
| 1 | 6 | 2 | 4 | 5 | 3 |
| 3 | 5 | 1 | 2 | 6 | 4 |

## Page 318

### CUBE VOLUME

Answer: 1232 cubic centimetres. Each little cube measures 2 x 2 x 2 cm, or 8 cubic centimetres, and there are 154 little cubes left. 8 x 154 = 1232

### DICE PUZZLE

Answer: 27. Add the top and side faces, then multiply by the front face

# ANSWERS

## Page 319

### KILLER SIX

| | | | | | |
|---|---|---|---|---|---|
| 6 | 1 | 4 | 2 | 3 | 5 |
| 5 | 3 | 1 | 6 | 4 | 2 |
| 4 | 2 | 6 | 3 | 5 | 1 |
| 3 | 4 | 2 | 5 | 1 | 6 |
| 1 | 6 | 5 | 4 | 2 | 3 |
| 2 | 5 | 3 | 1 | 6 | 4 |

### MATRIX

Solution: Each vertical and horizontal line contains one leaf pointing top left and two pointing top right. Each vertical and horizontal line contains two images where the ladybirds are facing in different directions and one where they are facing the same way. Each vertical and horizontal line contains a total of 45 spots on all ladybirds

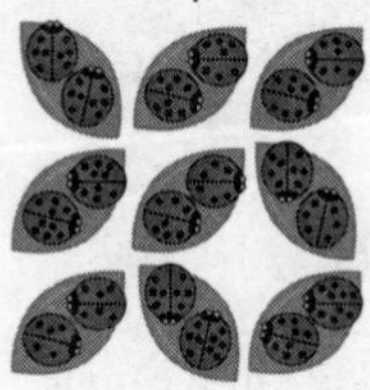

## Page 320

### KILLER SUDOKU

| | | | | | | | | |
|---|---|---|---|---|---|---|---|---|
| 1 | 7 | 3 | 2 | 8 | 5 | 6 | 4 | 9 |
| 5 | 9 | 8 | 1 | 4 | 6 | 2 | 7 | 3 |
| 2 | 4 | 6 | 3 | 7 | 9 | 1 | 5 | 8 |
| 4 | 1 | 5 | 9 | 6 | 8 | 3 | 2 | 7 |
| 6 | 2 | 7 | 4 | 1 | 3 | 8 | 9 | 5 |
| 3 | 8 | 9 | 5 | 2 | 7 | 4 | 1 | 6 |
| 7 | 6 | 1 | 8 | 5 | 4 | 9 | 3 | 2 |
| 8 | 3 | 2 | 7 | 9 | 1 | 5 | 6 | 4 |
| 9 | 5 | 4 | 6 | 3 | 2 | 7 | 8 | 1 |

### MASYU

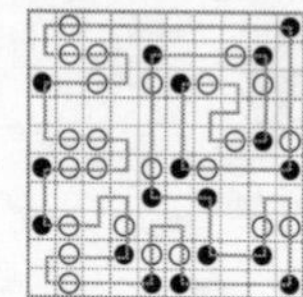

## Page 321

### SUM PEOPLE

42.

## Page 322

### SMALL LOGIC

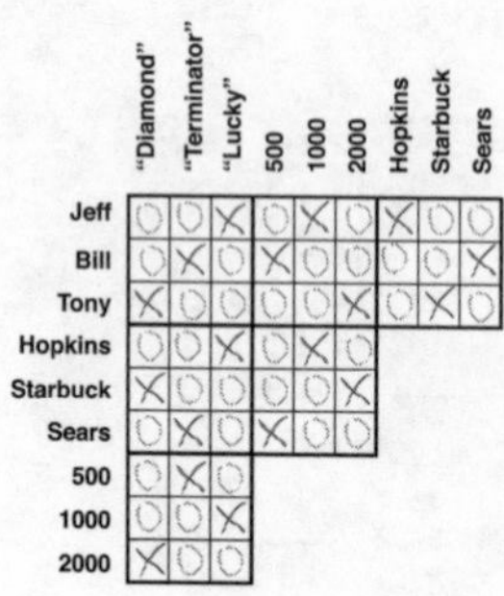

**Page 323**

## RIDDLE

Answer: Poppy. If Katy or Holly's statements are true, then Poppy's must also be true. If Poppy is telling the truth, we can't tell who ate the pizza. So Amy is telling the truth, and Poppy ate it.

**Page 324**

## BITS AND PIECES

Miguel
de Cervantes

## CAN YOU CUT IT?

**Page 325**

## MASYU

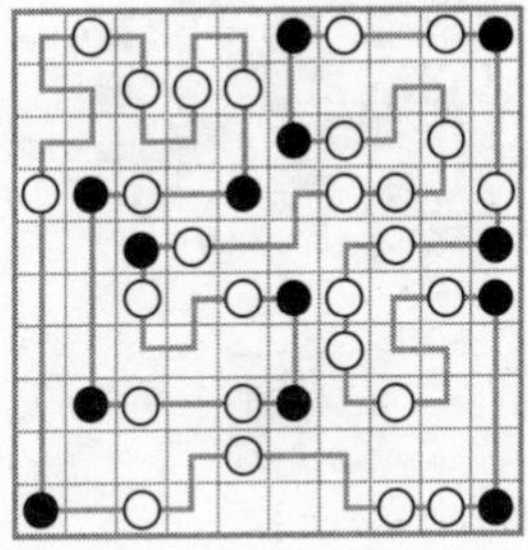

**Page 326**

## NUMBER MOUNTAIN

179

90 89

44 46 43

22 22 24 19

12 10 12 12 7

5 7 3 9 3 4

## MORE OR LESS SUDOKU

| | | | | | | | | |
|---|---|---|---|---|---|---|---|---|
| 7 | 1 | 3 | 6 | 9 | 5 | 4 | 2 | 8 |
| 4 | 2 | 5 | 1 | 7 | 8 | 6 | 3 | 9 |
| 8 | 9 | 6 | 4 | 2 | 3 | 1 | 5 | 7 |
| 2 | 4 | 1 | 9 | 8 | 7 | 5 | 6 | 3 |
| 5 | 6 | 9 | 2 | 3 | 4 | 8 | 7 | 1 |
| 3 | 7 | 8 | 5 | 1 | 6 | 2 | 9 | 4 |
| 6 | 8 | 2 | 3 | 4 | 9 | 7 | 1 | 5 |
| 1 | 3 | 4 | 7 | 5 | 2 | 9 | 8 | 6 |
| 9 | 5 | 7 | 8 | 6 | 1 | 3 | 4 | 2 |

# ANSWERS

## Page 327

### NUMBER FILL-IN

| | | | | | | | | | | |
|---|---|---|---|---|---|---|---|---|---|---|
| 1 | 6 | 0 | 5 | ■ | 2 | ■ | 4 | 4 | 5 | 9 |
| 0 | ■ | ■ | 6 | 2 | 7 | 2 | 0 | ■ | ■ | 6 |
| 9 | 1 | 2 | 0 | ■ | 2 | ■ | 8 | 5 | 4 | 7 |
| 5 | 1 | ■ | ■ | 3 | 5 | 4 | ■ | ■ | 9 | 6 |
| ■ | 1 | ■ | 9 | 9 | ■ | 5 | 5 | ■ | 6 | ■ |
| 4 | 4 | 8 | 8 | ■ | ■ | ■ | 7 | 2 | 7 | 6 |
| ■ | 4 | ■ | 1 | 8 | ■ | 2 | 8 | ■ | 4 | ■ |
| 5 | 0 | ■ | ■ | 2 | 2 | 5 | ■ | ■ | 2 | 6 |
| 4 | 0 | 4 | 5 | ■ | 4 | ■ | 1 | 5 | 4 | 7 |
| 4 | ■ | ■ | 3 | 5 | 5 | 3 | 2 | ■ | ■ | 8 |
| 2 | 2 | 6 | 4 | ■ | 0 | ■ | 1 | 9 | 9 | 0 |

### BITS AND PIECES

## Page 328

### SMALL LOGIC

| | Venus | Saturn | Jupiter | Black hole | Asteroid | Meteor | South | West | North |
|---|---|---|---|---|---|---|---|---|---|
| Bradley | O | X | O | X | O | O | O | X | O |
| Green | O | O | X | O | X | O | O | O | X |
| Fujyama | X | O | O | O | O | X | X | O | O |
| South | X | O | O | O | O | X | | | |
| West | O | X | O | X | O | O | | | |
| North | O | O | X | O | X | O | | | |
| Black hole | O | X | O | | | | | | |
| Asteroid | O | O | X | | | | | | |
| Meteor | X | O | O | | | | | | |

## Page 329

### CUBE VOLUME

Answer: 4347 cubic centimetres. Each little cube measures 3 x 3 x 3 cm, or 27 cubic centimetres, and there are 161 little cubes left. 161 x 27 = 4347

### KILLER SUDOKU

| | | | | | | | | |
|---|---|---|---|---|---|---|---|---|
| 5 | 2 | 9 | 1 | 6 | 8 | 3 | 4 | 7 |
| 1 | 3 | 7 | 9 | 2 | 4 | 6 | 8 | 5 |
| 4 | 6 | 8 | 7 | 3 | 5 | 1 | 9 | 2 |
| 6 | 7 | 1 | 4 | 5 | 9 | 2 | 3 | 8 |
| 3 | 9 | 4 | 2 | 8 | 1 | 5 | 7 | 6 |
| 2 | 8 | 5 | 6 | 7 | 3 | 4 | 1 | 9 |
| 7 | 1 | 6 | 8 | 4 | 2 | 9 | 5 | 3 |
| 8 | 4 | 3 | 5 | 9 | 6 | 7 | 2 | 1 |
| 9 | 5 | 2 | 3 | 1 | 7 | 8 | 6 | 4 |

## Page 330

### SMALL LOGIC

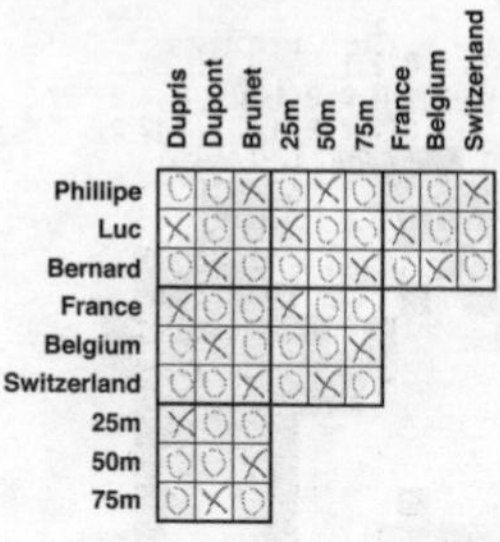

| | Dupris | Dupont | Brunet | 25m | 50m | 75m | France | Belgium | Switzerland |
|---|---|---|---|---|---|---|---|---|---|
| Phillipe | O | O | X | O | X | O | O | O | X |
| Luc | X | O | O | X | O | O | X | O | O |
| Bernard | O | X | O | O | O | X | O | X | O |
| France | X | O | O | X | O | O | | | |
| Belgium | O | X | O | O | O | X | | | |
| Switzerland | O | O | X | O | X | O | | | |
| 25m | X | O | O | | | | | | |
| 50m | O | O | X | | | | | | |
| 75m | O | X | O | | | | | | |

## Page 331

### LATIN SQUARE

| | | | | | | | |
|---|---|---|---|---|---|---|---|
| B | E | C | A | F | G | D | H |
| D | H | G | B | E | A | C | F |
| F | D | A | C | B | H | G | E |
| G | F | H | D | A | E | B | C |
| H | G | E | F | C | B | A | D |
| C | B | F | E | G | D | H | A |
| A | C | D | G | H | F | E | B |
| E | A | B | H | D | C | F | G |

### MORE OR LESS

| | | | | | | | | |
|---|---|---|---|---|---|---|---|---|
| 4 | | 2 | < | 3 | > | 1 | | 5 |
| v | | ^ | | | | ^ | | v |
| 1 | | 3 | < | 5 | | 2 | | 4 |
| | | | | | | | | |
| 2 | < | 4 | | 1 | | 5 | > | 3 |
| ^ | | ^ | | | | | | |
| 3 | | 5 | | 2 | | 4 | | 1 |
| | | | | ^ | | v | | |
| 5 | > | 1 | | 4 | > | 3 | | 2 |

**Page 332**

## MINI NONOGRAM

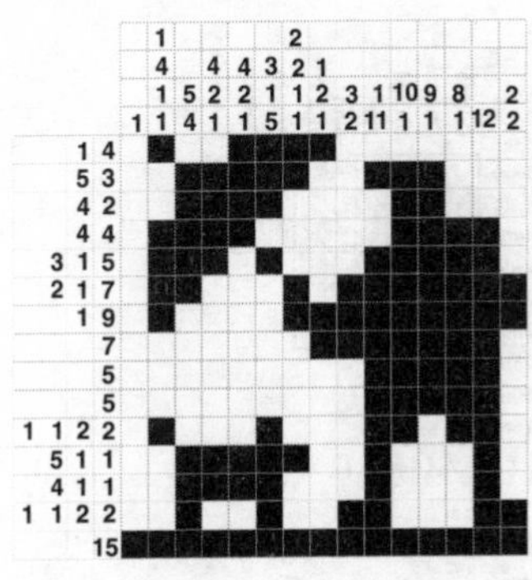


**Page 333**

## SCALES

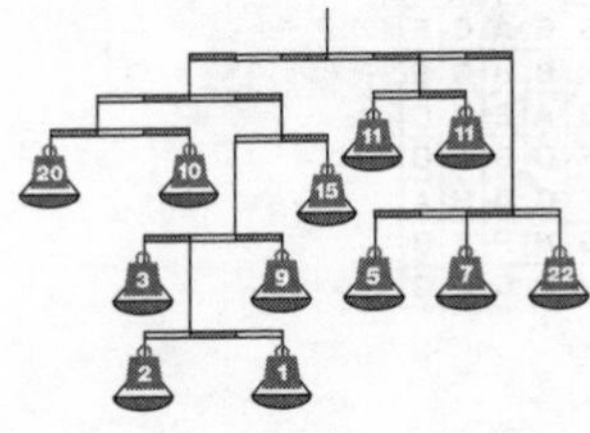


## SHAPE STACKER

Answer: C

Count the sides on each shape. Where shapes overlap their values are multiplied together.

(A) 4 x 4 x 6 x 10 = 960

(B) 1 x 3 x 4 x 5 = 60

960 divided by 60 = 16, as does C

**Page 334**

## CAN YOU CUT IT?

## CUBISM

Answer: 4

**Page 335**

## SMALL LOGIC

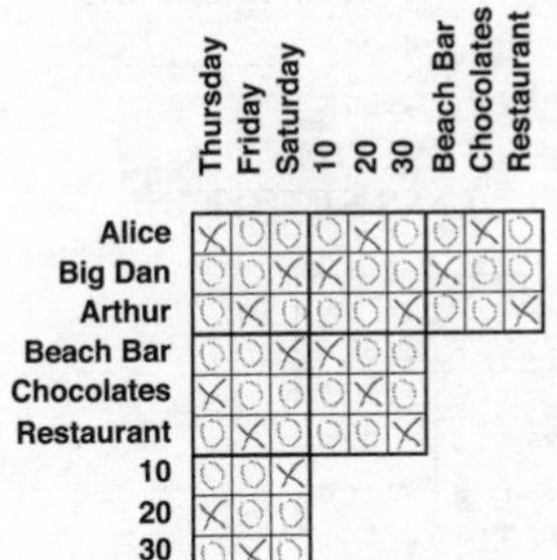

ANSWERS

## Page 336

### SCALES

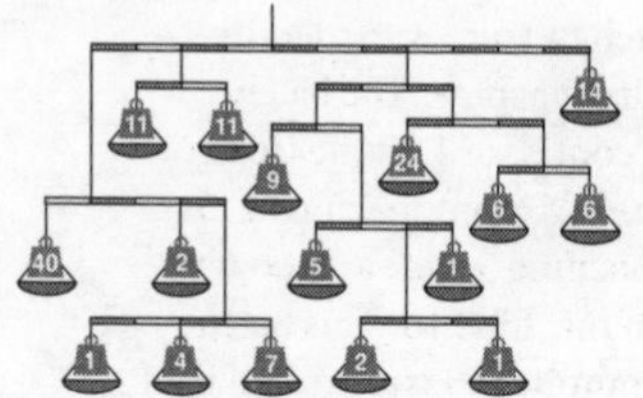


### LOOPLINK

| 2 | | 2 | 3 | | 2 | | 3 |
|---|---|---|---|---|---|---|---|
| 2 | 0 | 1 | | 0 | 3 | 2 | 2 |
| | | 3 | 2 | | 2 | 1 | |
| 3 | 0 | 2 | 1 | 2 | | 2 | 2 |
| 2 | 0 | | 2 | 3 | | 2 | 1 |
| | 2 | | 1 | | 2 | | |
| 2 | | 3 | 2 | | 2 | 3 | 2 |
| | 1 | | 2 | 3 | 2 | | 2 |

## Page 337

### MORE OR LESS SUDOKU

| 9 | 2 | 4 | 1 | 6 | 8 | 5 | 7 | 3 |
|---|---|---|---|---|---|---|---|---|
| 1 | 3 | 5 | 9 | 2 | 7 | 6 | 8 | 4 |
| 8 | 6 | 7 | 3 | 4 | 5 | 1 | 9 | 2 |
| 3 | 1 | 6 | 2 | 5 | 9 | 7 | 4 | 8 |
| 2 | 5 | 8 | 4 | 7 | 3 | 9 | 1 | 6 |
| 4 | 7 | 9 | 8 | 1 | 6 | 2 | 3 | 5 |
| 6 | 4 | 3 | 5 | 9 | 1 | 8 | 2 | 7 |
| 5 | 8 | 1 | 7 | 3 | 2 | 4 | 6 | 9 |
| 7 | 9 | 2 | 6 | 8 | 4 | 3 | 5 | 1 |

### NUMBER MOUNTAIN

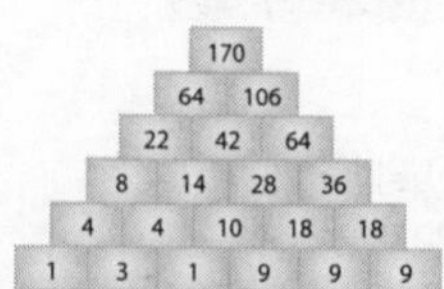


## Page 338

### NUMBER CHUNKS

| 8 | 9 | 8 | 7 | 6 | 4 |
|---|---|---|---|---|---|
| 9 | 3 | 6 | 1 | 5 | 7 |
| 7 | 1 | 9 | 4 | 7 | 3 |
| 9 | 2 | 9 | 5 | 6 | 3 |
| 2 | 1 | 2 | 9 | 9 | 3 |
| 5 | 5 | 5 | 5 | 9 | 7 |

### SAFECRACKER

| 4D | 1R | 2L | 2L |
|---|---|---|---|
| 2R | 1D | 1D | 2L |
| 1U | OPEN | 1R | 1U |
| 3R | 1D | 2L | 1D |
| 2U | 1R | 1U | 4U |

## Page 339

### PRICE PUZZLE

Answer: Also six.
6 bears (29.28) + 2 cars (24.94) +
4 trains (23.88) +
6 dolls (21.90) = £100

### CORNERED!

Answer: 68. Add the left hand red corners together and subtract the total from that of the right hand corners multiplied together.
3 + 1 = 4. 8 x 9 = 72. 72 – 4 = 68

## Page 340

### SYMMETRY

### SUDOKU

| 7 | 1 | 3 | 6 | 9 | 5 | 4 | 2 | 8 |
|---|---|---|---|---|---|---|---|---|
| 4 | 2 | 5 | 1 | 7 | 8 | 6 | 3 | 9 |
| 8 | 9 | 6 | 4 | 2 | 3 | 1 | 5 | 7 |
| 2 | 4 | 1 | 9 | 8 | 7 | 5 | 6 | 3 |
| 5 | 6 | 9 | 2 | 3 | 4 | 8 | 7 | 1 |
| 3 | 7 | 8 | 5 | 1 | 6 | 2 | 9 | 4 |
| 6 | 8 | 2 | 3 | 4 | 9 | 7 | 1 | 5 |
| 1 | 3 | 4 | 7 | 5 | 2 | 9 | 8 | 6 |
| 9 | 5 | 7 | 8 | 6 | 1 | 3 | 4 | 2 |

## Page 341

### SILHOUETTE

Answer: F

## Page 342

### RIDDLE

It will only be necessary to weigh one batch of truffles to identify the faulty machine. The batch should consist of 1 truffle from machine 1, 2 from machine 2, 3 from machine 3, etc., and finally 10 from machine 10. This batch would number 55 truffles and if all machines were working properly, at 10 grams each, should weigh a total of 550 grams. If the actual weight was discovered to be only 549.5 grams there must be only 1 of the 9.5 gram truffles in the batch and therefore machine 1 is the faulty one. If it's 549 grams, 2 light truffles and machine 2 is faulty etc..

## Page 343

### MINI MONOGRAM

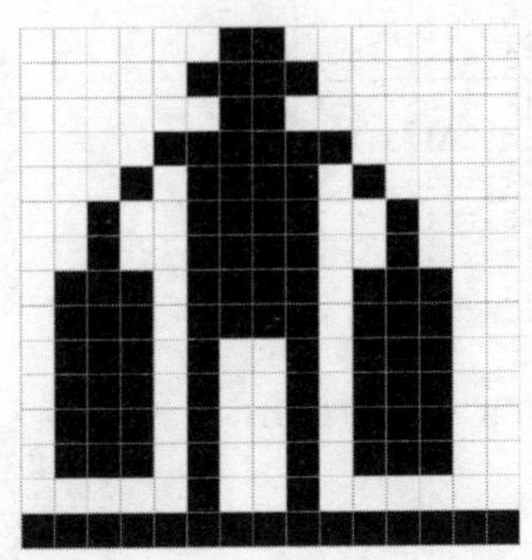

### DICE PUZZLE

Answer: D. The right hand 2 should be turned 90 degrees

## Page 344

### SCALES

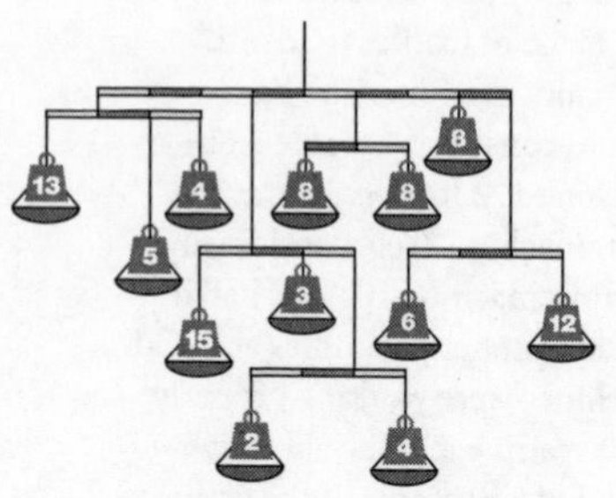


### MORE OR LESS

| | | | | | |
|---|---|---|---|---|---|
| 5 | 1 | 4 | 2 | 3 | 6 |
| 3 | 4 | 5 | 6 | 1 | 2 |
| 2 | 6 | 1 | 3 | 5 | 4 |
| 1 | 2 | 3 | 4 | 6 | 5 |
| 6 | 3 | 2 | 5 | 4 | 1 |
| 4 | 5 | 6 | 1 | 2 | 3 |

## Page 345

### MIRROR IMAGE

Answer: C

## Page 346

### SUDOKU

| | | | | | | | | |
|---|---|---|---|---|---|---|---|---|
| 2 | 8 | 9 | 6 | 4 | 7 | 3 | 1 | 5 |
| 4 | 5 | 7 | 1 | 8 | 3 | 6 | 2 | 9 |
| 6 | 3 | 1 | 9 | 5 | 2 | 7 | 8 | 4 |
| 1 | 9 | 4 | 2 | 3 | 8 | 5 | 6 | 7 |
| 8 | 7 | 2 | 5 | 9 | 6 | 4 | 3 | 1 |
| 5 | 6 | 3 | 7 | 1 | 4 | 8 | 9 | 2 |
| 9 | 1 | 8 | 3 | 7 | 5 | 2 | 4 | 6 |
| 3 | 2 | 4 | 4 | 6 | 1 | 9 | 7 | 8 |
| 7 | 4 | 6 | 8 | 2 | 9 | 1 | 5 | 3 |

### LOOPLINK

| | | | | | | | |
|---|---|---|---|---|---|---|---|
| 2 | | 2 | 0 | | 2 | | 2 |
| 3 | 0 | 3 | | 3 | 0 | 1 | 3 |
| 3 | | | 1 | 3 | 2 | 3 | 2 |
| | 1 | 2 | 2 | | 1 | | 2 |
| 2 | | | | 1 | | 3 | |
| 2 | 2 | 3 | 2 | 2 | 3 | | 1 |
| | | 3 | | 1 | | 3 | |
| 2 | | 2 | 2 | 2 | 3 | 2 | 2 |

## Page 347

### CORNERED!

Answer: 32. Using opposite red corners, subtract the smaller number from the larger. Then multiply the two totals together: 9 – 1 = 8, 7 – 3 = 4, 4 x 8 = 32

### REVOLUTIONS

Answer: 45 revolutions of cog A. This will in turn make exactly 90 revolutions of cog B, 80 revolutions of cog C, 72 revolutions of cog D and 40 revolutions of cog E

# YOUR PUZZLE NOTES

YOUR PUZZLE NOTES

YOUR PUZZLE NOTES

# YOUR PUZZLE NOTES